D. W. Griffith

D.W. GRIFFITH

His Life and Work

ROBERT M. HENDERSON

New York OXFORD UNIVERSITY PRESS 1972

Biograph and Griffith stills by
arrangement with Paul Killiam, proprietor of the
Biograph Collection and the D. W. Griffith Estate.

Photographs and stills have been provided by the
Film Library of the Museum of Modern Art and by
the New York Public Library, whose cooperation
is gratefully acknowledged.

Preface

In May 1942, two years after David Wark Griffith's career had been celebrated in a major retrospective at the prestigious Museum of Modern Art in New York City, but while he was still "at liberty" (out of work) in the motion picture industry, Griffith answered a request for biographical information from Barnet Bravermann:

> In your story, when you come to the period around 1899, why not put it this way,
> "D. W., I would like to know just what you did during this period?" D. W. answers,
> "So would I."
> Perhaps the dear readers would prefer nonsense. Somehow I don't think they are going to have much interest in any phase of my life.*

Griffith was not exhibiting false modesty. He was aware of the recognition, even adulation, accorded his works by the writers and critics whose articles appeared in film magazines with tiny circulations. He appreciated the recognition accorded by the Museum of Modern Art, and its publication by Iris Barry of *D. W. Griffith, American Film Master* as an outgrowth of their film retrospective. The world that mattered to him, however, was the world of Hollywood, the film industry, and he knew it wasn't interested. He was free to visit almost any studio in Holly-

---

*Letter from D. W. Griffith to Barnet Bravermann, May 28, 1942, in possession of the Museum of Modern Art Film Library.

v

wood. There were Griffith alumni working in the industry everywhere. They would welcome him, offer a chair, ask advice, invite
him to drop in any time, but never offer a job. The heads of the
studios masked their disinterest behind flattering words about
the great pioneer. The "realities" of the motion picture business
were that a director, or producer, was only as good (and as employ-
able) as the success of his last picture. While Griffith was grateful
for the encomiums of the new breed of film "historians," he would
have gladly traded them all for a film to direct. None was offered.
His career had died with the dismal failure of his independent
production, *The Struggle,* in January 1932.

There is no end to genuine creativity. Almost forty years since
Griffith's last film, and nearly a quarter of a century since his
death in 1948, the work and career of David Wark Griffith still
tower over that of any other motion picture maker. No one else
has done so much. In every film made by anyone anywhere, there
is the mark of Griffith. His films can be analyzed, deprecated,
dismissed as quaint voiceless antiques, but his mind and spirit
sit in every director's chair and every editing room.

In this attempt to tell of the life and times of David Wark
Griffith, I am grateful to the small band of loyal supporters and
friends, the critics and historians, the archivists and the "film
buffs" who have kept his movies and memorabilia alive and
fresh. It is from their memories of Griffith, their records, letters,
and documents, as well as the pages of the press and magazines,
that this account is constructed. There are gaps in this story despite
the mountain of material that exists. Griffith, the public man,
was highly visible, particularly after the triumph of *The Birth of
a Nation.* Griffith, the private man, was cautious, circumspect,
and even devious in concealing his affairs. He submitted, not
only willingly, but enthusiastically, to the published distortions
of his press agents. It mattered little that his family history was
distorted, his birthdate altered, his education bedecked with un-
earned academic degrees, and his rise to prominence muddied
with exaggerations and fictions. Griffith was a man of fertile imagination, a man of self-constructed romance, and, in time, he came
to believe his own constructions. His real story, stripped of the
romantic concoctions, is more interesting than the fiction.

This book is an attempt to sort out the reality of Griffith from the legend. It is not intended as a book about the films he made, except as they relate to his life. The substance of Griffith's creations was derived from his experience and life. To understand the nature of his films, we must look to his life. To know his films is to understand his vision, but not to know how that vision was built.

My personal gratitude and appreciation must be extended to those who generously assisted in the research for this book, particularly to Mrs. Eileen Bowser of the staff of the Museum of Modern Art film department. Mrs. Bowser has always cheerfully extended every courtesy and sound advice to me as she has to so many others who are investigating the early history of films. I am deeply appreciative of the research work on Griffith, the books and monographs, of those who preceded me: Katherine Long, Iris Barry, Seymour Stern, Barnet Bravermann, and Lillian Gish. I am grateful for the assistance of the staffs of the Theatre Collection of the New York Public Library and the Library of Congress. I owe a special debt to Griffith's actors and co-workers who remembered: Florence Lawrence, Blanche Sweet, Bessie Love, Richard Barthelmess, Karl Brown, Anita Loos, and, again, Lillian Gish.

Special thanks for invaluable assistance are due to Dr. Lester Predmore, once a boy at the reins of a Biograph prop wagon during the hot summers at Cuddebackville, New York, who was also there when it all began.

New York   R. M. H.
September 1971

Contents

Illustrations follow pages 86 and 214.

D. W. Griffith

1

From Playwright to Screen Writer

All drama must of necessity be conflict—battle, fight. How are we to protect the right unless we show the wrong? Unless we show the evils of a vicious past, how are we allowed to be the means of guiding the footsteps of the present generation? [1]

Clutching a new copy of the October 1907 issue of *Theatre Magazine* against a copy of *Pearson's Magazine* under his arm, balanced against a battered suitcase, the tall, imperial-nosed young man in checkered suit, derby, and high-buttoned shoes guided the young lady aboard the train for Washington, D.C. The *Pearson's* had a marker at the beginning of E. Phillips Oppenheim's new novel, *The Missioner,* and a corner was turned down in the *Theatre Magazine* at an article, "Interviews with Authors No. 11, Eugene Walter—the Insurgent Dramatist," on page 272.

As they settled back against the hard mohair-covered seats, the young woman pointed out an advertisement for the Miller Brothers 101 Ranch, enthusiastically wondering whether it might not be a wonderful place for a future vacation. She pointed out that the advertisement said they had "private rooms and comfortable accommodation for ladies and gentlemen." The young man, in his rich baritone tinged with a slight drawl, pointed out that the advertisement didn't include actors. Their conversation turned to memories of those parts of the West that they had visited, San Francisco, Los Angeles, and smaller towns in between, where they had been members of traveling theatre companies.

The young man, turning the pages of the latest *Theatre Magazine,* pointed out an article on the coming theatre season in New York. Grace George was to appear in Ibsen's *Lady from the Sea* at the Lyceum. Margaret Anglin would repeat *The Great Divide.* He pointed to a listing of the plays to be produced by James K. Hack-

3

ett, Maeterlink's *The Blue Bird,* Charles Rann Kennedy's *The Servant in the House,* and after a dramatic pause, in his rich actor's voice, he read the next play, "a new play marking the return to the American theatre of Fannie Ward, *The Fool and the Girl."*

She expressed disappointment that the name of the playwright, David Wark Griffith, was not mentioned. They agreed that after a triumph in Washington that name would never be forgotten again. The possibility of failure for the play was dismissed with a discussion of the producing capabilities of James K. Hackett and the cast that had been assembled to support Fannie Ward, Allison Skipworth, Frank Wundelee, and other competent players. A momentary frown came over the young lady's face as she wondered why her husband had not found a part for her. He smiled, reassuringly, and told her that her name, Linda Arvidson Griffith, would someday be as well known as his own.

Her attention turned back to her copy of *Pearson's Magazine.* They shared an excerpt from an E. Phillips Oppenheim story:

> He opened the gate. She stepped almost into his arms. Her white face was suddenly illuminated by the soft blaze of summer lightning which poured from the sky. He had no time to move, to realize. He felt her hands upon his cheek, his face drawn downward, her lips, soft and burning, pressed against his for a long exquisite second. And then—the darkness once more, and his arms were empty.[2]

She snuggled closer to her husband. He told her that he liked the lightning effect, but his attention had wandered to his own magazine and a profile of the Broadway playwright Eugene Walter, a success at thirty-three. His wife pointed out that he was only thirty-two, and with the success of *The Fool and the Girl,* he would be a year ahead of Walter. If Eugene Walter could write a play in three weeks as the article stated, David Wark Griffith could do the same, and she could star in it.

The Washington-bound train that carried the budding playwright and his wife was not bringing them to their hoped-for triumph. The possibility of failure was real. *The Fool and the Girl* opened on September 30, 1907, and, despite the best efforts of the experienced James K. Hackett, it failed. Fannie Ward's return from London to the American threatre was not triumphant.

The play, a serious melodrama about migratory pickers in the California hop fields, fell victim to unfavorable reviews and general audience apathy. The review that stung the young playwright the most was written by Hector Fuller in the *Washington Herald,*

> It may be said that the dramatist wanted to show where his hero's feet strayed; and where he found the girl he was after to make his wife, but if one wants to tell the old, old and beautiful story of redemption of either man or woman through love, it is not necessary to portray the gutters from which they are redeemed. . . .[3]

Despite the assurance that his play would run for the promised two weeks, Griffith reacted to Fuller's criticism with an angry letter to the *Herald*'s editor,

> In the name of justice, I ask you the courtesy of printing this letter. I am the author of *The Fool and the Girl* now being presented in your city. In the criticisms of no other Washington paper was there the faintest suggestion that anyone was hurt by the immorality of the play. But in Wednesday's issue of the *Washington Herald,* the most vicious, false, and hypocritical criticism is made by an alleged critic who signs himself, Hector Fuller. In our scenes in this prologue, we have not one essential piece of business, not so much as an embrace between man and woman, nor is one profane or foul word used, not even the much hackneyed *damn,* and the most terrible crime committed is the sipping of a little colored water which is supposed to represent champagne which up until this time we thought might be done upon the stage without causing any great outcry.[4]

Despite his defense, the audiences for *The Fool and the Girl* dwindled. The President did not attend. Hackett gave Griffith a handshake and sent him back to New York. Griffith clung to Hackett's parting admonition to bring his next play around for a reading.

The return trip to New York was depressing. Once again the young Griffiths were faced with the necessities of finding acting jobs that would meet the rent on their grim railroad flat. David Griffith was convinced that his future lay in writing plays. With some luck he might sell another one before Hackett's money ran out. His mind worried a subject during the entire train ride. Perhaps a bigger subject, a patriotic subject, might be the answer.

Something more important than the trials of migratory hop pickers.

There were certainly some strong points in his first play, but the actors hadn't been too successful in achieving the acting quality he had asked for.

> . . . care must be taken to get that natural, careless, slurring personal note, a feature of this class of women, white, common, free from too much harshness or coarseness, merely breezy good-nature and overflowing animal spirits.[5]

The big dance scene had not worked quite as he had envisaged it. It had become stiff and jumbled. He had asked for a dancer in a semi-Mexican costume to execute

> . . . a wild solo dance upon the platform, during which some of the figures on the stage move in and out between her and the front of the stage chatting and drinking while watching the dancing, parting now and then so the audience gets a full view of the dancing and then closing up so that she is lost in the picture in order to keep away from the idea of the dance being a speciality.[6]

Hackett had managed to give him the lighting effect that he'd wanted for Eva's room at the climax in the fourth act,

> It is sunset and red lights fall through the window. The room is dim with the evening light. Effie is seen distinctly in the white light from the street which falls in latticed splashes of white upon the floor.[7]

All that is done, he thought, but the next play will be just right. A big play about the American Revolution would be the answer. Griffith even had a title, *War,* simple, direct, and salable! He would begin the research as soon as they got home.

The thousand dollar fee that Hackett had paid Griffith for his play would not stretch very far, but for a time it was enough to give him free time for *War.* He spent every day at the New York Public Library reading about the American Revolution. Before leaving for the library, Griffith would do setting-up exercises with some battered Indian clubs and then take a brisk jog through Central Park. Physical fitness had become something of an obsession with him.

Griffith felt that the opportunities for a young playwright in New York were very bright. He thought that he now had a major contact with a sound management. Hackett's other major productions of the season were successful, Maurice Maeterlinck's *The Blue Bird* and Charles Rann Kennedy's *A Servant in the House,* starring Walter Hampden. A young playwright, Clyde Fitch, had two comedies running successfully, *Girls* and *Toddles.* The latter had a young member of the Drew acting family, John Barrymore, as its star. A critic had noted that young Barrymore "exhibited uncommon cleverness."

Not all the young playwrights were successful. Two young members of the Henry De Mille family, Cecil B. and William C. De Mille, were represented in April by a joint effort, *The Royal Mounted.* Their notices were as bad as Griffith's, ". . . filled with situations interesting to the idle, yet empty as a play can be." 8

While the Griffiths were long on hope, they were increasingly short of money. The last of the money from *The Fool and the Girl* was soon used up. A little money was earned by Griffith from a brief acting engagement in Brooklyn, and for both husband and wife from a slightly longer run in a pageant in Virginia. Griffith played John Smith to Linda's Pocahontas.

When his funds were low once again, Griffith met a former acting colleague and friend from his early days in the theatres of Louisville, Kentucky—Max Davidson. Max told Griffith that a few dollars might be picked up by selling stories to the motion picture companies springing up in the city. Max insisted that with Griffith's reputation as a "produced" playwright he would be able to sell them anything. Another actor-friend, Harry Salter, had given Griffith a similar suggestion.

Max Davidson allayed Griffith's fears that damage might be done to his good name as a playwright by association with the cheap film companies by telling him that authors' names didn't appear on the films, and, further, Griffith should sell the stories under his stage name, Lawrence Griffith.

Griffith wasn't certain that selling stories to the movies was a good idea, and Linda had similar doubts. Something had to pay the rent, however, so Linda grudgingly helped him look up the addresses of the motion picture companies. The best known company

was the Edison Company. The Griffiths agreed that he might as
well start at the top.

The Edison Company was not only the oldest film company,
with a direct connection back to Thomas Alva Edison's West Orange laboratory, but it also had the services of the then most successful motion picture director, Edwin S. Porter. Porter had firmly
established his claim by directing the influential *The Great Train
Robbery* in 1903. Griffith knew that he would have to sell his stories to Porter.

Max Davidson had said that Griffith might get as much as five
dollars for an acceptable story. Davidson pointed out that the stories didn't have to be plays. A one-page story was probably enough.

Griffith was only dimly aware of what a motion picture was. The
store-front theatres that housed them were popping up all over,
and Griffith was aware of their existence, but neither he nor Linda
had paid much attention to them. Griffith agreed with his idol,
stage producer David Belasco, who dismissed film and its possibilities in these terms:

> . . . always when you look at a picture on the screen you will be
> conscious of its lack of living quality. And this the celluloid
> drama will never be able to surmount. You will always have the
> subconscious knowledge that it is mere photography after all.[9]

It took little persuasion by Davidson and Salter to convince Griffith that the film companies would buy any ideas, even borrowed
ideas.

The list of film companies considered by David and Linda probably included, in addition to Edison, Vitagraph, Pathé, Lubin,
Kalem, the Essanay Company, Selig, and Williams, Brown, and
Earle. Griffith studied the posters outside some of the store-front
theatres to see what sort of material was being purchased. He saw
that Pathé was presenting *The Curse of Drink, The Cabby's Wife,*
and *The Gambler's Fate.* The current Edison films were *Romance
of a War Nurse, The Face on the Barroom Floor, Life's Game of
Cards,* and from Vitagraph came the dramatic gems, *The Washer-
woman's Revenge, A Kind-Hearted Bootblack,* and *How Simpkins
Discovered the North Pole.* Griffith saw no reason for looking at
any of the films. The stories were transparent enough, plots dis-

cernible in many instances from the title alone. Further, Griffith, remembering his research and labors in writing a four-act play, thought that turning out a brief story for a ten- or twelve-minute film would be relatively simple. A so-called major film effort of the time by Selig Poliscope was a condensed version of *A Tale of Two Cities.* In Griffith's mind that was only time enough for Sidney Carton's last speech. But then there wasn't any speech. So much the better, thought Griffith, that made everything easier.

The Film Index, a new trade magazine aimed at this infant industry, noted in 1908:

> . . . the chief forte of the moving picture at present is to amuse rather than to instruct, for the populace are quick to give the cold shoulder to any institution that assumes to educate or elevate it.[10]

David Griffith was certainly not interested in educating "the populace." He would write and sell as many stories as he could to the film companies for that purported five dollar fee.

What Griffith and the other members of the theatre profession could see of the operation of the motion picture business in 1908 was not likely to inspire respect. A typical scene of a film company at work near Borough Hall in Brooklyn would have reinforced their feelings of disrespect.

A large crowd, estimated later at four thousand people, had gathered to watch the posting of baseball results on a bulletin board. Some of the crowd had spilled out into the streets and over the trolley tracks. The police were kept busy trying to clear the tracks. A young man dressed in small boy's knickers and cap, an old woman, a stage manager, and a cameraman stationed themselves along the curb, ignoring the baseball results. As the next trolleycar came clanging down the street, the stage manager yelled, "Now, go!" The old woman dashed out on the tracks apparently tripping and falling in the path of the trolley. The man in boy's clothing jumped into the street on a second command. At curbside the cameraman cranked away, photographing the action against the crowd. The trolley screeched to a stop. The motorman, not an actor, jumped out to help rescue the old lady. The stage manager frantically waved him back shouting, "Let the boy save her!"

The baseball fans were photographed watching the "boy" carry the "old woman" to safety, unaware that they had just become unpaid extras in *Life of a New York Lad,* a production of the American Vitagraph Company.

Despite the contempt of the legitimate theatre for the motion picture business, its growth had already been phenomenal. New York City had over six hundred store-front movie theatres. Washington, D.C., had only a handful of legitimate theatres, but it had over forty of the small, dark movie theatres. While the newspapers, prestige theatrical magazines, and the leaders of society raised money for the establishment of a "national" theatre, non-English-speaking immigrants who could understand the silent films, the poor who could not afford the grand theatres of New York, and a lower middle class interested in novelty flocked to the movies.

Griffith's understandable contempt for the movies was revealed when he paid his first visit to a motion picture studio to call on Edwin Porter. He had drawn up a quick resume of the plot for Puccini's opera *Tosca* and attempted to pass it off as his own work. Griffith had misjudged his man. Edwin S. Porter had been a theatre director before his involvement with film, and he easily recognized the story as belonging to Sardou and not "Lawrence" Griffith.

Porter did not confront Griffith with his knowledge of the story's source. Such plagiarism was common in the film industry. Plots were freely stolen from everywhere. Porter, however, was not going to pay for something that could be had free. Griffith was given a brief no.

Porter was interested in Lawrence Griffith the actor. He liked the aquiline good looks and strong physique of the young man. He asked Griffith if he would like a role in a new film, *Rescued from an Eagle's Nest.* Porter would pay five dollars a day for Griffith's services as an actor. Five dollars was the amount Griffith had come for, and if he couldn't get it for *Tosca,* then why not for a brief acting job?

Griffith found himself playing a hero. His task was to rescue a baby from the depredations of a stuffed eagle, wire-controlled, that somehow looked more like a turkey. Griffith dutifully fought off the imitation bird, but the process seemed so ridiculous that Griffith resolved never again to become involved in such a charade. Once more he offered himself as a writer to Porter. Porter was still uninterested. Griffith took his slip to the pay window, picked up his money, and went home.

Linda suggested that he try his luck at another company on their list, the American Mutoscope and Biograph Company at 11 East 14th Street. Griffith shrugged. Max Davidson had mentioned "Biograph," so why not?

While working for Porter, Griffith had continued to work on his second play. He told Linda that he hoped to show the sweep and scope of the American Revolution, but it turned out that the script had too much sweep and scope in that it involved a cast of fifty-six principals and an equal number of extras. The play was submitted to a number of managements including Henry Miller's. After a brief interest the Miller office turned the play down because of the large cast and potentially high production costs. Henry Miller was able to avoid commenting on the play's quality. The plotting was in the worst tradition of melodrama, and the dialogue was stilted and wooden. Griffith did manage to project lively and imaginative scenes for the ensemble, which revealed a strong sense of spectacle. He opened his third act in the Red Fox Inn at Trenton on Christmas Eve. Griffith's manuscript referred to it as "the Red *Fix* Inn." As Linda continually pointed out, spelling was not one of David Griffith's strong points. Griffith had described the scene:

> Room is lighted with great candelabra set in walls R & L holding lighted candles, giving the soft, flickering lights that make shadows in the room, as the bright glare of the ordinary footlights would destroy entirely the atmosphere of the act.
>
> Opening of act, all possible brightness, and wild, half-drunken hilarity. In the center of the stage, six men and six women dancing the Morris dance to the air of the "Beggar Daughter of Bednal Green"—around the figure of a hobby horse which is fantastically made up over a man, musicians are playing wildly on wall seat. . . . A girl, gaudily dressed, highly rouged, patched, and powdered has her hed [sic] resting on a pillow which a civilian, fairly well dressed, rather disheveled, coatless, holds in his arms. A very small, dissipated-looking, old man of about sixty is being driven around the room by a young girl of about eighteen; she has bridle reins about his neck, and she strikes him with a driving whip, calling "Get up, get up, get up horsie, kick

nice horsie, kick," at which the old man squeals, kicking up one leg and then the other in imitation of a horse. Two men carrying an immense metal punch bowl half full of punch pass in and out among the crowd, all of them have pewter mugs which they dip into the bowl and drink at pleasure. Two re-faced [sic], fleshy, middle-aged men, decidedly the worse for liquor, follow the punch bowl, singing in time to the music:

> Oh, my beak, oh, my beak
> The punch is wet,
> And the punch is weak.[11]

Whatever else the manuscript reveals, it shows that Griffith had a fine sense of orgy, and the British and Hessian soldiers were not to be mistaken for the heroes.

For the time being the play was set aside. Griffith told his wife that he might be able to cut the cast down, although he thought that trying to show the Revolution in the proper way really needed more people than could be jammed on even the biggest stage.

On a bright May morning, following a meager breakfast of corn-meal mush, a piece of bacon, and black coffee, Griffith was ready for his visit to the American Mutoscope and Biograph Company on 14th Street.

Linda asked if he wished to take his one published poem with him as an example of his work. The poem she referred to was one that appeared in *Leslie's Weekly,* now propped open on top of the curly-maple dresser. It had been published on January 10, 1907, and represented the high mark in Griffith's literary life until he sold James K. Hackett his play. It was entitled *The Wild Duck.* Griffith glanced at his poem, swiftly re-reading it.

> Look—how beautiful he is!
> Swift his flight as a bullet
> As he comes in from the sea in the morning.
> For the wind is from the sea in the morning.
> See! He is bound for the hilltops,
> The gold hilltops, the gold hilltops.
> There he will rest 'neath the flowers,
> The red flowers—the white and the red,
> The poppy—the flower of dreams,
> The crimson flower of dreams.
> There must be rest in the morning.

His eye skipped to the last stanza.

Look! He is falling, falling out to the sea.
Ah, there is mist on the sea!
There is always mist on the sea in the evening.
Perhaps his nest is beyond, I know not.
Perhaps it is built of the mist, I know not.
Only with tired wings wearily beating,
And his eyes turned back to the mainland,
To the red and white and red
Waving and blowing together.
He is falling out, out to the sea
Poor little wild duck! Poor little wild duck!
In the evening when the wind blows out to the sea!
Ah me! Ah me! Ah me!
In the evening when the wind blows out to the sea.

He rejected the suggestion, saying that it would be meaningless to the motion picture people. Griffith crossed to the door, asking Linda how he looked. He was wearing a light tan suit, black patent leather shoes, a black derby, and was carrying a cane. Linda nodded her approval, wishing he didn't have to wear "wardrobe." There was an old theatre axiom which the Griffiths knew well. An actor preserved his best clothes, in the trunk, for future stage roles and did not wear them out in street wear. Griffith kissed his wife goodbye and walked jauntily out the door twirling his cane.

As he began the long walk to 14th Street, he made an appraisal of their situation. The money from Hackett was gone. The money from the Virginia pageant hadn't lasted very long, and the remnants of Porter's money jingled in his pocket. Linda had used up a small sum of her own and was now threatening to write to David's brother Jacob in Kentucky for something to help out. Griffith's mind wandered as he walked along. How would his father, the cavalry hero of the Confederacy, have faced this situation? Griffith could conjure up the face of his father, Colonel Jacob Griffith, but it had the dimness of an old photograph. His father had died when David was ten. Still he knew well the legends of his family, heroes all who knew how to step lively into the future. An unaccustomed wave of homesickness swept over him.

Home for David Griffith was Floydsfork in Oldham County, a short distance outside Louisville, Kentucky. His mother, sisters, and brothers were still living there, and in Louisville. And there were relatives all over the area. Griffith remembered his father as the head of the clan, a dashing ex-soldier, a two-term member of the Kentucky legislature, the embodiment of all the lost virtues of the ante-bellum South.

Late in life Griffith wrote about his relationship with his father:

> I often wondered if he cared anything about me particularly. I am forced to doubt it. As far as I can remember, he never seemed to show anybody his feelings toward them . . . what he did, which he did only occasionally, was to put his hand on my head and said [sic] "Son, how are you this day?" This simple action seemed to me an overwhelming miracle of some kind.[12]

Griffith felt that if it didn't work out at Biograph, or one of the other companies, Linda and he would just have to pack up and go back to Kentucky. He twirled his cane jauntily, remembering his old yellow dog. He had been a great dog, but his father had to shoot him.

> We called them sheep dogs—why I don't know because their principal business was supposed to be to go out and unaided by anyone, bring in the cows to the milking place.[13]

The dog had gotten sick.

> I heard the news that the execution was about to come off. Then I saw them lead the dog down to the side orchard with a rope around his neck so they could tie him to a tree. Then I saw my father go into the house to get a gun.[14]

Griffith stepped across 23rd Street, avoiding the horse droppings in the road.

> I knew it wouldn't be long now for the dog because father had been a colonel in a couple of wars, and a captain of one, and fought Indians, and most anyone who came around . . . and was a good shot. When I saw him go down into the orchard with the gun, I started running in the opposite direction. I didn't want to see the execution, but I couldn't run fast enough to get away from the report of the gun.[15]

It was 14th Street, and Griffith, at a slower pace, turned and walked toward Fifth Avenue. The Biograph studio was just around the corner from Fifth Avenue. A trolley clanged by, wheels grind-

ing. The thought of riding the rest of the way was suddenly appealing, but the right hand jingling the few coins in his pocket stopped
that notion. Even a nickel counted now.

> Colonel Griffith had a good aim. There was only one shot and I
> knew the poor old yellow dog was turning over on his back with
> his feet in the air like dogs generally do when the shot is cor-
> rected [sic] at the place. I asked afterwards what they did with
> the body, but nobody told me. That was the last of my first
> friend.[16]

Here was the American Mutoscope and Biograph Company at
last, a four-story brownstone with central steps leading to the film
company offices on the first floor above the street level shops. The
building occupied a typical New York fifty-foot front plot and had
obviously been converted from a former elegant residence. In fact
it had been the home of a member of the Cunard shipping family.
The building was now owned by the Buchman family, who had
leased it to the Chickering Piano Company for a first floor sales-
room. The upper floors were sublet as studio space by Chickering
to a miscellany of painters, sculptors, and musicians. In 1906, the
American Mutoscope and Biograph Company took over the Chickering lease and converted the three floors above the first floor
into a studio, offices, cutting laboratory, and costume and property
storage rooms.

Griffith started up the steps, paused outside the door, summon-
ing up his strength, and then plunged through the door.

2

All the Griffiths, Together

In my youth, this story as I heard it from my mother
—she was Scotch and would no more think of bragging
about anything than I would of jumping into the river.
. . . a certain Lord Brayington was exiled from Europe,
his title confiscated; also all of his property for some political offense. Mrs. Ray thinks this must have been Ber-
ington, but I am sure she was wrong in this. It may possibly have been Brotherton, but as I was an actor in my
youth with a man named John Griffith who did some of
the Shakesperean [sic] plays, and he did not want another Griffith on the program I took the name of Brayington. I was sure so this would seem to prove that this
was the name of my family. It seems that he had descended on one side of his family—I haven't the faintest
idea which, from the Griffith Princes of Wales; after he
had been thrown out of his position and title, he married
a lady named Griffith—I think the first name was Gy-
wain, whose father claimed to be a direct descendant of
AP Cyman Griffith, King of Wales, in 1079. . . .[17]

In the spring of 1875 the Reconstruction period was ending due to
the exposures of corruption in the administration of President
Ulysses S. Grant. The moribund Democratic party was beginning
to regain lost ground in both the North and South. In only ten
years' time the facts of the Civil War, or as the South preferred, the
War Between the States, were disappearing into the mists of legend. Old soldiers had begun to embellish their exploits. Exaggera-
tion was the rule. Nowhere was the need for legends more acute
than in the Border states. Every man who aspired to public office
felt that he would be asked what he had done in the war. It was as
important for local politicians to cloak themselves in heroics, even
if false, as it was for the Republican presidential candidate Ruther-
ford B. Hayes to let the constituency know he was a four-times-
wounded ex-Union Brigadier. In Kentucky, especially the rural

districts, a Confederate affiliation was more desirable than a Union one. In Oldham County, Kentucky, the local hero and aspirant to political office was former Colonel Jacob Wark Griffith, hard drinker, loud talker, barroom swashbuckler, and loafer. The colonel had failed to find a satisfactory vocation after the end of the war other than sitting on the front porch of his 520-acre farm watching his wife and daughters work the fields. He publicly announced his regret from time to time that his "war wounds" prevented him from doing more than occasionally supervising the work from horseback. The "wounds" apparently responded best to some therapy from the bourbon barrel sitting in the corner of the porch. Politics, on the other hand, was something for a man like Colonel Jake. No physical labor was necessary. The only requirements were the ownership of land and a more bombastic voice than the next man. The first requirement had been obtained through his marriage, and the second he had been born with.

Floydsfork, Kentucky, where the Griffith home was located, would have been described locally as a wide place in the road between Centerfield and Beard's Station. The latter name was changed by local decree in 1910 to Crestwood when the inhabitants tired of hearing train conductors call out "Whiskers" for their station. It was always Crestwood to which David Griffith referred as his birthplace, a much nicer name than Floydsfork, and certainly nicer than "Whiskers."

Jacob Griffith also had a touch of the local desire to upgrade his surroundings with an appropriate name. He called his plain dirt farm "Lofty Green," a name that away from Floydsfork, to the uninitiated, conjured up a vision of a great plantation. A farm of 520 acres was not a plantation, or even close. Still the colonel could sit on his front porch and imagine himself at the head of a great agricultural enterprise.

But it was from the war that Jacob Griffith derived his political opportunities. His favorite story, told with ever-increasing embellishments, was of a cavalry charge led by himself, convalescent from wounds, while driving a commandeered buggy. Jacob Griffith told the story with such spell-binding force that his family after his death repeated the story on his tombstone complete with a footnote authenticating the exploit which was supposedly drawn from a non-existent history of Kentucky. The colonel's imagination was much more forceful than mere fact. A good omen for a politician.

Jacob Griffith had another politically useful story. He described his promotion to brigadier general by Jefferson Davis, the President of the Confederacy, one day before the fugitive Davis surrendered. The colonel would point out that this was probably the last field promotion made by the Confederacy, and, of course, it was too late for it to be recorded in the official records. No record does exist of such a promotion, although Griffith was present at the side of Jefferson Davis.[18] It didn't matter in 1875. No one was checking on anybody's war stories. Jacob Griffith found that being a brigadier was much more impressive in Oldham County than a mere colonel.

One other ingredient was needed in Griffith's political stew. A successful politician needed an aristocratic background, some impressive lineage, to fit the Kentucky pattern. To support this desired image, he constructed a family tree that allegedly stretched back to the ancient Griffith chieftains of Wales. These, in turn, could be cross-connected with the then ruling houses of Europe.

> According to a book which I read in England, the name of which I have forgotten, this family was one of the oldest ruling families in the world, and it had been rulers for some 500 years before the 11th Century, and . . . they intermarried with a large number of the ruling houses of France and Great Britain. Incidentally, in mentioning this Prince Hohenzollern, one of the Kaiser's sons—the only one that has a chance of being put upon the throne of Germany, if such a thing should take place, as he married into the ruling family of Russia, and the other sons were not so careful about their wedding affairs—told me that his Aunt who was one of the Hohenzollern ruling family, told him that my family was much older than his own and he used to open the door for me to go through first.[19]

The colonel was equally willing to bolster the distaff side of the family. He let it be known that his wife was descended through her mother, Nancy B. Carter, from the wealthy Carters of Virginia. There was no connection other than the similarity of names.

To make a genealogical connection from the ancient kings of Wales, Colonel Griffith bolstered the family legends by turning a shadowy immigrant from England named Brayington, or Barring-

ton, no one was ever quite certain, into a Lord Brayington. David
Griffith outlined the legend,

> Now getting back to this Lord Brayington, or what have you,
> who married the Welsh lady named Griffith and discarded his
> own. It certainly could not have been great-grandfather Sala-
> thiel; it must have been his father. I know from one thing that I
> have heard from my family that it must have been close to the
> heart of my grandfather, Captain Daniel Weatherby Griffith (he
> must have been hard hearted) because he said that he would not
> have the name of England mentioned in his house, so the
> grudge must have been close in his memory.
> . . . Incidentally, my grandfather Captain Daniel Weatherby
> Griffith, was a Captain in Moultrey's Mounted Riflemen and
> fought with General Jackson at the Battle of New Orleans.[20]

Salathiel Griffith, the Colonel's grandfather, was turned into a
hero of the American Revolution, and his father, Daniel, created a
captain at the side of Andrew Jackson. In actuality Salathiel had
been a deputy constable in Maryland during the Revolution, and
following the war in 1786 was elected sheriff of Somerset County,
Maryland. His three-year incumbency was notable chiefly for his
ability to turn a small profit from the manipulation of the various
currencies, public and private, that floated about after the war, and
for the management of the small estates left, during probate, in his
charge. Salathiel gained little from these extra-curricular activities
except an estate consisting of three thousand dollars and several
small parcels of land in widely scattered locations. These properties, suspiciously resembling the properties in his official custody,
were left to his daughter Sarah Beauchamp and his five sons, Mer-
lin, Jefferson, Salathiel, William, and Daniel.[21]

Daniel Weatherby Griffith was six years old when his father, Salathiel, died. The net proceeds of his father's estate, after land sales,
amounted to roughly five or six thousand dollars to be used for the
education and apprenticeships of the five sons. Daniel, as the
youngest, received the smallest share, and, as a consequence, a
rather skimpy formal education.

The captaincy accorded Daniel by his son and by his grandson
D. W. Griffith never existed. It is doubtful that Daniel ever visited
New Orleans, and certainly not as a soldier. His less than illus-
trious military career consisted of an enlistment in George Hum-

phrey's Rifles of the Virginia Militia for the defense of Washington, D.C., in 1814. His total length of service was one month, from August 26 to September 26. His unofficial mustering out seems to have coincided exactly with the American defeat and rout at the Battle of Bladensburg just before the British captured and burned Washington. Daniel, then twenty-two, didn't stop the mustering out process until he was deep in Virginia far south of Washington. His highest rank was private.[22]

Daniel settled in Charles Town, Jefferson County, Virginia, married twice, and fathered five sons. Colonel Jacob Griffith was the son of Daniel's first wife, Margaret Wark. Margaret Wark had brought a small piece of property to her marriage. After her death, Daniel managed to dissipate the proceeds from his first wife's estate, forcing him to follow his eldest son, George Weatherby Griffith, to Kentucky. George Griffith had become a tailor in Floydsburg, Kentucky, in 1836. Twenty-one-year-old Jacob had joined him in 1839. Daniel and the rest of the family came later.

Young Jacob Griffith had received only a charity school education and was without a trade. He was apathetic to his brother George's offer of an apprenticeship in the tailor shop. Instead, he talked his way into an apprenticeship with a local doctor, John Grove Speers. Dr. Speers, himself, as was common practice, had earned his medical credentials by serving a two-year apprenticeship with a Dr. Hiram Weathers. After two years the fledgling doctor was free to set up his own practice. It was considered desirable, but unnecessary, to take some courses at Louisville Medical College. After two years at the side of Dr. Speers, Jacob Griffith became Dr. Griffith. It would have taken more time to become a good tailor.[23]

The potential patients seem to have been better judges of the new doctor's qualifications than the law. After four years of practice as a physician, Jacob Griffith's sole taxable possession was a gold watch.[24]

Since medicine didn't seem to provide an income, Jacob looked about for something else. The steady pay of military life seemed appealing, so on June 9, 1846, he enlisted in Captain Pennington's Company G, First Regiment of the Kentucky Cavalry. Within a few weeks his loud parade-ground voice and commanding presence brought him promotion to sergeant.[25]

Jacob Griffith's enlistment was also a patriotic act. Congress had declared war on Mexico on May 13, 1846, and the Kentucky Cavalry was dispatched to join the forces of General Zachary Taylor in Texas. Jacob's medical training, such as it was, caused him to be assigned medical duties at both the bloody battle of Buena Vista and at Saltillo.[26]

His patriotic fervor had dissipated by the end of his one-year enlistment, and despite the continuing war, Jacob took his discharge at New Orleans. Before the war was over, Jacob Griffith was back in Floydsburg, basking in a self-inflated reputation as a war hero and expert marksman.

Despite his newly acquired military glory, there were still few patients for his revived medical practice. His colorful war stories did impress attractive young Mary Oglesby, a cousin of Dr. Speer's wife, Sarah. Griffith married Mary Oglesby on September 18, 1848, and moved into his father-in-law's house.

This arrangement was a little wearing on Thomas Oglesby, Mary's father, and as soon as possible he built a five-room cottage on his farm for the young couple. He did continue to support them. Jacob Griffith was expected to assist his father-in-law in the operation of the 495-acre Oglesby farm, and Griffith could expect to inherit the farm after Thomas's death, in the same fashion in which Thomas had inherited the property through his own wife. Until that event, however, Thomas Oglesby made it clear that Griffith's status was that of a hired hand.[27]

On December 5, 1848, President Polk announced the discovery of gold in California. Gold fever swept the nation. One of the first to make the trek to California was Thomas Oglesby's brother Richard. Late in 1849 Richard Oglesby returned to Floydsburg with tales of the California gold fields. The contrast between the glittering promise of California and his present life behind a mule and a plow was too much for Jacob Griffith. He announced his intention of making the next trip to California with Richard Oglesby.

On May 2, 1850, Griffith in the company of Dr. Speer, Richard Oglesby, Miller Oglesby, and four others left for the West in a four-wagon mule train. Griffith said goodbye to his bride of twenty months, promising her, in the tradition of such moments, to return rich.

The group appointed former Sergeant Griffith to the command of the expedition, but barely one day past Lexington, Kentucky, Griffith was relieved of the command. The principal objection to Griffith by the other members of the party was his explosive temper which treated man and mule alike.

Jacob Griffith was no more successful as a gold prospector than as a physician. He spent two years in California with little success. Dr. Speer generously gave him an interest in a claim that yielded about $16 a day for them both which Speer purchased from another prospector. Griffith and Speer had remained in the vicinity of Nevada City. Richard Oglesby had left them and prospected near Palo Alto.

After two years Richard Oglesby returned and gave Griffith $8,000 to take back to Kennedy and deposit in a bank for him. Later Jacob Griffith claimed that he had managed to save $16,000 of his own money, an extraordinary claim in view of his $8 a day share from the Nevada City mine. At the final stop on the trip home, at Louisville, according to the Oglesby family, Griffith lost his own and Richard Oglesby's money in a card game. The Griffiths claimed that Jacob had lost only his own money, and that the Oglesby money was turned over to his father-in-law intact. In any event, the tax records for 1852 show that Jacob Griffith's only possessions were two mules valued at $120. They were probably the same mules that had brought him back from California.[28]

The unsuccessful gold hunter once again became Dr. Griffith, physician without patients, and part-time field hand. It was noted that Jacob's assistance on the Oglesby farm consisted of much noise, bustling about, but actually little work. He much preferred lecturing on the California gold fields at church socials, where his stories, appropriately embellished with dramatic gestures and operatic voice, rapidly gained him a reputation as an orator.

The next logical step was politics. Jacob Griffith took it. He became a candidate for the Kentucky legislature and was elected as the representative of Oldham and Trimble counties in 1854. Once again he said goodbye to his wife, moving to Louisville, and taking up residence at Mrs. Blackburn's boarding house.[29]

During his one session as a legislator, Griffith was informed of the death of his first-born son, Thomas Jackaniah, and the birth of his daughter Matta. The burden of both the death and birth fell on Mary Griffith.

Thomas Oglesby died in 1856 leaving a deed to his property that Jacob had helped him prepare. The deed provided for the equal division of the farm between Mary and her half-brother, Miller Woodson Oglesby. Miller Oglesby fought the terms of this division for seven years on the grounds of Jacob's undue influence. He finally gave up the battle for the property in 1863. Not until then did Mary receive a clear title to 264½ acres, five slaves, and miscellaneous cattle and horses. Jacob Griffith then took over the inheritance as trustee for his wife, listing himself, as he had during the court battles with Miller Oglesby, as her "agent." For the first time Jacob Griffith was a man of property, a slave owner, and consequently by Southern standards of the day, a gentleman.

Farms, even with slaves, still demanded a great deal of work from the owner. The seven years of operating the farm after his father-in-law's death had been most unpleasant, and Jacob was quite prepared to seize any opportunity for escape. The vote for secession in Kentucky at last provided him with his chance. He moved his wife and two children, Matta and baby William, off the farm into Floydsburg, where they would be near relatives, and enlisted in October 1861 at Horse Caves, Kentucky, in his old regiment, the First Kentucky Cavalry. Since it was customary for cavalry enlistees to provide their own horses, Jacob took Mary's horse with him.

The war years proved to be the high point of Jacob Griffith's life. He began again as a sergeant, drilling recruits. The regiment helped cover General Johnstone's retreat toward Nashville, Tennessee, and then was detached to guard railroad bridges near Decatur, Alabama. It fought in the bloody battle of Shiloh, joined General Forrest's advance into Kentucky, and participated in sharp engagements at Hewey's Gap, Tennessee, and in the Sesquatchie Valley. In the last engagement Griffith was wounded and promoted to captain.[30]

In March 1863 Griffith was promoted to colonel. He led his regiment at Chattanooga, McKinville, Hills Gap, and assisted in covering the Confederate retreat from Missionery Ridge.

During an engagement at Charlestown, Tennessee, Griffith's reg-

iment was allegedly asked to make one more charge. It was this
charge out of which Colonel Griffith's favorite story, the leading of
the charge while riding in a buggy, was born.

> I know this story of his leading a charge in a buggy is true [his
> son later wrote]. It was told me first by Major General Lord
> French of the British Army and have read it in some early his-
> tory records when I was in Kentucky—I think perhaps it was
> Rudd's History of Kentucky or it might have been Colonel
> Polk-Johnson, but I know this story is true as I have heard it
> from some of the men who fought under him.[31]

There is no evidence of such an action by Colonel Griffith taking
place during the war. As mentioned earlier there is no *History of
Kentucky* by Rudd. The only mention of the incident appears in a
subscription book alleged to be a history of Kentucky where the incident is mentioned in the biographical sketches of both Colonel
Griffith and D. W. Griffith. The language of the entries, however,
shows it to be a standard press release of the Griffith Company during the period of the book's preparation.[32]

Colonel Griffith returned to his home in June 1865, following
the surrender of Jefferson Davis. He found that Mary Griffith had
done an excellent job of managing the farm in his absence. The
former slaves, now technically freedmen without a place to go, had
remained in their little cabins and accepted employment as hired
hands at a small yearly salary. Mary had permitted them to stay on
the land, raise their own vegetables and chickens, and avail themselves of the services of a cow. The farm had been untouched by
the war, not even once threatened by Union guerillas. During the
colonel's absence, life on the farm had proceeded much as before.

Jacob reclaimed his favorite spot on the front porch, pretended
complete bewilderment at any and all chores, and continued to let
Mary run the farm. Those household chores that were physically
beyond Mary or the children, such as repairing cracks in the house
walls, were taken care of by Mary's relatives.[33]

When the three Griffith daughters, Mattie, Ruth, and Anna
Wheeler, were old enough, they joined their mother in the fields
and did chores such as milking cows, caring for the horses and
chopping wood. Meanwhile, the war hero Colonel Jake politicked
and got drunk on the porch.

One thing that mitigated against the colonel's behavior was the love of his family and the trust of his neighbors. The latter, impressed by his seeming leadership qualities, entrusted him with the sale of their produce in Louisville. He sold the produce and then gambled away the proceeds. His neighbors listened to his excuses for losing the money in silence. They did not ask him to handle their affairs again. His family remained loyal and uncomplaining, and he also was capable of expressing a fondness for his children, sometimes in impulsive ways.

He sold some cows for the collateral necessary to securing a loan. The loan proceeds were then used to buy a piano for his daughter Mattie. He also insisted that Mattie attend Millersburg (Kentucky) Female College, an unaccredited school that prepared and supplied teachers for the one-room rural schools.

After a time, Mattie was hired to be the regular teacher at the Walnut School, a one-room building between Beard's Station and Centerfield, where she taught all grades and all subjects. Mattie Griffith also took personal responsibility for the education of her younger sisters and brothers.

Despite the loss in confidence by his neighbors, Colonel Griffith was re-elected to the Kentucky legislature in 1877. He conducted his campaign from a new forty dollar carriage, an expenditure that the family could ill afford. After the election he left home to take up residence in Frankfort for the term of the legislature.

In January 1878 he wrote to Mattie,

> Dear Daughter,
> This completes the week of my legislative labor. So far all goes well. I have met a host of old friends who seem to have been more than glad to see me, all agreeing that I look nice and as when I was first flashing my sword in the great *Lost Cause*. . . .
> The question here is not asked is he rich but is he a man of brains. I want to prepare you for life, to be able to meet and act with life—to be able to hold "the mirror up to nature." Force upon your brothers and sisters the dire necessity of cultivating their minds.
>
> Your loving *pa*
> J. W. Griffith

There were five other Griffith children commended by Colonel Griffith to Mattie's special attention as the oldest child, two girls: Ruth and Anna Wheeler; and three boys, William, Jacob, Jr., and three-year-old David Wark Griffith. One other boy was added to the family later—Albert.

Little David was the apple of his father's eye. The colonel had written to Mattie while she was attending Millersburg Female College that little David "is one of the first in point of beauty and sense." David was born on the night of January 22, 1875. Some relatives remembered David as a baby who never cried and was "the homeliest brat they had ever seen." [34]

Mattie took seriously her father's charge to cultivate the minds of her brothers and sisters. They formed the nucleus of the classes that she conducted both at home and in the Walnut Grove School. Mattie was particularly concerned with young David because he had a pronounced lisp until about eight years old. His babyish name for Mattie, "Thith Mat," became her nickname for all the rest of the family. Mattie's cure for David's speech problem was to insist on, as well as encourage, his giving recitations. It is doubtful that the constant recitations cured the lisp; it was rather due to the passage of time and maturation, but young David did acquire a taste for performing.

Shortly after David Griffith's birth, the family moved into a new five-room house, the old house being razed after the move. It was this house that David Griffith was to remember as his first home.

> Indeed, like many others when far away from this farm, we would call it a lovely palace, the true Kentucky estate, without any fear that anybody was going to correct our slight exaggeration. In reality, this small palace had four small rooms downstairs and one garret above. It had a very cheerful outlook from the front of the house, looking from the front windows on the left towards the main road, a sloping meadow and a field where they generally grew wheat, and on the right, at the corner line, a graveyard. What physical strength I may have today I got from the exercise of running by the graveyard. We had to go to school a couple of miles away, crossing a creek seven times, and particularly in the winter time when we were getting home, it was almost dark. After what was something over two miles walking, we would put on all speed to get by this graveyard. [35]

In addition to his formal schooling under his sister, young David was also impressed, along with his sisters and brothers, with his father's tales of family exploits. The colonel's embroidered tales of

great-grandfather Salathiel and grandfather Daniel, and their alleged contributions to American history, as well as his own exploits
on behalf of "the lost cause," were terribly exciting. The colonel
added tall tales of his adventures in the California gold fields. The
stories were reinforced by the presence of the colonel's sword, and
pistol holsters engraved with "US" on the leather indicating that
they had been liberated from the enemy forces. David remained an
attentive audience long after the other children became bored. "I
remember he had a way of saying things so everybody paid attention to it. He had a voice of terrific power. He was called 'Roaring
Jake.' " [36]

David was also impressed with opinions expressed by others
about his father.

> I also imagine he was sort of a pet with the women because I
> remember at a dance which they were giving at our house. . . .
> There was a sofa in the corner of the room. I cautiously crept
> underneath it to see and hear what was going on. Near the sofa
> were a couple of young girls and one of them said, with real fer-
> vor, "Goodness gracious me, I would like to get a dance with
> Colonel Griffith." He was then far along in his sixties. Since I
> was the only one near enough to hear them and carry the com-
> pliment to the Colonel, I knew they meant it. It never seemed to
> make much difference whether he had money or not, he always
> managed somehow. You could have more fun riding with him in
> an old farm wagon with some straw on the floor than in the best
> pullman car that was ever made.[37]

The mementos from the War Between the States were sufficient
proof for young David of the truth of his father's stories. When the
colonel offered the excuse that the "family tree" and the family papers had been lost in a fire during the war, this, too, was accepted.
Griffith never doubted his father's stories throughout his life, and,
when he could afford it after his film success, he paid geneologists
to attempt to find the information that would link his family with
the ancient kings of Wales. No such links were ever found, but a
colorful family crest was found, or invented, that David Griffith believed was a true one. The search for ancestors always foundered
on the mysterious Mr. Brayington who had changed his name to
Griffith.

David Griffith was equally fond of listening to a cousin, Charles

Griffith, relate his exploits as a member of an unsuccessful posse on the trail of the notorious Jesse and Frank James. The family stories never suffered in the telling, and young David listened, wide-eyed, from his favorite spot under the sofa.

David Griffith's first experience with the theatre took place on a cold November evening in the Walnut Grove School. An itinerant performer with a magic lantern show and a strongman act rented the one-room school for a performance. Slides were projected on a large white sheet hung at one end of the room, and when the pictures ended, the strongman lifted his weights in the white light of the projector, his shadow cast large behind him on the sheet. David was excited by the strongman's finale in which a large rock balanced on his chest was shattered by repeated sledge hammer blows. The suspense of waiting for the rock or the man's chest to shatter was almost unbearable. At the conclusion David was swept away with hearing his first applause.

A more frequent source of entertainment for the Griffith family came from the regular visits of Isadore Kahn, an elderly Jewish peddler. Kahn's visits not only gave Mary Griffith and her girls an opportunity to shop, but also provided an evening of pleasure in listening to Kahn's stories of his travels. The peddler would be invited to stay for the night, and, like the troubadours of old, pay for his supper by playing an ancient concertina, singing Jewish folk songs, and telling Bible stories. All of the Griffith children were allowed to stay up late when Mr. Kahn visited.

The Griffith family, as was the custom for most rural families, provided much of their own entertainment by holding reading nights. The colonel, loving the sound of his own voice, did most of the reading. Other members of the family were pressed into service occasionally. Most frequently the colonel read from the poems, plays, and stories of Edgar Allan Poe, Oliver Goldsmith, Sir Walter Scott, and Shakespeare. The colonel would read with great vocal stress on the rolling phrases, the lofty sentiments, and the concepts of social caste.

Sometimes the reading nights included the Oglesby cousins and other neighbors, severely crowding the tiny house. David would listen from under the sofa, or for a change, would transfer to a spot under the dining table. He was unable to see a good deal of the time, but he was enthralled with the sound of the voices. The effect of the readings was enhanced by the flickering light of one or two candles next to the reader.

Two months after David's seventh birthday, the effects of Colonel Griffith's irregular habits and fondness for whiskey caught up with him. In March 1882 the colonel awoke in the middle of the night looking for something to eat. His choice of pickles, washed down with whiskey, resulted in a sudden painful attack. He wakened his daughter Mattie and sent her for the doctor. The rest of the family stood by while Mary Griffith attempted to soothe her husband's pain. The doctor arrived and administered a sedative.

David Wark Griffith remembered this event as it had been explained to him by his mother.

> This last illness was caused by a bullet wound he had received during the war. He had had many, but this one bullet had gone through his belly and he lay on the ground for several hours with his insides hanging out on the ground until a surgeon came.
>
> . . . He pulled his insides back in and sewed him up. At that time, the North, through the blockade, were holding out all drugs including morphine, catgut, etc. The catgut with which the surgeon sewed him up was not so good, and finally, after a lapse of years, it rotted and broke and nothing could be done for him so he lay in the darkened room dying from a blow of the past.
>
> I was outside, standing on the rear porch, when the country doctor came out and told one of the country cousins there was no hope. He was dying, and it was only a question of a few hours. I went around the house and got behind the chimney in my favorite corner when I was in trouble and, of course, I broke out in tears. Perhaps, I was always sentimental. Little while afterwards, they came and got me and took me inside. The poor old negroes were standing in the back, at the foot of the bed, weeping. I am quite sure they really loved him.
>
> Around the bed the family was gathered. As was the custom in the old South, he had a word of goodbye to say to each one of us. When it was my turn, I came beside the bed. He looked at me for quite a long time with those brave eyes that now seemed so soft and tender. Finally, he said, as I grew close to him, "Be brave, my son, be brave."
>
> Then after he had said goodbye to the last of the family, it was only a short time until he laid still forever. And then they

took him away, that which I loved more than anything I have
ever loved in my life.[38]

A cold gray rain fell outside as seven-year-old David stared at his
father's face for the last time.

Funeral services for Colonel Jacob Griffith were held in the
Mount Tabor Methodist Church, attended by relatives and neighbors from many miles around. Isadore Kahn, the peddler, came.
The colonel's old comrades from the Kentucky First Cavalry
formed a double line outside the church as Jacob's body was borne
from the services.

Colonel Jacob Wark Griffith had been a charming, dramatic
figure, a seeker of adventure in preference to work. To his son
David he was to remain a shadowy figure that embodied the brief
glory of the Confederacy and stood, with his romanticized ancestors,
in the mainstream of American history. There is a theory that the
fundamental concepts of a human being have been formed before
he is five. Certainly, David Wark Griffith's ideas and philosophy
seemed not to change after his father's death.

3

Biograph: The Beginning

> . . . the Motion Picture director has a material advantage over the old-time stage director. The latter is confined and limited in his scope. He can only show certain scenes in the limits of three walls, and at best has only a few square feet in which to place his characters.
>
> In Motion Pictures we operate in a larger field. On the stage so-called "effects" are imitations. The film-play shows the actual occurrence and is not hampered by the size of the stage nor the number of people to be used.
>
> For a film-drama we can go afield and get anything we want. If there is a shipwreck to show, we also picture the angry sea and the restless waves.[39]

A few years before the American Mutoscope and Biograph Company had moved to 14th Street, Henry Norton Marvin, the film company's general manager, and one of its founders, engaged a sometime stage director, George McCutcheon, to follow the pattern of a single incident without characterization set by Edwin S. Porter in making story films. McCutcheon was a man of small imagination and was quite content to imitate the films of other companies in New York. The task of hiring actors or writers had been delegated by Henry Marvin to McCutcheon and to Lee Dougherty, an ex-newspaperman hired originally to write publicity and advertising, and to supervise the acquisition of stories. Dougherty had also taken on the job of interviewing actors in McCutcheon's absence.

The company itself was in a perilous position. It was some $200,000 in debt to Leroy Barton, president of the Empire Trust Company. Barton had placed his own man, Jeremiah J. Kennedy, in control of the company as president to preserve their interests. Since Kennedy was interested only in the financial position of the company, he left the day-to-day operations in Marvin's hands.

Kennedy occupied himself with the sharp conflict between the

handful of independent film companies and those others that had
allied themselves with the Edison interests. The Edison group had
attempted to assert a stranglehold on the infant industry by securing the patent rights to the motion picture camera. Various attempts had been made by film entrepreneurs to evade the Edison
patents. One of the successful evasions had been conducted by
Henry Marvin and his partner, Herman Casler. The two men, associated in the Marvin & Casler Electric Rock Drill Company of
Canastota, New York, had with the help of a former Edison assistant, William Dickson, constructed a camera that did not violate
the Edison patents. Dickson's undercover help was most valuable
because he was probably the principal inventor of the Edison camera and knew exactly how to avoid trespassing on his own previous
work. One technical item was shared by the two systems, a special
device, called a Latham loop, that enabled the film to pass
smoothly in back of the lens, pausing for each exposure, without
destroying the sharpness of the image. In the face of the Edison attempt to freeze out any competition not licensed by themselves,
Marvin and Casler found that the shrewd J. J. Kennedy had acquired the rights to the Latham loop.

The legal standoff, maneuvered by Kennedy, was in 1908 on the
verge of a settlement with Kennedy gaining an upper hand. The
American Mutoscope and Biograph Company was to join the Edi-
son group in an association to be known as the Motion Picture
Patents Company. The member companies were Edison, Biograph,
Pathé Freres, George Melies, Vitagraph, Kalem, Essanay, George
Kleine, and Lubin. The new agreement was to take effect on Janu-
ary 1, 1909. Frank L. Dyer had been elected president, and show-
ing Biograph power, Henry Marvin was elected vice-president, and
J. J. Kennedy became the secretary.

The official statement of the new trust said:

> It is hoped by this movement to do away with the vexatious
> litigation which has long harassed the business, to guarantee to
> the renters and the exhibitors a sufficient quantity of the best
> American and foreign films and to prevent the demoralized state
> of affairs which now prevails abroad where no organization ex-
> ists. All licensees of the new Patents Company must compete for
> the business of the country on their own merits.[40]

While Kennedy's maneuverings on the business front brought some financial stability to Biograph, the company was in a poor competitive position in terms of films. The Biograph films were not being well received. George "Old Man" McCutcheon seemed most concerned with finding employment for seven of his children and grooming his eldest son, Wallace, to take over as director. Wallace had little interest in making films, much preferring to pursue a career in musical comedy.

Henry Marvin decided in the spring of 1908 that action was needed to improve the Biograph product. He hired another ex-newspaperman, Stanner E. V. Taylor, to write stories. Taylor had been quite skeptical of working in films, but when Biograph bought two of his brief 300-word stories, and paid thirty dollars for each of them, he decided to stay for some of that easy money.

The directorial problem was complicated for Marvin since George McCutcheon's health was declining, the result of acute mastoiditis. McCutcheon pushed Wallace forward to direct, but Wallace was willing to direct only one film a week. The company wanted at least two films each week, and in the best of circumstances three. The films were, of course, one-reelers running from five to twelve minutes, and some were still intended for use in the company's Mutoscopes, a peep-show machine still extant in some amusement park penny arcades. Stanner Taylor tried his hand at directing and accounted himself a failure. Marvin agreed. No one else on the staff was interested in directing. Neither of Biograph's two cameramen would consider it. Biograph's first cameraman was Arthur Marvin, the general manager's brother. The second cameraman was Gottlieb Wilhelm "Billy" Bitzer. Arthur Marvin was a light-hearted easy-going man, quite content to take and follow orders. Billy Bitzer had joined Biograph in the nineties as an electrician and, having a love of machinery, had made the transition to cameraman easily. Both men considered that their contributions to making a film were infinitely more important than those of a director. They felt the director merely moved the actors into place for the camera. Becoming a director would be a demotion for them.

Henry Marvin was inclined to agree with his cameramen. He thought that the only real requisite for a film director was energy, stamina, and some knowledge of actors.

When David Griffith stepped through the Biograph front door at the top of the brownstone steps, he found himself in a marble-floored foyer, a relic of the house's days as the Cunard mansion. On that main floor were the doors leading to the paymaster's office, Lee Dougherty's office, and, directly to the rear, past the stairway leading to the upper floors, the former Cunard ballroom. This large room, approximately fifty by thirty-five feet, had been converted by Biograph into the film studio.

George McCutcheon appeared promptly to look Griffith over. McCutcheon was a chunky fifty-ish man with an ample wad of tobacco in one cheek. The corners of the foyer were its frequent target. McCutcheon was friendly to the newcomer, introducing him to everyone who passed through the hall—Billy Bitzer, Arthur Marvin, Eddie Shulter, who painted scenery, and two actresses, Marion Leonard and Florence Auer. Finally McCutcheon introduced Griffith to Stanner Taylor. He had given a brief job description to Griffith of each person as they were introduced. Taylor was "the writer." Then McCutcheon turned Griffith over to his son Wallace for a tour of the building.

The first room on the tour was the studio. Wallace pointed out the banks of Cooper-Hewitt mercury vapor lamps mounted on the ceiling and the Aristo "flaming arc" lamps. Wallace mentioned how these lights enabled the company to film indoors without regard to weather, a considerable improvement over the old roof-top studios of the past, dependent upon daylight and subject to inclement weather.

Along one wall Eddie Shulter was painting canvas-covered stage flats for scenery. His painting techniques were the same as those used in the theatre. In one corner stood the camera mounted on a five-by-five-foot rolling platform. Wallace responded to a question from Griffith that the rolling platform was used to get the camera into position for each scene. It was then held steady in order to get the best exposure, the same as a still camera.

Enclosed between banks of Cooper-Hewitt lights stood a small interior setting. Griffith was unimpressed with the set. He had worked with much finer scenery during his stock company days, particularly during his engagement with Nance O'Neill's Company. This tacky studio made him wish he was back with a legitimate theatre company.

McCutcheon then led Griffith up the stairway to the upper floors. The first stop was the cutting room behind a wooden partition. Griffith was introduced to Edward Scott, the cutter, and his assistant, Joseph Aller. Wallace told him that the cutter's job was to assemble the individual scenes into one whole film. The processing and printing of multiple prints was handled in a factory in Hoboken, New Jersey.

Next to the cutting room was a shipping room run by Dan "Truck Horse" Shay. Shay had acquired the nickname from carrying heavy loads of film back and forth to the Hoboken laboratory. Griffith met Shay's young helper, James Edward Smith. Jimmy Smith did the packing, labeling, and general errand-running.

A small projection room was next, then another small room housing a job printing press on which Lee Dougherty produced the broadsides advertising Biograph films. Henry Marvin's formal office was also on the second floor, although he preferred to use a suite of three rooms on the third floor. Wallace didn't take Griffith to the fourth floor, explaining that it was just used to house some machinery that Marvin and Herman Casler had invented.

Returning to the first floor, Wallace McCutcheon showed Griffith the tiny dressing rooms last. The grubby, rat-infested little rooms would not have impressed a visitor, although the gas rings for heating coffee or soup, the layers of grime and dust, the empty whiskey bottles in the corner, looking like most theatre backstage areas, were familiar to Griffith. He had seen and lived in their like in theatres from coast to coast. The basement, McCutcheon mentioned, was for props and old scenery.

At the conclusion of the tour, Griffith was delivered to Dougherty and Taylor. Griffith identified himself as a writer, mentioning his published work. Dougherty was unimpressed with Griffith's poem, noting for Griffith's benefit that both Taylor and himself were ex-newspapermen. Dougherty was more impressed with Griffith's play and after its mention asked if Griffith had anything for sale. Over the next few weeks Griffith sold Dougherty a number of the brief stories and synopses that provided the plots for Biograph films. His stories that were filmed included *Old Isaacs, the Pawn-broker, The Music Master, At the Crossroads of Life, The Stage Rustler,* and *Ostler Joe.* Feeling safe to point out that he was also an actor, he was hired to appear in the films made from his own script, and he coached a fight scene in *The Stage Rustler.* Griffith mentioned that he knew a bright young actress, Linda Arvidson, who would be just right for the company, and Linda was also hired. The two appeared together in the leading roles of a highly condensed version of *When Knighthood Was in Flower,* directed by Wallace McCutcheon.

At last the wolf at the Griffith door was at bay. Both David and Linda received five dollars a day for the acting jobs, a sum that went a considerable distance in 1908, and the synopses brought in thirty dollars each.

While working on the films Griffith made a number of percep-tive comments in the presence of Arthur Marvin. Arthur was suffi-ciently impressed to mention to his brother that Griffith might be the director Henry was looking for.

Griffith was called into Dougherty's office and asked if he would direct a film. Griffith had watched Wallace McCutcheon closely and had decided that there wasn't anything difficult in directing a film. He even had some of McKee Rankin's old directorial manner-isms on tap. Rankin had been Nance O'Neill's director. He agreed to try. Thumbing through a stack of synopses on Dougherty's desk, he found one called *The Adventures of Dollie* that interested him.

Dougherty made certain that Griffith knew he would be direct-ing on trial. If the picture succeeded, he would be given another to direct. This arrangement left Griffith feeling insecure, so he hesi-tated, and then said that he would think it over and let Dougherty know the next day. Griffith wanted to go home and talk it over with Linda. His fear was that if he failed at directing, he might lose his acting jobs.

At home Linda encouraged him to accept, pointing out that he would be able to use actors of his own choice, even herself. After a thorough discussion, they decided he should accept, but with some conditions.

The next day Griffith returned to Dougherty, and after pointing out that he had responsibilities and would not jeopardize his writ-

ing or acting career, he said that if Dougherty would guarantee
that his other employment would not be endangered by failure,
he'd accept the directing job. Dougherty agreed and handed him
the synopsis for *The Adventures of Dollie*.

The synopsis was probably close to the description that Lee
Dougherty wrote for the Biograph bulletin announcing the production's release, July 14, 1908:

> On the lawn of a country residence we find the little family
> comprising father, mother and little Dollie, their daughter. In
> front of the grounds there flows a picturesque stream to which
> the mother and little one go to watch the boys fishing. . . .
> While the mother and child are seated on the wall beside the
> stream, one of these Gypsies approaches and offers for sale sev-
> eral baskets. A refusal raises his ire and he seizes the woman's
> purse and is about to make off with it when the husband, hear-
> ing her cries of alarm, rushes down to her aid, and with a heavy
> snakewhip lashes the Gypsy unmercifully, leaving great welts
> upon his swarthy body, at the same time arousing the venom of
> his black heart.
>
> . . . [The Gypsy] seizes the child and carries her to his
> camp where he gags and conceals her in a watercask.
>
> [Later] as they ford a stream the cask falls off a wagon into
> the water and is carried away by the current. Next we see the
> cask floating downstream toward a waterfall, over which it goes;
> then through the seething spray of the rapids, and on, on until
> it finally enters the cove of the first scene, where it is brought
> ashore by the fisherboys. Hearing strange sounds emitted from
> the barrel, the boys call for the bereft father, who is still search-
> ing for the lost one. Breaking the head from the barrel the
> amazed and happy parents now fold in their arms their loved
> one, who is not much worse off for her marvelous experience.[41]

David Griffith saw that this synopsis offered him the best opportunity for concealing his inexperience. The entire film could be
made away from the studio where the bosses would not be able to
see any mistakes. Arthur Marvin, assigned as his cameraman, had
suggested that they go to Sound Beach, Connecticut. Marvin
pointed out that it had been used before, and everybody knew
their way around. The people at Sound Beach were used to movie-
makers and would leave them alone. The other cameraman, Billy
Bitzer, had also taken Griffith aside, and with the assistance of an

old shirtboard, outlined his concepts of how a film should be made. Bitzer had also offered to write any special action scenes that Griffith might require. Griffith had listened attentively but had confidence that his own theatre experience was more valuable in seeing him through this experience than ideas garnered from cameramen. He did accept the idea that the film should be shot at Sound Beach.

It was the responsibility of the director to cast the film. David confided to Linda that he didn't think any of the men he had seen at the Biograph studio was right for the role of the father. He thought it should be someone younger, more handsome, a juvenile. Linda had no suggestions, but thought she could do the mother role.

Griffith assented, still thinking about the problem of a leading man.

The next day Griffith began making the rounds of the theatrical agents. From his own experience he realized that he would have to avoid saying that he was looking for an actor to appear in a film. The agents wouldn't pay much attention to him, or steer him to any of their good people. He thought that it would be best if he just looked over the people waiting in the outer offices.

As he climbed the steps of one agency, Griffith passed a young man who was leaving. When Griffith entered the office, he asked the clerk if the young man he'd passed was an actor. The office clerk thought he might be. Griffith turned and left, spotting the young man down the block, and pursued him to the corner.

"Hey! Are you an actor?"

The young man turned and stared at his hawk-nosed, checkered-suited pursuer. "Yes. So . . ."

"What's your name?"

"Arthur Johnson. What's yours?"

"Lawrence Griffith. I'm directing a motion picture, and I may have a part for you!"

Arthur Johnson was interested in Griffith's proposition, particularly since he was "at liberty." Johnson, not being a novice, suggested that they discuss the deal over free lunch and a few drinks at the nearest saloon. Griffith agreed.

When they parted, Johnson had accepted the part.

"I don't know anything about film acting."

"You don't need to know," Griffith smiled with false bravado, "just meet me at the Grand Central depot at nine o'clock tomorrow morning."

"What do you want me to wear?" Now the actor in Johnson had taken over.

"Wealthy young businessman! Wear whatever you've got that fits." Griffith waved goodbye.

Griffith completed his casting with Biograph regulars. Charles Ainsley was cast as the evil Gypsy, and Mrs. Frank Gebhardt, the wife of another Biograph actor, was to play the Gypsy's wife.

Although Arthur Marvin had been assigned to the picture to keep a company eye on Griffith, he later said that he'd been chosen over Bitzer because he was two inches taller. There was to be a camera set-up in the water, and Marvin claimed that Bitzer would have been in over his head. Bitzer was amused by Marvin's remark since he knew that he was permanently assigned to the "experienced" director George McCutcheon or his son Wallace.[42]

The pattern of Griffith's first picture followed that of the other films made by Biograph, and, for that matter, the other studios of the day. Each scene was photographed with the camera in a fixed location. The scene was played exactly as it would have been on the stage. The actors were photographed in what was to become known as a medium shot with all of them visible in their entirety. Entrances were made, as on the stage, from left or right. There were about twelve scenes in the film, and each scene was a single shot.

Griffith completed the film's shooting in two days, on June 18 and 19, 1908. The processing of the film was completed in the Hoboken laboratory on June 22. Griffith and Linda waited impatiently for the results. Griffith attempted to reassure himself and his wife, "If the photography is there, the picture will be all right; if it looks as good on the negative as it looked while we were taking it, it ought to get by . . ."

Arthur Marvin brought the first strip of film for Griffith's inspection.

"How is it?" Griffith asked nervously.

"Looks pretty good, nice and sharp."

"Think it's all right?"

"Yeh. Think it is."

The quality of the film as listed in the laboratory records was less enthusiastic. It stated that the film was only "fair."

The next step was to project the film upstairs in the tiny projection room. In this narrow six-by-fifteen-foot room, a picture roughly four by three feet could be projected on the end wall. Linda Griffith remembered:

> No sound but the buzz and whir of the projection machine. The seven hundred and thirteen feet of the *Adventures* . . . was reeled off. Silence. Then Mr. Marvin [Henry] spoke:
> "That's it—that's something like it—at last!"
> Afterwards, upstairs in the executive offices, Mr. Marvin and Mr. Dougherty talked it over, and they concluded that if the next picture were half as good, Lawrence Griffith was the man they wanted.[43]

The little projection room became the hub of Griffith's examinations for all his films. It had been the practice largely to judge the quality of a film by running the negative through the hands quickly enough to get some idea of the motion. Only a few films were worth examining in the projection room. Griffith changed that and decided to look at all of his films before they were released. The screenings in the little stuffy projection room became special occasions, remembered by Marion Leonard, a leading Biograph actress, as a place where "we all thrilled with the glow of triumph."

The official first showing of *The Adventures of Dollie* took place at Keith and Proctor's Theatre, Union Square, New York, on July 14, 1908. Despite some kidding that this was Bastille Day, the Griffiths anticipated a glamorous, exciting affair, but:

> The house filled up from passers-by—frequenters of Union Square—lured by ten cent entertainment. These were the people to be pleased—they had paid out their nickels and dimes. So when they had sat through Dollie's seven hundred feet, interested, and not a snore to be heard, we concluded that we had a successful opening night.[44]

Although his first film really had given little sign that Griffith had anything special to contribute, it had shown that he could handle actors, deliver the film on time, and display little temperament. That was good enough for Henry Marvin, and he assigned another film to Griffith, *The Redman and the Child*. Marvin was the one least concerned with public acceptance of Griffith films, or, for that matter, anybody else's. Biograph was selling only about twenty copies of each film made, a poor sales record, but there was no reason to think that Griffith's would do any worse. As a result of Marvin's attitude, by the time the first showing of *The Adventures of Dollie* had taken place, Griffith had completed one film started by Wallace McCutcheon and five more of his own.

Henry Marvin had found his director. He was quite willing to delegate to Griffith the authority to select his actors, stories, and locations. Griffith enjoyed this freedom, although it meant arguing at the paymaster's window about expenses. He hired his friend Harry Salter for *The Redman and the Child,* and took the company across the Hudson River on the Weehawken Ferry, and then by train to Little Falls, New Jersey, for the primitive scenes on a river. The first scenes were shot on June 30, processed in the laboratory on July 1, and examined by Griffith. They were properly exposed and technically satisfactory, so Griffith returned to Little Falls on July 3 and finished the picture.

With his third film, Griffith had gained enough confidence to work in the studio, and he began *The Tavern Keeper's Daughter* there on July 2. In addition to Biograph regular Frank Gebhardt, Griffith cast Marion Sunshine, a vaudeville performer, in this film.

After the Independence Day holiday, on July 6 Griffith started his fourth film, *The Bandit's Waterloo,* in the studio, finishing it on July 8. The fifth picture, *A Calamitous Elopement,* followed on July 9 and 11. Griffith then returned to *The Tavern Keeper's Daughter* and shot the last scenes on July 13. A pattern of having more than one film in production had been set up.

Griffith was now caught in an expanding work pattern that left him very little free time at home. He completed ten pictures in the month of July. Wallace McCutcheon had seen that he was no longer needed and gladly departed. George McCutcheon was too ill to return, and so Griffith became Biograph's sole director by default.

Although the other Biograph cameraman, Billy Bitzer, had dis-

played little interest in the new director, now that the McCutcheons were gone, it was necessary for him to split the filming
assignments with Arthur Marvin. Bitzer discovered that Griffith
was a man who listened patiently to suggestions and thought about
them, but in the end proceeded to follow an independent course.
There had been no problem between Griffith and Marvin because
Arthur Marvin was quite content to let someone else do all the
thinking. Bitzer, however, had ideas of his own and clung to them
stubbornly. He soon learned that Griffith was a firm leader. Once a
course of action had been decided, Griffith would not alter it. Billy
Bitzer would just have to swallow his unused ideas.

The increased tempo of production at Biograph meant that Griffith had to expand the company of actors. Harry Salter, whom
Griffith had known in their days as stock actors, became a regular. Griffith then felt that he needed a leading lady. He had a very
specific type of woman in mind, but when he discussed this with
Linda, he found that she was more than a little put out at not being
automatically considered for the job. Griffith explained that he
needed her for the character ingenue. Griffith saw actors in the
traditional stage categories.

Linda was not happy about accepting her husband's definition of
her abilities and acting type. A small wedge had been driven between them. Griffith had forgotten the old theatre axiom, actress
first, wife second.

Two actresses that better suited Griffith's definitions of leading
ladies were added to the Biograph roster during July, Marion
Leonard and Florence Lawrence.

Marion Leonard had been at Biograph before. She had made a
few films for the McCutcheons, but left to take a job with a touring
play. Griffith, impressed with her strong featured resemblance to
Sarah Bernhardt, persuaded her to return—an easy task since Marion was down to her last eighteen dollars.

Florence Lawrence was a different matter. Griffith had not originally planned to hire her. He had screened some Vitagraph pictures in the little projection room and noticed the work of an
actress named Florence Turner. He sent Harry Salter to find her
and ask her to come to Biograph. Salter pretended that he couldn't
find Florence Turner, but he did find his girl friend, dark-haired

pretty Florence Lawrence. Salter promised to put in a word for her and introduce her to Griffith.

Florence Lawrence was the first popular favorite in the Biograph acting company. She had been acting in the theatre since childhood, when, managed by her mother, she was billed as "Baby Flo, the Child Wonder-Whistler." Linda Arvidson recalled:

> . . . she never minded work. The movies were the breath of life to her. When she wasn't working in a picture, she was in some movie theatre seeing a picture. After the hardest day, she was never too tired to see the new release and if work ran into the night hours, between scenes she'd wipe off the make-up and slip out to a movie show.[45]

Griffith had been particularly interested in Miss Turner because she could ride a horse. Salter told Florence Lawrence to mention her role for Vitagraph in *The Dispatch Bearers* in which she rode a horse, because Griffith was looking for this skill.

When Florence Lawrence presented herself at the 14th Street studio the next day, she asked for Harry Salter. A rather lanky, tall young man approached her and asked if she was Miss Lawrence. He introduced himself as Larry Griffith and asked about her ability to ride a horse. Harry Salter had done his job well; Florence was able to lead into a discussion of her equestrian ability in *The Dispatch Bearers*. Griffith indicated his approval of her performance and some mild approval of the film itself, opinions derived from thin air since he had not seen the film. He did pride himself on judging actors in the flesh, and, after excusing himself for a moment, found Salter in the next room. As Florence Lawrence waited, as close to the door as possible, she overheard Griffith tell Salter that she might be the very person he was looking for.

> Hardly a minute had passed when he re-entered the room accompanied by a great, big, dignified man who stepped just inside the door, looked me over from head to foot, spoke a few words to Mr. Griffith, and disappeared back into the recesses of the studio. As Mr. Griffith came forward I came near asking who the dressed-up individual was, then thought better of it. At the Vitagraph studio I had learned that it didn't pay to be inquisitive. But Mr. Griffith knew what I was about to ask.
>
> "That was Mr. Kennedy," he explained. "He said he hoped you could ride as well as you look."[46]

Florence Lawrence's first picture for Griffith was *A Calamitous Elopement,* his fifth film. This simple marital farce didn't require any riding ability, but she was called back at the end of the month for the leading role in *The Girl and the Outlaw.*

> I was dressed like a cow-girl—knee-length skirt, leggings, blouse waist with sleeves rolled above my elbows, pistol holster swung about my waist, a water pouch slung carelessly over my shoulder, and a big sombrero on my head. My hair was loose. The camera was clicking off a scene for *The Girl and the Outlaw.* Charles Ainsley was the outlaw and I was the girl.[47]

The company was taken to Coytsville, New Jersey, a town that has now been absorbed by Fort Lee, for this ersatz Western. It was common to make films in New Jersey that were supposed to represent the wide spaces of the West. There was actually little resemblance in terrain, but audiences of city people, without a frame of reference, did not object. One of the great difficulties was keeping telephone poles out of the background. Sometimes these weren't discovered until the film had been processed. At that point it was too late, and the poles stayed in the finished film. It was not always objects as obvious at telephone poles that could ruin a scene.

> In *The Girl and the Outlaw* one of the scenes was supposed to represent a section of primeval forest on a mountain side. The finished print showed some perfectly lovely and well pruned maple trees on the slopes of the towering mountain.[48]

Florence Lawrence had rather oversold her horsemanship and found herself eating from the proverbial mantel. She backed away from the next outdoor drama that would require riding. Her refusal to do another outdoor film didn't bother Griffith. He had an abundance of ideas for films that could be shot in the studio.

Florence Lawrence made forty-seven films under Griffith's direction in 1908 and 1909 before leaving the company for more lucrative roles and her name on the credits of her films. It was always the policy at Biograph when Griffith worked there that no names of players, nor even Griffith's name, as director, appeared on the films. Miss Lawrence did achieve a measure of fame, however, under the title The Biograph Girl. Satisfaction with such anonymity could not last long for an ambitious actress.

One of the major problems that had to be overcome when the company worked on an outdoor location, a problem that still exists for film-makers today, was the crowd that collected. Griffith found that it helped to slip the first policeman who appeared on the scene a five dollar bill to disperse or, at least, to hold back the crowd. He found that the price began to escalate, however, as more policemen appeared whose upturned palms had to be filled.

The crowds could be held back, but children who would dart around the policemen to push their faces into the camera lens were equally annoying.

Florence Lawrence said:

> I always felt very foolish when we were doing comedy business in the open. Mr. Griffith used to trick the crowds by concealing the camera in a carriage. We would drive to our location, hastily going through our parts, get back into the carriage and be off before very many people could collect.[49]

The slap-dash performances that were customarily given by his actors didn't appeal to Griffith. He had been used to the extensive rehearsal system used in the legitimate theatre. The press of time and the need for more films to be turned out prevented him from scheduling elaborate rehearsals. In the studio he made it a practice to have at least one rehearsal, called a "mechanical rehearsal," before playing the scene for the camera. In the rehearsal the actors would go through a pantomime of the scene, learning where they were to move and what physical business had to be accomplished. Griffith would also tell them something of the nature of the characters they were to portray. Then the scene would be shot. As he gained confidence and authority, Griffith increased the rehearsals to three, using the second and third to inject some emotional content into the scene. He was anything but satisfied with even this and frequently expressed to the company that someday he would be able really to rehearse the company. The filming pace would not permit it, nor was there anyone in the Biograph administration that would have cared for the improved product that might have resulted. On a typical studio day Florence Lawrence remembered:

Once Mr. Griffith directed me in a scene for a comedy—*The Road to the Heart*—I think it was called—in the morning, in several scenes of a problem melodrama called *What Drink Did,* immediately after luncheon, and we completed the day's work by re-taking a scene for a near-tragedy—*The Romance of a Jew-ess.* This is one of the most trying experiences that happens to the moving picture player who conscientiously tries to feel his part.[50]

Miss Lawrence's memory had the films in the wrong sequences. The ones she remembered were made a month apart, but the principle was the same.

A day on location began with a subway ride to the 125th Street station on the west side of Manhattan, followed by a brisk hike to the ferry building. The company was expected to catch the 8:45 a.m. boat for New Jersey. Some of the company would leave even earlier in order to have a breakfast at Murphy's, a saloon with a separate family room, near the dock. On the opposite shore some rooms had been rented in one of the small inns. The actors would don costumes and make-up and then be picked up by carriage to be driven to the location for the day's shooting. The first light of the day was thought best for shooting so the company was expected to be ready at sunrise. All the costumes and props had been packed at the studio the night before and placed in the charge of Hugh Ford, the propman. Hughie would set out with the wagonload of equipment while it was still dark in order to arrive ahead of the company.

An advance man would have been sent out several days before to scout out the appropriate locations for the films. One of the people that Griffith used for this job at Biograph was a woman, Gene Gauntier, who later became a successful screen writer, after a career as an actress for Kalem.

As the light began to increase with the rising sun, Arthur Marvin or Billy Bitzer would get the camera ready. Two young errand boys, Johnny Mahr and Bobby Harron, would unload the prop wagon quickly and distribute the props to the actors as needed.

The camera was usually located out of the hot sun, perhaps under a shady tree. The location of the appropriate tree frequently determined the angle of the shot.

Griffith was not pleased with this technique of camera placement, but he had little success in getting either of his two cameramen to change their ways. Arthur Marvin was more tractable, but Bitzer was stubborn and capable of inventing all sorts of technical reasons for not moving.

The problem with Bitzer was solved when Griffith sent one of the boys to get some beer. Dangling a beer bottle over the spot where he wanted the camera placed, Griffith tried to entice the cameraman to move out of the shade. With one bottle he had no success. For two bottles Bitzer moved the camera to the position indicated.

Between ten and eleven o'clock in the morning shooting stopped. The shadows that made the photography interesting had gone. The noon sun tended to flatten out the images and show the often grotesque make-up at its worst. It was possible to shoot in the afternoon, but the shadows then fell the wrong way. After the morning session the company would then start the trip back to the studio. The constant moving back and forth from the studio to a location and the resulting loss of a half-day's shooting did not appeal to Griffith. He put his mind to work to find some way to get more work done.

Griffith was well aware that, despite being the only director at Biograph, he was still on trial. He was now more relaxed in the presence of the general manager, Henry Marvin, but he saw little of Jeremiah J. Kennedy and was extremely nervous when the Biograph president came around. Kennedy was fortunately not a frequent visitor, but on one occasion sent word that he would visit the studio. With the help of Harry Salter, Griffith began a frantic clean-up of the main studio. Florence Lawrence arrived and was pressed into action with a dust cloth, a gesture at best in the disarray of the large room. As the three worked to make some order out of the chaos, Kennedy, unnoticed, had entered at the back of the room. When the cleaners turned and saw him watching them, they reacted like guilty children at the cookie jar. Kennedy smiled.

"My children are industrious today" was Kennedy's sole remark as he walked out of the room.

The company that Griffith had inherited at Biograph consisted of Mr. and Mrs. Frank Gebhardt, Charles Ainsley, Ashley Miller,

David Miles, Anita Hendrie, Harry Salter, John Cumpson, and Flora Finch. Griffith added Florence Lawrence, Arthur Johnson, Mack Sennett, Herbert Prior, Marion Leonard, and his wife, Linda Arvidson. Others floated in and out of the company for brief appearances.

Linda was increasingly unhappy with her casting. She also regretted an arrangement that she and David had made. They had agreed not to reveal to anyone that they were married. Harry Salter knew, but he had been sworn to secrecy. The purpose of the agreement was to give David a free hand in using his wife as an actress without arousing any antagonisms among the company or accusations of nepotism by the front office. Griffith played the bachelor role to the hilt, sometimes overdoing his neutrality by working Linda somewhat harder than the rest of the cast.

After one trying session in which a scene was shot again and again because the film was buckling in the camera, Linda fainted under the pressure, and Griffith walked away, leaving Florence Lawrence to revive her.

When he left the studio at night, David would avoid Linda and walked with another member of the company. He was particularly fond of having Mack Sennett as a walking companion, using Sennett as a sounding board for his developing ideas of film-making. Sennett was a stocky young Irish-Canadian, born Michael Sinnott, who had assumed the stage name Mack Sennett during his brief career as a stock company actor and strongman. He was twenty-four. Griffith first used him in a small part in *Balked at the Altar* in late July. Although Griffith didn't regard him as much of an actor, he found Sennett a willing assistant, and Sennett's somewhat crude country humor seemed to please him. They would take a circuitous route and part just before reaching Griffith's own building. Linda expressed vigorous dislike for this subterfuge, but Griffith insisted that they did not dare do anything else. Actually he rather liked this pretense of freedom.

Griffith continued to press the pace of filming in order to please his bosses. When some of the company objected to the fast tempo of work, Griffith told them that since the exhibitors purchased the film by the foot, they were entitled to have as much action as possible in the limited footage. His favorite phrase to the company became, "We're not making illustrated song slides." He would cry from the sidelines while the shot was being made, "Faster, faster! For God's sake, hurry up! We must do the scene in forty feet."

By the end of December 1908 Griffith had directed and completed fifty-seven films. The stories he had been fed by Dougherty, Taylor, and a new writer, Roy McCardell, as well as some stories by himself and one or two suggested by members of the company, fell into a pattern that he continued to repeat during the next four years at Biograph. Some of these were Indian pictures featuring his own concept of the red man as a noble hero. Frequently the Indian was the hero and a white man was the villain. He made short comedies of the physical, slapstick variety, paralleling those made by the other companies. One group of comedies did become very popular with the public, the so-called "Jones" comedies featuring Florence Lawrence and John Cumpson. The Jones comedies were constructed around a single situation in which Mr. Jones would prove to be the butt of the incident. In *Mr. Jones at the Ball*, Jones is having his torn pants repaired in the ladies' room. The onslaught of the women trying to enter the room drives him into hiding in what seems to be a closet. Instead he finds himself, trouserless, back in the ballroom. Clutching a rug before him, he leaps from a window onto the head of a passing policeman. Jones is last seen being wheeled away by the policeman in a barrow to the police station. This may well have been the first comedy series. The list included social dramas, frequently showing the evils of drink, mystery stories with a beauty imperiled by burglars, and Griffith's first Civil War film, *The Guerilla*. The last had a climax built around a faithful Negro's ride for help. The servant's horse was shot from under him, but he managed to get through with the message.

Under Griffith the range of locations for filming had been extended, with less and less work done at the studio. Griffith liked the effect of real mountains, woods, rivers, and city streets. The company went to northern New Jersey, the Jersey shore, and Central Park and various city streets in Manhattan. The contrast between these real locations and Eddie Shulter's painted scenery was readily apparent. Griffith liked the reality.

Griffith pressed Lee Dougherty to intercede with Henry Marvin for larger film budgets. When he began, the allowance was about three hundred dollars a film, including the salaries. With the increasing prosperity of Biograph under the impending Motion Picture Patents Company agreement and the already apparent success of the Griffith pictures, Dougherty was able to get the budgets increased to around five hundred dollars a picture. This was only the production budget and did not include laboratory or distribution and promotion costs.

Griffith had tried one significant innovation in editing during this first half-year. In his ninth film, *The Fatal Hour,* as described in the Biograph bulletin, Griffith cut between two scenes that were happening simultaneously, an editorial device that came to be known as cross-cutting. He used it in achieving increased suspense, a method that was to become one of his major contributions to the development of film technique.

> . . . Certain death seems to be her fate, and would have been had not an accident disclosed her plight. Hendricks after leaving the place is thrown by a streetcar and this serves to discover his identity, so he is captured and a wild ride is made to the house in which the poor girl is incarcerated. *This incident is shown in alternate scenes.* There is the helpless girl, with the clock ticking its way towards her destruction, and out on the road is the carriage, tearing along at breakneck speed to the rescue, arriving just in time to get her safely out of range of the pistol as it goes off.[51]

The company stopped filming for the Christmas holidays of 1908, and David and Linda spent their most prosperous Christmas together since their marriage. Although Griffith was exhilarated by his success at Biograph, he still talked of going back to the legitimate theatre and of finding a producer for *War.* Linda was more practical and suggested that they stay at Biograph until they were on their feet. It hadn't been very long, she reminded him, since they had not known where the rent money was coming from and they had been preparing to go to Kentucky. He replied that if he went home, it would just be for a visit. Griffith showed that an actor's optimism increases with a steady paycheck. Linda agreed that she had had enough barnstorming for a long time.

4

An Actor Prepares

Poor mother and the rest of the family, they didn't even think it was right to attend the theatre much less become an actor. I am afraid their alarm over the latter part, my being an actor, was very far-fetched. But they took it seriously. But the tempter had opened the gates and I went flaring to the everlasting lights of fame and glory. I soon discovered that there may be lights out there, but they were a long distance away.[52]

Jacob Griffith's death brought down his creditors upon Mary Griffith demanding payments. The farm was double mortgaged and the unpaid interest amounted to 60 per cent of the value of the loans. An unpaid gambling debt appeared. Mary Griffith's brother asked for the deed to eighty-nine acres that had been purchased from Jacob in 1868. Jacob had failed to deliver the deed. The accumulated debts loomed large against the net worth of the farm, then between five and six thousand dollars.

Mary Griffith tried to fight back, but the Oldham County Court ordered the farm sold to satisfy Jacob's creditors. Mary's household goods and some livestock were exempted from the sale, possessions valued at only $434.50. At the auction Mary was able to buy back Mattie's piano, with the help of her brother, for twenty dollars.

The forced sale brought a total of $5,447.28 in cash and a note for $1,552.28 payable by December 1885. Half of the money received was needed to satisfy the creditors. Mary Griffith didn't receive payment on the note until 1897.

Mary Griffith's oldest son, William, had married Ann Crutchers shortly before the sale of Lofty Green. He and his bride lived in a five-room house built by her parents as a wedding gift. William moved his mother and the rest of the family into his house.

The move to a new town and cramped quarters had an unsettling effect on seven-year-old David. He was enrolled in a new school, the Cassaday School, and his sister was no longer his teacher. Instead he had a male teacher, Mr. Kootch, assisted by two other men and one woman. David, who had been an extroverted child, now kept to himself, reading instead of playing with other children. He even refused to go swimming with his cousins.

Griffith wrote of his new home:

> It had only one advantage. It had a creek that ran all around it and in the creek were lots of sun perch. Also it was supplied with more rocks than were ever on any farm of its size—than I have ever seen. Where it didn't have rocks, it was generously supplied with stones.[53]

At school David Griffith found himself bullied by the older boys. One boy particularly delighted in tormenting him.

> I think the lady school teacher sort of had a little sympathy for me during this period. She would let me out of school a little early sometimes—I think to escape the persecution of this young gentleman.[54]

Griffith's tormentor liked to wait until David was crossing the branch of a small stream near the schoolyard and then pepper him with snowballs. The bully had iced the snowballs during the day in the stream to make them rock-hard.

> . . . I have come to believe he must have been a boy of great intelligence and perception in working so seriously in attempting to knock my block off.
>
> Sometimes, in a moment of weakness, he managed to miss my head, but he seldom failed to get me somewhere, despite the fact that I was running and dodging at the same time to the best of my ability. Thus I got more energy to build up my constitution.[55]

When Griffith was eleven, he developed his first crush on a girl.

> I see her being a very beautiful girl. Just what type, I don't know, but she was very thin and could run like hell. This made her greatly desired by the captain of the prisoner-base teams. My God, how I loved her! I really do remember that she was little and slim, and that she had beautiful legs, and she could use them.[56]

This first love was thwarted when David missed the word "deceive" in the spelling bee, losing to his arch-rival both the contest and the girl.

> . . . he actually had the nerve to walk home with her while I
> cautiously lingered a little behind, wishing I could tell her what
> a grand person I was, but never got the chance.[57]

This schoolhouse was as small as the Walnut Grove School, one room with eight benches on each side of a center aisle. Griffith was usually assigned to a back bench.

> . . . having to cross the stream seven times, we always came in
> wet. I would have preferred to have a bench up near the stove. I
> suggested once in a bold moment that my feet were wet. I stood
> up to do it. She said sit down and let them dry, which I did.[58]

For the next four years Mattie Griffith urged her mother to leave William's home and move to Louisville. Mattie insisted that the opportunities for the whole family would be greater in the city. The second oldest son, Jacob, Jr., had already settled in the city, practicing the printer's trade which he had learned as an apprentice on the Spencer County *Courier*. Jack Crutchers, William Griffith's brother-in-law, had given Jacob that opportunity.

Mary Griffith had resisted her daughter's arguments because she felt that the family should stay with William in Southville long enough to help him get his farm established. With the help of Dr. R. B. Cassaday, Mary was collecting an eight dollar a month pension as the widow of a Mexican War veteran. Dr. Cassaday had certified that Mary was suffering from organic diseases of the heart "producing hypertrophy without dillitation, causing palpitation upon the slightest exertion." Despite the doctor's grim diagnosis, Mary Griffith collected her pension for over thirty years.

With her small income assured, Mary Griffith finally gave in to Mattie's wishes. She found a small boarding house to rent in Louisville that would provide some additional income and moved her three girls and the remaining two boys, David and baby brother Albert, into it.

The boarding house proved largely a failure. All the children had to turn to and help the family income as best they could. David delivered papers, the Louisville *Courier-Journal*, after school. There was little money for clothing, and David frequently had to go to school with holes in his shoes, frayed coat sleeves, and worn shirts. He longed for the day when he might wear clothes as fine as those he saw on the gentlemen of Louisville.

> I went quite a time to this school and couldn't get any idea what it was all about. I seemed to be in a haze, until I got a new teacher by the name of Wasabeer. Then with the aid of my sister at night time, I grew a little out of the haze. When we got the schoolbook edition of *Tales of Homer,* I seemed to see a light.
>
> This was a rather busy time, going to school in the daytime, selling papers after school, and doing my sister's efforts to get some ideas through the dumb skull. So finally, to my great surprise, after the examinations, I skipped two grades, and fell, slightly wondering, into the high school.[59]

Griffith's stay in high school was brief. The failing boarding house forced him to seek a better-paying job than selling newspapers. He found a job as the operator of a wire-controlled elevator in the J. C. Lewis drygoods store.

> The elevator I attacked was run by wire ropes, and it needed a good strong tug to go, and a strong grip to stop it. Beginners generally tore off a little flesh in the palms of their hands until they got them toughened. As there was not enough cash around to buy gloves, you had to stick it out until your hands got good and tough.[60]

One day a Negro boy observed Griffith talking animatedly with some of his friends and suggested that the elevator boy should be on the stage. David's friend Frank Coyle, with a malicious twinkle in his eye, solemnly agreed, telling David that he should join the amateur show being put on at the Broadway Baptist Church. Coyle said, keeping his face blank, that they were looking for someone to play a dunce.

David took Frank Coyle's suggestion seriously, went to the church that evening, and volunteered for the part. The church players were happy to cast him. The role consisted of sitting on a high stool throughout the performance. It had one line, "The breeze from the lake blows chilly tonight."

Despite the brevity of his role, David tried for as much authenticity as he could manage. He wrote to his cousin, Woodson Oglesby, and asked for Woodson's oldest country clothes and boots for a costume. He promised Woodson a complimentary ticket for the performance.

After the performance, Frank Coyle came backstage and offered his sly congratulations. He told Griffith that his acting was natural, his voice carried beautifully, and that he should continue in the theatre. Griffith took the tongue-in-cheek compliments seriously and began to daydream about becoming a professional actor.

David Griffith's new objective was reinforced by a new friend, Max Davidson. Davidson was a German-Jewish boy who had already appeared in one full-length play, *The District School,* and, in consequence, seemed to Griffith a theatre expert. Max fanned Griffith's interest by giving him glowing accounts of the theatre in Germany, particularly the "people's theatre," attended by workers and their families. Max described the growing popularity of this theatre despite the opposition of the German commercial managements.

His interest fanned to a fever pitch, David wrote to the managers of the Louisville theatres offering his services as an usher or stagehand. He avidly read the newspapers for theatrical news. He noted that visiting actors seemed to stay at the best hotels, dine at the best restaurants, and be lionized by Louisville society. The theatre seemed to be a very dignified and glamorous way to make a great deal of money. It was certainly better than running an elevator.

At home David rummaged through his father's old books, saved from the sale of the farm, the Shakespeare plays, the Walter Scott novels, and the Dickens novels. He began declaiming them in stentorian tones at night in his room. His voice was loud enough to attract the attention of the neighbors, some of whom wondered if the Griffith boy was losing his mind. He paced his room between the high walnut bed and the opposite wall which he had decorated with a Confederate flag, his father's picture, and a coat of arms drawn by his father after the escutcheon of the ancient Griffith kings of Wales.

David told his mother about his theatrical ambitions, but she refused to take him seriously. Mary Griffith told her son that the family had never been disgraced by an actor. However, she was tolerant toward David's nightly recitations, and was even willing to hold the book while he declaimed from *The Lady of the Lake.*

Mary Griffith did maintain a strict house for her children. She refused to permit her sons to smoke, and with the colonel gone, she found even the smell of beer on someone's breath offensive. David's younger brother, Albert, once stayed out all night rather than come home with the smell of beer on his breath.

A cousin, Albert Shipp Oglesby, had been working in Flexner's Bookstore. He was studying at night and had to find another job. He suggested that he could introduce David to the store's proprietor, Bernard Flexner, and David might be able to succeed him at the job. Griffith jumped at the chance.

> It would pay five dollars a week which was more than I was getting as an aviator in the elevator shaft. I interviewed the bookstore and got the job. I was much troubled in spirit, thinking I might have made a big mistake in leaving the elevator shaft.[61]

The Flexner bookstore was a more congenial place to work than the drygoods store. Griffith was delighted by this seeming introduction to the world of letters. The store was occasionally visited by a local novelist, Mary Johnson, and once by James Whitcomb Riley. One customer who made a lasting impression on Griffith was Adolph Klauber, afterwards a critic for *The New York Times* and the husband of actress Jane Cowl. Above all, there was the opportunity to read. Griffith took full advantage.

> The only reprimand I remember receiving was, "David, don't you think you would do better if you spent less time in reading the books and more time in selling them? A little attention to the customers, and, perhaps, if the books and shelves were dusted a little more frequently, it might be a step in the right direction." [62]

The Flexners impressed Griffith as a family. The bookstore proprietors Bernard and Washington Flexner were scholarly men. Their sister Mary Flexner was a playwright. Lincoln Flexner was a school principal, Jacob Flexner a physician, Jane Flexner a librarian, and Abraham Flexner owned the Flexner School. Another brother, Simon Flexner, later became associated with the Rockefeller Foundation.

The bookstore, located at 330 Fourth Street in downtown Louisville, was host to lectures held in a room at the rear of the store. David would set up the chairs for the afternoon or evening audience of thirty or forty people who had come to hear a visiting poet or novelist.

Through visitors to the bookstore, Griffith was able to obtain passes to the theatre and concerts from time to time. Max Davidson would also take him to a public forum held in a Market Street hall, unofficially dubbed "Freedom Hall" because it had become the home of speakers advocating socialism, populism, the single tax, and trade unions. Griffith was not terribly impressed by these speakers, but he admitted to Max that some of their ideas did sound like sense.

The Adolph Klauber that visited the store was the son of Edward Klauber, a society photographer whose studio and store were next to the bookstore. Griffith was very impressed with the Klaubers, father and son. They were both handsome men, elegantly dressed in high silk hats, gloves, and with flowers in their buttonholes. Griffith tried to strike up a friendship with Adolph despite the six years' difference in their ages. He didn't succeed too well, although he was allowed to visit the Klauber studio and examine the camera equipment, art supplies, and the displays of etchings, paintings, and photographs. Since the Klaubers catered to a wealthy clientele, Griffith was able to observe the manners of visiting Louisville society ladies. He was increasingly aware of the social and economic gulf that separated the Griffiths from the society of Louisville.

David fell in love for the second time.

> She was a blonde. I don't know how it is, but somehow blondes seem to have a fatal effect on me. I did her a lot of good anyhow. I had to walk about forty blocks to get to her house from where I lived.
>
> . . . her father objected to book clerks in her life . . . we had to meet unbeknownst [sic] as it were. My courtship gave her a splendid physique because in pleasant weather, I walked her miles and miles up and down the canal. I had a terrible temptation here because I wanted to kiss her, but I thought it was wrong and never did it. Instead I took it out in walking. Then when she became exhausted at this overamount of excercise, we would rest on the bank. We did hold hands, however, and I talked her to death.
>
> I think she always labored under the idea that I was sort of queer—dumb in everything except my mouth, a physical instructor whose aim in life it was to promote her powers of locomotion. However, one night, returning too near her house, her

> father turned the hose on me. As this happened to be very late
> in the summer, and it was a chilly night, my ardor was some-
> what cooled. He was a very good marksman and got me several
> times with his powerful cold water.[63]

During their walks Griffith quoted passages from his school text
version of *Tales of Homer,* passing them off as his own and telling
her that he hoped to become a writer.

> . . . her answer was to the effect that I would do marvelously
> well in such stories as "Deerfoot" and "The Indian Runner,"
> popular stories running in *The Boy's Home Companion.* The
> little blonde may have been right at that.[64]

Jacob Griffith, Jr. had been taking vocal lessons from Mrs.
Annie H. Baustead, convinced that his real career would be that of
a singer, not in his present job as a printer. He had an easy task
convincing David and Albert that they should join him for the lessons. With the addition of Frank Coyle, Mrs. Baustead found herself teaching a quartet. Although the boys frequently were unable
to pay for their lessons, Mrs. Baustead liked them enough to extend credit. Mrs. Baustead told David that his voice had enormous
power and volume. With equipment like that, she said, he should
be a singer and not an actor. Frank Coyle was busily undermining
this advice by telling Griffith that a singing career would only last
fifteen years while an actor could work all his life. Mrs. Baustead
was primarily interested in popular music, and she influenced Griffith in his own musical taste.

David Griffith was twenty, and felt that he must now give some
thought to his future. He was still unsure what that should be.

> There was a man named Ellis that lived in Louisville. He had
> gotten some people interested in amateur theatricals and at-
> tached to himself a dough-guy [financial backer] with the idea
> of going out on a short tour.[65]

Griffith was invited to join Ellis's company. Ellis was a blacksmith,
and rehearsals were held in the back of his shop. The company was
named the Twilight Revelers, and enough money was raised to
begin a brief tour. The troupe gave its first performance across the
river from Louisville in Jeffersonville, Indiana.

> . . . what a fuss was made at home where, at the proper time, I
> announced that I was going out with the Twilight Revelers.
> Some members of the company had casually mentioned that we
> were going out on a shoe string, which meant nothing to me at
> all. In fact, I had boasted around that I was going out with a
> real theatrical troupe on a shoe string.[66]

The opening performance in Jeffersonville met with some small
success. Griffith commented: ". . . the benignant [sic] citizens of
this city must have had some curiosity of what the hell was a Twilight Reveler for we did fair business." [67]

Ellis did not try to direct his troupe. That chore was turned over
to Edward Risley, who claimed experience as a blackface comedian
on the riverboats. Risley was the only member of the company who
claimed previous theatre experience until Griffith brought his
friend Max Davidson into the group. The others in the company
were employed as a carpenter, blacksmith, harness-maker, waiter,
and a barber. The barber did play the banjo with a fair amount of
skill.

Griffith later thought that all might have been well with the
Twilight Revelers if they had stopped after the Jeffersonville performance and returned to Louisville, but the blacksmith entrepre-
neur took them farther away from home.

> We struggled along to such few villages as would let us enter.
> Then things went from bad to worse. We couldn't get enough
> money in the house to pay the board bill. We had long since
> given up the idea of laundry bills. My roommate and I escaped
> out of one small hotel, from the second story, the day after the
> performance. We got a rope, tied it to our two rather inexpen-
> sive valises, as we called them then, and let them out of the win-
> dow, and with the aid of an adjoining window and some vines,
> followed the valises. Then with the haughty manager, leading
> man, and leading lady—beautiful, very beautiful, also blonde,
> we caught a train before the whole town woke up.[68]

In the next town, as they were preparing their performance, the
hotel manager from the previous town appeared to demand his
money. Ellis persuaded him to wait until the evening receipts were
in, and borrowed his watch. Business was bad. The troupe moved
on quickly just a step ahead of the hotel proprietors.

So finally we landed, absolutely stranded, with five hotel managers that had followed us hoping we would play to some business somewhere. The most woeful members of the hotel managers' group being those who had lost their watches, the watches having been pawned to buy railroad tickets.[69]

Griffith had a crush on the leading lady. She had fallen for the leading man. "[When] I thought I was getting right into the inner circle of her confidence . . . I was again out in the cold." [70]

The Twilight Revelers were, at best, an inept group of amateurs. In an all too typical instance Griffith missed an entrance cue. Max Davidson was on stage, successfully opening a safe. Griffith was to appear, saying: "You devil, get away from that safe, or I'll blow you to kingdom come!" Griffith was pacing back and forth repeating his line off stage and didn't hear Davidson give his cue. Davidson gave it several times and then exited from the stage to see what was the matter. At that point Griffith entered and gave his line to an empty stage and howls of embarrassing laughter from the audience.

The tour ended with Risley attempting to persuade the sixth innkeeper to take a share in the company in lieu of rent while the other members of the company decamped to make their way back to Louisville individually.

Griffith returned to his job at the bookstore more stage-struck than before. He was finally able to get some work as an usher and occasional stagehand in the Louisville theatres. He also became the best pass and free ticket grabber on the staff of the bookstore.

One of the first plays that Griffith saw in Louisville was *The Two Orphans* with Kate Claxton. Miss Claxton had starred in the original production of this American version of the Adolphe d'Ennery-Eugen Corman French play. The translation had been done by N. Hart Jackson, an assistant to the producer Albert M. Palmer. Kate Claxton, whose real name was Katherine Cone, made a career out of this story of the trials of two orphan girls in the years just before the French Revolution. The role of the villainous Jacques Frochard was played by McKee Rankin. Kate Claxton played Louise. Kitty Blanchard, eventually Mrs. McKee Rankin, played the other sister, Henriette. Kate Claxton appeared regularly in the play for over twenty-nine years. David Griffith loved it.

While ushering at the Macauley Theatre, Griffith was able to watch performances by De Wolf Hopper, Lillian Russell, Ada Rehan, Julia Marlowe, Olga Nethersole, Nat Goodwin, and other touring stars of the decade.

Griffith worked in the bookstore for two years, until shortly after the store was sold to Charles Dearing. Dearing was not so taken with a stage-struck clerk who spent most of his time reading the stock. Griffith was fired.

Instead of feeling despondent, Griffith felt that this was his destiny beckoning. He applied for a job with John Griffith's Strolling Players, then performing *Faust* in Louisville. The company was about to leave for an engagement in Albany, Indiana, followed by a tour of Michigan. Mr. St. John, the stage manager, listened to Griffith's audition and hired him. St. John was also influenced by Griffith's willingness to work for very low wages. One problem existed. St. John explained that there could only be one Griffith on the playbill, and that was the boss, John Griffith. David Griffith would have to use a stage name. Griffith christened himself Lawrence Brayington. The "Lawrence" he borrowed from the well-known stage star, Lawrence Barrett, and the "Brayington" came from his supposed family history.

The Strolling Players usually gave one-night stands, but in some of the larger towns they managed to stay for as much as a week. In January 1897 Griffith wrote to his mother from the Sweer Hotel in Grand Rapids, Michigan:

> Dear mother:
> When I left Louisville and came into eastern Indiana, the road followed along the river for miles before we reached Cincinnati. On both sides was water and nothing but water except here and there the roof of some shed or barn able to left themselves above the muddy flood. The mist is heavy and it is raining softly, but steadily, with a regular beat like a small clock, on a car window . . . and Cincinnati, with her 400,000 people, is but a few starlight beams in the darkness. Then, too, they are gone and we speed along in the starless night.
> I arrive at Columbus where I am directed to a cheap room for the night, and impress on the clerk the importance of calling me at 6:30. Columbus has buildings 11 to 12 stories high.
> I last saw St. John in a peculiar cut of long coat, and am waiting for him. Asked the clerk for telegrams and was told there

were none. So I stroll back to my position, first examining my-self on account of the sharp nose in the mirror. I don't blame him much. I don't look like a leading man, or much like a man of any kind. I begin to wish I was back at 625 First Street.

Our next town is Abilene, about 1200 or 1500.

I find myself watching, as the play goes on, the leading female part with more interest than is absolutely needed, as by no possi-ble chance could I ever play with any degree of success the tender part of Marguerite. But after the words, "She loves me, she loves me not, he loves me, he loves me not." (in the flower scene), I begin to wonder what kind of a Faust I would make at the line "Oh, Faust, thou king of all the world." I am smitten with the impression I was born in May for no other purpose than nightly readings of the tender lines of Faust, providing, of course, I could have the proper support with a good Mephis-topheles and others, not to mention Marguerite.

The next day at rehearsals, I find Grif to be a rough, but good-natured sort of man, a hard stage manager. In the last part of Marguerite, he told her she acted that particular line like a chippie. She came near fainting but held up to the end of the part when she broke into sobs.

Battle Creek [Mich.] is a beautiful town around which, and through part of the town, Battle creek flows. I stood on the bridge at sunset and saw the gold from the west float softly down until it fell a glowing light on the clear waters and sweetly murmured below me. My thoughts went back to the old farm where I have so often watched the water in the selfsame way when I should have been doing something else.

Should I ever be fool enough to marry, I would never marry an actress even if I got the chance. Write to me as Lawrence Brayington, c/o J. Griffith Company, Grand Rapids, Michigan.

St. John wants us to go to good hotels here. Of course, I have received no money yet and he pays the board. I go where they go, except Grif and St. John who go to the finest everywhere. But *my* this is fine enough. Have a beautiful room and steam heat for $1.25.

Your son,
David Griffith [71]

The Strolling Players ceased strolling in Kalamazoo, Michigan, shortly after the Grand Rapids engagement. As was commonly the case in the days before Actors Equity could demand a salary bond from producers, the managers, John Griffith and St. John, disap-peared leaving the actors to make their way home without funds.

David Griffith walked, rode freight cars, begged food along the way, finally managing to return to Louisville, clothing tattered and shoes worn out, his ardor for the theatre undampened. With a few days of rest and Mary Griffith's cooking, he was again declaiming lines from *Faust* at the top of his voice in his room.

One thing had been acquired by his first professional tour, in addition to a stage name, an actor's ego. Only a dedicated actor could possibly think that he could play not only Faust, but also all the other male roles, and additionally, but for a few slight problems such as a too-prominent nose, the role of Marguerite. Lack of pay, starvation, shoes with holes, such trifles could not hold back an actor. Griffith had even learned to swagger in the hotel lobby and ask the desk clerk for non-existent telegrams. "I'm expecting word from Mr. Belasco!"

The little professional touches were all that was needed to get Griffith jobs in the Louisville theatres. In February 1897 he was hired by the Cummings brothers, Ralph and Robert, for a role in their production of the Belasco melodrama *Men and Women*. The play opened in March at Colonel Meffert's Temple Theatre for a two-week engagement, two performances a day. Griffith was paid ten dollars a week.

Griffith continued to be known in the theatre as Lawrence Brayington, although he didn't conceal his career from his family and relatives. The Oglesbys and the Griffiths came to Louisville to see him act. Griffith had the small role of Stephan Rodman, the governor of Arizona. He was pleased with the dignity of the role.

The Cummingses told Griffith that they had no further work for him at the end of the run of *Men and Women*. Griffith was not too unhappy for the moment. He was proud to have played twenty-four professional performances at the Temple Theatre. The Cummings brothers didn't last much longer at the Temple than Griffith. They both arrived at the theatre drunk and were promptly fired by Colonel Meffert.

Two weeks after the end of *Men and Women,* Griffith was engaged to play the lover in *East Lynne* opposite Ada Gray. Ada Gray had been an actress of promise and some success. She was now in her seventies and still trying to play youthful roles. The play was given for one week at the Avenue Theatre and then embarked on a tour beginning in New Albany, Indiana. The company then did the production on a showboat along the Ohio River. Again a company manager disappeared with the receipts, stranding the company. Griffith hiked back to Louisville.

There was no work for Griffith in the Louisville theatres. After a time of sitting around his mother's house, he took a part-time job acting as a collector and salesman for *The Baptist Recorder*. Most of the time he haunted the theatres.

Griffith learned in August 1897 that a new company was being formed by Colonel Meffert for his Temple Theatre. Meffert had engaged Oscar Eagle and his wife, Esther Lyon, to act and direct. Oscar Eagle was a professional with a solid reputation, having been stage manager for both Melbourne MacDowell and Fanny Davenport. Colonel Meffert had given them the ultimate accolade of paying a substantial salary for their services, $175 a week for both.

Griffith tried to make the acquaintance of actors in the company in hopes that they would get him a job. He had little success. He had gotten to know some of the backstage workers during his stint with the Cummingses, and one of these, Tony Sivori, the chief property man, hired Griffith to help shift furniture, serve as call boy, and run errands for twenty-five cents a performance. David was also to help the prompter whenever the stage manager was busy elsewhere. Despite the humiliation of falling from the magnificent salary of ten dollars a week, Sivori's job did give Griffith a reason for hanging around the theatre.

The opportunity to get back on stage as a super came along, and then Oscar Eagle found some small parts in which Griffith could be used. His pay went up to a dollar a performance when he had one or two pages of lines.

Griffith's eagerness and energy in studying even the smallest part caused him to stand out from the other young men who worked backstage or appeared as supers. He was always asking for acting advice from members of the company. Two people who were particularly attracted to him were Adolph Lestina and Kate Toncray. Max Davidson was also a member of the company.

A ten-year-old local boy, Henry Hull, son of the city editor of the *Courier-Journal,* was hired to play the title role in *Little Lord*

Fauntleroy. One other part was open, the role of a butler. Eagle asked Sivori's advice about casting a butler.

Sivori replied, "What the hell's the matter with Griffith? He looks like a butler!" Griffith got the part.

Other roles followed in 1897. Griffith played Marks in *Lights of London,* a servant in *The Wages of Sin,* a walk-on in *All the Comforts of Home,* Parker Serrant in *Lady Windermere's Fan,* Mr. Randolph in *The Wife,* and Captain Woodford in *Held by the Enemy,* a Civil War melodrama.

In 1898 Griffith repeated his role of Thomas the butler in *Little Lord Fauntleroy,* a "villain" in *The Count of Monte Cristo,* Lord Drelincourt in *Jim the Penman,* and Frank Bedloe in *Shenandoah,* another Civil War melodrama. In the spring of 1899 he played his largest role with the Meffert Company, Athos in *The Three Musketeers.*

At the end of the season the Eagles left the Meffert Company, announcing that they were returning to New York where Oscar was expecting to direct several big musicals. Griffith was very impressed with the Eagles's departure. He wished that he could get on the train with them, knowing that there was employment at the other end.

With the company disbanded for the summer, Griffith looked for some sort of fill-in employment to tide himself over until Colonel Meffert engaged a new company for the fall.

During the summer, he acted as a runner for Will S. Hayes, who wrote a column, "Stage of the River," for the *Courier-Journal.* There was little future, less money, and less excitement in gathering news of incoming barges for Hayes. Even those expeditions into "the district," Louisville's red-light section, to secure news of a different sort for Hayes's column, were not particularly stimulating. Griffith had no contact with the regular staff of the newspaper, nor did he try to get employment there. In later years he claimed that he'd been a reporter for the paper, but faced with the evidence that no one there had ever heard of him, he admitted that his job had been most peripheral. He had been paid by Hayes directly.

As he worked at his boring job, he thought about all the allegedly wise advice he'd received from the actors in the Meffert company. Even Lestina and Kate Toncray had said that an actor had to go to New York in order to achieve success in the theatre. By the fall of 1899 Griffith had stood all the barge news he could and decided to strike out for New York. He sold his brother Jacob's bicycle for nineteen dollars, said goodbye to his family, and sneaked aboard a freight train for the trip to New York.

The ride ended in Atlantic City, not New York. When the train slowed down in the Atlantic City freight yard, he jumped and ran. Traveling hobo-style had its economic advantages as long as you weren't caught by the railroad police. Griffith walked to the Atlantic City depot and washed off the railroad grime in the public washroom.

Atlantic City was a change from Louisville with its fresh ocean breeze and boardwalk. It was a little late in the season, and many businesses were shuttering for the winter. There was no reason for Griffith to stay. He spent the night in the station, and then paid for a short train ride into New York.

Inquiries at a few of the better hotels showed Griffith that his tiny stake from the sale of the bicycle would not last very long. He inquired of a policeman where he might find inexpensive lodgings. The policeman directed him to the Bowery where he might find lodgings for as low as ten or fifteen cents a night. The policeman added laughingly that, of course, your bed partner might be either a rat or a cockroach.

Griffith found a flophouse that he could afford on Houston Street and lived there for the next two months, moving to another on Davidson Street near the Brooklyn Bridge.

If David Griffith had thought his own family was poor, he now saw a sea of poverty and broken human beings that made his own family seem almost affluent. His room at the Houston Street flophouse contained two rows of cots covered with bedspreads stained with cockroach corpses smashed during the night. His roommates were the dregs of New York, broken men, thieves, alcoholics, homosexuals, and a very few, like himself, who hoped to rise above that place. Griffith, a striking-looking young man, became the target for some tentative homosexual advances. He rebuffed them, making it plain that any further attempts would be met with violence.

The day began at 7 a.m. when the flophouse manager pulled a stout chain dumping the cots to the floor. Griffith would get out as quickly as possible and would look for a cheap breakfast. Then he would make the rounds of the theatrical agents. He made an unsuccessful attempt to find Oscar Eagle.

Despite his best efforts to play the role of a successful young actor fresh from triumphs in the Middle West, the display of his Meffert company programs, the agents looked askance at his rumpled suit, and lost interest when they saw the Houston Street address. He was given all the standard excuses: no casting today, too tall, not wide enough. One agent told him that vaudeville and the theatre were dying, as witnessed by Koster and Bial's use of films between the acts.

The money soon gave out. Griffith was forced to take work with a city street gang. This way he could manage to earn enough to keep going. He was grateful that he'd always taken good physical care of himself.

At last a small part turned up in a touring company that was opening in Tonawanda, New York. Griffith jumped at an opportunity to get out of New York. This wasn't the opportunity. The company expired in Tonawanda, and Griffith thought he was lucky to get a job as an iron ore shoveler. He earned enough money at this hard physical labor to get back to New York.

Fortune seemed to smile once again. Another touring company of *London Life* was going out on the road. Griffith was hired. This company expired in Minneapolis, Minnesota. This time Louisville was nearer than New York, and Griffith followed the now familiar route of walking and hopping freights until he got to Louisville.

He remained in Louisville for two years working at odd jobs and haunting the local theatres. At last he decided to try Chicago. He was hired by the Neil Alhambra Stock Company there. He discovered that his physical type could be in demand. The Alhambra Company was producing *The Ensign* and needed an actor to play Abraham Lincoln. Griffith's bony physique was a natural for the role. It is possible that his casting as Lincoln, and the hard work he put in to understand the part, contributed, despite his Southern sympathies, to his later sympathetic handling of Lincoln in two of his films.

After the closing of *The Ensign,* he joined the cast for Catherine Osterman's production of *Miss Petticoats.* This production was taken to California, closing in San Francisco. Using his slight connection with Oscar Eagle, he was able to secure a job with the Melbourne MacDowell Company.

With the MacDowell Company, Griffith was cast in several small roles. He appeared in *Fedora, The Financier,* and as Allessandro in a stage version of Helen Hunt Jackson's novel *Ramona.*

> This played at the Mason Playhouse in Los Angeles, throughout California, and ended the engagement in San Francisco.
>
> While playing Allessandro in Los Angeles, I meandered into a Spanish town, picked up three Spanish Mexicans who played the guitar and other rippling string instruments and translated *La Golandrina.* I have been told that this was the first introduction of this song in the U.S.A., but that is merely rumor. During the action of the play, I sang a couple of serenades in what I thought to be Spanish—I had studied assiduously with a Spanish musician—In fact I sang this serenade not only on the stage, but with the accompaniment of my three Spanish conspirators, we serenaded practically all of the girls in all the towns in that part of California.[72]

During the run of *Fedora,* Griffith found himself drawn to the company's ingenue, Linda Arvidson. She was equally taken with him and especially admired his deep resonant voice. The only thing that Linda didn't like was his stage name, Lawrence. She was relieved when he told her that his real name was David. Linda was a brunette.

The MacDowell season came to an end when faced with dwindling box office receipts. Now Griffith was stranded in California, much too far to walk to Louisville. He was forced to look for whatever unskilled labor was available as in Tonawanda. There was no ore to be shoveled in California, but there were hops to be picked. He joined the harvesters near Ukiah, California. It was from this experience that the outline for a play, *The Fool and the Girl,* began to form in his mind.

His rescue from the hop fields was effected by a message from Los Angeles to play Allessandro in *Ramona* once again. Linda Arvidson was also in Los Angeles. The two young people were able to spend a great deal of time together. Romance blossomed on visits

to the historic sights in the Los Angeles area, including the San
Gabriel Mission.

When *Ramona* closed, Griffith returned to San Francisco and
joined up with a company being put together by Nance O'Neill.
Miss O'Neill had just returned from a tour of Australia and was
eager to put together a new assault on the East. The tour promised
to get Griffith back to New York. Griffith was cast as Francis Drake
in *Elizabeth, the Queen of England*. In 1906 he played with
Walker Whiteside and in parts in Ibsen's *Rosmersholm* and Sudermann's *Magda*. The Nance O'Neill repertoire was designed to
show off the star in appropriate roles. Everyone else was subordinate. In *Magda,* Griffith replaced the company's director and leading man, McKee Rankin. Griffith remembered Rankin well from
Kate Claxton's production of *The Two Orphans*. That seemed
such a long time before. The part in *Magda* was that of Hefter-
dinct, the pastor. Griffith received good, although small, notices.
Miss O'Neill promised him more important roles.

The O'Neill Company began moving gradually eastward, touring Iowa, pausing in Des Moines, and finally finishing in Boston.
The company had a six-week booking in Boston. Nance O'Neill
had played in Boston in 1904, two years before, to an excellent reception. This time the reception was similarly warm.

With the security of success, Griffith sent for Linda, who was
still in San Francisco. Linda had survived the great earthquake
that demolished the city on April 18, but had lost most of her wardrobe. She was delighted to have a chance to leave.

Linda arrived in Boston the second week in May, and without
any further delay, Griffith proposed, and their wedding took place
in the Old North Church.

Although Griffith's name appeared in a number of cast lists for
the O'Neill Company, his performance was reviewed only once. It
was noted in a review of *Magda* that "Lawrence Griffith as the pastor was remarkably simple and true." Griffith had dropped the
Brayington name in California. During the Boston engagement, he
also played Ulric Brendel in *Rosmersholm,* and did a part in another Sudermann play, *Heimath*.

One of the plays that Nance O'Neill was planning to revive was
Judith of Bethulia, a dramatization of the biblical story of Judith

and Holofernes that she had commissioned from Thomas Bailey Aldrich. This was a major piece in her repertoire. The play was discussed with the company, even bits were rehearsed, and its production was much anticipated. Griffith became thoroughly familiar with the script. The engagement ended, however, before *Judith* could be produced.

Griffith was now hard at work on his own play, *The Fool and the Girl*. At the close of the O'Neill engagement, Griffith and his wife went to New York. He was hired almost immediately for a role in a road try-out of *The One Woman* by Thomas Dixon. Dixon had just previously successfully dramatized his novel of the reconstruction days in the South, *The Clansman*. Griffith's performance was found wanting, and he was given notice just two weeks before the New York opening. A small role in a production of *Salome* turned up and Griffith made his only acting appearance in New York. It went unnoticed. His play, however, was accepted by James K. Hackett for later production.

5

On Location: Perfecting the Art

When I first photographed players at close range, my management and patrons decried a method that showed only the face of the story characters. Today the close-up is employed by nearly all directors to bring a picture audience to an intimate acquaintance with an actor's emotions.

I adopted the *flash-back* to build suspense, which till then had been a missing quantity in picture dramas. Instead of showing a continuous view of a girl floating downstream in a barrel, I cut into the film by flashing back to incidents that contributed to the scene and explained it.[73]

After the brief Christmas holiday of 1908, Griffith returned to the Biograph studio and began an almost incredible work schedule. In the entire year he was to direct one hundred and fifty-one films, almost three films a week. True to his word to Linda, he expanded the company to meet the new pace, at the same time dropping those actors who didn't fit into his style of working, or with whom his personality clashed.

Something more than a personality clash brought about the departure of Charles Ainsley. Griffith demonstrated a fight scene with Ainsley somewhat too vigorously. Ainsley lost his temper during the mock blows and struck Griffith on the jaw. Griffith retaliated by knocking Ainsley to the floor. The actor picked himself up and walked out of the studio.

Griffith was not dependent on one actor. There was no lack of new players to take the places of any who left. He hired Violet Mercereau and Stephanie Longfellow to play ingenue roles, Clara T. Bracey as a character woman, and a handsome young Irishman, Owen Moore, as a leading man.

Toward the end of April, a young Canadian actress, Gladys Smith, came to the 14th Street studio looking for work.

> As I crossed the marble-floored foyer of the old mansion occu-
> pied by the Biograph Studio, a man came through the swinging
> door opposite me and began to look me over in a manner that
> was too jaunty and familiar for my taste.
> "Are you an actress?" he demanded at once.
> "I most certainly am," I retorted.
> "What, if any, experience have you had, may I ask?"
> "Only ten years in the theatre, sir, and two of them with Be-
> lasco," I said icily.
> "You're too little and too fat, but I may give you a chance.
> My name is Griffith. What's yours?" [74]

Gladys Smith replied with her stage name, Mary Pickford, a name
that she had assumed at the request of stage producer David Belasco when she worked for him in *The Warrens of Virginia*.
Gladys's temperament and slight testiness at being given "the treatment" by this movie director were understandable. She had spent
almost ten years in the theatre pushed along by a tough-willed
mother since her first child role in her home town, Toronto.

After her father's death when she was four, her mother had first
attempted to support her three children—Gladys, and a younger
sister and brother—by running a small candy store. The store allegedly failed when baby brother Jack fed the store's stock to the
dog.

The lack of success as a merchant, however, was really of secon-
dary importance to Gladys's mother. She had ambitions to become an
actress and went to the manager of Valentine's Stock Company in
Toronto for a try-out. There was a part for a small child, and the
Smith family always insisted that it was the future Mary Pickford
who suggested that she play it. This infant effrontery amused the
manager and he hired her.

Gladys Smith then passed from one stock company to another,
including her appearance in the Belasco production, until that
point in April 1909 when she appeared at the Biograph studio.

David Griffith's manner in greeting prospective members of the
acting company was also not surprising. He was perhaps imitating
the manner in which he had been treated during his own career by
directors such as Oscar Eagle and McKee Rankin. With new power,
insecure power actually, sometimes comes a certain arrogance. It is
interesting to note, however, that Mary Pickford was the only one

to remember this phase of the new director's career. The others remember him as soft-spoken, courtly, and a gentleman.

Griffith took Mary to one of the small, dirty dressing rooms, applied make-up to her face himself, and then made a brief test of her for the principal role in a forthcoming film, *Pippa Passes*. Mary was then shown about the studio and given a small role in the film then shooting, *What Drink Did,* in which Tony O'Sullivan, Harry Salter, and a child actress, Adele de Garde, had the major parts. Mary's vignette could serve only as an additional screen test because it was cut from the final print of the film. She was asked to return the next day.

Mary came back to Biograph the next day and was cast in another small role in *Her First Biscuits,* a slapstick comedy. This film was of a length called a split-reel, running only five or six minutes, an inauspicious beginning for the future "America's sweetheart."

With an enthusiasm for a new face that became a characteristic, Griffith continued to cast Mary Pickford regularly. Within a week she played a principal role in *The Violin Maker of Cremona* as the daughter of Herbert Miles, and opposite Owen Moore, and had begun another part as Marion Leonard's daughter in *The Lonely Villa*.

During the making of *The Lonely Villa* another actor appeared who was to become a fixture with the Biograph Company, James Kirkwood. Kirkwood had just returned from a road tour of William Vaughn Moody's *The Great Divide*.

He was an old friend of Harry Salter's, and Salter was pleased to introduce him to Griffith. In the same manner in which he had used Mary Pickford immediately, Griffith put Kirkwood into *The Lonely Villa* as a villain behind the cover of a false beard. Kirkwood was reluctant at first, but Griffith assured him that no one would recognize him behind the crepe hair. Kirkwood then joined the scene, adding his weight to a door-breaking scene being filmed.

It was Kirkwood, in his turn, who brought Griffith another male actor, one who was to become the most famous of all the actors who worked with Griffith, Henry B. Walthall. Walthall had appeared with Kirkwood in the road company of *The Great Divide*. Both men, at that moment, merely regarded the films as a way to pick up eating money while waiting for a break in the theatre.

They would probably have been surprised to learn that their motion picture director, the seemingly assured "Larry" Griffith,
looked at it the same way.

A small corporate event of 1909, one which meant little to Griffith or the acting company, brought about the official change in
the company name from the American Mutoscope and Biograph
Company to the simpler, and popular, Biograph Company. The
films themselves had long been referred to as Biographs. The company had gone out of the business of making photographic flip
cards for the peep-show mutoscopes and was concentrating solely
on theatrical films.

With the arrival of spring, Griffith was able to schedule more location trips for the company. In May films were made in Fort Lee,
Leonia, and Coytsville, New Jersey. The company went to Green-
wich, Connecticut, and in New Jersey, to Edgewater along the
Hudson, and Shadyside.

Griffith's personal style as a director was developing with the
same rapidity as the pictures being shot. He discovered that a direct confrontation with his actors would seldom give him the results he wanted. Subterfuge and gentle trickery frequently worked
best. He discovered that he would have less trouble with his actors
if he told them as little as possible about what was being filmed.
Without the handicap of a script, as in the theatre, to permit an
actor the opportunity to develop his own concept of a character or
situation, Griffith could control, almost completely, the outcome of
a film. Only *he* knew how a given scene would fit into the finished
picture. The secretiveness about his intentions that he developed
for these films became a Griffith technique that he would use
throughout his career. He also discovered that he could maintain
the best relationship with his company if he remained aloof from
the horseplay indulged in by its members. Griffith assumed easily the role of director as father-figure. He would, however, employ
any technique that produced results. With some of the ingenues in
the company, Griffith found that he could invent an outrageous
story about seeing their boy friend with another girl. With Bitzer
or Marvin tipped off to hold the camera in readiness, the momentary passage of jealousy on the young girl's face could be captured
on film. When the camera stopped, Griffith would put his arm

around the girl and confess that the story was only a joke and so restore good feeling within his company.

As a self-taught director, Griffith's approach was always pragmatic. He had read no theories of directing, nor had he had an opportunity in his stage career to direct. His training as an actor had depended on observation of his fellow actors, and as a director he depended on his observation of those directors for whom he had worked. His approach to the development of characters in film plays was also based on his observation of people's behavior in the streets. His own checkered working career between theatre engagements had given him a rich store of such observations. He tended to equate the society figures of his scripts with those people he'd observed in Louisville. His farmers were from Kentucky and California. His city people were a mixture of New York and Louisville. He would ask the actors to build their parts through the same sort of observation.

> He told us to watch animals, children, grown people under stress of emotion. We were all made to visit hospitals, insane asylums, death prisons, houses of prisoners to catch, as he put it, humanity off guard so that we would know how to react to the various emotions we were called upon to portray.[75]

Griffith also demonstrated for the individual actor, and for the company, how he would like a role played. Many members of the company found Griffith's impromptu performances so good that they despaired of equaling them.

To keep within the grueling schedule, it was sometimes necessary for Griffith to use mass psychology on his company. The technique was probably more derived from *Tom Sawyer* than from any other source, and while he didn't in one instance need a fence whitewashed, he did need a path cleared through some tall grass to the door of an old house being used as a background. The heat of the day was almost unbearable, and the entire company, retreating into the nearest shade, refused to budge. No one was willing to take up a shovel and build the path. After a time Griffith picked up a shovel himself and started to clear the path. After a few moments he paused and casually remarked that it certainly felt a lot cooler after some moments of physical exertion. He then began

shoveling with great vigor, then pausing, repeating his earlier remarks. The company, reacting like Tom Sawyer's friends, picked
up shovels and quickly cleared the path. When they finished, such
was the power of Griffith's suggestion, they admitted that they did
feel cooler after the workout.

Griffith's greatest asset as a director in working with a company
of actors was his infectious enthusiasm. The actors were swept away
by his confidence and energy. Any doubts that he had were saved
for his conversations after work with Linda; while on the set he
gave the impression that he viewed each task as one of great signifi-
cance. He was not one to label even the potboilers as just that, but
he regarded them as potential comic masterpieces. He had learned
another lesson well from his days with repertory companies—never
look back. A play once done was done, and the next one was the
only one to concentrate on. He transferred this attitude to his film-
making. When it came time to recall his Biograph films in 1913 for
the purposes of a trade press advertisement, he was able to list only
a quarter of his films, and he omitted some of those in which significant contributions to the development of film had been made.

The rule in rehearsals for Griffith was the use of great patience.
His rare outbursts of temperament were calculated to achieve some
immediate directorial effect. He usually spoke softly and carefully
coached the members of the cast individually, and then assembled
the whole performance with a minimum of attention to the company as a total entity. He came to know thoroughly the talents and
temperaments of each member of the company, and, as a result,
could take advantage of his full capabilities.

Sometimes during rehearsals in the studio, Griffith would leave
the room after instructing the actors to work out a piece of business on their own. When he returned, he would select from a run-
through those moments that he felt worked and asked the actors to
discard those that didn't.

In one early studio film the scene to be filmed was a bachelor
party in a wealthy home. Eddie Shulter had dressed the setting
with a number of potted palms, a device that always spelled wealth
to scene decorators with little actual experience with the wealthy.
The actors were dressed in rented dress suits, variously fitted,
mostly bad. Owen Moore looked splendid, his suit fitting neatly.

The other actors were, however, convinced that Moore would have looked elegant in a feed sack. Mack Sennett and Tony O'Sullivan managed to look the worst. Tony was overweight in an underweight suit, and Sennett gave the impression of a walking cadaver who had forgotten, like the old vaudeville business, to remove the hanger from his coat. The actors translated the awkwardness of the costumes into an awkwardness in playing the scene. Griffith turned the problem over to the company and left the room.

Billy Bitzer, the cameraman, ever eager to assert himself as a director-without-portfolio, tried to solve the problem by arranging the company in a tableau, a sort of frozen hotel lobby. All hands rejected Bitzer's approach. They remembered Griffith's parting words as he left the room that he would intercede with the front office, if the scene worked, to have everyone's pay raised from five dollars a day to ten. With this in mind one of the actors suggested a facetious solution. When Griffith returned, the actors said they were ready to run the scene.

With Griffith watching, they hoisted Owen Moore to their shoulders, carried him across the room, depositing him on top of a table, and then raising their glasses, half-turning toward Griffith near the camera, shouted with enthusiasm:

"Biograph!
Hah! Hah! Hah!
Ten Dollars, Ten Dollars,
Rah! Rah! Rah!"

They were all astonished when Griffith announced that they had achieved the proper effect. It was then repeated even more enthusiastically for Bitzer to photograph.

Griffith kept his word to the company and the pay scale was doubled for those members of the company who were present. New actors joining the company, however, continued to be paid at the five dollar rate throughout 1909 and 1910. Griffith was allowed to make special deals with individual members of the company when it was necessary.

Griffith never showed favoritism among his actors, and at no point was even a hint of the star system encouraged. The hero of a film made on Tuesday might be cast as a villain in Thursday's film.

As the popularity of individual performers in the Biograph films became apparent to other film companies, overtures would be made behind the scenes to hire some of them away from Biograph. Such defections were rare among the companies like Biograph that belonged to the Motion Picture Patents Company, but nothing prevented the pirate companies from trying to lure away Biograph players. Some of the more experienced players, the ones who had worked for other companies before joining Biograph, were the easiest to reach.

The first major defection was, almost inevitably, Florence Lawrence, The Biograph Girl. During the summer of 1909, Florence, with the assistance of Harry Salter, secretly negotiated with Carl Laemmle, the founder and head of the Independent Motion Picture Company, known as IMP. When the negotiations were discovered by J. J. Kennedy, he promptly fired them both. Griffith was not consulted. A kind of warfare had erupted between the licensed and unlicensed film companies. IMP was the enemy to J. J. Kennedy, and even a hint of desertion to the other side was anathema to him.

Laemmle signed Florence Lawrence and Salter with a flourish in the trade press that "the Biograph Girl was now an IMP." Solter was transformed into a "distinguished director" who would continue to be responsible for Miss Lawrence's film successes. Laemmle knew well that truth seldom can catch up with a big enough press campaign. It was unimportant that Salter had not directed a film, nor been responsible in any way for Florence Lawrence's films. The public didn't know who had been. Griffith's name was nowhere to be seen on any Biograph films, so Solter could be indirectly given credit for them.

The effect of this deceitful publicity was not lost on Griffith. He complained bitterly to Linda, although he kept his counsel at the studio. The effect of Laemmle's agreement to give Florence Lawrence screen credit and publicity for her films was also not lost on the acting members of the Biograph stock company. They hoped that Biograph would change its policy and give them individual credit. It did not, holding fast until after 1913 when the decline of the studio had begun. To gain recognition, the Biograph actors discovered that they would have to follow Florence Lawrence's and Salter's lead.

This first defection didn't take place until the summer of 1909, after Griffith had followed up a suggestion of Kennedy's that he take the company to a small town in New York's Orange Mountains. Kennedy had once stayed at a small, charming rural inn overlooking the Delaware and Hudson Canal just a few miles north of the New Jersey-Pennsylvania border. The town was called Cuddebackville, but the proprietor of the inn preferred a French version of the name, calling his establishment the Caudebec Inn.

On June 22 Griffith accompanied by R. H. Hammer, the secretary of Biograph, Lee Dougherty, Harry Salter, and a driver scouted the area and spent the night at the inn. Griffith thought the area had enormous possibilities. The brooding hills overlooking the Neversink River, the graceful little village built around a canal pond, and the ancient pre-Revolutionary houses appealed to his imagination.

Arrangements were made to house the company with Mr. Predmore, and four days later Griffith brought the company by train to Cuddebackville. The company was more excited by this trip than they had been by the short day-trips to Fort Lee. The prospect of working in the mountains seemed almost like a vacation with pay.

The ferry to Weehawken carried the company to meet connections with the Ontario and Western Railroad. They changed trains in Summitville near Middletown, New York, for a branch line carrying passengers twice a day through Port Jervis, New York, to Cuddebackville. The entire trip took about half a day from New York.

As was true of later visits, the company arrived in the evening at the little one-room station and began a lengthy walk up to the Caudebec Inn. The innkeeper, Charles Predmore, did meet the train with his impressive automobile, a big red Thomas Flyer, and drove Griffith, Mary Pickford, and one or two others up to the inn.

Frank Powell had been designated as company manager, and in that capacity he signed the company into the hotel register. The company on this first visit in June 1909 consisted of: Griffith; Billy Bitzer and his wife; Florence Lawrence; Harry Salter; James Kirkwood; Owen Moore; Henry Walthall; Mr. Russell; Mr. Shafer; Mr. Stanhope; Tony O'Sullivan; Mr. Martin; Lottie Smith, Mary Pickford's sister; G. Pickford, Mary still using her real first name, Gladys; Billy Quirk and his wife; Mr. Smart; Johnny Mahr; Bobby

Harron; an Indian adviser, Young Deer, and his wife; Miss McCloy; Henry Behrman; Stanner E. V. Taylor; Gladys Egan; Miss Mullen; Arthur Johnson; and Mack Sennett. Alfred Paget joined the company on the following Thursday, July 1, arriving on the early train in time for breakfast. At its largest, the company totaled thirty-three people.

Linda Griffith did not make this first trip to Cuddebackville. She had gone to visit her husband's relatives and her mother-in-law in Kentucky.

As the Thomas Flyer pulled up in front of the Caudebec Inn, the proprietor's wife stood on the long front porch waving her apron in welcome, calling, "Glad to see you come!" This cry, coupled with an equally fervent, "Glad to see you go!," became the punctuation for each visit of the Biograph company to Cuddebackville.

The inn was substantial for a summer hotel, although small by city standards. It had three floors and a number of outbuildings capable of holding eighty guests, provided that some of the guests were willing to sleep on cots along the halls. It had originally been built to serve the boaters on the Delaware and Hudson Canal that passed through the heart of the village a few hundred yards below the inn.

Griffith was assigned the best front room with the Pickford family directly across the hall. Since Mary Pickford's mother usually didn't make the trips, she insisted that the Griffiths keep an eye on her children. Some of the men were given single rooms, but most were doubled up, and as many as four were assigned to a slightly larger room.

On the company's second visit that summer, beginning on Sunday, August 1, Mrs. Smith, Mary Pickford's mother, did arrive on Tuesday, August 3, to put her stamp of approval on the surroundings, and brought her younger children, Lottie and Jack, with her.

Linda Griffith accompanied her husband on the third trip to Cuddebackville that summer, but the fiction of their separate status was maintained by assigning them separate, although adjoining rooms, with Linda signed in the inn register as Miss Arvidson. Linda chafed at these arrangements and insisted that the subterfuge should now be dropped. On all subsequent visits, with her husband's agreement, they were registered together as Mr. and Mrs. Griffith.

There was one unfortunate concomitant of Griffith's open acknowledgement of his marital status: the number of roles assigned to Linda began to decrease. At first Linda was happy to play the boss's wife and company hostess, but her feelings as an actress were not to be denied. She expressed herself vehemently to her husband. He simply insisted that he had to cast the stories in the way that seemed best.

New faces were added to the company on the third trip. Salter and Lawrence were gone, but old hands Marion Leonard and Kate Bruce had come along. Other first-timers included William Beaudine; Edith Haldeman; Billy Quirk; George Nichols; and a number of extra men including Mr. Cortez, Mr. Landers, Mr. Gibbs, Mr. Foote, and Mr. Buckley. Guy Hedlund, another actor, arrived on August 22 and, as last man in, was assigned a cot in the hall.

The physical and geographical nature of Cuddebackville somewhat dictated the kind of films that Griffith could make there. Several of the special local features made excellent locations: the old canal; the Neversink River passing through uninhabited hills; rocky cliffs above river rapids; the large canal pond, called "the Basin," near the inn; and several colonial stone houses still in reasonably good repair. The pattern dictated by these surroundings was a sequence of Indian films, colonial or Revolutionary War films, bucolic comedies and romances, and anything that seemed suitable to an outdoor rural setting. No attempt was made to film indoor settings. These, if needed, were saved for the return to the 14th Street studio. In most cases the films were planned without interior shots in order to save time.

Griffith developed a passion for his own idea of authenticity, particularly in filming Indian stories. It was for this reason that he hired a genuine Indian, Young Deer, and his wife to act as advisors and to keep the Indian props and costumes, the bows, arrows, and canoes, in good condition. In the evenings, for the amusement of the company, Young Deer and his wife would teach the willing authentic Indian dances.

A typical day began shortly after an early breakfast with Griffith preceding the company on location. The property boys, young

Bobby Harron and Johnny Mahr, would load a wagon driven by Lester Predmore, the innkeeper's son. Lester, using his own horse Jerry, found this an excellent way to earn some summer money. Johnny Mahr would then help Billy Bitzer with the camera and tripod. The actors were picked up in front of the inn by a hay wagon driven by Elton Cuddeback, a descendant of the village's founder, Major Cuddeback, a colonial soldier.

The company would work until noon and then take an hour break for lunch. Griffith did not tolerate any extension of the lunch period because each hour of sunlight for filming was precious. Sandwiches were brought out from the inn for the company. Only Griffith was driven back to the inn for lunch. He would take Bitzer with him so that a conference on the afternoon's work could be held without interference from the company. Griffith always returned before the hour was up ready for work.

When the sunlight was too faint for photography, the company returned to the inn. Griffith would retire to plan the next day's shooting and leave the company to their own devices. The absence of city pleasures deterred only a few members of the company. Charles Predmore did keep a comfortable Mission-style bar in the front of the inn, and it was well patronized by the men of the company. For others of the men, card-playing became the chief form of recreation. Genteel games, in which some of the ladies participated, were played in the inn's parlor, but across the street in a small building, called Tammany Hall because it was used as a polling place in local elections, a poker game was always in progress. If bad weather prevented filming, the poker game became an all-day affair.

After the first trip to Cuddebackville, while Linda was still visiting in Kentucky, Griffith had written to his wife:

> Dear Linda:
> Well, I am back in New York. Got back at twelve o'clock last night . . . I have accounts to make out for eight days, imagine that job, can you?
> Haven't talked with Mr. Kennedy yet, as I have been away, but expect to on Tuesday or Wednesday as soon as I can see him. Lost six pounds up in the country, hard work, if you please. . . .
> And then I want to go back to that place again and take you

up this time because it is very fine up there. I am saving a great automobile ride for you—if I stay. . . .[76]

The last "if" in his letter was a reference to Griffith's renegotiation of his contract with Biograph. A new contract was signed in August maintaining Griffith's minimum salary of $100 a week, but raising his commission from one-twentieth of a cent for each finished foot of film sold to one-tenth. J. J. Kennedy well understood the impetus that a commission arrangement would give Griffith in turning out a great volume of pictures.

When Linda Griffith did make the trip to the Caudebec Inn that August, she got her automobile ride, although she was somewhat unimpressed with the Thomas Flyer which she promptly labeled, "the red devil." She *was* impressed with the inn, describing it as:

> . . . a comfy place, three stories high, with one bathroom, a tiny parlor, rag-rugged, and a generously sized dining room whose cheerful windows looked upon apple orchards. It was neat and spotlessly clean.[77]

Although Linda didn't seem particularly bothered by that one bathroom, the morning stampede by thirty people was undoubtedly frightful.

Charles Predmore introduced Griffith to a wealthy local landowner, Mr. Goddefroy. Griffith was warned that Goddefroy had no use for automobiles and other modern inventions, so Griffith turned on his Kentucky country-boy charm and a firm friendship developed between the two. Two immediate results of this new acquaintanceship were permission to use an old stone house on the Goddefroy property as a background for *1776, or the Hessian Renegades,* and the rental of horses to be used by the company. Griffith had arranged for horses to be shipped up from New York, but they hadn't arrived. The stone house still stands today, looking much as it does in Griffith's film.

Although the resemblance between the Orange Mountains and Kentucky is somewhat remote, Cuddebackville did substitute for Griffith's home state in one film, *In Old Kentucky,* a story of two brothers fighting on opposite sides during the Civil War. The most dramatic moment in the picture was the homecoming of the de-

feated brother, ragged and footsore, during a gala party celebrating
the other brother's success. The emotional highpoint came when
the brothers reached out their hands in reunion. The ragged, de-
feated brother was played by Henry B. Walthall. Walthall was to
play a similar scene in Griffith's *The Birth of a Nation,* a moment
remembered as the most touching scene in that film.

In between the trips to Cuddebackville, Griffith made films in
New York at the studio. The most notable of these studio films was
Pippa Passes, based on the poem by Robert Browning. Mary Pickford had been tested by Griffith for the title role when she first
came to Biograph, but he decided to cast Gertrude Robinson.
Linda Griffith remembered his reasons for not using Mary: "David
thought Mary had grown a bit plump; she no longer filled his
mental image of the type." [78]

The element that made *Pippa Passes* more significant than the
other films Griffith was turning out with such rapidity was its
lighting. Griffith had very specific ideas about the effects to be used
in the film. Bitzer balked at trying to achieve these effects. Bitzer
stated positively that they couldn't be done. Griffith turned to Arthur Marvin, as always more compliant, and

> . . . figured on cutting a little rectangular place in the back wall
> of Pippa's room, about three feet by one, and arranging a sliding
> board to fit the aperture much like the cover of a box sliding in
> and out of grooves. The board was to be gradually lowered and
> beams from a powerful Kleig shining through would thus ap-
> pear as the first rays of the rising sun striking the wall of the
> room. Other lights stationed outside Pippa's window would give
> the effect of soft morning light. The lights full up, the mercury
> tubes a-sizzling, the room fully lighted, the back wall should
> have become a regular back wall again, with no little hole in
> it.[79]

Everyone was skeptical of the effect until the results were seen as
they watched the film in the tiny Biograph projection room.

> At first the comments came in hushed and awed tones, and
> then when the showing was over, the little experiment in light-
> ing effects was greeted with uncontrolled enthusiasm.[80]

While Griffith's experiments in lighting seemed unusual and exciting to the company and were not to be seen in anyone else's

films of the time, they were really only variations of standard stage practices. Griffith had seen them used in the theatre. He had asked for similar effects in the stage directions of his two plays. The only new element was that they were being translated to film by a camera.

Billy Bitzer was most impressed by Griffith's demonstration and its success. Never again was Bitzer willing to cling to his own ideas of what would work with the same stubbornness. He came to believe that any effect Griffith might desire could be worked out, and Bitzer wanted to be the one to work it out.

Griffith's ideas were not accepted with unanimity by other members of the company. One idea made an actor very unhappy, and his muttered expletive gave Griffith a nickname. Young Bobby Harron, prop boy and part-time actor, passing the unhappy actor, heard him mutter, "The bastard!" Bobby misunderstood. He thought the actor had called Griffith "the Master." Harron picked up the reference and began calling Griffith "the Master" himself. Those members of the company who were most respectful toward Griffith picked up the phrase and began using it.

Griffith was proving to be a thoughtful leader, however, in ways that earned the respect and gratitude of most members of the company. It was the custom of other film companies to pay actors by the day. If shooting were canceled because of inclement weather or for other reasons, the actors were not paid, even though they had been called and had spent the day sitting around. Griffith wanted his actors paid, and he resorted to the subterfuge of telling the studio that he had paid them from his own pocket and demanded reimbursement.

Eddie Shulter, the scene painter, whose work was not very satisfactory to Griffith, was replaced by an Englishman with architectural training, Harry McClelland. Shulter had painted all the interior sets in a peculiar shade of brown which was sometimes politely referred to as "Biograph brown," but normally by earthier and less flattering names. Now with Griffith's encouragement, McClelland experimented with the use of a warm gray color that enabled Griffith to use lighting more effectively. By 1910 this warm gray tone was used for most Biograph sets.

From the moment that Griffith became the Biograph director,

he directed all of the films with the exception of a brief comedy that Mack Sennett had been allowed to make in Cuddebackville at the railroad station. The tall, awkward-looking young Irish-Canadian had become a special favorite of Griffith's. Sennett was one of the first actors Griffith hired. Sennett had joined Biograph in July 1908, at twenty-four, after some brief experience in stock companies shortly after leaving his home town of Richmond, Quebec. His first appearance in a Biograph film was a small part in *Balked at the Altar,* Griffith's eleventh film, made on July 19 and 30, 1908. Griffith used him primarily as an extra, but he found congenial Sennett's ebullient spirits that were combined with a perpetually dour expression, and he used Sennett as an assistant, a "gopher." This meant that Sennett was dispatched to go for coffee, props, actors, or whatever Griffith required. When Sennett requested the use of a free camera and some idle actors, including Mary Pickford, at Cuddebackville to try out an idea of his own, Griffith readily agreed. The film was *The Little Darling.*

In November Griffith asked his quondam company manager, Frank Powell, to direct. Powell was a solid, efficient character actor and Griffith was impressed with his ability to handle actors when Powell assumed the job of company manager. Griffith gave Powell a film, *The Day After,* to direct with Blanche Sweet playing the lead as the spirit of the new year, and another in December, *All on Account of the Milk,* with both Blanche Sweet and Mary Pickford in the cast.

Griffith directed an average of twelve or thirteen pictures a month in 1909.[81] The stories for these films generally followed the patterns established in 1908 by his Indian pictures, contemporary melodramas featuring last-minute rescues, and miscellaneous costume films in vaguely Renaissance settings. He also made two films with the Civil War as a background, one film about the American Revolution, and one film with the French Revolution as a background. He made fewer comedies, and planned, at the end of the year, to turn over the production of these short films to Frank Powell. In 1910, the majority of the thirty-five Biograph films not made by Griffith were directed by Frank Powell.

It made little difference to Griffith what the source of his film stories was. He was as willing to accept a story idea from a member

Colonel Jacob Wark Griffith

"Lawrence" Griffith,
D. W. Griffith as a young actor.

David Wark Griffith in 1919.

Linda Arvidson Griffith, D. W.'s first wife.

Linda and David Griffith in their only joint film appearance in *When Knights Were Bold* for Biograph. Griffith's directorial career was about to begin.

The Biograph studio at 11 East 14th Street, New York. One of the basement stores was the head-quarters of the Automatic Weighing Machine Company whose owner, Leroy Baldwin, held a majority interest in the Biograph Company.

The interior of the Biograph studio at 11 East 14th Street showing the overhead Cooper-Hewitt lamps.

BRUTE FORCE

ON ladies' night at the club, a discussion of man
evolution and possible re-incarnation arises betwee
the young author and his clubmates. Piqued by h
sweetheart's flirtation with a rival, the young man drain
his first cocktail to the dregs and falls asleep over th
tale of "Weakhands and Lilywhite." This is a story e
prehistoric days, founded upon the famous Biograp
picture, "Man's Genesis," in which Weakhands is show
triumphant over his enemies through the invention of th
stone club. The author dreams that he is Weakhand
leader of the Stone Club men, who inhabit the uppe
caves of a great antediluvian mountain. With Lilywhi
and his band, he is living peacefully when Monkeywal
leader of the Low Cave men, seeks another dwellin
place and invades the territory of the Stone Club
Monkeywalk's men have just come through a devastatin
war and there is only one woman left in the tribe. S
the Low Cave men covet the wives of Weakhands' me
and attempt a raid. Thanks to the stone club, they a
beaten off; but they appropriate Weakhands' idea, fashic
clubs of their own, and by superior force abduct th
women, Lilywhite included. Weakhands and his me
after futile attempts at rescue, are practically besieged i
their cave by Monkeywalk, and are facing annihilatio
when Weakhands makes another invention. While sittin
moodily he flicks the string of a whip. The idea of th
bow and arrow is evolved. The weapon does suc
terrible execution among Monkeywalk's men that th
Stone Clubs are emboldened to make another attempt
freeing their women. They are successful; Lilywhite an
her companions, after several attempts to escape, ar
rescued; and Weakhands is again acclaimed a hero.

THE CAST

Weakhands.......Robert Harron
Lilywhite.............Mae Marsh
Monkeywalk....Charles H. Mailes
Cave woman ....Jenny Lee
Cave man............W. J. Butler

A dramatic spectacle of the dawn of civilization, comparable only with "The Battle at Elderbush Gulch" and "Oil and Water"

Biograph Re-issue
Number 20

IN TWO
REELS

Directed by
W. GRIFFITH

Biograph re-released *In Prehistoric Days* (1913) in 1915 as *Brute Force* to capitalize on Griffith's fame. None of the advertising when he worked for Biograph carried his name or those of the actors.

In Old Kentucky (1910) was also re-released by Biograph in 1915 with credits for Griffith and the cast.

Another Biograph re-release, originally filmed in November 1912.

The Musketeers of Pig Alley (1912), a realistic film partially made on the Lower East Side of New York City. Lillian Gish at left, Dorothy Gish center.

The Girl and Her Trust (1912) with Dorothy Bernard, and Griffith in a small role, a re-make of Griffith's earlier *The Lonedale Operator* (1911).

The new (1913) Biograph studio in the Bronx, showing the glass-enclosed studio on the roof. Griffith filmed some of the interiors for *Judith of Bethulia* there. It is still in use as a film studio.

The Biograph company at the Caudebec Inn in 1911. Mrs. Bitzer is seated in the rear of the Thomas Flyer. Griffith (hand to mouth) is facing Mary Pickford, and Young Deer is on the porch.

Henry Walthall and Blanche Sweet in *Judith of Bethulia* (1913).

Judith of Bethulia (1913). Lillian Gish and Blanche Sweet

Griffith in his first film role, *Rescued from an Eagle's Nest* (1907), directed by Edwin S. Porter for the Edison Company.

Linda Arvidson Griffith and Mary Pickford in *The Unchanging Sea* (1910).

Linda Griffith in 1913.

Florence Lawrence
as "The Biograph Girl."

Dorothy Bernard

Claire MacDowell

Mary Pickford

Lillian Gish in *Orphans of the Storm* (1921).

Dorothy Gish
in *An Unseen Enemy* (1912).

Mae Marsh

Marguerite Marsh

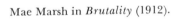
Mae Marsh in *Brutality* (1912).

Gertrude Robinson

Mabel Normand

Blanche Sweet

Blanche Sweet in *The Lonedale Operator*.

Constance Talmadge

Miriam Cooper

Kate Bruce

Charles Hill Mailes

William J. ("Daddy") Butler

Jetta Goudal in *Lady of the Pavements*.

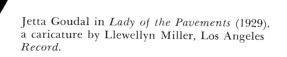

Jetta Goudal in *Lady of the Pavements* (1929),
a caricature by Llewellyn Miller, Los Angeles
Record.

Henry Hull

Richard Barthelmess

Harry Carey

Charles West

Neil Hamilton

Hal Skelly

Phyllis Haver

Evelyn Baldwin, Griffith's second wife.

Initial Feature Films, 1915-20

Rehearsal for a long shot of the Union Army on the march, *The Birth of a Nation* (1915).

The Union Army attacking the Confederate trenches, *The Birth of a Nation*.

Henry Walthall as the "Little Colonel" stands off the Union attack in *The Birth of a Nation*.

The set for Ford's Theatre in Washington, *The Birth of a Nation*.

Raoul Walsh as John Wilkes Booth catches his heel on the flag while making his escape after the assassination, *The Birth of a Nation*.

Henry Walthall
as the "Little Colonel."

The surrender at Appomattox. Howard Gaye as General Lee and Donald Crisp as General Grant, *The Birth of a Nation*.

The Klan attacks the black militia, *The Birth of a Nation*.

The newly formed Klan masses.

The feast of Belshazzar from the Babylonian sequence of *Intolerance* (1916).

The giant walls of Babylon, a setting for *Intolerance.*

Awaiting the final assault by Cyrus, *Intolerance*.

The Babylonian revelers await their fate, *Intolerance*.

Cyrus's army thunders toward Babylon for the final assault, *Intolerance*.

The attack on the gates of Babylon with swordsmen and a flamethrower, *Intolerance*.

Mae Marsh, *Intolerance*.

Margery Wilson, *Intolerance*.

Constance Talmadge, *Intolerance*.

Shots from the final sequences of Intolerance.
Griffith intercut each story in an intricate pat-
tern of increasing tempo, concluding with the
modern story, the only one to have a happy
ending, and an allegorical Armageddon
halted by the intervention of heavenly hosts
signifying an end to man's intolerance.

¶ The Boy's last dawn.

¶ The hangman's test.

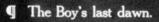

DG

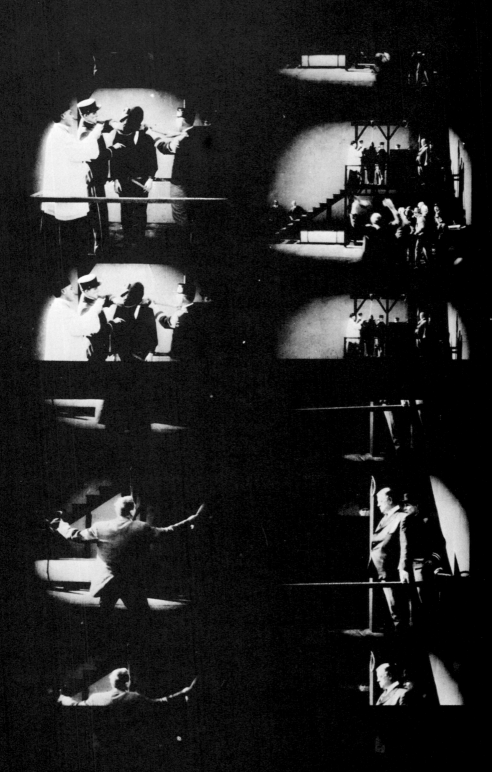

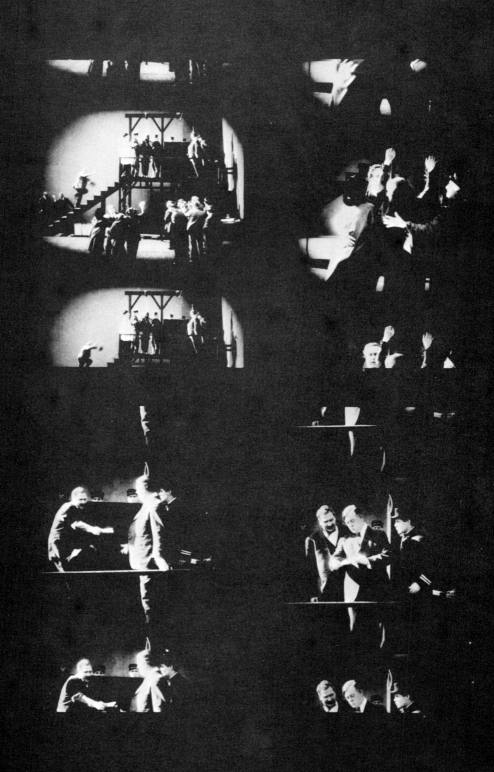

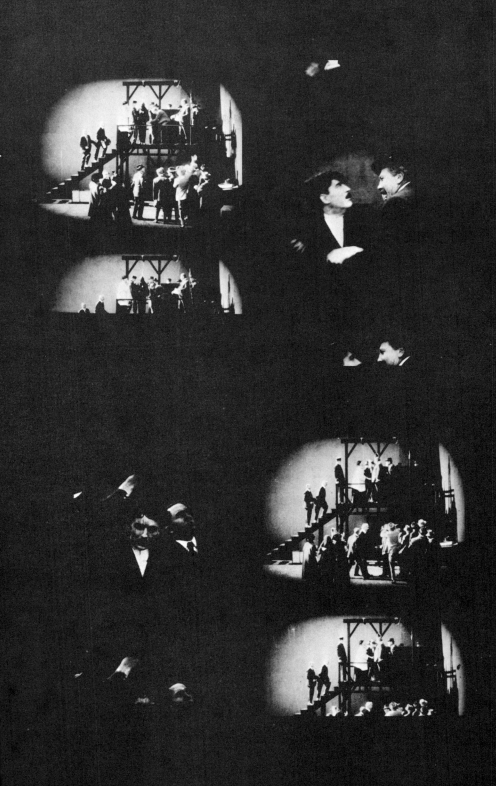

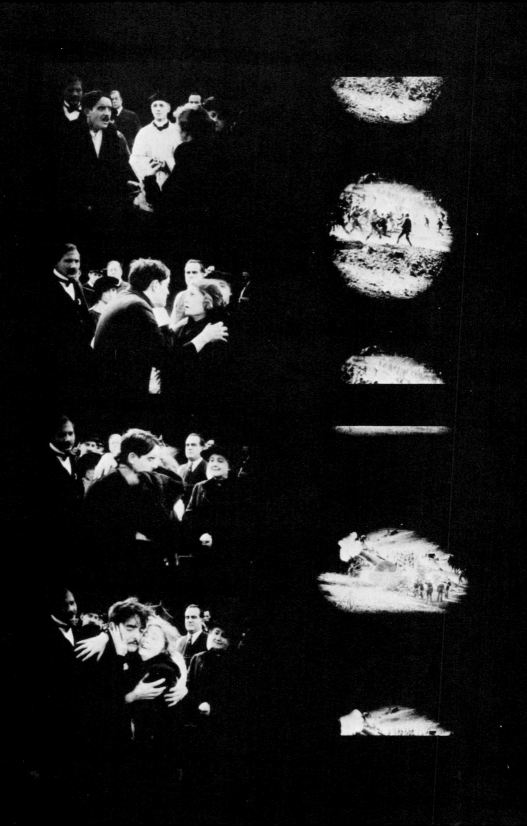

Lillian Gish and Robert Harron in *Hearts of the World* (1918).

Above, Griffith explains a scene in *The Great Love* (1918) to a group of English society ladies, including Lady Diana Manners. Below left, *The Greatest Thing in Life* (1918), Lillian Gish and Robert Harron. Below right, Clarine Seymour and Robert Harron in *The Girl Who Stayed at Home* (1919).

Robert Harron and George Fawcett in *The Girl Who Stayed at Home.*

Lillian Gish in *True Heart Susie* (1919).

Carol Dempster in *The Love Flower* (1920).

Richard Barthelmess as the Chinese boy in *Broken Blossoms* (1919).

of the acting company as from Dougherty and the Biograph story department. Both Sennett and Pickford sold Biograph story ideas that were filmed. Stanner Taylor supplied many plots, and Griffith borrowed directly from the works of James Fenimore Cooper, Robert Browning, William Carleton, George Eliot, and Mark Twain.

Griffith's ability to tell an increasingly complex story within the confines of the one-reel format had been enhanced by strengthening and refining the technique of cross-cutting, now used throughout the film rather than just in the chase sequences. The close-up, a shot showing one detail covering the entire screen, was used as a natural extension of the story to reveal significant detail. Both were part of a structure of parallel editing that moved simultaneous actions forward toward a joint resolution, sometimes, as in November's *A Corner in Wheat,* to make an effective social commentary. In this film Griffith interspersed shots of the hungry poor unable to buy bread because of inflated prices with shots of the successful wheat speculators celebrating at a lush banquet. The ability of a film to editorialize without words was effectively demonstrated.

Griffith was pleased when Linda reported, after her trip to Kentucky, that his family, especially his older brother Jacob, was enormously pleased with his success. Despite his salary and commissions, Griffith and his wife continued to live in their tenement apartment on 100th Street. He was now able to send some money home to Louisville to help his family.

The work week at Biograph now stretched to a full seven days for Griffith. Even Sunday afternoons were occupied with meetings of Griffith, Stanner Taylor, and Lee Dougherty in a saloon near Union Square where, for four or five hours, they would discuss the stories for the next week's films. One of the matters to be decided was which stories would be made a full reel in length and which would be limited to a half- or split-reel. In later years Griffith remembered those meetings taking place at Luchow's, the famous German restaurant on 14th Street, but more likely they were held in Halloran's, a working man's saloon on Sixth Avenue. Richard Barthelmess, when a school boy, got his first glimpse of the Biograph Company in Halloran's while on a visit to a 14th Street theatre managed by the father of a school friend.

Linda complained to her husband that she was not seeing

enough of him. Griffith replied that they would be able to shed their poverty as soon as he could make enough money, and with the commission, turning out more films was the way to make money. As logical as Griffith felt this explanation was, Linda was not really convinced. When Linda began to berate him for his lack of attention to her, Griffith would find that he had to go to a conference and would leave the house.

As though to compensate for the questioning of his authority and motives at home, Griffith assumed an increasingly patriarchal attitude toward the Biograph Company. He would bring his actors little games to play while they were waiting for filming to begin. In his days as an actor, Griffith had always tried to be "one of the boys" and join the poker games. Now if a crap game began in a corner of the studio, he would join for an experimental pass or two, merely to demonstrate that he knew the game, and then withdraw. This procedure gave the members of the company the feeling that Griffith was an expert. He always managed to have a story ready about some past exploit that would heighten this impression. He alluded to events and experiences sufficiently vague to prevent checking. Slowly, and to a certain extent unconsciously, Griffith built a fantasy world out of his past that would bolster his directorial authority.

6

California: The New Horizon

For a film-drama we can go afield and get anything we
want. If there is a shipwreck to show, we also picture the
angry sea and the restless waves. For romance we have
but to pick out some sylvan dell and bring our lovers
there. Let them act as two people very much in love
would be expected to behave in like circumstances, and
the audiences weave their own romance and do the larger
share of acting for that scene. On the side-lines we can reveal roses blooming in the sunlight, with a snow-crested
mountain for our background. In our drama the trees
sway in the breezes, and the blades of grass, damp with
real dewdrops, become a part of the action.[82]

With his contract renewed at a higher commission, David Griffith
entered his second full year as a motion picture director in 1910
filled with confidence. He had begun to recognize his importance
to the Biograph Company. His films were the only real prop supporting the company. None of Kennedy's financial manipulations
meant a thing without successful films. Griffith was aware that the
exhibitors were giving preference to Biograph films, his films, not
just for any artistic merit they might have, but because they made
more money than the competition.

While Griffith was not ready to exercise his growing power by
demanding more money, he did begin to ask that the successful
filming expedition to Cuddebackville be followed with a similar
jaunt to California during the winter. He pointed out to both
Henry Marvin and J. J. Kennedy that he was an old California
hand and knew the state from San Francisco to Los Angeles. He
described the lush backgrounds that could be used, the incompara-
ble sunshine, the warmth, and he compared this paradise with the
winter of slush and snow in New York that kept filming largely
confined to studio pictures. All of his dramatic powers were un-
leashed and at last his bosses were convinced. Permission was given

for the company to go to California. R. H. Hammer was to be sent as the management representative to oversee the business arrangements and keep the presence of the Biograph front office alive.

Griffith began to select the company to make the California trip. Frank Powell was, again, designated to act as the company manager. The others selected included Linda Griffith, Marion Leonard, Florence Barker, Mary Pickford, Dorothy West, Kate Bruce, Eleanor Hicks, Dell Henderson and his wife, Mr. and Mrs. George Nichols, Arthur Johnson, Alfred Paget, Arthur Marvin, Billy Bitzer, Eddie Shulter, Bobby Harron, and Johnny Mahr.

About January 15, the Griffiths started for California ahead of the acting company, accompanied by Mr. Hammer. Linda Griffith remembered the trip:

> Four luxurious days on luxurious trains before we could sight the palms and poinsettias that were gaily beckoning to us across the distances.
> The company departed via the Black Diamond Express on the Lehigh Valley, which meant a ferry to Jersey City. A late arrival in Chicago allowed just comfortable time to make the California Limited leaving at 8 p.m.
> The company was luxurious for just three days.
> It was only Mr. R. H. Hammer, my husband, and myself who had been allotted four full days of elegance. We *de luxed* out of New York via the Twentieth Century Limited.[83]

All was not so smooth for the company led by Frank Powell. As the company prepared to embark, young Jack Smith, who had now adopted the name of Pickford too, who had not been included on the company roster, threw a tantrum at not being allowed to accompany his sister Mary to California. Only Mary was scheduled to go. For the first time her formidable mother was letting her go without a chaperon. Mary's mother was willing to let Jack board the train and go with Mary despite Mary's protest that her brother had no luggage. The train began to pull out of the station with Mary in the doorway, still protesting. Her mother deposited Jack on the slowly moving step calling, "Look after your sister, Johnny!"

While Mary was most concerned about her brother's lack of extra clothing, including fresh underwear, young Jack took his mother's parting instructions quite literally and began to plague his sister with commands. He continued to issue dicta throughout the stay in California, in particular warning Mary about staying away from this or that man.

There were other departure disturbances. Arthur Johns and Charles West arrived hatless, breathless, and showing the effects of an all-night farewell party. They staggered aboard the train with great whooping cries.

Owen Moore was at the station to say goodbye to Mary Pickford. A romance had developed between the two at Cuddebackville, but they were attempting to conceal it from Mary's mother. Griffith had asked Moore to make the trip, but Moore had made his joining the company contingent on a ten dollar raise. Griffith had refused, as he refused a similar request from Mary Pickford. Moore was hoping that Frank Powell would tell him that Griffith had changed his mind. Powell saw Moore from a distance and gave him a negative shake of the head. Mary had also refused to go to California without the raise, but when Griffith merely shrugged and said he would give her parts to Gertrude Robinson, Mary's resistance disappeared and she was ready to go. This may well have been the last time that Mary Pickford was ever bested in financial negotiations.

The company arrived in Los Angeles, by way of San Bernardino, around January 20, 1910, and checked into the Alexandria Hotel following Mr. Hammer's suggestion. Hammer had agreed to pay for accommodations out of company funds for the first few days until the members of the company could get settled in their own accommodations.

Griffith was not the first to bring a film company to California. The Biograph visit had been preceded in 1907 by Francis Boggs and Thomas Persons who had settled long enough to make a crude one-reel version of the durable *The Count of Monte Cristo* for the Selig Company. Two erstwhile bookies, Charles Bauman and Adam Kessel, dubbing themselves the New York Motion Picture Company, had settled into an abandoned grocery store on the outskirts of Los Angeles in 1909. Bauman and Kessel were fleeing the repressive arm of the Motion Picture Patents Company to avoid seizure of their motion picture cameras. California was far enough for the moment to operate with some impunity.

With Griffith's approval, R. H. Hammer rented a loft for property storage and a vacant lot for outdoor filming at the corner of Grand and Washington Streets next to a lumberyard and a ball park. The lot, about an acre in size, was fenced. On the lot Griffith had Eddie Shulter construct a large wooden platform. Above the platform cotton shades were hung on wires, like clotheslines, to control, in a limited way, the amount of sunlight.

The actors were to don their make-up and costumes in the hotel and then make the trip to the lot. No dressing rooms were provided. The property loft was used for rehearsals. It was furnished with a battered kitchen table and three chairs, one of which was reserved for Griffith. During rehearsals the company had to sit on the floor.

After some protests from the actors, four small dressing rooms were set up on the lot, and Griffith had Frank Powell buy a tent to provide more of them. The stage was about fifty feet by fifty feet, open to the elements except for the cotton shades. Little protection was offered to the wind. When an interior set was being used, action had to cease until the wind died down so that it would not seem that a hurricane was blowing through someone's parlor. Even though this stage was outdoors, representing a return to the techniques of rooftop filming that had been common in New York in the earliest days, Griffith used it only for interiors, as he had done with the 14th Street studio in New York. For exterior filming Griffith called on his own knowledge of California to take advantage of those scenic and historical backgrounds readily available.

The first of these location visits was made to the San Gabriel Mission for a film called *The Thread of Destiny*. Subsequently trips were made to the Sierra Madre Mountains, Pasadena, the beach at Santa Monica, and to that suburb of Los Angeles later to be known as Hollywood.

At Santa Monica and at Port Los Angeles, Griffith made *The Unchanging Sea,* a variant on the Enoch Arden story, featuring his wife, Linda Arvidson Griffith. In the course of the film Linda, while waiting for her lost husband to return, was aged with make-up. Mary Pickford appeared as her grown-up daughter toward the end of the picture. Griffith convinced his wife that this was a real challenge for an actress. Linda had reservations about appearing as an old woman. She pointed out that she certainly wasn't old enough to be Mary Pickford's mother. Still the idea of a challenge appealed to her and she agreed to the part.

San Juan Capistrano, legendary home of the returning swallows, was to be a March location. The film to be made was *The Two Brothers*. Hammer was persuaded to hire a special two-car train with an attached baggage and horse car. For once the usually superb California weather failed. When the company arrived at their destination, a heavy rain was falling. The company dashed from the train to the hotel, arriving on the veranda thoroughly soaked. Filming was out until the rain stopped. For three days the rain continued. Griffith paced continually up and down the lobby, pausing only to badger Bitzer for weather reports. On the last day of the rain, the equally restless company watched from the hotel windows as an Indian funeral procession passed for services in the semi-ruined mission.

On the fourth day the sun came out, and the company was rushed into the street for the first scene of the film. This was to be a religious parade in which some of the actors were to appear in borrowed ecclesiastical garments. As the rehearsal began, Griffith noticed the sullen looks and mutterings of townspeople watching the film-makers. He realized that the spectators must have thought the actors were mocking the previous day's funeral procession.

As the fake procession neared the mission, the crowd's anger rose, and they rushed at the actors. Their particular target was old W. Christie Miller, playing a priest, who was carrying a large cross. The actors, whose bravery was confined to a script, saw the crowd closing in and ran for the safety of the hotel. The crowd gathered outside the hotel door with seeming intent to lay siege to the hotel. Griffith asked the Spanish-speaking hotel manager to go out on an upper balcony and try to calm the crowd. The hotel manager was finally able to explain what the film company was trying to do and that they were not mocking the funeral. The unruly crowd refused to be mollified unless some of the "cowboys" came out and entertained. The would-be mob now began to enjoy the movie company's discomfiture. They brought forward a horse, a bronco, and demanded that one of the "cowboys" ride it. Griffith was in luck. If such a confrontation had taken place in New Jersey, it would have

been likely that his Eastern cowboys would have been sent flying
from the back of this mean horse, but he had hired some genuine
cowboys in California to take care of the company livestock. One of
these, Art Acord, was an experienced rodeo performer. Acord volunteered to ride the horse.

Acord mastered the horse and easily won the crowd's support.
Then the other real cowboys put on an exhibition of rodeo tricks
in riding and roping. At last Griffith was able to bring the entire
company out of the hotel and resume filming. Some of the crowd
were even willing to help by marching in the restaged procession.

The next to last film made on this first California trip was a version of Helen Hunt Jackson's *Ramona.* Griffith was able to combine his special insights gained as an actor in a stage version of the
novel with the scenery near Peru and Camulos, California, some
seventy miles from Los Angeles. Griffith insisted that the film be
made under Helen Jackson's title, even though that meant that film
rights had to be secured from Little, Brown and Company, the
publishers of the novel. There was some front office opposition because it had always been easier, and cheaper, to borrow a plot, even
characters, and merely change the title. Hammer backed Griffith
up with appropriate telegrams to New York, and Biograph finally
followed through, purchasing the rights for one hundred dollars.
This was an unprecedented sum, even though it seems an absurdity in light of today's vast sums given for film rights. At that time
twenty-five dollars seemed an adequate payment for story rights.

Mary Pickford was cast as the Indian maiden, a role that didn't
seem strange to her because she had been the heroine of a number
of Griffith's earlier films having Indian characters. Griffith's attitude toward all of these films developed around stories of Indian
life was summarized in one line of the description of *Ramona:* "It
most graphically illustrates the white man's injustice to the
Indian." [84]

One more film, *Over Silent Paths,* about a lone miner and his
daughter making the trip to California by prairie schooner, was
made in the San Fernando Valley, and the company returned to
New York the second week of April. All the members of the company enjoyed the California stay and expressed their hopes that
they could return. Griffith promised that he would do his best to

persuade the bosses to finance another expedition the next winter.

It was inevitable that an acting company would attract its quota of characters. Mack Sennett had occupied the position as the chief buffoon almost from Griffith's beginnings. Despite the crudity of his humor, Sennett was a great favorite with Griffith. He could be counted on to play any part, undertake any assignment, and, despite his dour face, exude a spirit of cooperativeness that affected everyone in the company. It was equally inevitable that new members of the company who appreciated Sennett's humor, or who shared his antic view of life, would be attracted into his coterie. One of these newcomers with a special affinity for Sennett was Henry Lehrman. Lehrman had appeared at the studio in New York in 1909, affecting an absurd French accent, and claiming that he had considerable experience with the French film company Pathé. The available evidence would indicate, however, that Lehrman was a streetcar conductor on the 14th Street line who became enamored of film people while transporting them to work.

Griffith was not taken in by Lehrman's accent and false story, but he thought he was amusing and was willing to give him a try as an extra.

Mack Sennett later described "Pathé" Lehrman's first screen role as typical of the zaniness that attracted him to the former streetcar conductor.

> The scene called for French soldiers to capture a three-story building, rescuing some damsel in distress. Lehrman immediately distinguished himself. He not only ran into the building with the other extras, but suddenly appeared on the roof—and leaped into space.
>
> The fall would have splattered an ordinary man like a scrambled egg, but Lehrman lit with his backside, rolled twenty feet, bounced, and came up grinning weakly.
>
> Griffith was indignant.
>
> "You were not on camera," he hollered.
>
> "I was just rehearsing," Lehrman said. "I'll do it again." And he did.[85]

On the first Biograph trip to California, Lehrman became Sennett's roommate at the Alexandria Hotel. When Sennett left Biograph in August 1912, to begin his own producing company, he took Lehrman with him as a comedy director.

In July 1910 Griffith brought his company back to Cuddeback-ville. Mr. and Mrs. Griffith were assigned room 11. The company was a large one including Miller, Butler, Clarges, the Bitzers, Wal-thall, Mahr, Harron, Paget, Douglas Joss, Sennett, Lehrman, Billy Quirk, Grandon, O'Sullivan, Eddie Dillon, Craig, Stanhope, Beau-dine, Yost, Powell, Jim Evans, and among the women, Mary Pick-ford, Claire McDowell, Longfellow, Van Buren, Davenport, Kibbe, Hulme, and an old friend from his stock days, Kate Toncray. A total of forty-nine people made the trip to Cuddebackville from New York.

Griffith's directorial technique continued to be founded on prag-matism. In *Wilful Peggy,* Kate Bruce, playing Mary Pickford's mother, attempted to marry her daughter to an older man. Mary insisted to Griffith that if someone attempted to do that to her in real life, she would react by giving her "mother" a good shaking.

"Go ahead and do it," said Griffith.

After Mary had given Kate Bruce a thorough shaking, Griffith asked the character actress, "What would you do if your sixteen-year-old daughter shook you like that?"

"I'd grab her and spank her good and proper!"

"Well, what are you waiting for?" said Griffith. Mary backed away.

"If you think I'm going to submit to this nonsense, you're very much mistaken!" Mary turned and ran around an apple tree with Kate Bruce in full pursuit. Kate suddenly stumbled and fell. Mary looked back and with the filming forgotten for the moment, re-turned and, kneeling, threw her arms around Kate, giving her a kiss. Bitzer captured the entire scene with his camera, and Griffith used it in the final print of the picture.[86]

The evening activities at the Caudebec Inn after a busy day were much as they had been the previous summer. Some of the company gathered in the parlor to listen to W. Christie Miller, the company patriarch, read Shakespeare.

Guy Hedlund, a relatively recent addition to the company, dem-onstrated his variety act, a fake séance complete with a hypnotized medium and mysterious table tapping. One evening the tapping seemed to come from the ceiling. The new tapping from an unex-pected direction turned out to be Griffith pounding his shoe on the floor above in an attempt to quiet some of the parlor noise. Hedlund held his next séance in the nearby cemetery.

"Big Jim" Evans became the leader of the gambling forces meeting in "Tammany Hall" across the road. Poker was abandoned briefly for a crap game. Griffith wandered in and discovered that some of the company members who could least afford it were losing heavily. He promptly outlawed any game with dice, warning that only poker would be tolerated. Naturally the winners at the dice game weren't happy with Griffith's dictum, but by this time Griffith's authority was almost unquestioned. And all were aware that flouting that authority meant the loss of their jobs.

Borrowing the Predmores's Thomas Flyer, Griffith himself would drive the Pickfords, Mr. and Mrs. Bitzer, Linda, and himself off to another country inn near Port Jervis on the New Jersey border for dinner. Sometimes they would call on the Goddefroys. Goddefroy became an unofficial gadfly to the group, particularly bringing Griffith to task for paying his people in excess of the local wage scales. He did make himself popular with the company by bringing them his special drink when they were on hot, dusty locations. The drink consisted of a mixture of Bass's Ale and ginger ale mixed in a milk pail and sitting on a block of ice. The company was delighted to stand in line for their turns with the tin dipper at Goddefroy's "shandygaff."

Upon returning to the inn, the company was further bolstered by a round of drinks on their director, and a second round sponsored by Billy Bitzer. Only the adult members of the company were included in these invitations.

The company spent part of August 1910 in a second foray to Cuddebackville, and then returned to work in the 14th Street studio. At the beginning of November Griffith solicited Lee Dougherty's backing for his most ambitious project up to that time. He began two films simultaneously, in which each film told successive parts of the same story. Griffith argued that both films, *His Trust* and *His Trust Fulfilled,* should be released as one film. Anticipating a turn-down, he had made each film so that it could stand on its own. This was wise because Henry Marvin, Hammer, and Kennedy were against the notion of longer releases. Still Dougherty was able to announce both films in the Biograph bulletin:

> *His Trust* is the first part of a life story, the second part being
> *His Trust Fulfilled* and while the second is the sequel to the
> first, each is a complete story in itself.
>
> In every Southern home there is an old trusted body servant,
> whose faithful devotion to his master and his master's family was
> extreme to the extent of laying down his life if required.[87]

The first film began with the charge given to the faithful black
servant to protect his master's wife and daughter while he is fighting with his regiment in the Civil War. The husband is killed in
battle, and friends return his sword to the grieving family. The
sword is hung above the mantel. When the house catches fire, the
faithful servant remembers his trust and saves the child, then returns and rescues the sword. The homeless widow and child are
taken to the servant's little cabin with the black man standing
guard over them from his doorway.

In the second film it is four years later. The war is over. The
child has grown up and is a student in a seminary. The servant's
money is the means to pay her expenses and tuition. When the sav-
ings give out, he is tempted to steal to help the girl. He cannot
bring himself to commit a crime. His faithfulness is observed by
the girl's English cousin who then takes over the financial burden.
The cousin and the girl meet, fall in love, and marry.

> Old George at a distance views the festivities with tears of joy
> streaming down his black but honest cheeks, and after they de-
> part for their new home, he goes back to his cabin, takes down
> his master's sabre and fondles it, happy in the realization that he
> has fulfilled his trust.[88]

There is little doubt that Griffith was actively perpetuating a
popular Southern myth about the faithful black with these two
films. These were preliminaries to his attitudes expressed even
more forcefully in his later *The Birth of a Nation*. His attitude was
sincere, as was that of his co-workers. He believed in the "truth" of
his story. That a statement such as Dougherty wrote in the bulletin, "black but honest cheeks," implying that black cheeks were
usually *dishonest,* was racist would never have occurred to him.

Griffith completed eighty-six films in 1910. In the two and a half
years at Biograph, he had made two hundred and eighty-eight
films. That he made fewer films in 1910 than in 1909 was more at-

tributable to the use of other directors for Biograph than any slowing down of his own activities. He was now able to take more time with each film, rehearsing in more depth, and, of course, time not actually used in production was spent in the cross-country trip to California and back.

The only changes in the pattern of films made during 1910 was the addition of subjects which utilized the particular settings of California. He did depart from routine with one film by playing a medieval drama against the backdrop of Lambert's Castle, an imitation keep in Paterson, New Jersey.

As a film-maker, Griffith had solidified his position during 1910. He was fully in charge of his destiny. As a husband, he was failing. He had once had the insight to state that he would never marry an actress. He had. The relationship between Griffith and Linda was deteriorating in direct proportion to the drop in the number of roles in which she was cast. Linda Griffith had been given only two significant roles during the past year, and she had increasingly withdrawn from contact with other members of the company. Some of this withdrawal was a part of being the director's wife, but some was in response to her own lack of participation. Some of the newer members of the company were barely aware of who she was. In 1911 she was again cast in only two films, *Fisher Folks* and a two-reel re-make of *The Unchanging Sea,* now using its source's title, *Enoch Arden.* In both Linda played essentially character parts, and she still fancied herself as a glamorous leading lady. There were no domestic battles. It takes two to fight, and Griffith walked away, or stayed away, from any open quarrels.

With the wind, sleet, slush, and snow beginning again in December 1910, Griffith prepared the company for a second trip to California. Following the holidays, the company boarded the train for Los Angeles.

A newcomer in 1911, making the trip to the West, was a minor poet for *Smart Set* magazine who had decided to become an actor, Donald Crisp. Florence Barker and Joseph Graybill had also joined the company. Some old faces had disappeared. Marion Leonard had married Stanner Taylor, and the two went to work jointly for Reliance Films. Henry Walthall, Jim Kirkwood, and Arthur Johnson had also gone to Reliance. Griffith was sorry to see

Johnson leave. He considered the leading man one of his finest actors, but Griffith had to admit that Johnson's fondness for the bottle was making him increasingly unreliable.

The entire Pickford clan had also left Biograph in December. A secret deal had been negotiated on behalf of Mary with Carl Laemmle. Laemmle promised to double Mary's salary. While her mother was attempting to further Mary's career, Mary herself was not paying very much attention to it. She had been in love with handsome Owen Moore almost from their first meeting. Secretly, at Cuddebackville as well as in New York, the romance had grown. Now Mary slipped off to Jersey City and married Moore. In an attempt to look more mature, Mary had borrowed, without permission, a pair of her mother's high-heeled shoes and combined them with an oversized sealskin coat.

The impact of Mary's departure, coupled with the rumor that she would be receiving $175 a week from IMP and IMP publicity releases identifying Mary as the star of Biograph films, had a stunning effect on the remaining Biograph actors. Almost without exception, they braced Griffith to fight for more money for them with the Biograph front office. Biograph refused to begin publicizing its actors, but it submitted to some demands for increased salaries; they did agree to pay Wilfred Lucas a salary of $150 a week. Lucas had threatened not to make the impending trip to California without the raise. The demand was met when Griffith assured Henry Marvin that Lucas was a key member of the remaining company.

A new outdoor studio had been prepared for the company in Los Angeles. The new stage, at the corner of Georgia and Girard Streets, was double the size of the old one and made of smooth boards instead of the undressed lumber from which its predecessor had been built. The muslin scrims, used as light diffusers, were installed on an overhead trolley system. Dressing rooms, offices, and a projection room were housed in a one-story building next to the stage. The ultimate luxury was the installation of a telephone on the stage. Two large black limousines were hired to transport the company on location trips.

Responding to his wife's nagging, Griffith cast Linda in the leading role of *Fisher Folks,* the first film to be made in California in

1911. Linda played the dramatic part of a young crippled girl in love with a fisherman. The part was a good one, but the character aspects did not really appeal to Linda's self-image as an ingenue. She was also increasingly jealous of her husband's attentions to the other young women in the company. Her feelings were fortified when she saw the roles she wanted going to Blanche Sweet.

The second film of 1911 in California was *The Lonedale Operator,* a story of a beautiful young railroad telegrapher saved, at the last moment, from thieving tramps. The concise editing, particularly of the fine rescue sequence, has made this film almost the epitome of Griffith's Biograph style. Griffith intercut the shots of the distraught telegrapher, Blanche Sweet, trying to summon help, with the tramps' attempts to break into the office, and with the train crew coming to the rescue. The tempo of cutting speeded up, with each shot cut shorter and shorter, until the moment when the heroine was momentarily holding the villains at bay, then Griffith extended the train sequences, holding the suspense to an almost unbearable degree, before swiftly finishing with the rescue. Not a moment was wasted on extraneous detail.

Griffith directed five films in January, six in February, and five in March. It wasn't until late in March that Griffith used his wife again. He asked her to repeat her earlier role in *The Unchanging Sea.* Griffith had now decided to expand that film, no longer relying on the Charles Kingsley poem as a source, but following the original Tennyson poem and taking the original title, *Enoch Arden.* The two reels of *Enoch Arden* were shot in four days beginning on March 24. The cast included Wilfred Lucas, Frank Grandin, Florence LaBadie, Bobby Harron, Jeannie MacPherson, and Grace Henderson. The scenes were shot in Santa Monica in the same area where *The Unchanging Sea* had been made.

Billy Bitzer made excellent use of backlighting in *Enoch Arden.* Bitzer always claimed that he had discovered this technique by accident while filming Mary Pickford and Owen Moore sitting at a table with the sun at their back. The shot had been meant as a prank. Bitzer expected that the result would be a silhouette of the lovers, but enough of the sun was reflected from the white tabletop to bring out their faces against the sunbright halo about their heads. Griffith was invited to see the shot as part of Bitzer's joke.

The director recognized the beauty of the technique at once and asked that it be used again in an appropriate place in a regular film. To duplicate the effect in *Enoch Arden,* Bitzer substituted reflectors for the white tabletop.

Improvisation was still the ruling spirit for Griffith, and he used the fishing shack that had been requisitioned as the women's dressing room as the bridal home in the film. The men's dressing room in an abandoned horse car, stuck fast in the sand, was not used. A horse car didn't seem at all appropriate to the film.

George Nichols, a character actor, was sent all the way to San Francisco to get the costumes from Goldstein and Company. Griffith had used costumes from this company the previous year in *Ramona,* but his knowledge of their stock stemmed from his acting days in San Francisco.

When the film was finished, Griffith requested that both reels be released as a single film just as he had done with *His Trust* and *His Trust Fulfilled.* There was as little interest in New York this time as there had been before. Griffith pressed as hard for this longer format as he could. Henry Marvin finally compromised and permitted the two reels to be released as Part One and Part Two. Exhibitors were encouraged to show the first reel on one day and the second on the day following. Audiences demanded that both reels be shown together, and the exhibitors began to give in. This simultaneous showing of both reels made *Enoch Arden* the first two-reel film to be made by any unit of the Motion Picture Patents Company. It was not the longest film made up to that time, since J. Stuart Blackton had made a *Life of Moses* in 1909 in five reels, but all reels had been released and shown as separate films. Blackton had also made a three-reel version of *Uncle Tom's Cabin* in the same year, but this, too, was intended for single-reel release. Paul Panzer, later to gain fame as the villain in Pearl White's *The Perils of Pauline,* had directed a three-reel film on the *Life of Buffalo Bill,* with the real William "Buffalo Bill" Cody as himself, for Harry Davis and John P. Harris of Pittsburgh the same year.

Although the independents had beaten Griffith in the development of the longer film, Griffith's *Enoch Arden* had greater impact. It was a superior film, and it received more extensive distribution through the licensed theatres affiliated with the Motion Picture Patents Company.

An addition to the Biograph acting company in 1911 was a young man from a prominent theatrical family, Lionel Barrymore. His sister Ethel was already an established stage star, and his younger brother John was viewed as a promising young leading man and light comedian. Lionel, who would have much preferred to be a musician and composer, nevertheless made his career as an actor. He first called on Griffith at the 14th Street studio looking for work. Griffith, on hearing his name, at first refused to take Lionel's application seriously.

> "I'm not employing stage stars," said Griffith.
> "I'm not remotely any such creature," said Lionel. "I will do anything. I mean absolutely anything. Believe me, I'm hungry. I want a job."
> "All right," said Griffith, "We'll put you on. . . ." [89]

In the first printing of Iris Barry's *D. W. Griffith, American Film Master,* a photograph of Lionel Barrymore was erroneously identified as showing him in Griffith's *Fighting Blood,* and for a long time it was accepted that this was his first film for Griffith. In the later edition edited by Eileen Bowser, the same still was correctly identified as coming from *The Chief's Blanket* made in 1912, not under Griffith's direction. Recent viewers of *Fighting Blood* have not found any sign of Lionel Barrymore in that film. Barrymore's first work for Griffith did begin in the early part of 1911 in California.

To gain time for his own work, while still maintaining the amount of film product that Biograph demanded, Griffith turned over some of the directorial chores during 1911 on a regular basis. Frank Powell was given a schedule of typical melodramas, each following the pattern and style set by Griffith, and Mack Sennett was given responsibility for the split-reel and one-reel comedies. Powell had the use of the regular Biograph actors when they were not cast in a Griffith film. Sennett, on the other hand, surrounded himself with those Biograph players with a special affinity for slapstick comedy, Mabel Normand, Fred Mace, Ford Sterling, and his former roommate "Pathé" Lehrman.

In many ways the most ambitious film made by Griffith during the California trip of 1911 was *The Last Drop of Water*. Eight prairie schooners, a generous contingent of extras to play soldiers and Indians, and a mixed collection of chickens, dogs, horses, and a lone cow were used to give this brief Western story an authentic look. The entire complement of the company was used, in large and small roles. The featured actors were Blanche Sweet, Charles West, Bobby Harron, Dell Henderson, W. Christie Miller, Jeannie MacPherson, Joseph Graybill, and William Butler. Linda Griffith described the scene:

> We set up camp in the San Fernando desert—two huge tents, one for mess, with cooks and assistants who served chow to the cowboys and extra men. Two rows of tables, planks set on wooden horses, ran the length of the tent—there must have been at least fifty cowboys and riders to be fed hearty meals three times a day. The other tent contained trunks and wardrobe baskets, and here the boys slept and made up.[90]

After the conclusion of *The Last Drop of Water,* the company was preparing to depart for New York when it was discovered that a common problem of the time, film static, had ruined the last shots of the picture. Another trip to the San Fernando location had to be made to re-take the ruined shots. Then, and only then, was the company able to board the train for the East Coast.

The Last Drop of Water was a somewhat ironic title in another way because it became the last film in which Linda Arvidson Griffith was to work under her husband's direction. On the return trip to New York they quarreled bitterly, not only about the small number of roles given to Linda, but more importantly about the attentions that Linda alleged Griffith was paying to the other girls in the company. Griffith denied her accusations, but when Linda threatened to make the sort of public scandal that might threaten his job at Biograph, he agreed to sign a "confession" of his infidelity. Linda announced that she was leaving him when they arrived in New York. He agreed to continue giving Linda a substantial portion of his income for her support.

Linda, ever the ambitious actress, had no intentions of discontinuing her career. She intended to capitalize on her Biograph connection in the same way that the Pickfords had. She also decided to put away the "confession" for the day when it might be needed as a defense of her rights. She had no intentions of giving her husband a divorce. It was to avoid this possibility with its attendant scandal that caused Griffith to accede to her wishes.

When they parted in New York, Griffith headed for a hotel. He felt confused, but more than a little relieved. Increasingly Griffith had been assuming the role of surrogate father for his acting company, a role accepted by all but Linda. Now there would be no further private challenges to his authority. There would be no further dinner table protests against his casting by the strong-minded Linda.

Griffith made his last trip to Cuddebackville in July 1911. The company of forty-two included Mabel Normand, Claire McDowell, Kate Bruce, Edwin August, Alfred Paget, Guy Hedlund, Donald Crisp, Mack Sennett, Lehrman, Fred Mace, Beaudine, and Griffith's Indian adviser Dark Cloud and his wife.

Griffith always retained fond memories of Cuddebackville and the Orange Mountains, but when he finished filming there in 1911 he never returned. The mountains, valleys, and deserts of California were more spectacular and cinematic than the low tree-covered hills of New Jersey for the outdoor locations that now came to Griffith's mind. Other members of the company, once introduced to the little town, did return, and in the case of Billy Bitzer continued to correspond with Charles Predmore, their host.

One film made at Cuddebackville on this last trip had a notable technical innovation. *The Squaw's Love* featured a fight scene between two Indian maidens, played by Mabel Normand and Dorothy West. The end of the fight came when Dorothy pushed Mabel over the edge of a cliff. Mabel Normand, a superb athlete, was to execute a back dive into the Neversink River. Mabel was fearless, but she also announced that she would do the stunt only once. To make certain that the shot wouldn't be missed, Griffith had Bitzer set up three cameras to film the action. Bitzer would operate one, and a new cameraman, P. Higginson, would operate a second. Arthur Marvin, Griffith's first cameraman, had died the previous February 11th. Higginson had been hired to work primarily with

Frank Powell. The third camera was operated by the former office and prop boy turned actor Bobby Harron.

The fight came to its climax, and Mabel executed her dive perfectly into the river. She was promptly pulled from the water, bundled into the Thomas Flyer, and driven back to the inn for a reviving brandy or two. In the editing of the film, footage from only one camera was used, perhaps accounting for the subsequent overlooking of this first use of multiple cameras.

Griffith and the company left Cuddebackville on August 3. At that point he was still speaking of the possibilities of returning. Billy Bitzer sent Charles Predmore a postcard from New York:

> Expect to be up with the Indians in a couple of weeks. Anything I can do for you, you know the number is 11 East 14th Street. We are going to do a big war picture at Fort Lee this week, then an easy one, then Cuddebackville.[91]

Billy Bitzer had become very fond of young Lester Predmore, son of the inn's owner, and when the Biograph troupe made their next trip to California in 1912, he wrote and asked if young Lester might be allowed to go with them. Charles Predmore, ever a practical man, replied that his son had to complete his education. Instead of becoming a movie star, Lester Predmore became a dentist and career officer in the army.

The "big war picture" that Bitzer referred to in his postcard was *The Battle*. Although Griffith had already made a number of films with the Civil War as a background, they had tended to focus on individual stories with the war merely a peripheral factor. Now he was ready to stage and film his first battle scene. The Biograph bulletin outlined the plot:

> In the days of '61 how many brave soldiers were urged to deeds of valor and heroism by thoughts of "the girl he left behind." This story tells of the transforming of a pusillanimous coward into a lion-hearted hero by the derision of the girl he loved. The battle takes place outside her home, and he, panic-stricken, rushes in, trembling with fear, to hide. She laughs in scorn at his cowardice and commands him to go back and fight. Her fortitude inspired him and he manages to rejoin his company before his absence is noticed. Ammunition is low and somebody must take the hazardous journey to procure more

from another regiment, which he volunteers to do. This undertaking cannot be described, for the young man faces death at
every turn. The most thrilling part of his experience is where
the opposing forces build bonfires along the road to menace the
powder-wagon.[92]

With the use of artillery pieces, the action scenes were a small-
scale rehearsal for Griffith's later epic, *The Birth of a Nation*. The
principals in the cast included Blanche Sweet, Bobby Harron,
Charles West, Donald Crisp, and Spottiswoode Aiken.

In many ways 1911 was a watershed year for Griffith. He had
managed to consolidate many of his directorial techniques, now
commanding complete obedience to his own purposes from the
company. He was free of any domestic responsibilities and could
devote his time entirely to film-making. Significantly, too, he had
shifted from his connection with the acting profession to directing
by symbolically signing his first contract with his real name, David
W. Griffith. His 1910 contract had first been signed Lawrence Griffith, and then "Lawrence" was crossed out and David written over
it. Although his income was still tied to a base of $75 a week, his
total income had risen from salary and royalties to about $3,000 a
month.

Griffith made seventy films in 1911, some sixteen fewer than in
1910. They showed the improvement in his use of editing, cross-
cutting scenes and shots, not only for suspense and for climactic
chases, but also as a standard technique of story telling. Increasingly he had employed a moving camera, mounting it on a train.
The close-up was now a preferred method of adding visual punch
to the climax of a carefully constructed sequence of shots rather
than for its novelty or shock value. He had learned to employ
larger and larger casts effectively in his films, as in *The Last Drop
of Water* and *The Battle*. He had discovered the advantages of
multiple cameras. Now he was ready to continue polishing his art
and to dream of its further possibilities.

7

Graduation from Biograph

I interested myself in the short-story pictures in much the
same way as a painter interests himself in smaller works
in order to earn the wherewithal to devote his time to a
more ambitious effort.[93]

Mary Pickford returned to Biograph at the beginning of 1912,
joining the company in California after the Christmas holidays.
Her experience with IMP had not been a pleasant one, and, as she
was to testify at her later divorce trial, her marriage was equally
unpleasant. Moore's fondness for the bottle and an inability to be
reconciled with Mary's mother were probably the chief contribu-
tors. For the moment, Mary's memories of the company made her
turn to Griffith and Biograph for security, but circumstances and
Griffith himself had changed. Mary was welcomed back, but she
was no longer the leading ingenue of the company. Biograph
promised to release her name in connection with her films, although it was adamant that no credits would be given on the films
themselves.

The roster of young ladies who might be cast almost inter-
changeably, at least in Griffith's mind, included Blanche Sweet,
Marguerite Loveridge, Dorothy Bernard, and, as an addition to the
company in 1912, Mae Marsh. Mary Pickford was to make two related discoveries on this return to Biograph: Griffith did not need
her, and she did not need him. Still, Mary Pickford made some of
her most memorable Biograph films in 1912.

Mary played the lead opposite Charles West in Griffith's first
film of 1912, *The Mender of the Nets.* Blanche Sweet was cast in
the second film, *Under Burning Skies,* with Wilfred Lucas and a
newcomer, Christy Cabanne. Dorothy Bernard was given the leading role in the third film, *A Siren of Impulse,* with Charles West.
As Griffith juggled his casts, alternating the girls, considerable rivalry developed. Mary Pickford remembered: "I even noticed some

resentment when I returned to Biograph, especially among the girls who had stepped up during my absence." [94] This natural rivalry appeared in its greatest intensity among the mothers and guardians of the young leading ladies. Mary Pickford's mother and Blanche Sweet's grandmother were sometimes fierce and insistent on their offsprings' roles. Griffith, employing his most courtly quiet manner, was able to play these partisans off against each other and maintain his independence.

Griffith's continual experimentation with filming techniques continued. In *The Goddess of Sagebrush Gulch,* he included a shot of a man sliding down a bank showing the slide moving diagonally across the frame. Increasingly the beauty of backlighting was explored. His use of long shots exploiting the beauty of the scenery was becoming a regular scene-setting device, and more complicated editorial mixes of medium and close shots were used. Actors were given entrances that could be photographed in dynamic diagonals.

At the end of January Griffith decided to re-make a successful film from the previous year, *The Lonedale Operator.* The new version was titled *The Girl and Her Trust,* and Dorothy Bernard was given the role previously played by Blanche Sweet. The story was much the same as before, but Griffith introduced some slightly more sophisticated camera work. Shots were made with the camera mounted on a handcar intercut with shots of a pursuing engine made from fixed locations. Additional shots were made from an automobile riding parallel to the handcar and engine. The latter shots were of the type later known as "tracking shots." With the same breathless editing and shorter and shorter shots, the handcar and train were brought closer and closer without showing them in the same shot until the last shot showed the train catching up from the rear.

Despite a somewhat more finished technique, the earlier film is a better one. Blanche Sweet manages to convey the helplessness of the trapped young telegrapher in a much more moving way. The directness and simplicity of the editing of *The Lonedale Operator* gives it a more effective, dynamic pace. Both films illustrated the point that, despite Griffith's continuing experimentation, the development of his art did not consist of a long, steadily upward climb.

Between January and the end of March, Griffith maintained his usual pace, completing eighteen films. In *A Beast at Bay,* made in March, he filmed a race between an automobile and a locomotive, a sequence later repeated in *Intolerance.*

The constant demand for more and more films from Biograph had put great strains on Lee Dougherty, Stanner E. V. Taylor, and the story department. They were willing, as was Griffith, to accept a story from any source as long as they felt that it could be filmed. Stories from unknown authors were accepted and stories were equally welcomed from members of the acting company. The cameraman Billy Bitzer had contributed the story for Mack Sennett's first comedy hit, *The Curtain Pole,* and Sennett himself had written a number that were filmed. Further, Sennett convinced Mary Pickford that she should try her hand at writing. Mary was convinced that she should try, not so much by Sennett's arguments, but by his success. Mary had a rather low opinion of Sennett's intellectual abilities, and she felt that her own efforts could not help but be superior. One of Mary's stories, *Lena and the Geese,* was purchased by Biograph and filmed in April 1912. It was a rather unremarkable although charming film, notable chiefly for a blithe dance executed by Mary as she returned homeward with her geese. Griffith liked the little dance step for its symbolization of girlish innocence and made a mental note to use it, with variations, in future films.

There was one notable indirect effect of *Lena and the Geese.* Sometime after its release date, June 17, 1912, it was seen by two young sisters, Lillian and Dorothy Gish, in a Baltimore theatre. The Gish sisters and their mother were friends of the Pickford family from its vaudeville and theatre days. At one point they had shared an apartment in New York while both mothers promoted their daughters in the theatre. With great surprise, Lillian and Dorothy recognized their friend Gladys Smith, not knowing that she was now called Mary Pickford, and resolved to visit her at the Biograph studio in New York.

In late spring Griffith undertook to break out of the pattern of films in which he felt increasingly trapped and make a picture that would have more significant things to say. The vehicle was a story called *Primitive Men* about the dawn of time, or at least the dawn of man. Griffith insisted that the title be changed to *Man's Genesis*. Griffith saw the film as one showing man's fundamental nature, a universal comment seriously approached. Lee Dougherty disagreed, thinking that a film about cavemen could only be done as a farce. According to Linda Arvidson:

> . . . Mr. Griffith was determined that it should be a serious story; and he did it as such, although he changed the animal skin clothing of the actors to clothes made of grasses. For if the picture were to show the accidental discovery of man's first weapon, then the animal skins would have to be torn off the animal's body by hand, and that was a bit impossible. So Mae and Bobby dressed in grasses knotted into a sort of fabric.[95]

The "Mae and Bobby" in Dougherty's comments were Mae Marsh and Bobby Harron, the latter by then accredited as a full-fledged actor. Mae played the role of Lilywhite, the heroine, and Bobby Harron was Weakhands, the hero. Bruteforce, the villain, was played by Wilfred Lucas. This was the first important role for Mae Marsh. She had followed her older sister, who used the *nom de film* Marguerite Loveridge, to the Biograph lot in California. Marguerite Loveridge, née Margaret Marsh, had been cast by Griffith in January in *The Mender of the Nets*. Mae was still in school, but she spent her free time at Biograph. Dorothy Bernard pointed her out to Griffith, commenting on her resemblance to stage beauty Billie Burke.

The rival actresses at Biograph were not upset by the casting of Mae Marsh in *Man's Genesis* chiefly because they didn't think the costumes were particularly flattering. Their eyes were set on the principal role in the film to follow, *The Sands of Dee,* to be based on a poem by Charles Kingsley. Before casting Mae Marsh, Griffith had asked Mary Pickford to play the part. She refused, saying: "I'm sorry, Mr. Griffith, but the part calls for bare legs and feet. (In those days we even wore stockings and shoes in bathing.)"[96] Then the part was turned down successively by Blanche Sweet, Dorothy Bernard, and even Mabel Normand. Griffith was upset but managed to keep the company from seeing his displeasure. Whenever anyone attempted to question his judgment in casting, he became more determined to have his own way. This small rebellion was not to be tolerated. He determined to make the casting of *The*

Sands of Dee contingent on the casting of *Man's Genesis*. He called the company together and announced: "for the benefit of those who might be interested . . . as a reward for her graciousness Miss Marsh will also receive the role of the heroine in *The Sands of Dee*." [97]

The experienced actresses, who had vied for the role, were thunderstruck. The various mothers and grandmothers went into momentary shock. All of them, in the sort of generous spirit actresses generate from personal disappointment, hoped that little Mae would fall on her face. She did not. Her special radiance shown through and overcame her inexperience. Mary Pickford commented: "Miss Marsh gave a beautiful performance. Indeed we were all so stirred, we swallowed our pride, and gave her our sincerest congratulations." [98]

Granting Mary Pickford her best memory of the response to Mae Marsh's performance, Mary nevertheless decided that if untrained actresses could be instant successes in motion pictures, then it was time for her to return to something that demanded "real" professionals, the stage.

The company returned to New York in May and resumed work at the 11 East 14th Street studio. In June the young Gish sisters, responding to their resolve after seeing *Lena and the Geese,* came to the studio to find their friend Gladys Smith. The Biograph receptionist, a position denoting the company's new affluence, told the girls that no one by that name worked for the Biograph company. Lillian insisted that Gladys Smith had played the leading role in *Lena and the Geese*. The receptionist then told them that their friend must be Mary Pickford. Mary herself remembered this moment after she had been summoned to see her visitors:

> We were laughing and reminiscing gaily when Mr. Griffith came through the swinging doors into the hall. I beckoned to him and said:
> "I want you to meet three of my dearest friends, Mr. Griffith: Mrs. Gish and her daughters, Lillian and Dorothy, and I think they would be lovely on the screen."
> "You have courage to introduce me to two such lovely girls," said Mr. Griffith. "Aren't you afraid of losing your job, Mary?"
> "No," I said, "because if they can take it from me, it is obviously not my job."

"You'll be sorry," he told me teasingly as he went up the stairs.[99]

In 1940 Lillian Gish recalled a slightly different first meeting:

> Mary secured an engagement with the Biograph Company and one day out of curiosity I went down to the studio to see her work. Mr. Griffith was directing a picture at the time. He saw both Dorothy and myself and evidently thought we might become successful screen players. We were immediately engaged. . . .[100]

Lillian Gish recalled in 1968 more details about this first meeting. She described her anxiety as she stood under Griffith's steady blue-eyed gaze.

> "Mary, aren't you afraid to bring such pretty girls into the studio?"
> She retorted, "I'm not afraid of any little girls. Besides, they're my friends." [101]

Griffith then questioned the girls about their acting experience and ability, directing his questions toward their mother. Dorothy piped up: "Sir, we are of the legitimate theatre!" Griffith then summoned Henry Walthall, Elmer Booth, and Bobby Harron to meet the girls. Almost immediately they were plunged into rehearsals for *An Unseen Enemy*. Lillian Gish also remembered that Griffith had descended the stairs for this first meeting.

There are two other non-eyewitness versions of this meeting. One is told by Terry Ramsaye:

> Mary came down the hall and there was a chatterfest of busy little girls in the hall. As they stood talking, a serious sober-faced man came down the big stairs and walked past with a glance at the trio of youngsters.
> "That's Mr. Griffith," Mary whispered awesomely. "He's the director."
> They were still talking when Christy Cabanne, then an assistant to Griffith, approached and inquired if Miss Pickford's friends would like to help out in the making of a scene for the picture then in the works.
> This was an adventure. They certainly would.
> Up in the studio under the green-blue glare of the lamps, Lillian and Dorothy sat in the first row of an audience scene. They had made their start on the screen as extras.[102]

Linda Arvidson Griffith's version was also based on hearsay.

> Things were quiet in the theatre and Mary saw no reason why, when they could find a ready use for the money, her little friends shouldn't make five dollars now and then as well as other extra people.
>
> Lillian and Dorothy Gish just melted right into the studio atmosphere without causing a ripple. For quite a long time they merely extra-ed in and out of pictures. Especially Dorothy—Mr. Griffith paid her no attention whatever, and she cried because he wouldn't, but he wouldn't, so she kept on crying and trailed along.[103]

Griffith's own memory lacked the details of the other accounts:

> I remember one day in the early summer going through the gloomy hall of the Biograph studio when suddenly all the gloom seemed to disappear. This change in atmosphere was caused by the presence of two young girls sitting side by side on a hall bench. They were blondish and were sitting affectionately close together. I am certain that I have never seen a prettier picture . . . Lillian had an exquisite ethereal beauty. As for Dorothy, she was just as pretty as a picture in another manner; pert— saucy—the old mischief seemed to pop right out of her and yet with it all, she had a tender sweet charm.[104]

The varied versions of the Gish sisters' arrival at Biograph are not as important as the fact that they did arrive. Perhaps, as Lillian Gish recalled, they first met Bobby Harron in the hallway of 11 East 14th Street rather than a receptionist, Christy Cabanne, or Mary Pickford. The sisters did appear in a significant way for the first time in *An Unseen Enemy*.

Lillian Gish has recounted many times the story of Griffith's use of a red and a blue ribbon, one color for each girl, as a means of telling them apart. Examination of the photographs and films of the girls in 1912 suggests that they didn't look sufficiently alike to necessitate such a means of identification. It would rather seem to be an example of Griffith's use of psychology in handling two young actresses entirely too conscious of coming from "the legitimate theatre." The girls bore a strong family resemblance, but they were definitely not twins.

An Unseen Enemy was a re-make of *The Lonely Villa* in terms of basic plotting and general film design. *The Lonely Villa* had been Mary Pickford's third film in 1909.

The cast, in addition to the Gish girls, included Elmer Booth as their brother and Grace Henderson as a slatternly housemaid conspiring with the film's villain to rob the villa's safe. Griffith also used Bobby Harron and a new recruit, Harry Carey.

Griffith held a rehearsal for the film the day before shooting was to begin. He wanted to test the abilities and reactions of Lillian and Dorothy. Several times during the rehearsal he fired a track starter's pistol into the air in an attempt to get the girls to react with the proper amount of fear. He didn't bother to tell them that the pistol only fired blanks. Both girls reacted as Griffith wanted. " 'He's gone mad!' I thought as we scurried around the room looking frantically for an exit," Lillian Gish later exclaimed.[105]

Griffith was pleased with the rehearsal. He found himself enormously attracted to Lillian and had to force himself to maintain his professional composure. He told both girls to return the next day for the actual filming and turned away to busy himself with some inconsequential details.[106]

Griffith completed six pictures in July 1912, beginning with *Friends,* a Western filmed at Coytsville, New Jersey. Griffith used several close shots of Mary Pickford. When Mary saw the footage in the Biograph projection room she was highly critical of her make-up, particularly its artificiality. She was joined in her criticism by her fellow actor Lionel Barrymore, but he was more concerned with his own appearance, which he considered to be too fat. Lionel resolved to cut out drinking beer. Mary resolved to work for a more natural make-up.

Griffith used Lillian Gish in one July film, *In the Aisles of the Wilds,* shot along the banks of the Hudson River. Claire MacDowell, Harry Carey, and Henry Walthall were in the cast.

August was the month for renewing Griffith's contract. His talks with J. J. Kennedy took enough time to hold down film production to only two films. Griffith asked Kennedy for stock in the Biograph Company as part of a new contract. Kennedy refused, stating that there was no stock available. Griffith countered by asking for 10 per cent of Biograph's profits. Kennedy said he would consider it, although his intention was merely to stall the talks. Griffith had shown that he was aware of his value to Biograph. Kennedy was equally aware of Griffith's value, but he was reluctant to accord recognition to someone he considered to be only a cog in the business machine. Kennedy held long talks with Henry Marvin in order to examine the alternatives to Griffith's demands. Could Griffith be fired? Could he be replaced? The results from the exhibitors showed both men that getting rid of Griffith would be very bad business. They reluctantly admitted that Griffith's films were largely responsible for lifting Biograph from near bankruptcy. Kennedy knew that he would have to deal.

Other negotiations were going on that same August. Griffith's apprentice, Mack Sennett, was having talks about going into independent film-making with Charles O. Bauman and Adam Kessel. Sennett later claimed that the negotiations began because he owed the ex-bookmakers one hundred dollars from a losing bet on a horse. When Baumann and Kessel arrived to collect, Sennett, broke, quickly and nervously made a counter-proposal that they finance him in a new comedy motion picture company. Sennett, who somehow thought he might receive a broken arm as interest on his debt, was surprised when the bookmakers agreed to put up $2500 for the nameless comedy company. It didn't remain nameless for long. On a stroll, Sennett saw the logo for the Pennsylvania Railroad, a symbol of the Keystone State, and promptly decided that his new company would be Keystone too.

Sennett came to Griffith and said a reluctant goodbye. He also wanted to tell Griffith that he was taking with him those Biograph players whom he had used in the comedies he'd directed for Biograph: Mabel Normand, Fred Mace, "Pathé" Lehrman, and Ford Sterling. Griffith wished him well, although he couldn't resist saying that he thought Sennett might do better to remain.

Griffith's own negotiations were suspended, and he continued to work under his last contract from November 1911. Kennedy promised that the company would work out the details of a new proposal if Griffith would just be patient.

In September Griffith made *The Musketeers of Pig Alley* with exteriors shot on the streets of New York. The film was advertised as "a depiction of the gangster evil," and it has been called the first gangster picture, although its basic ingredients had been before by Griffith. Its crisp documentary realism presaged similar sequences in *Intolerance* and bore a great similarity to the last film of Griffith's career, *The Struggle.* Lillian Gish played the young wife who becomes the object of unwanted attentions from a neighborhood gangster, played by Elmer Booth. Walter Miller was Lillian's husband, and the cast also included Harry Carey, Bobby Harron, and Griffith's athletic trainer, "Spike" Robinson. Robinson had been hired to spar with Griffith in the latter's continuing quest of physical fitness. *The Musketeers of Pig Alley* still projects an excellent cross-section of New York tenement life in 1912.

While Kennedy stalled the contract talks, Griffith seemed to be answering with a slowdown of his own. He made only one other film in September. Kennedy now gave Griffith greater assurances that, while 10 per cent of the Biograph profits was out of the question, he would guarantee a satisfactory settlement. It would be dependent, however, on Griffith's turning out more films. Griffith believed Kennedy and in October plunged back into more active production, completing seven films.

Mary Pickford's last film for Biograph was made in October, *The New York Hat.* Mary had been offered a leading role in *A Good Little Devil,* a play to be produced by her old mentor David Belasco. Without telling Griffith that she was talking to Belasco, Mary accepted the role, and then informed Griffith she was leaving. Mary had thought the parting would be easy, but "suddenly realized how much [she] would miss [her] beloved Biograph and the guiding hand of this brilliant man." [107] With tears in his eyes, Griffith said, "God bless you, Mary. I'll miss you very much."

The New York Hat was based on a scenario mailed to Biograph by a sixteen-year-old school girl from California, Anita Loos. Anita Loos was a show business child. Her father, R. Beers Loos, was the proprietor of a traveling stock company on the West Coast that specialized in melodramas. Biograph had no idea of the age of this author, and Lee Dougherty sent Miss Loos the $25 purchase price without hesitation.

The acting and production people at Biograph said goodbye to Mary Pickford at a party on October 25 in Mary's Riverside Drive apartment. Mary gave the party as much to celebrate her return to the stage as to say farewell to Biograph. She wasn't alone in leaving the company, however. Lillian Gish had also been offered and accepted a small role as a fairy in the same play. Lillian swore Mary to secrecy. She said that it would be better if she told Mr. Griffith later.

When Lillian approached Griffith and told him of her own impending departure, Griffith became very confused. At first he didn't quite know how to react. He asked Lillian how much Belasco would be paying her. When she replied that she would receive $25 a week, he offered to double her salary if she would stay at Biograph. But then, before Lillian could reply, he told her of his admiration for Belasco and said that she'd be foolish not to take this opportunity to work with him. Griffith seemed unsure what advice to give this beautiful elfin-faced girl. Perhaps he felt emotionally involved with her in a way that conflicted with his image as the leader of the Biograph acting company. Maybe if he was away from her for a time, he might be able to sort out some of his reactions.

Griffith's expressed admiration for Belasco was genuine. He still harbored a secret wish that he might be a member of Belasco's company. He was enormously pleased when much later in his career a press agent dubbed him "The Belasco of the Screen."

Lillian's acceptance of the role in *A Good Little Devil* posed problems for the Gish family. Griffith wanted to take Dorothy with the company on their forthcoming trip to California. Mrs. Gish had an offer to appear with a stock company in Springfield, Ohio, and was eager to resume her own acting career. Mrs. Gish finally agreed that Dorothy could go to California and share a room with Gertrude Bambrick. She would remain in New York with Lillian until the *Devil* company went on tour, and then she would go to Springfield. Mrs. Gish wasn't too worried about Lillian because the Pickfords would be able to keep an eye on her.

A Good Little Devil opened in Philadelphia. Griffith gathered a number of members of the Biograph Company and made the trip to see the play. After the performance they went backstage and congratulated their former colleagues. Griffith told Lillian that he was very proud of her performance, and repeated similar praise to

Mary Pickford. When the play opened in Baltimore after the Philadelphia run, Griffith took the train down to see it again. He found it hard to admit that he wasn't that interested in the play but wanted to see Lillian.

The last two months of 1912 became a whirlwind of film-making for Griffith. The answer for any personal problems that Griffith might face was work of such intensity that there was no time for any outside considerations. He directed fourteen films before the Christmas holidays, including *The Burglar's Dilemma,* based on a story concocted by Lionel Barrymore. The Griffith scoreboard at the end of December 1912 showed a total of four hundred and twenty-three films made since he had succeeded the McCutcheons. The overwhelming majority of the films had been one-reelers, but the scattering of two-reel films had also proven successful despite Henry Marvin's misgivings. As the company was about to leave for California, both Marvin and J. J. Kennedy cautioned Griffith against trying to stretch out his films into additional reels. They pointed out that the one-reel films were returning handsome profits at the box office, and success shouldn't be tampered with.

Griffith felt that his bosses were being a little hypocritical. He was aware that they had helped in the promotion and exhibition of a four-reel film, *Queen Elizabeth.* They were aiding a combine, the Engadine Corporation, in securing a license for the presentation of this French film, a *Film D'Art* production, starring Sarah Bernhardt and Lou Tellegen. The principals in the Engadine Corporation were Edwin S. Porter, Joseph Engel, and an ex-furrier, now treasurer of the Marcus Loew theatres, Adolph Zukor.

In Griffith's eyes *Queen Elizabeth* had only its stars and its length to recommend it. It had been first shown on July 12, 1912, in association with Daniel Frohman at a legitimate theatre and had proven to be merely a photographed stage play. Despite its four-reel length, there were only twelve shots, and photographically it looked like the short efforts of 1908. By way of contrast, Griffith's own *The Sands of Dee* had sixty-eight shots in one reel. There were no medium or close shots in *Queen Elizabeth.* Kennedy and Marvin were impressed, however, by the return of almost 400 per cent profit within a brief exhibition time.

J. J. Kennedy was willing to concede to Griffith that there was a place for longer films, but he didn't see Biograph becoming directly involved in their production.[108]

Kennedy was willing to approve a limited number of two-reel films to be made during the forthcoming California trip. He stipulated that their production had to be approved in advance from New York. R. H. Hammer, acting as company manager, would secure that permission. Griffith protested that the poor communications with New York would hold up production. He told Kennedy that the length of a film was something which had to flow from the requirements of the story, and this could be determined only when the film was actually in production. Kennedy was adamant about Griffith securing permission. Griffith left for California feeling, for the first time, that his directorial prerogatives were being threatened. The freedom that he had enjoyed at Biograph, the absolute control over his acting company, over the selection of stories to film, and the entire creation of his films, had led him to regard the Biograph executives as merely salesmen and paymasters. This assertion of administrative control was both frustrating and frightening to him.

The basic acting company for the California trip of 1913 consisted of Dorothy Gish, Elmer Booth, Harry Carey, Lionel Barrymore, Henry Walthall, Walter Miller, Claire MacDowell, Charles Hill Mailes, Joseph McDermott, Alfred Paget, Kate Bruce, Kate Toncray, Jack Dillon, Mae Marsh, William "Daddy" Butler, Blanche Sweet, Gertrude Bambrick, and W. Christie Miller.

Lillian Gish had taken a slight fall during one of her flying sequences in *A Good Little Devil* during the Baltimore engagement. She was merely shaken up, but Belasco, mistaking her pale, fragile look for an impending illness brought on by long rehearsals and skimpy meals as well as the accident, and fearful of a possible injury suit, dismissed her from the company and advised rest for her.

Lillian's seeming fragility was more surface than real. Underneath her ethereal appearance was the strength of a lion. She immediately caught the train for California to rejoin her sister and Griffith.

The company that Griffith took to California in 1913 had changed considerably from that of his beginning years. Former

Griffith players were now scattered about the industry. Flora
Finch, briefly a Biograph player, was a principal comedienne opposite John Bunny at Vitagraph. Harry Myers was working for
Lubin. Florence LaBadie and George Nichols, veterans of the
Cuddebackville trips, were working for Thanhouser. George Nichols had become Thanhouser's chief director, appointed on the
basis of his association with Griffith. He attempted to follow in
Griffith's footsteps, going as far as to take the Thanhouser acting
company to Cuddebackville in the summer of 1912.

Owen Moore, now separated from Mary Pickford, was playing
opposite Florence Lawrence at Victor. Marion Leonard and her
husband, Stanner E. V. Taylor, were at Monopole. The influence
of any single person on the history of any enterprise is difficult to
trace. There is little doubt that those who had worked with Griffith scattered throughout the industry, carrying his methods and
his ideas to other companies. In 1913 Griffith had already become
the man to watch and imitate.

When the company left 11 East 14th Street for California, they
said goodbye to their old studio with its dirty, prop-filled dressing
rooms, and its bright memories. A new studio was under construction on 175th Street in the Bronx and was expected to be ready for
their return. The old studio had been home base for Biograph for
seven years, and over five hundred and seventy films had been
made, edited, and distributed from its studio and offices. The new
studios were to have:

> . . . two huge stages—one artificially lit, and one a daylight stu-
> dio. There was every modern convenience but an elevator.
> . . . From the dressing rooms a balcony opened that looked
> down on the studio floor. . . .[109]

Griffith looked forward to the planned facilities at 175th Street,
but his last look at 11 East 14th Street was filled with memories. A
major link with his past was being broken. Some of his dreams of
the theatre, and his marriage to Linda Arvidson, were irrevocably
tied to the old building. He turned his back on the past, holding
his sentimental memories, but facing a future. For Griffith that future was work.

The passing of the old studio was also the end for Griffith at

Biograph. It would be easier to sever ties with this company when it seemed an impersonal machine in the new Bronx headquarters. Griffith was to use the new studio only briefly. A few interior shots for his last Biograph picture, *Judith of Bethulia,* were shot there. The new studio was to be used by other directors, other companies, right to the present day, but not Griffith.

8

The Climax at Biograph:
Judith of Bethulia

Griffith's productions were all experiments in picture
making. They might be vast experiments, or little experiments, according to the size of the bank account at the
time—but they were experiments nevertheless.[110]

Griffith plunged into a heavy schedule upon reaching California.
He directed nine films in January and February, beginning with
Love in an Apartment Hotel, based on a story purchased from a
William Marston of Harvard College, and concluding with *A Mis-
understood Boy* from a story submitted by Christie Cabanne that
gave a leading role to Bobby Harron.

The first film of March, *The Little Tease,* about Kentucky
mountaineers, was stretched to an extra half-reel when Griffith
found that he couldn't tell the story satisfactorily in a single reel.
The first official two-reel film, for which permission was obtained
by Hammer, was *The Yaqui Cur* made in April. A second two-
reeler, *The Mothering Heart,* was tailored for the talents of Lillian
Gish at the end of April. The finished film was also only a reel and
a half in length, but had to be shown in the two-reel format. All together Griffith finished six films in April and four in May. Some
responsibility for the Biograph product was removed from Griffith
when the trade press carried the announcement that as of April 5
Tony O'Sullivan would direct all the Monday releases, and Dell
Henderson would be the director of the mid-week comedies. Biograph was releasing three films a week for exhibition.

The luxury of the extra time afforded by O'Sullivan and Henderson carrying part of the load enabled Griffith to work out plans for
his most ambitious film up to that time. It was reported in the
trade press that Griffith was having an imposing western town constructed in the San Fernando Valley for a future film. The story

commented that the setting was unusual for both its authenticity and the strange fact (in film scenery terms) that it was being built three dimensionally. No announcement was made of the purpose of this elaborate setting, and Griffith himself did not explain it even to his company. The mock western town was for a two-reel film to be called *The Battle at Elderbush Gulch.*

It has often been stated that Griffith experienced a great deal of difficulty with the Biograph front office during 1913, but actually both Kennedy and Marvin recognized the value of Griffith to Biograph and were willing to appease him in small ways. They had finally given in and were willing to publicize their ace director, and even a few of the featured players, although not on the films themselves. They did feel it necessary to keep a tight rein on the money. They felt that the commission arrangement they had with Griffith was an eminently fair one, but Griffith indicated his displeasure with a policy that forced him to earn his money by merely turning out footage. Griffith was acutely aware that to take more time with the preparation and shooting of a film would have the effect of lowering his own income. The only way he could reconcile his artistic desires with his personal pocketbook was to turn out longer films.

Despite being in California, removed from the main exhibition center of New York, Griffith was aware, through the trade press, of the opening of an eight-reel Italian spectacle, *Quo Vadis,* and had learned about the acclaim for its rich decor and monumental sets. The actual film had virtually no influence on Griffith, but written descriptions of the film provided a spur to him to attempt something equally important. Griffith always denied that he had seen *Quo Vadis,* although Blanche Sweet remembers it being shown to the company after their return to New York from California. She thinks that Griffith was present. In any event it had little influence on him except in the press descriptions of Griffith's final Biograph film, *Judith of Bethulia,* which was something of a response to it.

As the time approached for the return to New York, Biograph's story editor, Lee Dougherty, informed Griffith that he had decided to stay in California and was resigning from Biograph. Before his resignation, Dougherty had arranged to purchase a story called *Judith and Holofernes* from a Grace A. Pierce of Santa Monica. This story, based on the Apocrypha, seems a little suspect in the context of Griffith's familiarity with the Thomas Bailey Aldrich play, *Judith of Bethulia,* based on the same story and commissioned for Griffith's former employer Nance O'Neill. Griffith wanted to make this film, and the Pierce scenario seemed insurance against a plagiarism suit. Biograph had no intentions of buying the rights to the Aldrich play when the basic story was in the public domain. Still, when Griffith finally began filming his *Judith,* the Aldrich script was by his side and was consulted.

Plans for *Judith* were being formulated by Griffith during June and the beginning of July. He directed only two films in June while carpenters were constructing sets in Chatsworth Park for *Judith.* Griffith did delegate some authority for the construction of sets, but he liked to visit the construction personally, each day if possible. He was simultaneously concerned with the western town for *The Battle at Elderbush Gulch.* The supervision problem for the latter was solved by scheduling the last film in June, *Two Men of the Desert,* a minor effort, to be made in the San Fernando Valley as well.

A modest two-reel film, *The Reformers, or The Lost Art of Minding One's Business,* from a scenario by Frank Woods, the former pioneer film critic of *The Dramatic Mirror,* was made at the beginning of July. The film was an exposé of the "uplifters," as Griffith termed the wealthy society matrons who played, simultaneously, "Lady Bountiful" and moral censor to the lower classes. Griffith had scant use for society reformers, and he was always capable of seeing beauty in the midst of poverty. He finished the film on July 6 and began work on *The Battle at Elderbush Gulch.*

Linda Arvidson Griffith, although not present during the shooting, described the film, mangling the title:

> The Battle of Elderberry Gulch [sic] was a famous picture of those days. The star was a pioneer baby all of whose relatives had been killed by the Indians. During the time the baby's folks were being murdered another party of pioneers, led by Dell Henderson, was dying of thirst nearby. With just enough life left in them to do it, they rescued the baby from its dead relations, staggered on a few miles, and they, too, sank exhausted in the sand and cacti.

> Another cornucopia sandstorm blew up.
> Kind-hearted Dell Henderson, now sunk to earth, had protect-
> ingly tucked the baby's head under his coat. But the tiny baby
> hand (in the story, and it was good business) had to be pictured
> waving above the prostrate figures of the defunct pioneers, to
> show that she still lived. Otherwise, she might not have been
> saved by the second rescuing party, and saved she had to be for
> the later chapters of the story.[111]

The lost baby was shown to have grown up in the person of
Blanche Sweet, although the actual baby, according to Linda Griffith, was a Negro baby selected by Griffith from a foundling home
for the quality of its photogenic black eyes.

For another film to follow *The Battle at Elderbush Gulch,* Griffith decided to re-make *Man's Genesis.* The new film was called at
first *Wars of the Primal Tribes.* When Biograph finally issued the
film late in 1913, it was re-titled *Brute Force.* Griffith was strongly
attracted to the story of primitive man and his struggles. Many
years later, in the thirties, Griffith made a last attempt to start up
his career with another re-make of the same general story for Hal
Roach, re-titled again *One Million B.C.,* starring Victor Mature
and Carole Landis. Griffith was removed from the picture long before it was finished, but the basic story remained Griffith's. The
story was re-made once again, long after Griffith's death, under the
last title and starred Raquel Welch.

The setting for *Judith of Bethulia* was now complete. It was in
an area, then, of approximately twelve square miles. The wall of
the city of Bethulia was built between two rocky outcroppings so
that it was unnecessary to have the city take on a circular shape.
The architectural verisimilitude of this strange location didn't
bother Griffith at all, nor did it bother him that the city, in such a
position, would have really been indefensible, since the enemy
Assyrians could easily have scaled the rocks to enter the city rather
than assaulting the city wall.

Griffith spent more time than usual in rehearsing for *Judith.* He
insisted that the extras also be transported to the location for rehearsals and prepared the horsemen for the battle scenes. All of
this was expensive and, at least to Biograph, an unheard-of procedure.

One of the crucial settings was a well. It was actually a dry fake, but Griffith insisted that two barrels of water a day be shipped to the location to preserve the authenticity of the well scenes. The water cost eighty dollars a day.

The cast for *Judith* was headed by Blanche Sweet as the Bethulian widow, and Henry Walthall, hidden by a large beard, as the Assyrian general Holofernes. Everyone else in the company was pressed into service including Lillian Gish, Dorothy Gish, Gertrude Robinson, Kate Bruce, Bobby Harron, Lionel Barrymore, Marshal Neilan, Antonio Moreno, and Thomas Jefferson.

Lionel Barrymore remembered many years later, and somewhat imprecisely, that he had played several roles in the film, changing beards and costumes as Griffith willed. Barrymore noted that Griffith employed a four-part construction for the film, a technique similar to the one employed in *Pippa Passes,* and with some alleged similarity to the four-part construction of *Intolerance.* The resemblance to the latter film is slight at most, other than the obvious similarity to the Babylonian sequences in *Intolerance.* Barrymore also remembered that Harry Carey was crucified upside down. Carey does, indeed, appear as a traitor and is disposed of by the unforgiving Holofernes.

Judith of Bethulia deserves greater study than it has been accorded to date. It was the crowning achievement of Griffith's career at Biograph, not for its length alone. *Judith* makes use of almost all of the cinematic advances that Griffith had perfected in his shorter films. He tells the story with sometimes incredible swiftness. His shots are pared to essentials. The opening sequence, the exposition and establishment of the drama's framework, is carried out with great economy.

SHOT 1   Medium long shot of the exterior of Bethulia's walls, angled to make the small set, built between real rocks, look larger.

SHOT 2   Close shot of Mae Marsh (as Naomi) at the well.

SHOT 3   Medium shot of Naomi lifting water from the well.

SHOT 4   Close shot of Naomi lifting the heavy water bucket.

SHOT 5   Medium shot of her lover, Bobby Harron, greeting her and helping lift the water jug to her shoulder.

SHOT 6   Close-up of Naomi looking at her love. Harron is almost outside the frame at right.

SHOT 7   Medium shot of the young lovers leaving the well and moving right out of the frame.

SHOT 8   The lovers enter the frame in close up from left, and exit into long shot and out of frame at right.

Then Griffith introduced his first explanatory title. In this brief opening sequence, he introduced three of the principal settings for the film, showed the importance of the outside well as a source of water for the Bethulians, captured audience interest with the human element of the young peaceful lovers, and placed the audience firmly on the side of the Bethulians before the introduction of the villains.

The introduction of Judith, a widow in mourning, reduced to observing the happy life of the village through her window, presents a major motif of the film, a motif that might be described as alienation. Judith is lonely and separated from her village. She longs to become a part of it again. Griffith heightened this feeling in a shot showing Judith admiring a tiny baby held by a young mother, played by Lillian Gish, and turning away in private anguish.

The disruption of this seemingly private story by the attack by the Assyrians comes swiftly. Following a brief historical title noting Holofernes's relationship to the king of Assyria, Griffith shows Holofernes in a single shot, in close-up against the long curving line of his army. This is followed by three shots of the Assyrian army beginning their attack forward toward the camera and leaving the frame in lower right, cutting to the attack across the fields, cutting again to the Bethulian women fleeing from the wells, and again to the Assyrians massacring the villagers, including a woman and child.

Not a single moment was wasted in development, and yet Griffith crowded these shots with telling detail that was amplified in the remainder of the film.

While the battle scenes showing the attack on the city concentrate more on sword-waving than on swordplay, they manage a tempestuous excitement and drive. The walls are attacked with rolling towers, battering rams, and ladders, and the defenders, a small number of actors, reply with arrows and spears. Griffith shows his mastery of tempo by cutting from the visual excitement of the battle scenes to the calm, closed-in, isolated room where Judith watches from her window. Griffith's constant intent to relate the bigness of spectacle to a small personal story has been given no better vehicle than this. Close shots of Blanche Sweet allow her tortured face to mirror the trials of the besieged city, and to develop her feelings of wanting to find some way to help. For Griffith, spectacle was always subordinate to concern for the problems of individuals. It is ironic that he should be remembered in the popular mind as the creator of spectacle, and that when he ceased making films with spectacular scenes it was commented that his direction had changed. Griffith himself always avowed that his film *America* was a failure because circumstances forced him to eliminate the stress on the personal stories in the film in favor of action scenes or motiveless melodrama.

In *Judith* Griffith continued the counterpoint of battle action against Judith in her room and against the waiting figure of Holofernes on his couch in an elaborate tent. The role of Holofernes was not a physically taxing one for Henry Walthall, who played it almost entirely lying on his couch. This languid waiting was not unlike a spider in the center of a web.

Griffith contrasts Holofernes's grim sentencing of a traitor, Harry Carey, and his subsequent crucifixion, with Judith's anguish and compassion for her fellow villagers as she watches from her window. Judith's decision to sacrifice herself in an attempt to kill Holofernes is played against his cruelty.

Before filming Judith's arrival at Holofernes's camp, Griffith spent an inordinate amount of time on a pseudo-orgy featuring an oriental dancer performing an imitation of the Ruth St. Denis style. The effect is about as orgiastic as a recital by a Saturday morning dancing class, but it does show Griffith's interest in specific effects, later amplified when he hired the Denishawn dancers for *Intolerance*.

The scenes in which Judith attempts to seduce Holofernes and discovers that she has fallen in love with him do not work very well. While it is useful to show Judith's inner conflict at carrying out her murderous mission, no real attempt is made to give her new feeling of love any proper motivation. In his play on which the film was based, Thomas Bailey Aldrich avoided this difficulty by providing motivation for Judith in his dialogue, but Griffith seemed to assume this was not necessary in the pantomime form. Griffith might easily have succumbed to the popular but false notion that a lonely widow falls immediately for any strong masculine figure in her path. All dramatists have, at times, employed stereotypes where the necessity for economy of action has seemingly prevented them from developing character properly. Emotional responses can also be assumed. But in a character that is otherwise well motivated, this is a significant weakness.

Griffith does show the pressures on Judith to continue her mission by cutting to shots of the now-starving village women, including Lillian Gish and the baby, advancing on their men with outstretched pleading hands. He also shows the failure of a desperate drive on the wells to seek water, and then shows that Judith must now continue despite her love for the enemy general.

The killing of Holofernes and the disintegration of the Assyrian forces is somewhat anti-climactic. It seems as though Griffith were now trying to complete the film quickly, as though the four-reel format, despite being his longest film to that moment, was hampering him. The feeling is almost inescapable that the motivation for Griffith's future long films can be found here. Four reels were not enough for his vision. If the promise of the depth of the opening reels were carried out, *Judith* might well have been a film of twice its released length.

When Biograph, long after Griffith's departure, re-released *Judith of Bethulia,* two reels of out-takes (rejected material) were added to make a six-reel film, re-titled *Her Condoned Sin,* but it was not mere lengthening that Griffith needed. He needed the longer form for the more complete telling of his story, while still using the same swift, economical pacing as before.

In another direction, the basis for Griffith's drive to develop the physical spectacle of his films can be anticipated in *Judith.* The Bethulian setting was a mud village compared to the magnificence of Babylon in *Intolerance.* Bethulia's set had to be photographed from restricted angles, to make it appear larger. Griffith longed to use sets that would give him more freedom of action.

As the film was being shot, the Biograph office in New York became aware of its steadily rising costs. Griffith had budgeted the film for $18,000, and even this had been questioned by the company accountant, J. C. "Little" Epping, in New York. While the film's final cost of approximately $36,000 seems an absurdity against the million dollar film budgets that have followed, it represented a tremendous rise above the film costs for 1913. Griffith's contract, despite its expiration, did give him authority over all aspects of production, and he was able to override Epping with charm and firmness. Griffith had quickly realized his dominance over Epping, and managed to keep him off balance whenever the accountant attempted to question expenditures. Griffith recognized Epping's ability, but his faith in his own judgment, now greatly increased since his timorous first steps into film, kept him from listening to any of Epping's advice when it ran counter to his own wishes.

Judith was finished during the first week in July except for some of the interior shots. Griffith planned these for completion in the new Bronx studios on the company's return to New York.

In New York at the end of July, Griffith faced a confrontation with Henry Marvin and J. J. Kennedy. After assuring him that his talent as a director was not in question, they stated that he would have to relinquish his control over budgets and expenditures. In an effort to sweeten this blow, Marvin told Griffith that additional directors would be hired and Griffith would be asked to supervise their work. Griffith would finish the shooting of *Judith* and edit it into a workable size, preferably four separate films for individual release, but would not receive an assignment for a new film immediately.

Griffith left the office extremely agitated with Marvin and Kennedy's plans. He strongly believed that Biograph's success, perhaps even its existence, was due almost entirely to his own efforts. The intricacies of manufacture and sale, the maneuvering with the trust, the keeping of books, were all extraneous matters in Griffith's mind. As he worked on the final scenes for *Judith* and began the arduous task of editing the film with his cutter Jimmy Smith and adding titles written by Frank Woods, Griffith became determined to find a way out of Biograph. He was acutely aware of the success of former members of his acting company with other film companies, the Pickfords, Florence Lawrence, and George Nichols —character man turned director. As for himself, he still didn't have a new contract with Biograph. He decided to have one more meeting with the bosses.

Griffith was unaware that during the spring Henry Marvin, with Kennedy's support, had negotiated a deal with the theatrical producers Klaw and Erlanger to film their plays as five-reel motion pictures in partnership with a new K & E subsidiary called the Protective Amusement Company. The long films would be shown in K & E legitimate theatres during the summer.

The work on *Judith* was finished. Griffith, stiffening his resolve, marched into Kennedy's office to test his value to Biograph. Before he could manage to tell Kennedy that he was thinking of leaving Biograph if his terms were not met, Kennedy announced that Biograph would be making longer films under the new arrangements with Klaw and Erlanger. Griffith would not have any part in this, but was welcome to continue with his production of one-reel films. Terry Ramsaye reported Kennedy's remarks:

> "The time has come for the production of big fifty thousand dollar pictures. You are the man to make them. But Biograph is not ready to go into that line of production. If you stay with Biograph it will be to make the same kind of short pictures that you have in the past. You will not do that. You've got the hundred thousand dollar idea in the back of your head." [112]

Kennedy had taken the wind out of Griffith's sails, and as Griffith left the office he realized that there was no answer except to leave Biograph. He thought of two steps to take. The first was to secure the services of a lawyer. He had to make certain that any contract he might sign would fully protect his interests. He was also acutely aware that his personal agreement with Linda when they had parted left him without protection from her demands. The second thing would be to spread the word, as subtly as possible, that he was open to offers. That special word should particularly be carried to Adolph Zukor. One of the members of his company who could be trusted to spread the story of Griffith's dissatisfaction was Tony O'Sullivan, and there were others as well.

Griffith's plan was successful. Zukor heard and approached him with an offer of $50,000 a year. This marked a considerable increase for Griffith, but several factors now militated against his acceptance of it. The terms offered by Zukor did not extend much in the way of the independence that Griffith now felt he had to have. Griffith was also wary of the small tie that existed between J. J. Kennedy and Zukor's production company. He decided to turn the offer down. Zukor was unhappy with Griffith's rejection, but his partners were delighted. They were convinced that the offer of $50,000 a year was ludicrous. Ironically, Griffith did go to work for Zukor some twelve years later at over three times that offer, a salary of $156,000 a year.

The next offer came through an introduction by O'Sullivan to Harry E. Aitken, the president of a film-distributing company called Mutual. Aitken was the head of film exchanges in Milwaukee, St. Louis, Joplin, and other cities in the Middle West. Film exchanges originally were organized so that exhibitors could trade films with each other, the films having been purchased outright from their producers. When the Motion Picture Patents Company limited the opportunities for new producers of films, a number of businessmen, recognizing the potential money in the new business, moved into the exchange business. By 1913 the film exchanges were buying films directly and renting them to the exhibitors. Harry Aitken was the second largest buyer of films in the United States.

The film producers in the Motion Picture Patents Company (MPPC) were acutely aware of the profits enjoyed by the film exchange middlemen and planned to move aggressively into this field. Plans were announced for the formation of the General Film Company, which would take over the direct distribution of all films. When Aitken heard of this challenge, he hastily summoned a meeting in Indianapolis of the independent film exchange owners. Aitken exhorted his fellow exchange owners not to sell out to General Film for a fraction of what their businesses were worth. Aitken's efforts were rewarded with the signing of an agreement to unite in their own protection and so fight the attempted take-over.

Aitken's meeting was supposedly secret, but when he returned to his operating headquarters in St. Louis, he found that the Motion Picture Patents moguls had been informed and in retaliation had canceled Aitken's rights to purchase films. Aitken's three hundred customers would be forced to turn to the new General Film Company for their pictures. Aitken's companies were facing immediate ruin.

Harry Aitken was a resourceful man with extremely quick, if sometimes erratic, business reflexes. He took the next train for New York City with the bare beginnings of a plan in mind. If he could not buy films from those companies belonging to the MPPC, he would have to deal with the handful of independent producers who were battling for their own survival. The MPPC was locked in both legal and extra-legal battles with the independents involving mainly their patent claims to the significant mechanisms of the camera. It was the practice of the MPPC to physically seize any unauthorized cameras. The independents fought back with their own squads of strong-arm men, and kept their cameras concealed within blinds or behind makeshift screens in secret studios.

The independents made their sales through a single marketing company managed by Jules Brulatour. Brulatour in return supplied the independents with their raw stock, blank film, purchased from foreign manufacturers. The principal firms in the group serviced by Brulatour were IMP, the Carl Laemmle Company; Reliance films, headed by Baumann and Kessel, and their subsidiary, Mack Sennett's Keystone; Yankee; Republic; Centaur; Nestor; Rex; Thanhouser; Great Northern; Solax; and a number of importers of foreign films including Harry Raver, Pat Powers, and others. Aitken headed straight for Brulatour's office.

Arrangements were made easily for Aitken to buy films from the independents, but Brulatour exacted Aitken's agreement to buy out the independent film exchange in St. Louis and hire its operator, Bill Swanson, at three hundred dollars a week. With bankruptcy staring him in the face, Aitken was delighted to agree.

The independents were equally pleased with their new arrangement with Aitken. Aitken's organization and clients provided them with enough outlets to bolster their fortunes in the fight against the MPPC. They decided to mount a direct challenge. A firm of aggressive patent attorneys was hired. The challenge was successful, and, within a year, the independents had won their case. The monopoly on the means of film production was broken.

Aitken was exhilarated by his business recovery. Like so many of the men attracted to the business side of film-making, Aitken relished the wheeling and dealing of the infant industry. If Griffith felt that he was dealing with a mechanized form of theatre, Aitken knew he was working with a business not much different from selling shoes. Aitken recognized that the way to success was to build a structure that would combine all the potential profits into one, to control both production and distribution. In this thought he was merely echoing the MPPC's plans for the General Film Company. Still the MPPC pattern meant that Aitken could fill his own theatres with a product that he controlled, and, as he thought, still not cross the infant antitrust laws. To establish a beachhead in New York, Aitken bought the Harsten film exchange on 14th Street from Powers, Ditenfass, and Harsten. With the assistance of Thomas Cochrane, he persuaded Mary Pickford and Owen Moore to join in forming a production company to be called Majestic Films. Through Majestic, Aitken would pay Mary and Owen each $275 a week. Aitken then followed this up with the purchase of the film exchanges owned by Bauman and Kessel, and the Reliance studios at 515 E. 21st Street. He hired new executives to operate his companies, J. C. Graham, J. V. Ritchey, and Frank Myers. Graham and Myers later became executives at Paramount. Ritchey's job was to control production at the Reliance studio for release under either the Reliance or Majestic brand name.

It was not all unimpeded progress for Aitken and his plans. The moment he stepped out of his role as a distributor and into production, some of the other producers felt threatened and moved to retaliate. Wily Carl Laemmle at IMP believed that Aitken had stolen Mary Pickford and Owen Moore from him. Laemmle initiated an attempt to abrogate Aitken's agreement with Jules Brulatour to purchase independent films. Aitken countered by organizing his own Majestic and Reliance into a new sales organization, sweeping in American Flying A, Gaumont, Great Northern, Solax, and a few other small companies, and hiring Joseph Miles from Brulatour's staff as manager. The newest Aitken company was dubbed the Film Supply Company of America, Inc.

A so-called "peace" meeting was held in the bridal suite of the Waldorf Hotel in which Aitken brashly tried to persuade Laemmle himself to sign up with Aitken's new organization. Laemmle refused and walked out of the meeting. Aitken afterward claimed, and Laemmle denied, that Laemmle had offered to sell IMP to him. Aitken's trump card was a Wall Street investment banker, Crawford Livingstone, a fellow resident of the Waldorf. With Livingstone's financial knowledge and assistance, Aitken's film exchanges and some thirty-five others were welded into another new company, the Mutual Film Company.

In his organization of new companies amalgamating production, distribution, and exhibition, Aitken secured the backing of some relatively new faces. He was joined by J. R. Freuhler, a real estate investor from Milwaukee; H. H. Hutchinson from American Flying A, who was a brother-in-law of the Roebuck of Sears and Roebuck; the Shallenberger brothers, patent medicine promoters from Iowa; two bankers from Chicago, Paul Davis and John Burnham; the bookies Baumann and Kessel; and from Wall Street, in addition to Crawford Livingstone, Felix Kahn, and W. B. Joyce of the National Surety Company. Without realizing its portent, Aitken had let Wall Street into the infant industry and, in doing this, had altered the fabric of the business.

With his new backing, Aitken was able to float substantial loans from the established banks, the Corn Exchange Bank, the Central Union Trust Company, and Title Guarantee and Trust. He hired a prestigious law firm, Cravath and Henderson, to handle his legal affairs, and retained Walter Seligsberg as his personal attorney, making Seligsberg the first attorney to work exclusively for a film company.

When Carl Laemmle walked out of the Waldorf, he was determined to continue the fight against Aitken. He summoned a meeting of the remaining independents that had not signed up with Aitken. He persuaded all of these to join a new company to be called Universal Pictures. A determined attempt was made to woo Baumann and Kessel back into the Laemmle fold, not so much for the services of the two former bookies as for their remaining assets: the services of Mack Sennett and Keystone, and the successful director-producer Thomas Ince. Ince had established a studio in California outside Santa Monica, called, with the modesty that became characteristic of the motion picture business, Inceville.

Laemmle discovered that Baumann and Kessel had already made their deal with Aitken, and had even provided their California properties, including Inceville, with armed guards to prevent any seizures by Laemmle. The business meetings of Laemmle's Universal in New York became so hectic and disrupted that at one point Laemmle had his books and records thrown from the windows of the board room to waiting employees in a taxi to prevent their falling into the hands of the opposition. The records were spirited away in the taxi to a secret hiding place.

Baumann and Kessel received new financing through Aitken and his bankers, guaranteeing that films by Sennett and Ince would be distributed through Mutual.

On the production front Aitken was also moving ahead. He purchased the Clara Morris estate in Riverdale, in the northwest corner of New York City, suitable for outdoor locations. J. V. Ritchey was using the 21st Street studio to do lithography, so Aitken rented a loft building on 18th Street as a temporary studio for filming interiors. The purchase of the Reliance studio and interests brought with it the services of the actors and directors on its staff. These included many of the members of Griffith's old Biograph acting company: Stanner E. V. Taylor and his wife, Marion Leonard, James Kirkwood, Henry Walthall, Dorothy Davenport, and Arthur Johnson. The intermediary who had introduced Griffith to Aitken, Tony O'Sullivan, was employed there as a director.

It was in this context of empire-building that Griffith met Harry Aitken, and the latter recognized that he had the opportunity of securing the services of the best director in films. Aitken, in addition to his dominating concern with the merchandising of film, was perceptive enough to recognize that ultimately good pictures made money, and good pictures were produced and directed by talented directors. He saw that Griffith was really Biograph's only significant asset, not the pretentious new studio in the Bronx, or the equally pretentious arrangements to produce films from the Broadway shows of Klaw and Erlanger. His judgment was assisted, of course, by his knowledge of the money-making record of Griffith's Biograph films. As a result, Aitken was quite willing to give Griffith the independence in film-making, including budgeting, that J. J. Kennedy and Henry Marvin were unwilling to do.

On the other hand, David Griffith knew little about the financial maneuvering and corporate inventiveness that Aitken was indulging in, and he was not interested in finding out. Griffith was only interested in making pictures, and the increasingly complicated way in which they were sold was beyond his understanding. He could rattle off the jargon of the business with an actor's glibness, but the complexities of financing were really incomprehensible to him. Aitken was a source from which the cash would flow for making pictures, and that was all Griffith really wanted to know. Aitken agreed to allow Griffith the privilege of making two independent films a year in addition to the regularly scheduled program features to be made under the Reliance-Majestic banner for distribution by Mutual. Aitken meanwhile added another invented production company to his package, Continental Features Corporation, for the production of long films, now known as "feature films" to distinguish them from the one-reel "shorts."

Griffith's break with Biograph was announced in the *Dramatic Mirror* on September 29, 1913. The separation was to be effective October 1st. The advertisement was prepared for Griffith by an attourney, Albert H. T. Banzhaf, who was styled as Griffith's personal representative. For the first time Griffith was taking credit for his work at Biograph in a public way and announcing that he was "producer of all great Biograph successes, revolutionizing motion picture drama and founding the modern technique of the art." This statement was followed by a list of Griffith's alleged pioneering achievements, taking credit for "the large or close-up figures, distant views . . . the switchback, sustained suspense, the *fade-out,* and restraint in expression. . . ."

The advertisement then listed one hundred and fifty-one films directed by Griffith, beginning with *The Adventures of Dollie* (misspelled as "Dolly") and ending with the unreleased *Judith of Bethulia.* The listing covered only slightly more than one-third of the films Griffith had actually directed, but it included those that he believed were the most important and had been the most successful at the box office.

Although Griffith was well aware of the work he had done, seeing the list in print had an exhilarating effect on him. He was well aware that he had overstated his accomplishments and contributions, but in the film world hyperbole had become a staple. One advertisement made Griffith feel that he was an important man, a towering figure in this new industry. Like Napoleon, he had stage-managed his own coronation, and it would be difficult, if not impossible, for him to recognize the real base for his success. The modest personal manner of his early days always remained, but the insecure actor looking for a weekend performance with any company that would hire him, the timid seller of story ideas, the tentative director trying to remember how McKee Rankin might have directed something were gone forever. David Wark Griffith knew he was the best in the business, a business that was bigger than the legitimate theatre—and the vanishing shade of "Lawrence" Griffith knew it too.

Griffith now set out to bring as many of "his company" under his new banner as he could. His actors had never been regarded by himself as employees of Biograph. They were members of his company. Making the transition with Griffith were Bobby Harron, Lillian and Dorothy Gish, Blanche Sweet, Edward Dillon, Henry Walthall, Donald Crisp, Mae Marsh, Spottiswoode Aitken, Jack Pickford, and George Siegman. Harron's departure from Biograph ended an association longer than Griffith's, for he had begun as a messenger boy and had been made an actor by Griffith. Lionel Barrymore passed up the chance to follow and decided to return to the theatre. Dell Henderson, now a director, remained at Biograph, and Griffith's cameraman Billy Bitzer also decided to stay. Bitzer told Griffith quite freely that he was foolish to leave the security of Biograph.

Talented as a photographer, Bitzer nevertheless was unimaginative about the future. There was no security at Biograph. Griffith was succeeded by second- and third-rate directors and, despite the momentary success achieved by the release of Griffith's last films, *The Battle at Elderbush Gulch* and *Judith of Bethulia,* in 1914, Biograph was beginning a decline. Both of these films did less well in 1914 than they might have if released in 1913, because they had lost much of their uniqueness in the swift changes occurring during that single year. Despite Marvin's and Kennedy's hopes, the Klaw and Erlanger deal proved a failure. Aging Broadway stars could not supplant the new fresh faces of films. Despite much vigorous thrashing about, including the re-issue of *Judith* in 1917 with the added two reels and new title, Biograph was really in its death throes. With Griffith's persuasion Bitzer was finally induced to leave Biograph and join his old director.

9

Creation of a Monument:
The Birth of a Nation

Most people considered a Motion Picture drama a ten-cent proposition. They measured everything by the standard of price. It was not surprising they overlooked the fundamentals of the case and were unprepared to pass judgement upon the undertaking. But, in all truth, there was neither daring nor venturesomeness in this move. You see, we knew what we had. This was an advantage the other fellows had failed to take into consideration.[113]

The process of settling into a new organization took Griffith and his company a few months. Despite Aitken's purchase of the Clara Morris estate and rental of the loft building on 18th Street, Griffith informed his new boss that he intended to take the company to California during the winter season as he had at Biograph. Aitken controlled only a tiny studio, the Heights Studio, and though Inceville was almost in the Aitken fold, there was no room there for another company. With Griffith's prodding, Aitken rented the former Kinemacolor studio at 4500 Sunset Boulevard in Hollywood. He announced through the press the acquisition of this property in early December 1913.

At the same time Griffith was preparing to shoot his first film under the new management, *The Escape,* with Blanche Sweet in the leading role. Blanche suddenly became ill, and the project was shelved. Griffith turned to *The Battle of the Sexes.* Quite openly Griffith told his cast that the film was a potboiler designed to bring in some quick money. The cast was a small one: Lillian Gish, Owen Moore, Mary Alden, Fay Tincher, Donald Crisp, and Bobby Harron. The plot, based on *The Single Standard* by Daniel Carson Goodman, was a stock melodramatic view of infidelity and its effects on wife, daughter, the "other woman," and the wandering husband himself. According to the Museum of Modern Art film

141

department, only a brief excerpt remains of this film. The accuracy of Griffith's description of the film cannot therefore be assessed. Billy Bitzer, under a three-year personal contract to Griffith, was behind the camera.

Harry Aitken was willing to let Griffith make each film four to five reels in length, but he tried to insist that the budget be held to $5,000 for each film. He did promise that a Broadway legitimate theatre would be rented for the opening of each film. Aitken kept his word. *The Battle of the Sexes* opened on April 12, 1914, at Weber's Theatre. Griffith's second film, *The Escape,* which had been picked up after Blanche Sweet's recovery, opened at the Cort Theatre on June 1, 1914, and the next two films began their runs at the Strand.

Aitken's business deals were outrunning his ability to maintain a cash flow from his backers. A "wait and see" attitude developed, forcing Aitken to pressure Griffith for more films. Griffith's former assistant director, Christy Cabanne, was given his chance to direct with *Until Death Do Us Part.* Griffith agreed to supervise the productions directed by others. Actually Griffith had little time to give attention to any other pictures than his own, but the Griffith cachet was a solid promotional plus for the company. The title of Cabanne's film was changed to *The Great Leap.* Griffith's part-time supervision extended to eight more films by other directors: *The Gangsters of New York, Dope, Ruy Blas, Frou Frou, Sapho* (sic), *Moths, The Mountain Rat,* and *The Floor Above.*

Griffith's second film for Aitken, *The Escape,* was announced in December 1913 as a "four-part" picture introducing Blanche Sweet in her first film for Mutual. Although the name of the production company for the Griffith films was the amalgam Reliance-Majestic, Aitken publicized the films as Mutual releases. He was determined to see that the product was always identified with the distributor. Production companies might come and go, but distribution would always remain.

The pace set by Griffith was almost as fast as that of his earliest days, and in some ways even faster. *The Battle of the Sexes* was shot in four days in such a driving fashion that the moment Lillian Gish's eyes seemed too bloodshot to be photographed, she was sent home for a few hours' sleep and then brought back to continue.

With the special promotion and advertising that Griffith demanded for his films, their release was delayed, and no income could be realized. When Griffith asked for the funds to take the company to California, Aitken found that he would have to mortgage the negative of his completed films to raise the necessary cash. Griffith refused to permit Aitken to raise money on any of his films in this way, so Cabanne's *The Great Leap* was nominated. While waiting for Aitken to raise the travel money, Griffith completed *The Escape* in New York during January 1914. He had brought Frank Woods over from Biograph and set him to work looking for properties suitable for filming. Among the possibilities brought up for discussion with Griffith by Woods and his assistant Russell E. Smith was a play by a Southern clergyman, Thomas Dixon, called *The Clansman*. This patchwork melodrama had had some small success in the theatre after Dixon had dramatized it from his own novel, but its theatrical success was slight enough to keep its price in a class where a motion picture company could consider it. The story of a Confederate soldier's return from the war appealed to Griffith. It had some slight similarities in detail to Griffith's own father's experiences, but, more important, it had an emotional appeal for Griffith's juvenile memories of Colonel Jake's war stories. Griffith reminded Woods that they had done well at Biograph with a few Civil War films. Griffith asked Aitken to look into the matter of purchasing the rights to the play from Dixon.

The Reverend Thomas Dixon was a man who prided himself on his fiscal shrewdness and promptly asked ten thousand dollars for the rights to his play. If his view of the future had been as confident as his view of himself, he would have asked for ten times that sum and more. Aitken, of course, did not have ten thousand dollars. Lack of cash hadn't stopped Aitken before, and it didn't this time. He persuaded Dixon to accept his personal check for $2,500 and a promise of a share in the profits from the film. Dixon, who knew the value of cash but not promises, accepted the check and reserved the right to take, or reject, the profit-sharing at a later date. In the meantime he would consider that Aitken owed him $7,500 for the balance of the rights.

Griffith was elated when Aitken reported his success with Dixon. The subject of the film was beginning to obsess Griffith, and he was eager to begin rehearsals, using the play's text as a beginning, while the company was still in New York. Actually, Griffith was only able to find time from *The Escape* for some brief readings.

With *The Escape* finished, and the mortgage money in from *The Great Leap,* Griffith entrained with the company for California and the Kinemacolor studio at 4500 Sunset Boulevard. Ironically, his entrance into that studio followed in the footsteps of his estranged wife, Linda Arvidson Griffith, who had been employed there briefly by Kinemacolor after their parting.

Almost without unpacking, Griffith went to work on *Home Sweet Home,* a quartet of stories tied together by the theme of John Howard Payne's lyric. The first story was loosely based on Payne's life. While it has been noted that this four-part construction resembled that of the later *Intolerance,* there is only a superficial resemblance. The individual stories were not intercut or interrelated beyond the general unification of the theme. To make the film, Griffith worked essentially in the same style as he had at Biograph with one-reel pictures. To the long-time members of his company were added Josephine Crowell, Miriam Cooper, Fred Burns, and Courtenay Foote. The film was notable for its increasingly complex use of technical devices, refinement of parallel editing, and at least once for a "ride to the rescue," a Griffith trademark, that failed. Griffith chose to close the tragedy of Payne's sweetheart's death with an allegorical ending in which Payne tries to reach his love, transformed into an angel, from a pit presided over by Lust and Greed.

Despite the visual symbolism used as an ending, it was the sentiments of "Be it ever so humble, there's no place like home" that appealed to Griffith in two ways: to his sentimental romantic temperament which he could never shed and to his strong sense of which dramatic materials would have broad popular appeal. Griffith felt that he had discovered during his Biograph period an ability within himself, a sureness, to select materials for and to understand popular taste. The public, in increasing numbers, had liked the Griffith films, not alone for their technical effectiveness but also for their stories. Late in his career, Griffith was attacked by critics on the grounds that he did not understand what the public wanted. It was charged that this was his major weakness. In 1914 it was his greatest strength.

Now that Griffith was being publicized by Aitken, the management of Biograph, Marvin and Kennedy, began releasing the last films Griffith made for them. *The Massacre* was released at the end of February, and a day or two later *Judith of Bethulia* began an engagement at the Tivoli in San Francisco. Griffith paid little attention to these films that now seemed part of a dead past. He was busy devising the allegorical ending for *Home Sweet Home* in which Henry B. Walthall, in the role of John Howard Payne, would be flown to heaven on the edge of the gown of his sweetheart, Lillian Gish, now transformed into an angel. Both Lillian and Henry were wired to fly, not a new experience for Lillian— she had been flown on stage in *A Good Little Devil,* the Belasco play starring Mary Pickford. She does remember hanging in the harness for what seemed an intolerable length of time while Griffith and Bitzer decided how the shot should be made. They had discovered that raising Walthall straight up gave a distorted perspective, and made his feet the dominant factor in the frame. At last it was decided that the actors would have to be flown backward to heaven. For Walthall it was an uncomfortable climax to a film in which he had already been well smoked in an artificial hell of smoke pots in Chatsworth Park.

One of the distractions that Aitken introduced into Griffith's schedule was the production of a short newsreel using a fashionably dressed model, Norma Phillips, to be known as "The Mutual Girl," introducing events and personalities of the day. Griffith agreed to direct the first of these in order to set the pattern, but refused to let Aitken use his name in connection with them.

Aitken had remained behind in New York, operating out of a ten-room apartment on 57th Street. Aitken used the apartment for invitational screenings of the films as they were forwarded from California in his constant search for investors. On his guest list of society and financial figures were artist Montgomery Flagg, Irvin Cobb, Charles Dana Gibson, George Randolph Chester, Mrs. Randolph Hearst, and Messmore Kendall. Aitken flattered many of his guests by using them as subjects for the Mutual Girl newsreel.

At the end of March Biograph released *The Battle at Elderbush Gulch* without Griffith being particularly aware of it. He had plunged into the filming of *The Avenging Conscience,* based on Edgar Allan Poe's *The Telltale Heart,* and *Annabel Lee* with Walthall, Sweet, Spottiswoode Aitken, George Siegman, Ralph Lewis, and Mae Marsh.

The increasing production tempo combined with the expense of constructing new laboratory buildings under Bitzer's supervision was putting a severe strain on Mutual's finances. Despite the lavish screening parties, Aitken was having difficulty feeding his corporate monster. In addition, the diversity of interests that Aitken had pasted together for his corporate body started to come apart almost as soon as organized. Aitken's Wall Street financiers wished to see their money handled in a responsible corporate manner. The film entrepreneurs managing the individual companies under the Mutual banner were selfishly interested in seeing their own films promoted, and their own profits boosted. Aitken managed to hold these elements together for a time by moving faster than anyone else. The two men most concerned with Aitken's methods of operation, and with his promotion of Reliance-Majestic at the seeming expense of the other production companies, were John R. Freuler and Samuel S. Hutchinson of the American Film Company. Aitken's dazzling footwork managed to keep them temporarily at bay, but they were waiting for the first stumble.

Despite his other work, Griffith was well along with his planning for *The Clansman* by spring. Lillian Gish remembers Griffith taking her aside after the other members of the company had left the set of *Home Sweet Home* to tell her about the purchase of the Dixon novel and play. He told her that he wanted to tell the "true story" of the losing side in the War Between the States. Griffith also outlined his plans to other members of the company—Mae Marsh, Miriam Cooper, Elmer Clifton, Henry Walthall, Spottiswoode Aitken, Bobby Harron, George Siegmann, Walter Long—and swore them all to secrecy. Griffith knew that telling this many people was no way to keep a secret, but he had long found it effective to slip out news of a forthcoming project as a way to arouse his actors' enthusiasm. The sole purpose of his secrecy was to keep the word from reaching another film company. It was still a custom to rush a half-baked version of someone else's story onto film ahead of the originator whenever possible. In this case secrecy about the fundamental idea was useless because news of the project had already appeared in the trade press. There was nothing particularly special about Griffith making a Civil War film.

Griffith's relationships with his actors were cemented through his sharing of confidences. He would take each aside and seemingly make that person the recipient of some private confidence binding the actor to him in a much stronger fashion than even money and legal contracts. Griffith's technique didn't work with everyone. Some, like the Pickfords, were well aware of the dollar's value and went their own way in its pursuit. It is also apparent from examining the changing roster of Griffith's players that he could quite easily drop those whose talent failed to fit in with his plans.

Griffith secured a commitment from Aitken for a $40,000 budget with which to produce *The Clansman*. This was four times the budget that Griffith had been given to produce the five-reel films then being completed. It seemed reasonable to both Aitken and Griffith that a ten-reel picture could be made with extreme ease for $40,000. Aitken's partners, especially John Freuler, were livid when they heard about this huge budget and promptly protested. Aitken secured the backing of his other financial directors, who were willing to go along more because they didn't like Freuler than because they thought it a wise expenditure.

Griffith had had almost nothing to do with the process of raising money for *The Clansman;* nevertheless he liked to give his actors the impression that he had raised the money. Since actors are notoriously unconcerned with the details of any theatrical management, they were quite willing to believe that their director, their leader, was responsible for all matters involved with the film.

While he finished the last moments of *The Avenging Conscience* in May, Griffith began rehearsals for *The Clansman*. Props and costumes were arriving at the studio in quantities. Griffith began carrying pamphlets, notes, and booklets, all research materials, in his pockets, studying them at every opportunity. In some instances his casting for the film surprised the company. He took Lillian Gish aside and told her that he wanted her to try Elsie Stoneman, the role of the Northern Senator's daughter. Backstage gossip had speculated that this role would go to Blanche Sweet. Sets were being constructed both at the Reliance-Majestic studio and at the "ranch," an outdoor area that eventually became the property of Universal.

Although Griffith was nominally living at the Alexandria Hotel, his real home became the studio. He would keep his cutters,

Jimmy and Rose Smith, working far into the night, running the film shot during the day. Since Griffith worked without a shooting script, he needed these special night sessions to refresh his sense of continuity. *The Avenging Conscience* was finished, replete with special effects, double exposures, special framing devices, extreme close-ups for symbolic purposes, all done almost as a try-out for later use. The film employed a long dream-nightmare sequence edited so that the audience would be unaware that it was not reality until the end of the picture. Griffith's exploration of the mind of his protagonist was remarkable not only for its achievements, long preceding similar experiments to come in the twenties, but also in that it was done so swiftly when Griffith's mind was occupied with other things.

The commitments Griffith was making for sets, costumes, livestock, and extras for *The Clansman* had used up the $40,000 budget quickly. Griffith called Aitken for more funds. Aitken was able to raise another $20,000, but this also was spent rapidly. Aitken suddenly found that all his charm and business sagacity were suddenly useless. He couldn't raise any more money. The film had only reached the half-way point. Aitken came to California to meet with Griffith. They held their worried conference in a short-order restaurant near the studio, covering napkins with endless columns of figures as Aitken made Griffith aware for the first time that the Reliance-Majestic Company was near bankruptcy. The lunchroom proprietor, a Mr. Wynpenny, overheard their discussions and interrupted to offer $3,000 from his savings as an investment. Aitken had thought only of raising money in large sums; now he and Griffith siezed on Mr. Wynpenny's offer as an example of how money might be raised in small amounts. They took Wynpenny's $3,000, raised another $15,000 from a Ford dealer in Pasadena, a Los Angeles businessman, and an adventurous widow, a Mrs. Granger. Other small amounts were contributed by studio employees who were willing to put their faith in Griffith. J. D. Barry, Griffith's acting secretary, had found the Pasadena car dealer, and Griffith had insisted that Barry keep a seven hundred dollar commission. Barry invested his commission in the film, a move that eventually brought him over $14,000 in profits. Eventually the total budget and fund-raising reached the then astronomical level of $110,000.

Aitken had managed to mollify the board of Mutual only by assuming complete responsibility for *The Clansman* and taking over the Mutual investment as his own. Freuler put on a seeming display of magnanimity, forgiving Aitken for his sin of over-indulgence in this folly. The other members of the board joined in the surety that Aitken had learned his lesson. Charles Hite, the head of Thanhouser Pictures, was the chief peacemaker between Freuler and Aitken. Hite seemed almost like Aitken's right arm. And then, suddenly, he was gone, killed in an automobile accident when his car smashed through the side rail of the Harlem River Bridge and crashed some fifty feet below. Killed with him was his wife, a former Biograph actress, Florence LaBadie. Hite's place on the Mutual board was taken by his partner, Dr. Wilbert Shallenberger. Without Hite's calm voice and advice, Aitken and Freuler were soon back at each other's throats.

Filming of *The Clansman* was underway. The interiors were shot at the studio on Sunset, the fir tree scenes at Big Bear Mountain, and the cotton fields in Calexico. The California heat became almost unbearable. Griffith made two personal concessions to the heat and the strong sunlight. He took to wearing a large floppy straw hat with small ventilation holes cut around the headband. A current superstition held that shaving the head was an excellent hair restorative. Griffith was becoming increasingly bald, so both for the superstition and the heat, he had had his head shaved. The result of the straw hat, the hot sun, and the little ventilation holes was a series of round sunburned spots on Griffith's pink scalp.

Young Karl Brown, beginning to learn his craft as a cameraman by assisting Billy Bitzer, remembered Griffith suddenly breaking into song while a scene was being shot, a wordless "Ya-ha! Ya-ho!" interspersed with bits of poetry, never identified for anyone. One phrase remained with Brown for life, "See this garment that I wear? It was knitted by the fingers of the dead! The long and yellow fingers of the dead!"

The battle between the Edison licensees and the independents still had not been resolved. Griffith now was working on the side of the independents. This meant that their camera had to be preserved from sudden seizure.

Although the numbers of actors and extras employed during the shooting of *The Clansman* were never as large as publicized, there were three hundred to five hundred extras, all of whom had to be highly organized. Griffith developed a system that came to be known as the nucleus system. Small groups of actors were placed under the leadership of individuals who would transmit action instructions from Griffith on a tower overlooking the location. Elmer Clifton, Henry Walthall, George Siegmann, Erich von Stroheim, and Andre Beranger each headed a unit. Each group was rehearsed separately and prepared to execute their movement on a signal from the tower. One mass rehearsal was held without gunfire. Since the first time that gunfire was to be used was also a take, everyone crossed their fingers in hopes that it would go all right.

The actions went as rehearsed, but the smoke bombs produced such a volume of smoke that details of the scene were obscured. The actors coughed and choked. Griffith sent word to the crew to cut down the size of the charges so that the smoke would be less. It still remained a difficult task for Bitzer to photograph through the haze.

Griffith had chosen to begin filming the picture with the Civil War battle scenes, for he rightly figured that this would be the most difficult, as well as costly, part of the picture, and the most impressive for any potential backers that might be brought to visit the locations. With his special sense of the symbolic, he had begun shooting on the Fourth of July, 1914. The total period of shooting extended to the end of October, stretched out with the pauses for additional fund-raising.

Since his days at the New York Public Library doing research for his unproduced play, *War,* Griffith had been concerned, at times almost obsessed, with research. He was fascinated with material, however, that bore out his own pre-conceived ideas. The notion of comparing sources and weighing their factual authenticity was unimportant to him. Nevertheless the practice of research for a film could be said to have originated with Griffith, and later he did establish a department specifically charged with this task. It has been said that Griffith always listened intently to "expert" advice from surviving veterans of the war, military advisers, and others, but from all this advice he winnowed only that material which seemed relevant to his own vision, a vision more Colonel Jake than history. The resultant motion picture is as much a fantasy as any turned out by Hollywood, and not a documentary—which in no way denigrates the film. It is its own reality, even though it turned out to be unpalatable for many who viewed it.

In later years Griffith was frequently castigated for using white actors in blackface, notably George Siegmann in the role of Silas Lynch, the mulatto politician, and Walter Long as the renegade Negro Gus. Lillian Gish has rightly pointed out that there were few Negro actors in California at that time. Griffith did use a number of blacks as extras, and one black actress, Madame Sul Te-Wan, remained a close friend of Griffith's from the time of her employment on this film until Griffith's death.

More damaging to blacks than Griffith's use of white actors in blackface was an attitude the film conveyed that could still be attacked more than fifty years later by Roy Wilkins, head of the National Association for the Advancement of Colored People:

> Since the film appeared fifty years ago, Negroes have made many a breakthrough. But all the Duke Ellingtons, Marian Andersons, Ira Aldridges, Jackie Robinsons, Bert Williamses, Fritz Pollards, the Olympic heroes and the heroes of two world wars, the scientists, scholars, technicians, political figures, poets, playwrights, entertainers, and diplomats have not succeeded in erasing the vicious image etched by the Griffith racial epic.[114]

The furthest thing from Griffith's mind that summer of 1914 was the making of a "racial epic." He would have been outraged if anyone had challenged him on his own bias. To Griffith this story was "the truth." While Griffith was a conscious apologist for the Southern cause in the hazy "roses and drums" tradition, his racial bias was almost totally unconscious. Lillian Gish had a surprisingly prescient feeling that the racial incidents in the film might cause difficulties after the picture was released. She asked Griffith whether the film might not be stopped because of them. Griffith replied, "I hope to God they do stop it! Then you won't be able to keep audiences away with clubs!" This bit of theatrical cynicism was probably uttered for its effect on Lillian and the others present and did not represent Griffith's real feelings.[115]

When the storm of criticism and protest broke over the film after its release, the extent of the research Griffith did for the film became an additional factor in his bitterness against his critics. He had re-created, in seemingly faithful detail, the Ford's Theatre setting, and even the precise place in that evening's play, *Our American Cousin,* for the moment of Lincoln's assassination. Other sets were done with the same degree of fidelity. The scene, admittedly biased and inflammatory, of the Negroes in a Southern legislature was based on accounts and evidence that Griffith considered factual. The battlefield representing Petersburg below Richmond, scene of the final struggle in the war, was re-created with the help of professional military assistance. Griffith was always unable to understand that his assembled "facts" were selected to serve his own bias.

None of these considerations really entered Griffith's mind during that hot summer of 1914. The sheer physical task of filming the picture was enough to occupy his time completely. Each day the film was returned to a special laboratory constructed at the studio. The negative was processed with great care by Abe Scholtz. Karl Brown characterized Scholtz as a photochemistry wizard who could produce "finer negative quality than anyone through the simple method of fine skill and infinite patience." [116]

The developed negative was then turned over to Griffith's cutter, Jimmy Smith. Today's extreme care in handling original camera negative with white cotton gloves in a dustless environment was then unknown. There was only one negative, no duplicate. Sections of this irreplaceable material were frequently carried out to location and run through gloveless hands to check on details from past shooting. This action, enough to give a present-day filmmaker the shivers, seemed to be necessary to Griffith and Bitzer because the positive prints were processed and printed in Chicago, and they would be delayed too much if they had to wait for them. Karl Brown, Bitzer's assistant, noted:

> Seems strange, these days, to think of a negative like that being stacked away in loose rolls, in cans, to be gone through by anybody who wanted to find out something. No gloves, no anything. . . . Hell, it was only a negative.[117]

The possibility that the picture would have to be halted for lack of funds was constantly in the minds of everyone as the shooting was taking place. Lillian Gish remembered that Johannes Charlemagne Epping, sometimes J. C., or more frequently "Little," appeared trembling before the company to announce that there was no money to meet the payroll. He assured the company that money was being raised, the picture would continue shooting, and all would be paid. Griffith was nowhere in sight, and such was the faith in him of most of the company it was automatically assumed that he was off fund-raising. The company went along for several weeks without a payday.

Occasionally fund-raising efforts were visible to the company. Griffith broke his shooting schedule for a day to stage a special scene for the benefit of William Clune, owner of Clune's Auditorium in Los Angeles. Clune represented both a potential backer and a potential exhibitor for the finished film. The scene was the one in which the Confederate volunteers march off to war, flags flying, families saying farewell, and a tiny band playing *Dixie*. Clune was least impressed with the band, but Griffith assured him that the magnificent orchestra at Clune's Auditorium would accompany the film to better effect. Then some of the company overheard Griffith tell Clune that all they needed was fifteen thousand dollars more to finish the film. Griffith and Clune walked away to confer in the office. When they re-appeared, both were smiling. The company assumed that all was well. Clune departed, and Griffith ordered the company back to work.

Griffith was driving the company in his quiet gentlemanly manner, and he was driving himself even harder. His attention to physical fitness was paying off, making it possible for him to work long hours, subsist on little food and sleep, and share his enthusiasm and energy with the company. According to Karl Brown:

> There was never any sense of futility or discouragement. Every scene was *the* big scene, the golden opportunity that would make everything right forevermore.
> And it wasn't an act. Griffith actually did believe intensely, with radiant fervor, in what he was doing, and could sweep everyone on the set into his own mood of extreme worth-while-ness [sic].
> He'd get tired, sure; and sometimes damnably weary of the whole thing—but it was he, Griffith, who was tired, and it was never anything wrong with the picture or the picture idea.[118]

Griffith was fortunate in having not only talented actors and actresses whose efforts are visible in the film but also in the loyal, equally talented members of the company who did not appear on camera. First among these was Billy Bitzer. Bitzer filmed the entire picture, although he had assistants with some of the auxiliary cameras, the decoys. Karl Brown gave a cameraman's assessment:

> Bitzer deserves a great deal of very real credit for Griffith's success. Not that Griffith would not have succeeded with another cameraman—but in Bitzer he had the best in the world.
> Bitzer had one thing which matched Griffith's art—a sort of instinctive know-how that defied analysis. He was absolutely foolproof in the matter of exposure for effect, as opposed to exposure for photographic correctness.
> He also knew, to perfection, how to work hand in hand with Scholtz and to get the most out of that cooperation.
> One thing that militates against any correct appraisal of Bitzer's real place in the Griffith career is—and always was—his refusal to take anything very seriously. He loved to kid about himself, the work, and everything around him, making a joke of the entire business, and in the meantime taking it very seriously indeed.[119]

Second among the assistants was tobacco-chewing Frank "Huck" Wortman, a short powerful boss carpenter. Like Bitzer, he had one ability above all else that made him invaluable to Griffith. Wortman was able to improvise, to take the sketchiest idea and turn it into a setting, all without head-shaking or displays of temperament. Wortman was unflappable. He was more interested in solving the construction problems posed by Griffith than in asking for reasons.

Following Wortman and his crew was another craftsman, "Cash" Shockey, a house painter converted by Griffith into a scene painter and placed in charge of a crew. In fairness to Shockey, it should be noted that he had some skill as an artist.

None of the men around Griffith had ego problems. They followed Griffith's lead willingly, contributing their ideas while content with anonymity. There were no individualists second-guessing the director. Around these men Griffith assembled a technical crew, not only for *The Clansman* but also for his future pictures.

Despite all of this expert help and assistance, the ultimate decisions, large or small, were made by Griffith. Austin Lescarboura reported a story from the filming in an article written for the *Scientific American* in 1917:

> Accuracy is an essential in the high grade production, and in taking his first classic motion picture Griffith paid particular attention to the small details. Rumor has it that during a big battle scene a dispute arose among the actors as to the color and kind of horse ridden by the famous commander-in-chief of the Confederate forces, Robert E. Lee, when he was campaigning at the head of the Army of Northern Virginia. Griffith was away at the moment.
>
> "Better stop 'taking,'" suggested one of the actors to the cameraman, "till we telephone in and have the facts about General Lee's horse looked up and verified."
>
> A high-powered touring car had glided up behind the group. In it sat Griffith himself.
>
> "What's the fuss about?" he inquired. When told, he smiled tolerantly. "Why, Lee's dappled gray charger 'Traveler,'" he remarked, "is one of the three most famous horses in history. Bucephalus' and Napoleon's nag were the other two, and I've got a horse as near like 'Traveler' as possible waiting in that stable yonder. Go on with your 'take.'" [120]

The actual production and shooting of the film, despite the momentary pauses for fund-raising, lasted from nine to twelve weeks. The smaller figure is usually given, but the memory of some participants, Elmer Clifton for one, remembered that it took a few weeks longer. An additional three months were spent by Griffith in cutting, editing, and developing a score for the film. Griffith worked closely with Joseph Carl Breil in developing a score that would enhance the film, a score suitable for the theatre orchestra at Clune's Auditorium. Breil had not been present during the filming and suggested to Griffith that he might have been better able to do his job if he had been. Griffith agreed and allowed him to have access to the sets on future films.

Griffith was proud of the results now beginning to take form and was quite willing to show parts of the film to visitors. Among these visitors was the distinguished stage actor George Arliss. The trade press reported that Mr. Arliss reacted by saying that he would never think of the movies as being crude again.

Work was finally finished at the end of January. Arrangements were made for the film's premiere at Clune's Auditorium for the

end of the first week in February. Clune's was, of course, the only
choice for the premiere, since William Clune had become an investor in the film.

Harry Aitken had been trying to extricate himself from his difficulties with the board of Mutual. As part of the arrangement in
which he took full responsibility for his "mistake in judgment" in
permitting *The Clansman* to become such a costly production, he
formed a new company to take over the film. On the same day,
February 8, 1915, that *The Clansman* opened in Los Angeles, the
Epoch Producing Corporation was incorporated at Eddyville, Ul-
ster County, New York, with William P. Scully as president, Fred
F. Weiss, vice-president, and Albert H. T. Banzhaf, Griffith's attorney, secretary-treasurer. Control of *The Clansman* was placed in
the hands of this new corporation.

The run of *The Clansman* that began on February 8 at Clune's
lasted for seven months, an unparalleled run for a film or, for that
matter, even for a legitimate play. Although the skeptics initially
praised the film, they were convinced that it would never make
money. William De Mille wrote: *"The Clansman* certainly establishes Griffith as a leader and it does seem too bad that such a
magnificent effort is doomed to financial failure." [121]

It was announced on February 13 that the Liberty Theatre in
New York City had been leased from Klaw and Erlanger for the
East Coast premiere. Griffith brought a print to New York for a
special showing at the Rose Gardens on 53rd Street on the evening
of February 20th. It was later recorded by Terry Ramsaye, and repeated by others, that it was at this preview that Thomas Dixon,
author of the play and books on which Griffith based the film, suggested enthusiastically that the film be re-titled *The Birth of a Nation*. Since this title had already appeared in the trade press, the
specifics of this story are doubtful. Whether the title was really suggested at some point by Dixon is possible. Griffith never denied
the story.

The film was scheduled to open at the Liberty on March 3. On
March 2 the first corporate meeting of the Epoch Producing Corporation was held. The original officers, nominated for incorpora-
tion purposes, stepped aside and formal elections were held. Harry
Aitken was elected president, Griffith became vice-president, and

Harry's brother, Roy Aitken, was elected secretary. Albert Banzhaf remained as the treasurer. Corporate control was thus equally divided between the Aitken and the Griffith interests. Actual control, however, remained in the hands of Harry Aitken.

The following night the film opened. *The New York Times,* in briefly reviewing the film, gave some indication of the storm to come.

> "The Birth of a Nation," an elaborate new motion picture taken on an ambitious scale, was presented for the first time last evening at the Liberty Theatre. With the addition of much preliminary historical matter, it is a film version of some of the melodramatic and inflammatory material contained in "The Clansman," by Thomas Dixon.
>
> A great deal might be said concerning the spirit revealed in Mr. Dixon's review of the unhappy chapter of Reconstruction and concerning the sorry service rendered by its plucking at old wounds. But of the film as a film, it may be reported simply that it is an impressive new illustration of the scope of the motion picture camera.[122]

Griffith was not mentioned until the fourth paragraph, where it was also mentioned by the *Times* reviewer that the film took a full evening to unfold and marked the advent of the two dollar movie. The reviewer also noted in his final paragraph:

> It was at this same theatre that the stage version of *The Clansman* had a brief run a little more than nine years ago, as Mr. Dixon himself remarked in his curtain speech last evening in the interval between the two acts. Mr. Dixon also observed that he would have allowed none but the son of a Confederate soldier to direct the film version of *The Clansman.*[123]

No note was taken of Griffith's own brief remarks at the premiere. Subsequently the film was opened in Boston on April 9, and in Chicago on June 4. Griffith attended both of these openings, taking at that time, as Bitzer later commented, his first "vacation" since his days before Biograph. Griffith would not have called his time "at liberty" before Biograph as a "vacation." The trips to Boston and Chicago were, of course, promotional. Griffith would appear on opening night to make a carefully calculated modest speech, and then, retiring to the projection booth, he would con-

tinue to study the film and undertake further editing. Griffith
would cut the film in the projection booth in response to audience
reaction, thus beginning a process that really prevented anyone
from ever again seeing the film that was first projected at Clune's.
In New York City, he was pressured, perhaps even forced, to eliminate some shots that aroused the ire of New York's Mayor John
Purroy Mitchel, and his license commissioner. Rumor has always
implied that these eliminated scenes were by far the most racist incidents in the film. There is no way to be certain of this today.

It is impossible to look at *The Birth of a Nation* through contemporary eyes and see what ingredients caused the tremendous
impact on the audience of 1915. The film made use of all of those
remarkable devices of filmic story telling that Griffith had developed at Biograph, now magnified in length and intensity. We can
guess that the audience was moved by the realism of the battle
scenes, the melodramatic viciousness of the carpetbaggers' menacing
the "Little Colonel" 's family, and certainly by the climactic excitement and sweep of the hooded Clansmen riding to the rescue.
These same ingredients served to stir the opposition to the film. It
is a film of emotional excess with the immediacy of the close-up.
The same situation would have far less impact on a remote theatre
stage. Griffith played on the fears of his white audience, appealed
to their prejudices, and perpetuated the Southern myth of Reconstruction that had grown since the 1890s. Above all Griffith
showed that an audience would accept fiction as a reality. Griffith
also demonstrated that an audience became most involved with the
"truth" of a motion picture when they were involved in the lives of
"real" people. The secret of *The Birth of a Nation,* perhaps, is that
the audience cared about the Camerons.

The box office success of *The Birth of a Nation* was sensational.
Aitken decided to follow a policy, later known as "road showing,"
which enabled Epoch allegedly to skim off the cream of the business through the control of all showings in the major cities. Following this, Aitken would sell the rights to exhibition in the small
towns and cities on what was known as a "states rights" basis. The
buyers of these rights would have the exclusive control of a particular state or group of states for the exhibition of the film. This decision ultimately represented one of Aitken's few errors in business

judgment. He thought that the returns from these subsequent showings would be small and insignificant. Epoch was to receive a percentage of the receipts from the states rights showings, but Aitken failed to set up an accounting system that would guarantee accurate returns. One of the results of this mistake was exemplified by the hustling young Massachusetts nickelodeon proprietor Louis B. Mayer, who purchased the New England rights, and, by filing understated reports of grosses, made his first million, launching himself on the chain of events that would place him at the head of Metro-Goldwyn-Mayer, the most powerful motion picture production company of the thirties and forties. Other fortunes were made by similar chicanery in territories purchased from Epoch on the same basis. The accounting system for the earnings from *The Birth of a Nation* was so chaotic that *Variety,* the show business newspaper, still refuses to list this film in its all-time list of money-making films, although it grants that it may have grossed more money than any other film ever made.

Instead of extending their congratulations, the members of the Mutual board, led by John Freuler, jealously ousted Aitken as president at their June 23, 1915, meeting. Riding on the rising success of *The Birth,* Aitken, undaunted, gathered together those elements of his old organization that would still follow his lead and organized a new company, the Triangle Film Company.

Aitken's departure from the board room of Mutual left Freuler with a Pyrrhic victory. Aitken took with him his own production company, Reliance-Majestic, and persuaded Baumann and Kessel to bring Keystone into the new company. Aitken then kept the services of Griffith, Mack Sennett, and Thomas Ince, the three premier creative talents in the industry. They were the only real assets that Mutual possessed.

The first meeting of the new company took place on July 20 at La Junta, Colorado, in a hotel suite from which Aitken had the furniture removed in order to have enough space. Among those attending, in addition to Aitken, were the three directors after whom the company was to be named, Griffith, Sennett, and Ince. Also present were Charles Baumann, Adam Kessel, Charles Kessel, Albert Banzhaf, W. N. Seligsberg, and Arthur B. Graham.

Although Aitken used the presence of his three directors as an excuse for calling his company Triangle, he was very careful to keep the control in his own hands. With the legal preliminaries out of the way, Aitken moved to supplement his directors with a roster of established stage actors. He recklessly engaged William Collier, De Wolf Hopper, Raymond Hitchcock, Eddie Foy, Sir Herbert Beerbohm Tree, Billie Burke, Weber and Fields, Marie Doro, Joe Jackson, and others with ample theatre and vaudeville reputations and no film experience. Aitken also signed a lease to use the Knickerbocker Theatre, a legitimate theatre in New York, for the exclusive showing of Triangle pictures.

The success of *The Birth of a Nation* continued to increase. The promotional tone of the film, from costumed ushers, half-page display advertisements in the newspapers, giant billboards, to "show trains" bringing people from the small towns and rural areas, set the pattern for the entire film industry. It seems as though Aitken missed hardly any effective promotional device. There were souvenir programs, contests, parades including Klan-costumed figures, bands, and assorted whoopla; even the mounting protests served to promote the film.

In New York City alone it has been estimated that over 825,000 people saw the film in 1915 at both its first run in the Liberty Theatre and subsequently at other theatres.

All of this attention, publicity, and increasingly theatrical exhibition did not pass without opposition. The removal of several shots from the film after its initial showings in New York has been mentioned. Griffith had reduced the film from a total of 1,544 shots to 1,375. Not only were the most inflammatory racist scenes trimmed, but also removed were references to the hypocrisy of New England abolitionists who had descended from the slave traders themselves, and a reference to a racist letter from Lincoln to Secretary of War Stanton stating that the black race was inferior to the white. None of this footage seems to have survived, and the excised print is now the "official" version. Leading the opposition and calling for the complete suppression of the film were the newly founded National Association for the Advancement of Colored People, particularly in Boston, and such distinguished citizens as Dr. Charles Eliot of Harvard, Jane Addams, Oswald Garrison Villard, and Francis Hackett. The latter most referred to Thomas Dixon as a "yellow clergyman."

Griffith was more disturbed by the attacks on *The Birth* than he was elated by its success. He was offended by the demands for removal of material from the film even while he reluctantly acceded to them. The campaigns to censor and repress the film seemed to him attacks on truth, attacks upon everything that he had always accepted about the War Between the States, attacks on civilization itself. He began mentally to organize some sort of reply, something that would re-affirm the need for art to exist without censorship, something that would re-state the case for examining any issue with an open mind, and with tolerance. The money flooding in from the film was destined to give him the backing for his reply. It has been estimated that the film's gross receipts topped $48,-000,000. Since Griffith was not as direct a participant in the profits as he seemed, his own returns were only in the vicinity of one million. Perhaps he could have retired as a wealthy man even at that small percentage, but money for Griffith was only a means to an end.

Griffith had returned to California following the Chicago opening of *The Birth* and reported to the Reliance-Majestic studio for work. The so-called vacation had left him tired and without a desire to begin another big project. It was announced that he would direct a modern story, *The Mother and the Law,* for his next film. The production of the picture was interrupted only for his side trip to La Junta, Colorado. *The Mother and the Law* was intended as a film much on the scale of *Home Sweet Home* and *The Battle of the Sexes,* a project that seemed relatively easy after *The Birth.*

Aitken was still busy playing the name-inventing business. The Reliance-Majestic trademark for the studio disappeared when the studio was re-named Fine Arts Pictures. The new Triangle enterprise began rapidly. Griffith made a major contribution, first, as the mentor of a number of bright young directors who had learned their trade as his assistants, William Christy Cabanne, Edward Dillon, Sidney and Chester Franklin, Paul Powell, and Lloyd Ingraham. Second, the services of Allan Dwan, Chester Withey, and John Emerson were also added, and Griffith contributed under his pseudonym Granville Warwick the scenarios for *The Lamb* and *The Lily and the Rose.* The former was directed by Cabanne, and the latter by Paul Powell. The first Triangle program opened in New York on September 23, 1915 (with the same two dollar top ticket as *The Birth*) and consisted of three films: *The Lamb,* starring Douglas Fairbanks, Thomas Ince's *The Iron Strain,* and *My Valet* with Raymond Hitchcock. *The Lamb* was billed as having been "supervised" by Griffith. Beyond his contribution of the scenario, he had had nothing to do with it. Griffith had agreed to permit Aitken to use his name as the "supervisor," or producer of Fine Arts productions. Aitken convinced Griffith that this additional publicity could only help his career. Within a year Griffith perceived that there was no value to himself personally in having his name attached to other people's films, particularly if they weren't very good, and he began to deny that he had ever supervised any other films. Despite these denials, there were six films produced at Fine Arts in 1916 that were alleged to have been derived from actually non-existent novels by Granville Warwick. Griffith was participating, giving advice to his disciples, but now keeping his own name away from any direct connection with their films.

Griffith was also engaged in other writing, his reply to the attacks on *The Birth of a Nation.* In the spring of 1916 Griffith published a lengthy pamphlet, *The Rise and Fall of Free Speech in America,* in which he wrote:

> The integrity of free speech and publication was not . . . attacked seriously in this country until the arrival of the *motion picture,* when this new art was seized by the powers of intolerance as an excuse for an assault on our liberties.
> The motion picture is a medium of expression as clean and decent as any mankind has ever discovered. A people that would allow the suppression of this form of speech would unquestionably submit to the suppression of that we all consider so highly, the printing press.[124]

The basic idea and attitude implicit in Griffith's counter-attack had been formulated in his mind throughout 1915. The operative word in his pamphlet was "intolerance." Griffith decided that *The Mother and the Law* should be expanded in such a way as to defend mankind against the inhumanity and intolerance of others. The new epic would be called *Intolerance* and would tell three other stories in addition to the modern one, *The Mother and the Law:* one set in ancient Babylon, one to tell the story of the St. Bartholomew's massacre in the France of Louis IX, and one to recount the final passion of Jesus. With the success of *The Birth,* any project that Griffith wanted to name would find approval from Aitken, and, even more important, would find all the financial backing necessary.

Once again Harry Aitken invented another company to distribute this new venture. In December 1915 he incorporated the Wark Producing Company. Investors pressed money upon him, and now that Griffith had his profits from *The Birth* flowing in, he could put a substantial share into this new company. If *Intolerance* could be turned into the bonanza that its predecessor was becoming, the Kentucky farm boy would become a multi-millionaire.

Approximately seven months had been spent in preparing, filming, and editing *The Birth of a Nation.* More than double that time was spent on the production of *Intolerance.* Karl Brown, now promoted from assistant to Bitzer to second cameraman, watched the growth of *Intolerance* out of *The Mother and the Law:*

> The growth of this picture was just one of those things that could only happen with Griffith. First, *Mother and the Law* shot and completed, ready for the theatre ahead of the release of *Birth.* A lapse of time—then another picture, on the same theme, parallel story but in a different period. This could have sufficed for his purpose of mounting suspense—but then came a third, bigger yet—and finally, Babylon in all its glory.[125]

Griffith's new and mighty effort required an expansion of the studio space at Fine Arts. It was severely crowded by the expanded shooting schedule for Triangle releases by the other directors. Harry Aitken, never averse to expansion, now had to find the capital to keep this growing film leviathan moving. The receipts from *The Birth* could be used, but expenses were outrunning them. Despite the willingness of investors to put money in Wark Producing, and to bet on Griffith, they were not quite as eager to back the other films being made under the Triangle banner. Aitken, aware that he must perform a financial dance *en pointe,* bravely offered Triangle stock on the open market. He opened an office in New York under the title The Loftberry Syndicate, and then, executing a neat gambit in reverse psychology, he took large advertisements in leading newspapers throughout the country to announce that the public should be warned *not* to buy Triangle stock unless they knew it was a gamble. Aitken's scheme worked well enough to raise the price of Triangle stock from an opening at $4\frac{1}{2}$ to $9\frac{1}{4}$. For reasons that remain unclear, Aitken suddenly tried to hold the stock at the $9\frac{1}{4}$ level by buying back some $200,000 worth. The professional buyers stopped trading, and the stock began to fall back. Realizing that he could no longer support the higher figure, Aitken, seeing his cash reserves dwindling, went quickly to the investment banking firms of F. S. Smithers and Company and Knauth, Nachod and Kuhne to seek a $500,000 loan to keep his studio production moving. To obtain the loan, he pledged all of the assets, both personal and corporate, controlled by himself and his brother Roy. The banks, to protect themselves, placed their own men on the Triangle board. The seeds of Triangle's destruction had been sown without Aitken's realization. The new board members, as representatives of their banks, were not speculators. They would want to see cash results from Triangle, and quickly, or they would vote for liquidation. Because of the independent financing of *Intolerance* through Wark Producing, the film was not affected by these financial maneuverings. Still Aitken had made free use of Griffith's name and the success of *The Birth of a Nation* in his stock-selling and fund-raising. When Griffith became aware of Aitken's maneuverings, and the use of his name, he became increasingly antagonistic toward Aitken. The friction surfaced in a relatively minor way. Aitken was convinced that Mae Marsh, as a star, had little or no box office appeal. Griffith believed just the reverse. When Mae Marsh was successfully hired away from Triangle in 1916 by Samuel Goldwyn, then sti'l Samuel Goldfish, Griffith wired Aitken: "I would suggest that you attend to managing Triangle which is conceded to be the worst managed business in Film History. . . ."

Griffith was a better critic than manager. He failed to see the contribution that Harry Aitken had made to the success of his own efforts. All that was apparent to him in 1916 was that his films were the trade goods that made Triangle run, and he saw little reason for continuing to support the Aitkens. To break his connection with them began to appear the only salvation of his future. To be hailed as a dramatic genius was an unsettling boost to Griffith's ego. To Griffith it seemed that his talent had been smothered too long by insignificant, untalented little promoters. Griffith would be much better off on his own. What Griffith could not see was that the Aitkens of the film business were necessary. His own business acumen and certainly his experience were nil, and, given his real interests, not likely to improve. His attitudes were shaped by those advisers immediately surrounding him, including Banzhaf. Griffith recognized that bookkeepers were necessary in film-making, but he preferred the easily dominated and cowed kind, like "Little" Epping. There was little time for involvement with Aitken's problems, however, because as much space at the Fine Arts studio as Griffith could find was being transformed into the giant outdoor settings for his new film, *Intolerance*.

10

Masterpiece and Failure: Intolerance

When motion pictures have created something to compare with the plays of Euripides, or the work of Homer or Shakespeare or Ibsen, or the music of Handel or Bach, then let us call motion picture entertainment an art—but not before then.[126]

It is probably impossible some fifty years after an event to determine the precise moment at which any decision was made, and certainly that moment when David Griffith decided to turn his melodrama *The Mother and the Law* into a gigantic four-part motion picture, re-dubbed *Intolerance,* cannot be pinned down. That Griffith had given intimations of interest in spectacle was evident even before his involvement with film, in his play, *War,* and one colossal bout with a motion picture on an epic scale had just been completed. It is the measure of this brilliant man that he could plunge into a project of the monstrous size of *Intolerance* without a visible moment of misgiving or self-doubt. Griffith had undoubtedly caught the fever that would afflict other film-makers in the future, that the bigger the statement of a theme, the more import, the more impact it would have. Griffith was to draw on all the resources, human and material, that the Fine Arts studio could produce, and to send out emissaries throughout the young industry in California to round up any other free agents who could be recruited into his cast and crew. The credited cast would number over sixty, with hundreds of extras uncredited. Griffith used almost everyone who worked on the Fine Arts lot, some of them in many appearances. Not only were the regular members of what had been the Griffith stock company used—Lillian Gish, Mae Marsh, Bobby Harron, Marguerite Marsh, Edward Dillon, Spottiswoode Aiken, Josephine Crowell, Ralph Lewis, George Siegman, Elmer Clifton,

Alfred Paget, and Kate Bruce—but many relative newcomers, some of them to become important actors and directors, were given a baptism of film-making—Erich Von Stroheim, Eugene Pallette, George Walsh, Constance Talmadge, Tod Browning, Miriam Cooper, Joseph Henaberry, Gunther von Ritzau, Elmo Lincoln, Tully Marshall, Monte Blue, Sam de Grasse, and Lloyd Ingraham. Griffith hired the Denishawn dancers, and their leading dancer, Ruth St. Denis. There was even a small role for Griffith's old roommate and stock company partner, Max Davidson.

There was no script, no plans beyond the pocketful of notes and research memoranda that filled a hotel room, that existed outside Griffith's mind. Now the physique built by running in the park, sparring sessions, and Indian club twirling was put to the test. Griffith was everywhere, constantly conferring with the leaders of his army of workers. A small village of shacks grew up across from the studio. Supplies were brought in by freight car—building supplies, and food for a constantly expanding force of carpenters, painters, plasterers, and eventually for the hordes of extras employed when shooting began.

The day would begin with a conference between Griffith and Huck Wortman. Griffith would give his master carpenter notes and instructions on scraps of paper. From these scraps Wortman would make, and pass along to his crews, the orders turning Griffith's dreams into three-dimensional reality. Giant reaches of scaffolding began rising to the sky, towering above the studio buildings. Karl Brown contemplated Wortman's problem:

> Consider a single element of the *Intolerance* set. Walls sixty feet high are no particular problem on paper. The engineering examples are all worked out for you in the examples of trestle construction and so on. But these were no ordinary walls. They are thick with plaster staff work, tricked out with towers, and upon the towers are massive [artificial] elephants—and now, ladies and gents, comes the trick of designing a structure to support these elephants, crowds of people, the stress of changing men, the impact of battering rams, and the thrust of living elephants against its gates. The fall winds and the winter rains must be considered. How much of a puff of wind will it take to send the entire structure crashing? What anchorage is needed to keep the top-heavy elephants secure from crashing down on the

mobs below? How, indeed, can you paint plaster so that it will stand the wind and sun and weather without peeling or cracking, high on those un-get-at-able [sic] towers? And—and here's the crux of all problems—how the hell are you going to guess what Griffith is going to think up next, out of the spur of the moment, to do on, around, or about that set? Or rather, how are you going to out-guess his every possible brain wave and be ahead of him? [127]

Brown was referring to the scenery for the sequence set in ancient Babylon, but settings were also constructed for ancient Judea and the Paris of Louis IX. To match these sets, to dress them, the property department under the direction of Ralph DeLacey, the propmaster, was growing at an equally rapid rate. DeLacey was building and collecting thousands of objects, pieces of furniture, decorative items, swords, guns, heads of livestock.

Griffith's cutters, Jimmy and Rose Smith assisted by Joe Aller, had their editing room expanded into a special building, staffed by rows of girls who would spend their entire day splicing film.

The studio still photographer, Woodbury, hired additional still men who augmented the staff already concerned with other Triangle films, and began operating a dark room on a twenty-four-hour-a-day schedule. An art department rapidly spread through two floors of a special building.

One addition to the staff was Benjamin "Bennie" Zeidman, who headed an expanding publicity department. Zeidman, employing a press agent's license for hyperbole, described the scene of set construction: "At night the twinkling lights create a veritable fairyland. . . ."

Karl Brown took great pleasure in informing Zeidman that lights were not supposed to twinkle, ". . . or if they do, you don't shoot!"

Frank Woods still directed the story department which had little to do with *Intolerance,* but Woods did exercise almost dictatorial control over the other films being made for Triangle. Woods would hold a staff meeting each day in the projection room, viewing the film footage shot the previous day. It was Woods who would determine which scenes should be re-shot. He was available to Griffith for consultation on problems in continuity, although Griffith did not need anyone's services as a writer.

Gentle, self-effacing Abe Sholtz, the wizard of the processing lab, had filled out his ranks with bearded Russian immigrants to turn the developing and drying drums. Sholtz personally still developed a test from each shot (a small number of frames) before going ahead with the processing of the day's film.

The man most closely resembling the legendary whirling dervish was J. C. Epping. Epping was charged with meeting the mounting payrolls, and making some attempt to keep up with the rapidly escalating costs. Most of the department heads, however, took their lead from Griffith and attempted to ignore Epping, except on payday.

As Griffith began shooting the film on the mammoth sets, disaster was sometimes only a hair's breadth away, seeming at times almost like the climax of one of Griffith's Biograph films. At one point Griffith insisted on making a shot with horses and chariots on top of the wall. They were to charge the length of the wall. The set was wide enough for the effect, but Huck Wortman had not built the wall to take the pounding of chariot wheels and horses' hooves. He protested vigorously and saltily, but Griffith waved away the protest. The set rocked like a ship at sea, almost on the verge of collapse, but the shot was made. Wortman's foresight in preventing the damages that might be caused by a possible windstorm saved the day. The set had fortuitously been braced with strong steel cables.

Karl Brown chuckled for years over the daily adventures of one of the actors, Howard Gaye, who played the role of Jesus in the Judean section of the film. Gaye had previously played Robert E. Lee in *The Birth of a Nation,* but was now embarked on a new characterization that would build a one-note career.

> Howard Gaye, for reasons of build and face, became a professional Christ. Griffith was always using Christ in some way or another, generally leaning out of a cloud and forgiving the erring father-son-mother-sister-wife, or what have you. This was standard practice and warranted keeping a regular Christ on contract.

During the long schedule of *Intolerance,* Howard made up every day and stood by during the filming of the Biblical story. He was in the habit of making up at home and riding to work all ready. Hollywood has not yet forgotten the sight of Jesus Christ riding down Sunset Boulevard at the wheel of a Model T. Ford.[128]

Griffith was indefatigable in pursuing every detail during the filming. He took time to keep the extras from pushing their beards up to their foreheads, to oversee hairdressers, and to convince the wig maker that false eyelashes could be made for Seena Owen. He devised built-up shoes for George Siegman, so that his role, Cyrus, the Persian conqueror, would have greater physical presence, and another pair for Alfred Paget to wear as Belshazzar, the Babylonian king. With everyone he exuded confidence. His natural graciousness, even courtliness, became more pronounced. There was no question about who was in charge. When Alan Dwan, an assistant director, questioned the actors' ability to stand up to the overwhelming size of the settings, Griffith smiled and remarked that if it worked, he, Dwan, would be doing it himself the next year.

The settings became a topic for even so non-theatrical a journal as the *Scientific American:*

Perhaps the greatest set that has ever been constructed. . . . On the front of this huge setting—the side that faces the camera —are gigantic walls painted to simulate stone, 100 feet high and adorned with reliefs of strange winged creatures and elephants, suggestive of the architecture of ancient Babylon. The towers of the set stand 135 feet high, and the various structures cover a ten-acre tract of land in Hollywood, California, just outside Los Angeles. For more than six months the carpenters, masons, concrete workers, and painters were busied with the set, and the cost of the work is reported to have been in excess of $50,000. The setting has been used for a production entitled "Intolerance," produced under the direction of D. W. Griffith. In the number of people employed the film is said to outrival the American classic production "The Birth of a Nation," which was produced by the same master director.[129]

The estimate of costs in the *Scientific American* report were on the low side. Some of the other costs included:

Banquet hall scene for the Feast of Belshazzar, $250,000.

Jeweled costume worn by the Princess Beloved, $7,000.

Payroll, four weeks, at $12,000 a week, $48,000.

Salaries to dancing girls at Belshazzar's Feast, $20,000.

Trailing cape worn by Princess Beloved, $1,040.

Daily payroll, "extra people," $8,000 a week, $48,000.

Building construction and costs of materials, $300,000.

Costumes and uniforms for 18,000 soldiers, $360,000.

These figures were not compiled by a publicity agent, but by Mr. Griffith's auditing department. It is a well known fact that "Intolerance" cost approximately $1,900,000.[130]

Griffith planned to direct and, in some instances, film the scenes on the giant Babylon set from the height of a tower in the same manner in which he had worked during the battle scenes of *The Birth of a Nation*. He would maintain, as he had before, telephone communication with the assistant directors who controlled individual groups of actors and extras. This initial tower concept, however, didn't seem to give Griffith the perspective that he wanted, and the idea was rejected in favor of using an anchored balloon. The balloon was erected, but proved an unsteady camera platform in the wind and a frightening experience for Billy Bitzer. The final solution was another tower, this time mounted on rails and including a camera platform on a self-contained elevator. Griffith wanted to provide for different camera positions vertically as well as horizontally. The rail idea was an adaptation, albeit on a giant scale, of the camera platform on rollers used in the old Biograph 14th Street studio. Once the rolling tower was finished, Griffith saw something new that could be done with the moving camera platform. A shot could be made with the camera in motion. This new technique was used for the opening shot of the Feast of Belshazzar, showing some 4,000 extras and the Denishawn dancers celebrating the beginning of the great feast. The camera, with Griffith, Bitzer, and Brown riding the platform, starting from a position about a quarter of a mile from the center of the set, was lowered during the shot and moved into the set until coming to rest in a medium shot of a miniature chariot, drawn by two white doves, carrying a white rose from the king to his princess. Bitzer managed to keep the entire shot in crisp focus, a difficult feat even for a very short moving camera shot.

Another innovation was Bitzer's use of magnesium flares for filming night scenes. Bonfires had been used for a somewhat similar effect in *The Birth of a Nation,* but Bitzer demonstrated to Griffith that the flares would produce a steadier and brighter light. J. C. Epping promptly warned Griffith and Bitzer that they should use the flares sparingly because they cost $20 each. Bitzer agreed that they would position the flares very carefully, both for the lighting effect that was desired, and also to keep the smoke from blowing into the setting. He assured Epping that he would try to make the shots with only one take. Epping departed satisfied. Once he was gone, Griffith indicated to Bitzer that they would get the shots right no matter what the cost of the flares.

The enormous outflow of money for *Intolerance* under the Wark Producing Company banner, and the needs of Triangle for more capital, were outstripping Harry Aitken's fund-raising ability. Thomas Ince was busily building $35,000 settings for his production *Civilization,* using thirty carloads of lumber, beginning in May 1915. In an effort to make some financial sense out of Triangle, Aitken hired H. O. Davis from Carl Laemmle's company to operate the studio, and Charles Parker as general manager. Parker's qualifications to administer a film enterprise consisted of having made a fortune in American Radiator. None of these moves, or men, could stop the financial crisis swiftly developing. Finally, Aitken had to tell Griffith that there was no more money. Griffith's response was to take his own money, the profits coming in from *The Birth of a Nation,* and pour them into the final phases of *Intolerance*'s production. Griffith insisted that he was not gambling. With supreme self-confidence, he told everyone that this film would surpass *The Birth* in earning power. His confidence led some fifty investors, including Lillian Gish and Mae Marsh, to put money, as much as they could, into the film.

One thing had become clear to Griffith: keeping his own counsel, he knew that he had to break with Harry Aitken. In Griffith's mind it was clear that the sole function of the businessmen involved with film was to raise the money for making pictures, and Aitken was failing in his job. Griffith thought that the pictures sold themselves. How to get away? That was uppermost in Griffith's mind. There was one possibility. Adolph Zukor seemed to be constantly in the background, offering contracts to many members of Griffith's company if they would join his Famous Players-Lasky. Zukor had not long before made a handsome offer for Griffith's services. Perhaps he would again. Griffith was also impressed with Zukor's success as an executive with the Marcus Loew vaudeville circuit, with his successful promotion of *Queen Elizabeth,* and, most appealing of all, with his connections with the New York theatre. The legitimate theatre remained Griffith's first love, and he regarded it as the fountainhead of any theatrical endeavor. He was still inordinately impressed with stage credentials rather than film credits despite the many stage stars he had observed to fail in the new medium. Griffith had watched the debut in film of the distinguished Sir Herbert Beerbohm Tree. Sir Herbert had come to Triangle to star in a film with his wife. The first session was a disaster. The stage star and his wife attempted to act for the silent camera by using their *voices.* When Griffith urged them to be more physically expressive, Tree responded that he would be happy to comply if only that black box in front of them could be removed. The black box, of course, was the camera.

Griffith decided to put out a few subtle feelers in Zukor's direction. He instructed his attorney, Albert Banzhaf, to make the necessary overtures. Zukor was pleased to deal with Banzhaf because he immediately recognized that, despite Banzhaf's legal knowledge, he was soft as a businessman, a poor judge of human character—in short, someone who could be easily bested in any deal. Zukor, through Banzhaf, forwarded an offer to Griffith.

Shooting finally was finished on *Intolerance* at the beginning of the summer of 1916. Griffith then settled down to the tedious process of editing the film with Jimmy and Rose Smith, with some eager assistance from Lillian Gish. Lillian had been all over the sets during the shooting of the film, staying as close to Griffith as she dared, and now she made herself equally at home in the cutting rooms. Griffith was both flattered and pleased by the young actress's attentions, and he responded to them in a fatherly manner. Given a free choice, that would not have been the manner of his response, but Griffith was well aware that he was a married man, and somewhere in the background was Linda Arvidson. Griffith was making regular payments to Linda on the basis of their informal separation agreement. Griffith was cautious in his relationships with other women, particularly those for whom he had a genuine affection, and he made certain that no hint of scandal could reach him. Still he liked having Lillian about. He liked taking her with him on location jaunts, or out to dinner, and he found her a receptive ear when he discussed his plans. One of Griffith's strong points as a director was his love of playing teacher, and he had few happier moments than sitting on the Fine Arts studio lawn with a group of actors about him while he lectured informally on the nature of drama and film. Lillian Gish was an excellent one-woman class.

Jimmy and Rose Smith had not yet been married, but the moment for them had arrived during the editing phase of *Intolerance*. They told Griffith that they wanted time off for their wedding, fully expecting great objections to be raised by the director. Griffith smiled and told them to go ahead with the wedding. Jimmy and Rose were elated, but then Griffith added one small proviso. They could have the weekend for the honeymoon, but Jimmy would have to be back on the job on Monday morning. He was.

The first rough cutting of *Intolerance* lasted for eight hours, and despite recognizing that the film would have to be at least half that long, Griffith began to have ideas of running the film in two parts. Trial balloons with a few selected exhibitors quickly showed that there was no interest even in a four-hour film. With some reluctance Griffith saw that he would have to cut the film to a single evening's showing. He managed to trim the original 200,000 feet of film to approximately 13,500 feet, a cutting ratio of about 20 to 1, a not unusual ratio even for contemporary films. The version available today, best exemplified by the Museum of Modern Art's preservation copy, has shrunk to 11,811 feet. This was a result of both Griffith's continuous editorial process while the film was running in its premiere exhibition, and its reconstruction several years later when Griffith attempted to restore the original from cut-up negatives. For purposes of re-release, the film was separated into *The Mother and the Law* and *The Fall of Babylon,* and to do this the original negative was cut. As a result it will never be possible to see *Intolerance* in the form in which it was originally screened.

Griffith had the film ready for previewing on August 6, 1916, in a theatre at Riverside, California. A score had been assembled by Joseph Carl Breil, with Griffith working as a close supervisor and collaborator. Further work needed to be done, and Griffith and Jimmy Smith put in another month trimming the film even more.

The New York opening took place at the Liberty Theatre on September 5, 1916. *The New York Times* reported:

> Ever since the remarkable film, "The Birth of a Nation," was unreeled before an amazed public more than a year ago, the question of whether it was an accident or whether D. W. Griffith, the man who directed the film, was really a new master of the cinema, has interested those who follow the personalities that manipulate the puppets of stage and studio. The answer came last night when D. W. Griffith's second big picture, "Intolerance," was exhibited in the Liberty Theatre before an audience that might have gathered to witness the premiere of some favorite dramatist's latest work, so dotted was it with prominent folk of the theatre.
>
> The verdict "Intolerance" renders in the controversy concerning its maker is that he is a real wizard of lens and screen.[131]

The *Times* expressed some reservations about the film itself, further commenting:

> For in spite of its utter incoherence, the questionable taste of some of its scenes, and the cheap banalities into which it sometimes lapses, "Intolerance" is an interesting and unusual picture. The stupendousness of its panoramas, the grouping and handling of its great masses of players, make it an impressive spectacle.[132]

The review in *Film Daily,* a trade paper with no real influence outside the industry, gave more of a boost to Griffith's hopes:

> Stupendous, tremendous, revolutionary, intense, thrilling, and you can throw away the old typewriter and give up with the dictionary because you can't find adjectives enough. Mr. Griffith has put on the screen what is, without question, the most stirring human experience that has ever been presented in the world. As a spectacle *Intolerance* is the greatest offering ever

staged. The hardest thing the film audience had to swallow was the revolutionary construction employed by Mr. Griffith in building four separate stories in such a manner that the audience could hold the thread of each and jump from one to the other in a manner that would have been considered impossible had most anyone else suggested it without being able to construct it.[133]

Most of the other reviews were equally enthusiastic. The Liberty Theatre was selling out. It seemed that Griffith had topped the success of *The Birth of a Nation*. The film had cost almost $2,000,000, twenty times the cost of *The Birth,* but Griffith, and those surrounding him, felt that this was a relatively paltry sum to recoup. For the first four months of its run at the Liberty, *Intolerance* did better business than *The Birth*. Suddenly in the fifth month, January 1917, business died. The same pattern was repeated in other cities.

Griffith had embarked after the New York opening on another marathon promotional tour across the country. He attended the opening of the film in Cleveland on October 2, the San Francisco premiere on October 9 at the Columbia Theatre, and on the 17, the opening in Clune's Auditorium in Los Angeles. Along the way, he paused to deliver some speeches about film censorship before ladies' clubs and civic groups, and to plug the film. As *Film Daily* reported, he explained:

> . . . that [in *Intolerance*] he was not attempting to follow the accepted ideas of continuity, but was rather offering his themes in a development much the same as thoughts might flash in one's mind.[134]

In December 1916 the *Moving Picture World* noted that *Intolerance* was breaking all records in San Francisco. The same month Griffith appeared in Philadelphia for the opening at the Chestnut Hill Opera House, and in January he went to Pittsburgh. He returned from Pittsburgh for a speech in Washington, D.C., before the National Press Club on his now favorite theme, screen censorship, and then left for an appearance in Chicago before the Women's Suffragette Party of Cook County. The militant women were more interested in persuading him to make a film on women's suffrage than in listening to his talk on film censorship. The Chicago speech was on January 22, and he was back in Washington, D.C., for another version of this same censorship lecture before the National Art League of America on January 25.

For the first time Griffith found a place for a member of his immediate family in his rising fortunes. His youngest brother Albert, now calling himself Albert Grey, was dispatched to Australia to open *Intolerance* there, and perform the same errand in New Zealand. Time was to prove that Griffith's fortune might have been improved if brother Albert had remained in the Antipodes.

Now, even more than during the run of *The Birth of a Nation,* Griffith found himself at the center of an enormous publicity campaign. A feature story on Griffith by Henry Stephen Gordon appeared in the November 1916 issue of *Photoplay.* He was a ceremonial guest of Governor Whitman of New York, offering his help in the planning of a campaign film for Whitman.

Griffith had been invited to the White House by President Wilson during the initial release of *The Birth,* but the reaction across the country to that film had convinced the Washington politicos that it would not be wise to invite Griffith this time. Nevertheless there was enough public adulation whipped up to have turned the head of a saint. Griffith was certainly many things, but a saint was not one of them. To find himself called "The Belasco of the Screen," accorded the mental stature of a genius, or on a minimum level referred to as a "master," was more than he could stand and still maintain his perspective. The high school dropout and part-time actor had reached a peak. As a result his personal pronouncements became more pompous and self-inflating, and he began permitting his press agents to undertake extensive embroidery on the facts of his early life. Now the legends of his descent from the kings of Wales, his days as an intrepid reporter for the Louisville *Courier-Journal,* and his wholly fictitious graduation from the University of Louisville began.

Before the pattern of box office failure for *Intolerance* could be seen, Griffith accepted an offer through Banzhaf for a deal with Zukor.

On March 17, 1917, Griffith sailed abroad for the first time to attend the London opening of *Intolerance.* He had been approached by representatives of the British government to make a propaganda film for them, and it was his intention to discuss that subject. On the same date as his sailing he released to the press his announcement that he was leaving Triangle and had signed an agreement with Artcraft, the producing company subsidiary of Famous Players-Lasky. Griffith did not announce that part of his deal with Zukor involved Zukor's financing of a film to be made in England in return for the distribution rights.

After the United States declared war on Germany on April 6, Griffith felt even more strongly about making a film in England that would be his contribution to the war effort. He cabled Lillian Gish and her mother along with other members of the cast of *Intolerance* to come to London. They were to help in the promotion of *Intolerance,* but mindful of the old stock company days, Griffith thought that he might use all of them if he made a film. London was a bit farther afield than Cuddebackville, but the principle remained the same. Lillian and Mrs. Gish crossed on the *St. Louis,* the first camouflaged ship to sail. Billy Bitzer, Bobby Harron, George Fawcett, George Siegmann, Dorothy Gish, and little Ben Alexander and his mother all sailed on the *S.S. Baltic* on May 28. They were certain that nothing could happen to them because General Pershing was also a passenger.

The wreckage of Triangle that Griffith left behind was not apparent to the public, but it was apparent to Harry Aitken. Aitken's realization that all three points of the "triangle" were deserting the company forced him to take the only action that seemed to make sense. He brought in more business help from the ranks of the exhibitors. Aitken was typical of those motion picture executives who had come into the business from exhibition and distribution. They all felt that any faults in production could be instantly cured by increasing the number of outlets for the product. They didn't really believe that the product itself was very important. As long as enough theatres would play their films, under a non-cancelable arrangement, solvency was assured. It was a different breed of executive, like the Zukors, who knew that while the business side could never be neglected and strong ties had to be established with the sources of money in Wall Street, the quality of the product would in the end determine success or failure. *They* were the survivors, not the Aitkens.

Looking back, Harry Aitken in 1941 remembered that he had made a last attempt to hold Griffith by offering him a large block of Triangle stock. Aitken wrote:

> I am wondering if Mr. Griffith has given you the information that I gave him the same amount of stock in Triangle that I received at no cost to him. A very large block that would have been worth millions shortly thereafter, but that he took the temporary income offered elsewhere and at the same time helped Douglas Fairbanks to get away from the three year contract he had with us, with two more years to run. The Triangle then not only had some 2500 stories and negatives but an international distributing system. The quality of the pictures from the three entirely different studios were leading the world so as I did it, it seems that it should be told as it happened.[135]

While Griffith avoided any involvement in Triangle's difficulties by staying in England, Aitken made desperate moves. He sought the financial backing of Superpictures, Inc., a new company organized by W. W. Hodkinson, Raymond Pawley, and S. A. Lynch. Lynch was the head of the biggest motion picture theatre chain in the South. Through Lynch, Superpictures, Inc. loaned Aitken $600,000 and thus enabled Aitken to wipe out Triangle's debts. But there was a price. Lynch now organized and controlled the Triangle Distributing Company through which all Triangle films would now have to pass. Aitken had to accept this, but he was made doubly unhappy when he discovered that Lynch was also distributing the Zukor films from Artcraft, and he began to suspect that the Triangle product would be short-changed.

In the process of liquidating the debts owed by Triangle, Percy Waters persuaded Aitken to sell the California properties: the Fine Arts studio where Griffith had worked, the lease on the film ranch at Inceville, the Culver City plant, and the studio in Yonkers, New York. In addition, without Aitken's knowledge, Waters also sold the foreign distribution system.

S. A. Lynch got into a fight with his two partners, Hodkinson and Pawley, and bought out their shares in the Triangle Distribution Company. As the sole owner, he now put this company up for sale. The only purchaser, perhaps the only one who knew that the company was on the market, was S. A. Lynch Enterprises. S. A.

Lynch was also the president of this company. His next move was to submerge the new arrangement into a states rights distributing company formed with two new partners, Louis B. Mayer and Sol Lesser.

Harry Aitken had decided that Europe, or at least that portion of it not involved in the war, was a calmer place. Upon his return after only four weeks, he found that Percy Waters and Felix Kahn had jointly instituted stockholders' suits against Triangle and himself. Aitken's brother Roy had engaged a new firm of lawyers who had never had any involvement with the motion picture business. Harry found the situation almost hopeless. When Felix Kahn offered him a way out, he jumped at it. Kahn offered to put Triangle on a sound financial footing, provided that Aitken turn over to him control of the Aitken common stock. Aitken agreed. An outstanding loan to the company made by Roy Aitken would be paid off in preferred stock. Further, Aitken had to agree to stay out of the business and let Kahn run it without interfering.

A few months later the restless Aitken discovered how far he had been led down the garden path when he met with Kahn to complain that Triangle's business had not improved. He wanted Kahn to give him back control over his stock. Kahn refused, but magnanimously asked Aitken what should be done with the company. Aitken suggested that it should be turned into a production company instead of a distribution company in order to protect and capitalize on the valuable trademark. Kahn smiled enigmatically and turned the knife. He told Aitken that they couldn't follow his suggestion because he, Kahn, was a director of Famous Players-Lasky, and he had an agreement that prevented him from producing films in competition with Zukor.

Aitken walked out of the meeting, head bowed, convinced that he had been a victim of a plot by Adolph Zukor to deliberately wreck Triangle. Now the affair was ready for the courts. Aitken and his naïve lawyers prepared a petition claiming that a conspiracy on the part of Lynch, Zukor, Kahn, and Waters had set out to wreck Triangle. The reply of Kahn and Waters was to throw Triangle into bankruptcy. Aitken later claimed that this was done despite the fact that Triangle's indebtedness, other than some tax liens, amounted to only $4,500.

The final act of this tragedy took place in 1918 when Lynch, barely recovered from an attack of the virulent influenza then sweeping the country, was accused of defrauding his exhibitor customers by raising money on film negatives that Triangle didn't own. There was a mysterious disappearance of prints and negatives from the Triangle vaults, followed by a partial recovery when some prints were discovered in San Francisco packed and labeled as "hardware" and consigned for shipment to Java. The studios were shut down.

Aitken himself was in court answering a stockholders' suit that alleged that he had artificially inflated the value of Triangle stock to $8, and then illegally transferred $400,000 of Triangle's assets to the Western Importing Company which he controlled. Aitken's performance on the stand during this suit was ineffective. The usually articulate Aitken suffered a loss of memory and answered most questions with, "I don't remember."

The case was finally settled out of court with a rumored settlement by Aitken of $1,375,000. There is no evidence that Aitken had that much money. The forced bankruptcies managed, in any event, to wipe out the debts.

The tangled affairs of Triangle and the seemingly shoddy standards and performance of the businessmen in films make Griffith's rejection of them understandable. Griffith watched Aitken's downfall dispassionately, convinced that ultimately the only answer for himself was to own and control his own studio. That way he could make his films without interference. The ease with which this might be done seemed apparent since Griffith found numerous investors for his projected film in Britain, and he saw no reason why he couldn't find more for any project that he might envisage.

11

The Road to Independence

> It was the prospect of sharing in a Griffith triumph that
> made any star proud to do anything he suggested. The
> feeling of being part of a great job in any capacity built
> a spirit through his organization that nothing else could
> create. The smallest bit might become an overnight sensa-
> tion. A single closeup in a Griffith picture might be the
> beginning of another Pickford career. To be with him
> was to enter the magic circle of success, where everything
> seemed to work, and nothing ever to fail.[136]

As Griffith prepared for his departure to England in March 1917,
the fact that *Intolerance* might possibly be a failure was just becoming apparent. He was not ready to discuss this with anyone,
and continued to display a cheerful, optimistic facade. Just before
departure he did ask the Gishes to hold a newspaper wrapped bundle for him until his return, or his further instructions. The
Gishes, despite natural curiosity, didn't open the bundle, placing it
in their safety deposit box. They always suspected that it contained
stocks and bonds, a nest egg hedging against possible disaster.

In England Griffith presented *Intolerance* at a command performance for the royal family before the official opening. The impri-
matur of a royal command performance helped gain the attention
of English society and political figures including the Prime Minister, Lloyd George. Griffith was invited to 10 Downing Street, the
Prime Minister's official residence, and was asked to make a film
that would assist in making America and the uncommitted world
sympathetic to the Allied cause. Griffith later told the Gishes that
the projected film was to assist in bringing the United States into
the war. This latter story was undoubtedly a fabrication after the
fact of America's entry into the war in view of the reticence of an
experienced politician like Lloyd George. Griffith was enjoying,
however, the flattery of the British request, and he could be for-

given for taking the broadest possible inference from it. As it turned out, the film that Griffith made in part in England was not finished until only a few months before the war ended. Since the British government did want a film that would reinforce their political and moral position in the war, they offered Griffith financial help and other cooperation, which extended to carefully guided trips to the front.

By the time Lillian Gish and her mother arrived in London, Griffith had already worked out the general details of the film in his mind. He explained it to them over dinner at the Savoy Hotel on their first night in London. The film would tell the story of a small French village suffering under German occupation. Griffith even had the title ready, *Hearts of the World.*

Griffith was thoroughly enjoying his new role of celebrity in English society. He was lionized at parties given by major notables in London. Upon his return from these affairs, he would regale the Gishes with stories of the evening's happenings, stories in which he was always the central figure. He told them that Winston Churchill persisted in trying to sell him stories for films. Lillian Gish asked if Churchill's stories were good. Griffith shrugged and replied that they were no better than his own.

One of the results of Griffith's mingling with English society was a filming session of a number of handsome ladies including Lady Diana Manners, Miss Elizabeth Asquith, and the Duchess of Beaufort, showing them transformed from their idle peacetime pursuits into dedicated war workers. The ladies were told that the footage would be used in *Hearts of the World,* but Griffith decided to hold this footage. It was used in *The Great Love,* his next film, made in the United States. Griffith had learned the value of stock footage that, if saved, might be useful in another film.

For the first time in his life Griffith found himself confronting a real war. Out of his fantasies and library research, Griffith had created the battle scenes of his Biograph films, and the great battle scenes of *The Birth of a Nation* and *Intolerance.* Now Griffith visited a bombed schoolhouse just after a London air raid and looked directly at the horrors of war. Tears came to his eyes, and he looked at Lillian Gish next to the tragic site: "This is what war is. Not the parades and the conference tables—but children killed, lives destroyed." [137] The bomb had burst in the kindergarten. Ninety-six children had been killed.

Despite his revulsion at the war damage and tragedies surrounding him, Griffith, the pragmatic director, knew that he must make use in his film of what he observed. He sent his actors to the London railroad stations to observe the soldiers and civilians. He told them to catch a walk here, a cast of countenance there, a reaction between two people, the emotions of mother and son, of sweethearts, all to be incorporated where appropriate in the performances by his actors. On a stroll Griffith and Lillian saw a girl with just the right walk for Dorothy Gish. They followed the woman for some distance until they could imitate the walk well enough to demonstrate it to Dorothy on their return. The results of this bit of observation and transmittal can be seen in Dorothy's performance as "the little disturber" in *Hearts of the World.*

Since the War Office Committee of the Ministry of Information was financing a significant part of *Hearts of the World,* it was easy for Griffith to make visits to the battlefronts in France. These were guided tours, safely out of range of actual shelling, not under fire as the Griffith press agents were later to claim. Nevertheless, Griffith was able to see and feel the reality of war's devastation. Because of this official sponsorship Griffith could also obtain actual battle film footage shot by army photographers. This was necessary because some anonymous War Office bureaucrats decided that a cameraman with a suspiciously Germanic name, Wilhelm Gottlieb Bitzer, shouldn't be allowed to photograph in a war zone. When the time for actual work in France came, Bitzer was not, at first, allowed to cross the channel. As a result Griffith was forced to work out of Paris with a French cameraman with unknown capabilities. Griffith took the Gish sisters, Mrs. Gish, and Bobby Harron into some of the bombed and shelled-out areas just behind the lines. Fortunately, the front was relatively stabilized.

To ease the travel problems behind the lines, Griffith affected a sort of khaki officer's uniform without insignia, even though he carried the necessary documents. It was just easier to gain some sort of recognition in the event of a military challenge rather than go through the time-wasting procedure of producing the documents. Bobby Harron traveled in his costume as a French private.

Mrs. Gish, with only a small role in the film, was not needed in any of the shooting in the countryside, but she refused to be left behind in Paris.

Various satisfactory locations were found: a semi-ruined village, shell-scorched orchards and fields. There were times when Griffith's little company was dangerously close to the front lines, well within reach of the German long guns. At times when they sat down for lunch in an abandoned dugout, the chicken was accompanied by the sound of distant artillery fire and flashes of shell bursts. Lillian Gish remained convinced that her mother's early death was hastened by the effects of a sort of shell shock induced by these seemingly hazardous conditions.

Only once was there any real danger, and that occurred during a scouting expedition for locations when Griffith went off with a military escort. He returned, ashen-faced, to report that his party had been under direct fire. Two of his guides had been killed, and he had witnessed a group of allied soldiers, crossing an open field to meet them, obliterated by shellfire.

After this experience Griffith wasted little time completing the shots that required his actors, and then sent them back to London. He remained behind, claiming later that he had filmed documentary footage of actual battle scenes, men dying, ordnance moving to the front, and other combat footage.

In the middle of October 1917 Griffith brought his company back to the United States to finish the film in the safety of California. While passing through New York, arrangements were made to purchase some film owned by a Captain Kleinschmidt, a German nationalist, who had toured the United States showing his films prior to the U.S. entry into the war. These consisted of shots of the German army in action. This film, which might well have been impounded, cost $16,000, and some of it was useful in the final editing of *Hearts of the World*.

Despite the footage shot in England and France, and the footage obtained from Captain Kleinschmidt, about two-thirds of the footage actually used in the film was shot in California after the company's return. This is plainly shown in the laboratory and film charge records. How much film Griffith shot in France will probably remain a mystery.

Karl Brown rejoined Bitzer in California as second cameraman. Brown picked up the raw stock each day and loaded the cameras. Because of the collapse of Triangle and the sequestering of all of their old equipment, the cameras were loaded with raw film borrowed from Cecil B. De Mille. The sets to be used were built by Huck Wortman and among them were the remains of the old *Intolerance* sets. Even a dark room was constructed in one of the Babylon towers. It was necessary to revert to complete sun shooting, and the schedule was made by Griffith accordingly. A group of bungalows facing the lot was rented to serve as dressing rooms.

Karl Brown observed:

> In many respects, *Hearts of the World* was the most revealing picture—as of Griffith—that he had ever made.
>
> Here was picture making reduced to its most primitive elements. I don't think there was ever a time in Griffith's career when he was forced to do so much with so little.
>
> Strangely, the very handicaps themselves made for a great picture instead of a merely good one. The naturally sunlighted sets looked real because they *were* real. There wasn't a floodlight coming in through the cafe window. It was sunshine, and it looked as real as it was. That was a real army outside, on a real street.[138]

The one false note in the film, one not readily apparent because it was a silent picture, was the use of a strange form of double-talk meant to be French. Griffith had the actors resort to this because English speech would make lip movements too easily recognizable.

Huck Wortman faced a strange problem with the setting for the inn. He had built a series of interconnected rooms for the stage inn that had little architectural reality. He found it a source of amusement to attempt on paper to show how this strange spider-like creation made some sort of architectural sense. The result showed each room opening into each other and all opening into the central room of the inn. What it lacked in verisimilitude it gained in photogenic quality.

An additional cameraman joined the staff for the film, Henrik Sartov, an erstwhile portrait photographer whose work Griffith had first seen when he examined the passport photographs for Lillian and Dorothy Gish. They had gone to the Hoover Art Company to

have the pictures taken, and the staff photographer assigned to take
their pictures was Sartov. Sartov used a favorite single element
lens, a spectacle lens full of aberrations, but when stopped down
to a certain point it produced a soft focus quality and sparkling
catchlights in the eyes of the subject that were enchanting. With
the same ability to recognize and capitalize on accidental discoveries
that had marked his early career at Biograph, Griffith hired Sartov
for one purpose, to make the close-ups of Lillian Gish and capture
the same quality shown in the passport photos.

Sartov's first results, no longer in miniature form but blown up
to full screen size, were disastrous. Griffith was not discouraged and
told Sartov to keep working. Finally the problem was solved, and
Sartov became a regular member of the camera team, although his
duties were still limited to the making of the special close-ups.

Most of the cast for *Hearts of the World* was hired in California,
including Erich Von Stroheim who appeared in several small German roles. Griffith used, with permission, an abbreviated version
of Von Stroheim's name, Von Strohm, for the villain, played by
George Siegmann.

The final editing of the film was completed in time for its first
review in Pomona, California, in March 1918. The official premiere of *Hearts of the World* was given at the 44th Street Theatre
in New York on April 4, 1918. The film was shown in twelve reels.
Once again Griffith's continuing editing, both for artistic reasons
and, after the armistice in November, to make it fit a new situation, reduced the film to eight reels. For the first time, however,
complete shot lists existed to show what the original film contained. The shot lists were made for the use of the cutters, since
Griffith was less able to supervise the cutting personally. Eliminated were sequences and shots that had been designed to arouse
the hatred against the Germans but now seemed superfluous in
peacetime. In addition Zukor, concerned with the distribution of
the film, had been pressuring Griffith to shorten it. Griffith had resisted Zukor's arguments, replying in a telegram: ". . . if picture is
big enough twelve reels is short enough. . . ." But with the
changed world situation Griffith found reason to give in and au-
thorize the shorter version.

In a review more than twice the length of those accorded *The*

Birth of a Nation and *Intolerance, The New York Times* reported on April 5, 1918:

> Mr. Griffith's film seeks to make the war a big reality, to bring as much of it as possible within the four walls of a comfortable Broadway theatre; and, if the demonstrations by which those who saw the picture manifested their succession of emotions can be accepted as faithful indications, the motion picture succeeds in its ambitious aim.

On the successful integration of the real documentary footage of the war with the fictional material created in Hollywood, the *Times* further comments:

> Sometimes one does not know whether what he is seeing is a real war or screen make-believe. The pictures of hand to hand fighting in the trenches, the bursting of shells from big guns, the demolition of buildings, the scouting trips and raids into enemy trenches are impressively realistic.

One of the final bits of reporting covered the appearance of Griffith on stage at the conclusion of the film:

> After "The End" had been flashed upon the screen the spectators stood and shouted for Mr. Griffith until he appeared on the stage. He said that he had no speech to make, but only wanted to thank those present. When he attempted to ask the spectators to pray for and support the men fighting in the war, which, he said, the flickering shadows on the screen represented in a small way, his voice broke and he never finished his sentence.[139]

It is interesting to compare Karl Brown's comments on Griffith's personal appearances for curtain speeches with the *Times* account.

> Griffith's personal appearances, for curtain speeches on opening nights, were strictly the Ham What Am—phony as Belasco's collar, and as effective. His shy little timid entrance, his murmured appreciation of their liking his little play, and his confused exit, dashing a tear away from an eye just before hitting the wings, was Standard Production Number One which had one golden virtue: it worked. You could hear the reaction in the exit crowd: Gawd, ain't he modest, though, Mabel? He actually busted out bawling! [140]

Despite the possible inference of callousness in such a performance, particularly on such a solemn subject, Brown also commented:

Griffith's attitude toward the public was always one of great respect. The use of tricks to gain public attention was not in any way necessarily rooted in contempt, anymore than the stage management of a political campaign by a sincere statesman reflects contempt upon a people he is anxious to serve. Whatever arrested attention and spurred interest in his product was good, however cheap it might be in the sight of latter day analysts.

This attitude was a direct reflection of his attitude toward himself and his work, to which he was dedicated as permanently as a surgeon to surgery, a lawyer to law. In order to grow, he must be consistently successful in serving his master, the public, with a quality of product that would induce them to buy eagerly more and better of the same.[141]

Hearts of the World was no more free of censorship than its two immediate predecessors. Newly created censorship boards in various cities and states began looking for things to remove. Morris Gest, a theatrical impresario and Belasco's son-in-law, who with William Elliott and F. Ray Comstock stood in for Zukor as the presenters of the film in New York, wired President Wilson to protest the cutting of two scenes from the film by the Chicago censors. Wilson was, of course, much too busy to take up the cudgels for two censored film scenes, and Gest knew it. The advantage of the wire was to make it available to the press. Morris Gest was no stranger to the flamboyant gesture.

The press had dutifully reported that the scenario for *Hearts of the World* was written by M. Gaston de Tolignac and translated into English by Captain Victor Marier. Both names were pseudonyms for Griffith. He chose the French name as appropriate to the story's theme and locale, and the "Captain" name seemed to lend a cachet to the military and war scenes. It also explained how Griffith, who spoke no French, could understand the alleged French scenario. Griffith fell in love with the "Captain Marier" image and kept it during his next three films, using it to mask his collaborations with his old friend Stanner E. V. Taylor.

After the New York opening Griffith worked his way back to California and made personal appearances at the openings along the way, including Chicago on April 22. When he arrived in California, he found that his increasing prominence in the industry entitled him to some extra-curricular accolades. He was elected chairman of the Motion Picture War Service Association on May 26 in

Clune's Auditorium, along with his old colleague Mack Sennett as treasurer, and Stanner Taylor as secretary. The association was formed to promote the sale of Liberty bonds for the support of the war effort. Griffith made a number of appearances to aid in the selling of bonds, and supervised a one-reel film featuring Lillian Gish, Kate Bruce, and a young dancer who had worked for him in *Intolerance* as part of the Denishawn group, Carol Dempster. Carol Dempster had just quit as a student of Ruth St. Denis after one brief West Coast tour with the company and decided on a career as a film actress. She was determined to be a star, and in particular, a Griffith star. The one-reeler was her first step.

The break-up of Triangle and Griffith's separation from Harry Aitken, combined with his loose arrangements with Zukor, left him without the support of a business organization. In a situation like that the safest course was to turn for help and support to a relative. Griffith had persuaded his younger brother Albert to work for him during the promotion of *Intolerance*. Griffith had felt increasingly a sense of family responsibility after the death of his mother in December 1915, and had willingly proposed to assume more responsibility for all of his family. From that point on Griffith regularly sent money to his relatives in Kentucky.

In June 1918 Griffith dropped the firm of Elliott, Comstock, and Gest who had been handling the distribution and promotion of *Hearts* and turned the film over to his brother. Albert's first move was to sell the states rights for California and the western states to Sol Lesser, then president of All Star Feature Distributors, Inc., for $200,000. Albert was less successful in his other sales. The New England territory brought only $75,000, and the combined rights for Pennsylvania and Illinois brought only $150,000. Still *Hearts of the World* had earned a profit of over $500,000 by the end of 1918.

Despite his public success and the adoration of his film company, Griffith became an increasingly lonely man. He clung to a personal relationship with the Gish family that provided him with a warmth missing in the cold hotel rooms of the Astor in New York and the Alexandria in Los Angeles. Since his break-up with Linda his only homes had been hotel rooms. He had seen Linda only once after 1911, at the time of the opening of *Intolerance*. It had been an awkward meeting for both. Griffith was not certain of Linda's intentions. He had told the Gishes that he hoped to get a divorce, but Linda made it perfectly clear that she had no intentions of divorcing him while his star was rising. She presented him with an agreement, prepared by her lawyer, calling for 15 per cent of his income as a support payment. Griffith was confused, and it seemingly never occurred to him to seek legal advice. With his strong sense of familial obligation, he signed the agreement. He warned Linda that there might not be very much income because of the amount of money tied up in *Intolerance*. Linda replied that she wasn't worried. Her money wasn't going to be used to finance films. It was to come off the top. At that moment *Intolerance* looked more lucrative than *The Birth of a Nation*. Besides, she told him, he was a "genius." Griffith knew from the tone of Linda's voice that there would be at least one person who would never believe the publicity handouts about himself.

Any hopes that Griffith had entertained about securing his personal freedom were now gone. This precluded his making any obvious alliances with other women. He saw that Linda was quite capable of making use of even the faintest hint of scandal for her own purposes. Further contact with Linda was made through third parties, usually Banzhaf, except for her letters demanding payments and accounts of his income for more payments.

The answer to any personal troubles for Griffith was to plunge into more work. His contract with Zukor's Artcraft called for six personal productions and the supervision of other films to be made by Artcraft. In December 1917 Artcraft had managed to cut through the red tape and lease the old Fine Arts studio, and once again it became a place of frenzied activity. Even before the release of *Hearts of the World,* Griffith had written a synopsis of a war film with Stanner Taylor to be called *A Hun Within.* The picture was assigned to Chester Withey as director, and was designed to make use of more of the stock footage of the war, including the Kleinschmidt material, left over from *Hearts.* Credit for the story appeared over Griffith's old pseudonym Granville Warwick. The cast included Dorothy Gish, George Fawcett, and Erich Von Stroheim, as well as other members of the Griffith company then available. The picture was set up as an independent production by something called the F-4 Company, and it was financed with Griffith's own money. He then sold the film to Zukor's Famous Players-Lasky for both a credit against his own obligations and a small profit of about $25,000.

Once *Hearts of the World* had been launched, Griffith began work on the films for Artcraft. He retained the rights to *Hearts,* but the Artcraft films all belonged to Famous Players-Lasky, a company soon to adopt the name of its distribution organization, Paramount Pictures. Griffith also arranged to produce, but not to direct, a comedy series to star Dorothy Gish. During the next five years, through 1922, seventeen films were made in this series.

Griffith plunged into work with all of his old energy and drive. During the early summer he made *The Great Love* with Bobby Harron, Lillian Gish, Henry Walthall, George Fawcett, and George Siegmann and had it edited and ready for release by August. The film told the story of a young American, horrified by the German "atrocities" in Belgium, who enlists in the British army. In London the young American falls in love with an Australian girl and saves her from an unscrupulous fortune hunter and "the machinations of German adventurers masquerading as radicals." Griffith worked into the film more of the war footage remaining from *Hearts,* and finally he was able to use the shots of Diana Manners and the other English society ladies taken during his trip to England. The program took full advantage of this vignette and listed Queen Alexandra of England and the Princess of Monaco in the cast. Actually none of these ladies had expected that their work before the camera would turn up in a commercial film. Lady Diana Manners was later inspired to seek a career as a film actress.

The Great Love opened at the Strand Theatre in New York on August 11, 1918. The reviewer for *Film Daily* liked the "Zeppelin raid," but thought that the "miniature spectacle" was "not so good because it was too long." *The New York Times* commented:

> One must bow to Mr. Griffith for the deftness with which he can link fact and fiction in an almost continuous chain. It is true that there sometimes seems to be missing links, and occasionally the theatricalities of the story make it somewhat too obtrusive, but when one remembers that the producer had to deal with the inflexible material of actual occurrences, the difficulties of his task are appreciated and his degree of success be-

comes much more prominent than the relatively small measures of his failure.[142]

The *Times* reviewer thought that both Lillian Gish and Bobby Harron gave better performances in *The Great Love* than they had in *Hearts of the World*. About Harron he noted that "he displays talent not noticed in his other performances." Lillian Gish, he says, "gives her part a humorous touch that is delightful."

Unfortunately, according to the Film Department of the Museum of Modern Art, there are no prints available today of *The Great Love* and of several of the subsequent films that Griffith made for Artcraft. The reason that has always been given has been the deterioration of the negatives in the Paramount vaults.

With only a short break for a quick trip to Washington, D.C., to film the House of Representatives in action for possible inclusion in a proposed government propaganda film, Griffith was immediately at work on his next picture. To fill out his contract with Zukor, Griffith was determined to hold himself down to the modest sort of program film which would cause the least production problems and which could be turned out in the shortest possible amount of time. The evidence of the box office also seemed to indicate that such modest, relatively low budget films would earn the greatest potential profit. The need for such profits, in view of the failing returns from *Intolerance,* were now obvious to him. In the vein of so many of the bucolic romances of his one-reel days at Biograph, Griffith made *A Romance of Happy Valley* with Lillian Gish and Bobby Harron as the young lovers. The setting was Kentucky and the image conjured up by Griffith might well have been the Floydsfork of his youth. The cast almost seemed like one from the Biograph stock company. There were roles for Kate Bruce, George Nichols, and Adolph Lestina.

In his almost manic ability to pyramid projects, Griffith simultaneously began working on his last war film, making use of the final remnants of the war footage from preceding films. The coming of the armistice and the subsequent change of feelings about war films were apparently sensed by Griffith. The war film *The Greatest Thing in Life* took precedent over *A Romance of Happy Valley* and was rushed for release. Lillian Gish and Bobby Harron were also starred in this film. It told the rather remarkable story of a Southern officer who loses his snobbish biased point of view in the enforced comradeship of the trenches. It has been alleged that it was in this film that Griffith included the scene in which Harron, as the Southern officer, pretends to be the mother of a dying Negro soldier and kisses him. This incident, which grew organically and centrally out of the theme of the film, was later seized upon by certain critics and commentators as Griffith's apology for the racism of *The Birth of a Nation.* There is no evidence that Griffith ever felt that an apology was necessary for *The Birth,* nor that this moment in *The Greatest Thing in Life* was so intended. The film could be thought of as an unusual one for a Southerner to make if one assumes that Griffith was a doctrinaire Southerner and ignores those films in which he displays a growing liberal and enlightened attitude. It was a screen moment that certainly showed Griffith's sense of showmanship because the kiss came shortly after the Negro character had rescued the prejudiced officer.

The story for *The Greatest Thing in Life* was written by Griffith and Stanner Taylor, credited to the mythical Captain Marier, but the title was suggested by Lillian Gish over a malted and cheese sandwich lunch.

The Greatest Thing in Life opened in Los Angeles on December 16, 1918, and at the Strand in New York on December 22, 1918. *Film Daily* liked the film, chortling: "DWG put it over again; it is both box-office, because it is human, and artistic." [143]

As was increasingly the custom for major film presentations, the opening in Los Angeles was preceded by a live prologue including dancers—a sort of ancestor of the Radio City Music Hall Rockettes. Among the dancers selected for this prologue were Clarine Seymour and Carol Dempster, both to appear prominently in Griffith films and in his life. Another dancer was billed as Rodolfo Di Valentina, who later simplified his name to Rudolph Valentino.

With *The Greatest Thing in Life* launched, Griffith returned to *A Romance of Happy Valley* and had it ready for release on January 26, 1919. Despite the Kentucky setting, there is a strong hint of the de Maupassant story of the son who returns home unrecognized and is murdered by his impoverished parents. In this film the son experiences a near miss, and Griffith makes all right with the world. Griffith included a bit of humor that as a plot device still elicits both surprise as well as a chuckle. The young man who leaves his puritanical home to make his fortune in the city accomplishes that task by inventing a mechanical frog, and even more remarkably, he sells the frog for $10,000 before returning home to rescue his parents from poverty and his sweetheart from spinsterhood. Even Griffith, whose career was based on an invention deriving from the nineteenth-century drive to progress through mechanics, could have fun putting down the whole ideal. *The New York Times* liked both Harron and Gish in the leading roles:

> The part of John, the wayward son who showed all the others the way to live, is played by Robert Harron, whose impersonation adds to the already accumulated evidence of his versatility as a screen actor. Lillian Gish, as his sweetheart, is sufficient reason for his returning home.[144]

Although only three films had been completed toward the six-film contract with Artcraft by the end of January, the trade press printed rumors that Griffith would sign a contract to produce and direct for the First National Exhibitors Circuit, Inc., a company set up by exhibitors who had been frozen out by Zukor. The rumor was promptly denied by the vice-president of First National, although Griffith was secretly negotiating for such a contract, to take effect when he had completed his contract with Artcraft.

The First National deal was not the only one in which Griffith was involved at that point. He had also been invited to participate in the formation of a new releasing company to be called United Artists in celebration of its founders, Charlie Chaplin, Mary Pickford, and Douglas Fairbanks. Each member of the quartet, including Griffith, would produce his films independently and release them through United Artists. Various secret meetings, in which Griffith was sometimes represented by Albert Banzhaf, were held before the signing of a formal agreement on February 5. The new distributing company was to be headed by Oscar Price, former Assistant Director of Railroads in Wilson's government, with William Gibbs McAdoo, President Wilson's son-in-law and then Secretary of the Treasury, as general counsel. McAdoo was hired for $50,000 a year, a considerable increase over his cabinet salary of

$12,000. Hiram Abrams, assisted by Benjamin Percival Shulberg, commonly known as B. P., was to be the general manager of distribution. The two top executives of the new company were without experience in the motion picture business. Abrams and Shulberg were already knowledgeable and attuned to the strange corporate in-fighting in the new industry.

Ten days after the ceremonial signing of the United Artists agreements, Griffith signed a contract with First National for three films. He was to receive $285,000 plus a percentage of the profits delivered from each picture to First National. Griffith's plan was to use the First National money as his investment in independent productions for United Artists release, and his new partners were so informed. For United Artists, he would be responsible, as would the other partners, for four pictures a year.

At this point in his career as the spring of 1919 began, Griffith was committed to a total of ten pictures for the coming year. If Griffith's piling up of commitments seems to border on a manic condition, it is important to remember his incredible capacity for work and the Biograph experience in which he had grown accustomed to turning out almost any number of pictures in a given short span of time. What was lost on Griffith for the moment was that the quality expected of a feature picture in 1919, in great part due to his own efforts, was much higher than that in the days of 1908 to 1913. The films also required longer shooting schedules, greater physical production, longer editing sessions. The audience, after seeing *Intolerance,* as well as the other large-scale films that followed it, would no longer accept the fakery of the one-reel production. For any film maker to turn out "quickie," ill-produced films was to court disaster. Griffith himself had come to like the luxury of lengthy preparation and research, longer shooting schedules with re-takes if necessary. All of these factors militated against Griffith's being able to keep his contractual promises without compromising the quality of his films. In fact, however, Griffith would never again have the luxury of the free flow of money keyed to whatever his imagination wanted to try in film. Like other film makers, he, too, would be held to tight budgets from that point on.

Griffith had changed along with the industry. He was not readily aware of the change. He still liked to think of himself as a simple country boy, or, perhaps, an actor with the worldly experience gained from barnstorming tours. The straw hat, high shoes, loud suits with the jackets cut overlong like a riverboat gambler that epitomized the successful image as he saw it about 1905 had now become his real image of success. The flattery of the press, with their "Shakespeare of the Screen," a step up from the use of Belasco in the same phrase, had had its effect. The sharp theatrical figure of 1905 with the humble country-boy manner had become Griffith in actuality. The poses of the publicity photographs were frozen into off-camera attitudes. Only with the Gishes and others of his old colleagues, and when he was working did this pose fall away. Griffith teetered on the brink of a massive self-delusion. He now believed that he could accomplish anything with film. Any story that he put his mind to, no matter how frivolous or derivative, would be a success through his efforts. For a time this feeling was reinforced. He did indeed achieve success from materials that others would have rejected, but in this success were the seeds of eventual failure.

Griffith designated his attorney, Banzhaf, to represent him on the board of United Artists. Banzhaf was unfortunately not the man to cope with the changes in the film industry or with the clever business dealings of the Abramses and the Shulbergs. He was not even in the same league, for all his legal training, with Mary Pickford. Mary handled her own affairs with brilliance that at times might have made her seem the logical successor to Hetty Green, the incredible female stock investor sometimes called "the Witch of Wall Street." Chaplin relied on the cockney shrewdness of his brother Sydney. Chaplin later gave his brother credit for the basic idea of United Artists, and for convincing him that certain proposed film company mergers would freeze out the artists and lower their salaries. Sydney had hired a young lady as a "researcher," charged with picking up a film executive in the Alexandria Hotel and pumping him for details of the rumored mergers. It would seem likely that the young lady earned her pay with a highly exaggerated report, but it was enough to convince Chaplin, Fairbanks, Pickford, and even Griffith that they should protect themselves by forming their own company.

The signatory meeting in February, previously mentioned, took place at Mary Pickford's house. Chaplin later described how each of the principals turned up with a lawyer and a manager:

> It was such a large gathering that what we had to say was like public oratory. In fact, every time I spoke it made me quite nervous. But I was astonished at the business acumen of Mary. She knew all the nomenclature: the amortizations and the deferred stocks, etc.

Chaplin also remembered: "On these occasions she saddened me more than amazed me, for this was an aspect of 'America's sweetheart' that I did not know." [145]

In January and February Griffith filmed *The Girl Who Stayed at Home,* in which more scraps of war footage could be used, as well as the footage shot in the House of Representatives the previous August. The government cooperated in allowing Griffith to use the latter footage apparently in a desire to popularize a selective draft amendment that had been debated during Griffith's filming session. The war was over, however, and Griffith wisely decided not to mention any government connection with the film. The change in the climate from war to peace was reinforced by Griffith, who could now include the character of a "good" German in the film. In casting the picture Griffith gave young Carol Dempster her first starring role opposite another newcomer, Richard Barthelmess. The real star of the picture was that young "old pro" Bobby Harron who played an unpleasant young cad reformed and matured by his army experience. It was ironic that Harron, who was kept in one uniformed role after another by Griffith, actually was exempted from the draft on Griffith's special appeal as being essential to the making of official war films.

Griffith couldn't resist one small touch of the old Confederacy. He cast his old colleague Adolph Lestina as an aged expatriate Confederate living in France and insisting on flying the stars and bars over his home. Lestina finally reacts to the war and the participation by the United States by hauling down the Confederate flag and running up the stars and stripes.

The Girl Who Stayed at Home was premiered at the Strand Theatre on March 23, 1919. It is interesting to note that *The New York Times* reviewer was struck, not by Carol Dempster's performance, a wooden one at best, but by that of Clarine Seymour:

Lillian Gish is missed, but Clarine Seymour, who takes the part she probably would have had, is never deficient.

. . . all the others do everything that could have been required of them.

The review also called attention to the use of selected focus, probably the result of using a long lens:

. . . in some way, which has not yet become general, he dramatically emphasizes the central figures of a scene by throwing all the other objects so out of focus that they remain to provide suitable background and environment for the action without competing with it for the interest of the spectators. This is an artistic development of the close-up. In certain scenes it has all of the psychological effect of the close-up and something else. It makes the action more eloquent by keeping it in its environment, it preserves the continuity of the story, and it adds smoothness and beauty to the picture as a whole. And when Griffith does make a close-up, it is a soft, delicately shaded portrait.[146]

Griffith was continuing to be receptive to experiments, drawing on the skills and suggestions of his crew, winnowing them, and then making use of those that had the greatest effectiveness. He had been the first to permit use of the newly developed "sun" arcs when making *Hearts of the World*. Now he was allowing the extension of Sartov's soft focus work in close-ups into larger compositions.

One irritant noted in this film was the sometimes redundant titling:

Why does Mr. Griffith, who can make such eloquent, intelligible pictures, go to such pains to spell everything out? Why, for example, when he has a wounded German soldier utter a cry which everyone knows instantly is an appeal for water, does he insert a subtitle reading "Wasser, Wasser," and then inform the spectators that the words mean "Water, water"? Certainly his text is often unnecessary and frequently mars the artistry of his pictures.[147]

While *The Girl Who Stayed at Home* was being edited, Griffith had begun work on his next film, this time with Lillian Gish, *True Heart Susie*. Keeping all the balls in the air like a circus juggler, Griffith had even begun work, between *The Greatest Thing in Life* and *The Girl Who Stayed at Home,* on a film based on Thomas Burke's *Limehouse Nights.* The film was to be called *Broken Blossoms.* The principal players were Lillian Gish, Richard Barthelmess, and Donald Crisp. The subject had a special appeal to Griffith, and, shortly after starting it, he stopped and withdrew it from the Artcraft schedule. His reasoning seems to have been that this picture should be made as one of his special films. Richard Barthelmess was switched, as already noted, into *The Girl Who Stayed at Home.*

True Heart Susie was completely a Lillian Gish film set in the Griffith-remembered countryside, a pastiche of his own past. Some have wondered how Griffith managed to have so many projects going at the same time, but it was his ability to produce films that could be easily done while he was planning his more difficult projects. He didn't need research for *True Heart Susie.* He was his own encyclopedia of rural America. As a result, this film rises above some of the "cute" antics given to the actors. Both Clarine Seymour and Carol Dempster were given small, generally insignificant roles.

True Heart Susie was quickly edited and scored and opened in New York at the Strand on June 1, 1919. The picture was solidly praised:

> Once more, D. W. Griffith, ably assisted by Lillian Gish, Robert Harron, and Clarine Seymour, G. W. Bitzer as photographer, and others, has brought meaningful humanity to the screen, more nearly pure, than it has been in a motion picture play, except in other works of Griffith, with the best of which, considering its pretensions, it holds its own.[148]

True Heart Susie contained one important ingredient besides Griffith's knowledge of country customs and people, and that was affection. Griffith always remained the country boy, and his returns to Kentucky were expeditions of renewal. That warmth and love shine through the film. A chief criticism of most of Griffith's work is that he was guilty of excessive sentimentality. What was sentimental in this and other films for others, was love and unconscious nostalgia for Griffith.

Griffith had temporarily turned aside from *Broken Blossoms* because he was having difficulty capturing the right atmosphere for the picture. With his own experience in London guiding him, he had a firm idea of what he wanted. He found his answer in some watercolor designs by an English artist, George Baker. Sets were not built directly from Baker's designs, but rather were used to set the mood and spirit of the picture. This was the first time that Griffith had worked with an artist who might be called a designer in any real sense.

The nature of the story itself, dealing, as it does, with the tragic romance between a boy and girl of different races, presented another problem. Some of those around Griffith warned him that the public was not ready for a story with even a hint of miscegenation. Karl Brown noted:

> This is the picture for which dire trouble was expected. The theorists found everything wrong with it. Mixed races—tragedy —murder and unrelieved death—and of all things, a Chinese lover.
>
> If Griffith ever had sound reasoning to back his judgement, *Blossoms* had the advantage of that reasoning. Hardly any element in that picture had not been done successfully by Griffith before. Yet he was the only one not to be surprised when it went out and cleaned up—beautifully.[149]

Billy Bitzer was still Griffith's principal cameraman, but with Griffith's desire to capture the quality of Baker's watercolors, he gave Henrik Sartov a larger role in working out variants of his soft focus effects. The experiments first tried in *The Girl Who Stayed at Home* were about to pay off. Great care was taken to produce effects exactly as Griffith wanted them. Several weeks were spent in painting and re-painting the sets to capture colors that would photograph in the right way. Almost the entire studio electrical department was turned out to solve the problems of getting the special effect of London fog, and the shadow effects in the prologue and epilogue required five cameras set at different angles to satisfy the director's requirements. *Broken Blossoms,* frequently described as a simple picture, managed to cost more money to produce than Griffith had spent on *The Birth of a Nation.*

The story for *Broken Blossoms* had been called to Griffith's attention by Mary Pickford and Douglas Fairbanks. He had immediately pictured it as a vehicle for Lillian Gish. Lillian's reaction to the idea was quite different. She was a big girl now and no longer saw herself playing what seemed to be a child's part. She told Griffith, quite positively, that she was not interested. She did say that she would be willing to coach any little girl in the role that Griffith might eventually select.

Griffith was not ready to admit defeat. He then employed all his arts of persuasion on Lillian. He pointed out that the closing scenes of the film would demand all the art that an experienced, talented actress could muster. No inexperienced child, even with superb coaching, could play those moments. Without further argument Lillian marched off to the wardrobe department to see about a costume. She was probably still not entirely convinced, although the appeal to her own vanity and her desire to please Griffith eventually overcame her doubts.

In the wardrobe department Lillian discovered something more vital than a costume. Mrs. Jones, the wardrobe mistress, noticed that Lillian looked pale and feverish. They were the first symptoms of influenza. Lillian was a victim of the flu epidemic that was plaguing the country. Before the illness broke, Lillian's temperature went up to 106. Despite her frail appearance, Lillian Gish was, and is, constitutionally strong. Others were not so fortunate in that great epidemic. Of the thousands of deaths across the country, Artcraft studios contributed five, including Bobby Harron's sister Tessie.

To play opposite Lillian, Griffith hired a young actor, Richard Barthelmess, from New York. Barthelmess was working in a picture with Marguerite Clark on location outside New York when Griffith's telegram offering the role arrived. Obviously another factor in the postponement of *Broken Blossoms* was Lillian's illness. It was Lillian's flu that also gave Carol Dempster her first real part. Barthelmess remembered that Griffith directed *The Girl* while wearing a gauze mask over his mouth and nose. Barthelmess's first impressions of Griffith were of his appearance, so much at variance with the pseudo-theatricality affected by other directors.

> Griffith habitually wore a business suit with a high starched collar and often high-buttoned shoes, and a slouch fedora hat. The dress was as characteristic of him as the riding breeches were with C. B. De Mille. If the weather was really hot, he

might replace the fedora with a farmer's straw hat, with a hole poked in it for ventilation. And later when we were making *Way Down East,* in the ice and snow, he changed his attire only by wearing laced waterproof boots. No matter where the location or the weather conditions, "The Master" looked more the banker than the popular conception of the movie director.[150]

Each member of the Griffith company had a favorite memory of some small Griffith eccentricity. Karl Brown remembered Griffith's strangely stage-British cry to Andre Beranger, "Ber-an-gah, get me thermos flahsk!" Barthelmess's memory was of a Griffith perpetually out of cigarettes. Griffith would put out his hand at intervals, assured that some assistant would put a cigarette in his hand and light it for him. Barthelmess also recalled that Griffith would take the company, after shooting had been finished, to an evening of dancing at the Alexandria Hotel. Griffith loved to dance, and loved to have the young ladies of the company show him the latest steps. Most eager of these young instructresses was the ambitious Carol Dempster.

Griffith had begun some rehearsals for *Broken Blossoms* before Barthelmess was hired. He used the character actor George Fawcett to rehearse the role of the young Chinese boy. Griffith was at a loss for the right actor to play the role. He had rejected Bobby Harron, who might have seemed the obvious selection, and it was Rose Smith, the cutter, who first told him about young Barthelmess. When Barthelmess arrived in California, he observed Fawcett rehearsing the role before he had the opportunity to step into it. Barthelmess was always quite candid in admitting that he copied the manners and style developed by the experienced George Fawcett in the rehearsals.

As part of the preparation for the film, Griffith escorted Barthelmess several times to Chinatown in Los Angeles, where they made visits to temples, restaurants, and shops. Griffith was encouraging Barthelmess to follow his very pragmatic method of acting. He was determined that Barthelmess would gain the right mannerisms, as well as feeling, for the role. Barthelmess later noted: "I absorbed a lot of Chinese atmosphere and ever since that day I have been a firm believer in this method of getting to know what to put in a characterization."

The rehearsal period was an extensive one, about six weeks. When the shooting began on the film only eighteen days were required. Barthelmess found that, ". . . the whole experience was a most pleasant one. Griffith was a hard taskmaster inasmuch as he would not be too kind in his criticism of his artists, in order to bring out an emotional quality which was necessary to a scene." [151]

Barthelmess was not present when the climactic scene was filmed in which Lillian Gish was trapped, terrified, in a closet. When the rushes were first viewed, the gossip around the studio was to the effect that Lillian's magnificent performance came as a result of Griffith's goading. Lillian's story is that she merely gave a completely unrestrained performance, and she remembered that if anyone was frightened it was Griffith himself. When the scene was finished he said, "My God, why didn't you warn me that you were going to do that?"

The third principal member of the cast for *Broken Blossoms* was Donald Crisp. Crisp had played the vignette role of General Grant in *The Birth of a Nation*. He had become a Griffith actor during Griffith's last months at Biograph. Crisp was also an ambitious, hardworking directorial aspirant. While rehearsing in *Broken Blossoms* for Griffith, he was directing a film for Famous Players-Lasky. When Griffith began the actual shooting, Crisp was still not available during the day, and his scenes had to be shot at night or on Sunday.

Griffith was no longer the free agent, able, for instance, to withhold *Broken Blossoms* from Artcraft. Now he had to go directly to Zukor. Luck was on Griffith's side. Lillian Gish reported Zukor's reaction: "You bring me a picture like this and want money for it? You may as well put your hand in my pocket and steal it. Everybody in it dies. It isn't commercial." [152]

This was probably one of the few times that Zukor's commercial intuition ever failed him. Griffith had to raise $250,000 to buy *Broken Blossoms* back and hold it for United Artists release. The magnitude of Zukor's mistake in letting this film go is shown by the fact that by 1934 the film had earned a profit of over $700,000 despite the high payment to Zukor. The actual cost of filming the picture was only slightly more than $88,000, so Adolph Zukor had made a small profit on the transaction.

Broken Blossoms opened at the George M. Cohan Theatre in New York on May 13, 1919. The musical theme for the picture had been composed by Griffith himself. He had whistled the theme for Louis F. Gottschalk. Gottschalk had then written it down. A recent playing of the song from a sheet music copy in the collection of the Americana section of the Music Division of the New York Public Library showed that Griffith's idea of music had more of old Kentucky in it than either of London or China.

For the opening the usual live prologue was planned, once again to be danced by Carol Dempster. Griffith decided to film the prologue. When *Broken Blossoms* was first screened before the opening, the colored stage lights for the prologue were left up. The colored tints were quite startling over the black and white film. As Griffith had done so many times during his career, he recognized a valuable innovation. The film was sent out to a laboratory, and selected sections were dyed in various soft colors.

On the opening night the conclusion of the film was followed by silence, no applause. Lillian Gish, Richard Barthelmess, and others hurried backstage to see and congratulate Griffith on a film that had so moved the audience that they were stunned out of any visible reaction. As they arrived backstage they were witnesses to an astonishing sight. Morris Gest, the one-time distributor of *Hearts of the World,* was throwing and smashing chairs against a wall. At first they thought that Gest was demonstrating against the picture, but it turned out that this was merely his idiosyncratic way of showing his wild enthusiasm and approval. Gest announced that the price of admittance to this film should not be $3 but $300.

The film was a resounding critical success. *Film Daily* reported: "This film is a poetic tragedy given a masterly production; it is a masterpiece of its kind, and it offers a chance to see if the public will accept a tragic ending." [153]

The New York *Call* reported: "He [Griffith] has far exceeded the power of the written word." [154]

During the trip to New York to open *Broken Blossoms,* Griffith had decided to take the next step in his quest for independence. He resented deeply having to pay such a large sum over cost to keep the rights to what he felt was his picture. He was more determined than ever that the only kind of front office he wanted to work for was his own. He wanted no more Marvins, Kennedys, Aitkens, or Zukors controlling him. While in New York he made arrangements to purchase a large estate on Orienta Point, a peninsula jutting out into Long Island Sound near Mamaroneck, New York. It was Griffith's intention to convert this estate into his own studio. Griffith's reasons for establishing his own studio in New York rather than California were probably at least two-fold. He wanted to get away from the burgeoning business atmosphere of California, and New York was a return to his beginnings. Why not start over for himself near where it had all begun?

12

Independence:
Griffith's Own Studio, Mamaroneck

The future of the picture is a topic that usually makes me go into ecstasies. The big things it is possible for a picture to do make one feel at a loss for words. Just think what could be done with a picture if it came into the hands of a great political party with a big issue like that of slavery before the voters. Think of the big stories that are yet to be filmed, the history of the world yet to be told in pictures for future centuries. And all of these things are not so far in the future as you may imagine.[155]

Griffith returned to California in June, making a few promotional stops along the way. One of these was at the Methodist Centenary Pageant in Columbus, Ohio. Griffith announced to the gathering that he would make a film of the pageant for special distribution among Methodist churches. The film would be dedicated to the memory of his mother. He also advised the church delegates to use film as a tool in advancing church work. The impression given by Griffith was that he would somehow personally develop a film from the material of the pageant, but the actuality consisted of having a film crew merely record the pageant in a newsreel fashion. The film, called *The World at Columbus,* was dedicated to Mary Griffith, but in no sense was it directed by Griffith.

At last back at the studio in California, Griffith had little time in which to bask in the encomiums coming his way from *Broken Blossoms.* The picture was evoking flights of fancy from the critics:

It is a strange combination of delicacy and brutality, of blooming flowers and sudden death, of the light and shade of life. Its terrific strength and profound emotion is quite the most startling New York has seen on the screen in years and establishes a new high record for David Griffith.[156]

Griffith's contractual obligations had not disappeared, and he had to begin a new film. As almost a form of release from the tensions of his preceding film, he chose a Western story, the first since his days at Biograph. The story was loosely based on the tales of Joaquin Murietta, the bandit scourge of the California goldfields who had assumed the outlines of a Western Robin Hood. Richard Barthelmess was cast as a romantic Murietta, called Alvarez. Carol Dempster was given the role of the heroine Lady Fair, the name being some indication of the usual insipidness of such roles, and Clarine Seymour was cast as Chiquita, a Mexican dance-hall girl, a far better role than Carol's. The company was taken on location to Tolumne County, California, during July. The film, from a scenario by Stanner Taylor, was called *Scarlet Days.* Taylor had outlined the plot for a Western to Griffith, setting the locale in Arizona in 1875. It was Griffith who then decided that it would be more interesting if they changed the locale to California in 1849, and gave the hero some of the characteristics of the legendary Murietta, perhaps using a few of his alleged exploits in the film.

Griffith had not automatically decided on using Barthelmess in *Scarlet Days.* Despite his success in *Broken Blossoms,* he didn't seem to have the open bravura of a Western hero. The other possibility was Rudolph Valentino, but Griffith decided that Valnetino's Italianate face would not have the romantic appeal for audiences that this character needed. This error in casting judgment might seem a small one, except that it was symptomatic of the way in which Griffith's personal audience analysis had begun to diverge from popular taste of the coming decade. Valentino was rejected, and, reluctantly, Barthelmess was given the role of Alvarez, the celluloid Murietta.

Scarlet Days was the last film under Griffith's contract with Artcraft. He assured Zukor that it would be a "big drama with lots of comedy, real scenery, big action." It was well received by the trade press. Unfortunately no prints are known to exist today.[157] Zukor was satisfied, and, with the exception of the Dorothy Gish comedy series, Griffith was free of his Artcraft contract. The making of the Dorothy Gish comedies were in the hands of other directors, so Griffith could turn his attention to the three films due under the contract with First National.

Griffith had sent his brother Albert back to the East to supervise the changing of the old Flagler estate outside Mamaroneck, New York, into a studio. This involved not only renovation of the existing estate, but also the erection of several new buildings. In California Griffith began work on *The Greatest Question,* a film that Griffith himself regarded as a potboiler. In order to work quickly, he made use of those old professionals, Lillian Gish and Bobby Harron, along with Josephine Crowell, Ralph Graves, George Fawcett, and George Nicholls.

It has seemed surprising to people since that Griffith allowed his name to be used in connection with these First National films, in view of the fact that he had so jealously kept his name from association with lesser films, denying his supervision of Triangle movies. The reason, of course, that Griffith had to put his name to these films was that his First National contract specified that his name be used, at least for promotional purposes. In fact it was not really necessary that Griffith direct these films, merely that his name should appear as the director in publicity and in the film credits.

Since Griffith saw these films as merely a quick way to raise the money for his projected independence in Mamaroneck, he was quite willing to walk away from the First National films and to leave the direction in the hands of one of his assistants. He was not worried, however, about the films' failure. After all, the story in *The Greatest Question* was the typical melodrama that he had made in one-reel form so successfully at Biograph. It wasn't much, according to Griffith, but it had sold. Griffith was now confident that anything that he made, particularly if the cost wasn't too high, would sell. The failure of *Intolerance* was a fluke. Griffith really refused to believe that it was a failure.

On September 5, 1919, Griffith informed the administrators of First National that it would be necessary to put the final touches on *The Greatest Question* in the East. Griffith was eager to get back to the East Coast and supervise the construction at Mamaroneck himself. There was no real need to shoot any footage in the New York area, but it was a wonderful way to put the transportation expenses of the company on the budget for a film that belonged to someone else. Griffith still retained the sharp eye of the itinerant stock actor for ways to get every nickel from an expense account. He never lost sight of the pennies, just the dollars. The company arrived in New York in October. Griffith took the company into the old Thanhauser studio in New Rochelle, New York, to finish some interior shots for *The Greatest Question* and to do the final editing on *Scarlet Days*. He would have liked to go directly into Mamaroneck, but it wasn't finished.

The last two films projected under the First National contract were also prepared in part, and certainly planned, in the rented New Rochelle studio. These were two tales of the South Pacific, *The Idol Dancer* and *The Love Flower*. Always the improviser, and fed up with the narrow confines of the New Rochelle studio after the final editing of *The Greatest Question* in November, and feeling the nip in the air that presaged a cold winter, Griffith chose these stories with the view to moving himself and the company into a warmer climate. He didn't want to go back to California, so that meant he would have to go to Florida. On November 17, the Griffith company entrained for Fort Lauderdale to begin shooting the exteriors for *The Idol Dancer*.

Richard Barthelmess, playing the leading role in *The Idol Dancer,* described the Fort Lauderdale of 1919: "Fort Lauderdale in those days had not been built into the lovely resort city, which it now is, and consisted largely of swamps and coconut groves resembling the South Sea Islands." [158]

In this Florida jaunt Griffith took, as his principal acting company, Barthelmess, Carol Dempster, Clarine Seymour, as well as some of the character people, Kate Bruce, Creighton Hale, and George MacQuarrie. Lillian Gish was left behind. She was given the opportunity to direct one of her sister's comedy films, together with a vague request to keep an eye on the building at Mamaroneck.

When the exterior shooting in Fort Lauderdale was completed by the first week in December, Griffith decided that it would be pleasant to take a side trip to Nassau in the Bahamas. On December 10 Griffith set out for Nassau on a yacht called *The Grey Duck,* along with the mayor of Fort Lauderdale and members of the mayor's staff, for the normally twelve-hour trip. A sudden and unexpected storm forced *The Grey Duck* to put into a safe harbor at Whale Key. The members of the *Grey Duck* party were out of communication with the world for three days.

When the normal twelve hours had passed for the arrival of

The Grey Duck, and more hours for good measure, it was feared that Griffith and his party were lost at sea in the storm. McAdoo persuaded the navy to launch an intensive search. They were finally found at Whale Key. There was considerable speculation that the entire episode was a publicity stunt, a device to publicize Griffith's new films. That this incident was not a publicity stunt was emphatically stated by Richard Barthelmess in 1944 while he was serving as an officer in the U.S. Navy. Barthelmess wrote:

> In passing, I want to make sure that no injustice is done to him [Griffith] and, for this reason, I make particular mention of the fact that the *Grey Duck* episode was not a publicity stunt. I was in Miami at the time and was personally aboard one of the rescue vessels which was sent out to find him—a 110 foot ex-submarine chaser from the last war, named *The Berry Islands.* The storm was so severe that once having started, the Captain could not stay out in the storm and made straight for Nassau. The storm was of near hurricane intensity.[159]

Once found, Griffith and his party were safely escorted to Nassau, where Barthelmess and his mother joined them, and all the group then took another ship in safer weather.

Back in Mamaroneck in the unfinished studios, Lillian Gish was directing her first film. She found herself frequently at odds with Huck Wortman, and dangerously close to going over the $50,000 budget for her film *Remodeling Her Husband.* Miss Gish thinks now that her difficulties with Wortman were caused, perhaps, by his nerves, shattered in the war. She has forgotten that Wortman's only war was the invasion of Babylon near Hollywood and Vine. Unfortunately Wortman has left no comments on Miss Gish's nerves, but it is likely that the master carpenter thought that he was in charge of finishing the studio. His faith in Miss Gish's ability to understand and oversee construction was also shaken when she gave him the wrong dimensions for the main set of *Remodeling Her Husband* so that no room was left for the camera! Wortman undoubtedly breathed a sigh of relief when cold weather, coupled with a complete lack of heat in Mamaroneck, forced Lillian and her company to retreat back to the Thanhauser studio in New Rochelle to finish her film.

Griffith was still in Florida when *The Greatest Question* opened at the Strand Theatre in New York on December 28, 1919. The comment from *Film Daily* was rather strange as well as unfavorable, "It contains too much horror." *The New York Times* thought that Griffith failed to answer "the greatest question."

> Mr. Griffith has apparently been dipping into psychical research, but only dipping timidly. He does not face the question squarely and answer it clearly one way or the other. The subject of survival [after death] comes into his story only twice briefly and each time in such a way as to leave the question answered. Once a youth appears to his mother at the moment of his death far away, and subsequently the dead boy stands before her and his father when she appeals to him for a sign of his continued existence. The woman and her husband are convinced, but the first case might be explained as telepathy or coincidence and the second appearance might have been a hallucination. Neither is real evidence of survival. The photoplay should have testified boldly to the fact of survival, denied it unqualifiedly, or admitted its uncertainty. As it stands, it ought to satisfy both those who want to believe in survival, and those who don't, but it contributes nothing to the solution of "the greatest question."
>
> The story of the photoplay is relatively unimportant, as Mr. Griffith, no doubt, meant it to be.[160]

Griffith returned with his company from Florida in January and finished *The Idol Dancer* and *The Love Flower* at his new Mamaroneck studios. Both films made use of the same pseudo-South Seas setting, the Fort Lauderdale-Miami coconut palms, and some shots at Nassau. *The Idol Dancer,* originally titled *Rainbow Isle,* gave vivacious Clarine Seymour her first starring role. Griffith didn't care much for the end results in this film, but he thought well enough of Miss Seymour's promise to tentatively cast her in a major role in *Way Down East* scheduled to be shot that winter. Unfortunately, Clarine, cast as Kate Brewster, died during emergency surgery just after Griffith began filming *Way Down East.* Mary Hay was the replacement in the part.

The Idol Dancer went to First National as the second picture under Griffith's three-film contract with them. The film was as weak as anything Griffith had ever turned out. Said *The New York Times:*

As the story progresses the religion of a white missionary and his nephew triumphs over the hostile spirits of a derelict beachcomber [Barthelmess] and an untamed girl of mixed and romantic ancestry. But the beachcomber throws his bottle of gin into the ocean and the girl casts her idol away. Also she consents to wear clothes, and it may be imagined, will go shopping on Fifth Avenue within a few months. All of which may indicate that, to the mind of one at least, "The Idol Dancer" is not convincing.[161]

The Idol Dancer had opened at the Strand on March 21. *The Love Flower,* the second South Sea romance, was scheduled as the third First National picture, and due to open on May 15, 1920. After a preview on April 2, Griffith was convinced that this was a much better film than the first. With some additional close-ups of Carol Dempster, it merited treatment as a major film to be released through his United Artists partnership. The preview had been given for a meeting of the American Newspaper Publishers Association. Griffith liked the assembled gentlemen's masculine reaction to the filmed Carol Dempster. After the preview Griffith made arrangements to buy the film back from First National. The added scenes, of Carol Dempster diving, did little to improve the film. The opening of the film, then released through United Artists, was postponed until August 22, 1920, again at the Strand Theatre. Some of the reviews of *The Love Flower* began to measure Griffith's direction against his past achievements. The comparisons could only be increasingly unfavorable. *The New York Times* said:

> Whenever a director sets out deliberately to use motion pictures for a certain purpose, it requires much subtlety and restraint on his part if his purpose is not to obtrude from his story and defeat its own ends by becoming detached from the realities and congruities of life which must be present, if at all, in the story and its people. This is the danger to which Mr. Griffith is especially exposed, for, though he has gone beyond other directors in many departments of motion picture work, he has not shown marked evidence of subtlety and restraint.
> . . . If "The Love Flower" had been produced by any of a hundred inconspicuous directors, the chances are that it would be universally judged a "pretty good melodrama," but coming from Mr. Griffith, from whom the public has been encouraged

to expect something exceptional, its shortcomings are not easily overlooked.[162]

Griffith's new heroine, Carol Dempster, didn't fare well, being called "merely sugary and kittenish." Barthelmess "had his scenes of genuineness and obvious acting."

Griffith was really thinking little about the critical, or even box office, reception of *The Idol Dancer* and *The Love Flower*. They had been produced to place their advance money in the Griffith till, from whence it could be spent on the studio in Mamaroneck. It is seldom noted in film histories that the completion and release of a film does not put money into a company's coffers for a considerable time, even when the film is a big hit. The spending of money on production, however, does take place within a short span. Griffith's resources were drained rapidly soon after he purchased and rebuilt the Mamaroneck property. Capital was also invested in the production of films which had not as yet brought in any significant returns. As time was to prove, only *Broken Blossoms,* alone, of all the Griffith films between *The Birth of a Nation* and *Way Down East*—the film that Griffith was working on as *The Idol Dancer* and *The Love Flower* were opened—managed to return a profit. Some profits were being realized on the Dorothy Gish comedy series, and Griffith was the recipient of advance payments on the films for First National, but he was using every cent for the new studio and for the first of his independent productions, *Way Down East*. In addition, both *Broken Blossoms* and *The Love Flower,* the rights to which he had bought back from their distributors, were mortgaged in the quest for more operating capital. An Aitken or a Zukor might have easily perceived impending financial disaster, but Griffith was only concerned with the production of his next film. Increasingly he relied on his brother Albert and his attorney Banzhaf to oversee the business side of his efforts. He had employed "Little" Epping, but no one paid any more attention to Epping now than they had when he was Aitken's accountant. Epping, however, was astute enough to provide for his own personal future by saving his money and not investing in films.

Another reason why Griffith had no real concern for the business of film production and distribution was that his experience told

Griffith conferring with Frank Woods with Billy Bitzer looking on.

A publicity shot of Griffith directing Henry Walthall. Bitzer pretends to operate the camera.

Griffith's camera crew for *The Sorrows of Satan* (1926).

G. W. "Billy" Bitzer in a self-portrait presented to Charles Predmore, the Cuddlebackville innkeeper.

Candid picture of Billy Bitzer in his office at the Museum of Modern Art by Arthur Kleinert (circa 1940).

The D. W. Griffith, Inc. studio at Orient Point in Mamaroneck, New York.

Griffith checks the sound during the filming of *The Struggle* (1931).

The camera mounted on a suspended platform above the falls to film the climax of *Way Down East* (1920).

Griffith poses with the actors in a scene from *Way Down East*.

An interior set for *The Sorrows of Satan* (1926). Adolphe Menjou (standing) and Ricardo Cortez at the left (seated).

Griffith directing W. C. Fields in an exterior scene for *That Royle Girl* (1926). The blurred figure is busy assistant director Frank Walsh. At the left is Field's stooge and aide-de-camp, known only as "Shorty."

Griffith directing a love scene between Walter Huston (Abe Lincoln) and Una Merkel (Ann Rutledge), *Abraham Lincoln* (1930).

Griffith with Cecil B. De Mille (left) and Mack Sennett (right).

Above, Erich Von Stroheim, who began his career as a Griffith assistant. Below left, W. S. Van Dyke, the director of *The Thin Man* and other films, who began as a Griffith assistant. Below right, Raoul Walsh. a Griffith actor and assistant who became a major director.

The signing of the agreement forming United Artists. Griffith, Mary Pickford, Charlie Chaplin, and Douglas Fairbanks in the foreground. In the rear are attorneys Albert Banzhaf and Denis O'Brien.

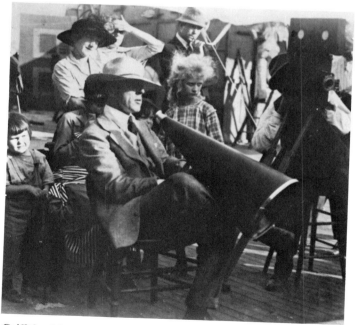

Griffith with megaphone.

The United Artist principals, Fairbanks, Griffith, Pickford, and Chaplin.

Griffith witnessing, with Merle Oberon, the presentation of an acting award to Bette Davis by Douglas Churchill in January 1940.

Lillian Gish wanders out onto the treacherous river ice in *Way Down East* (1920).

Later Feature Films, 1920-31

Richard Barthelmess completes the rescue of Lillian Gish from the river, *Way Down East*.

The French Revolution swirls through Paris, *Orphans of the Storm* (1921).

Griffith, in straw boater, sets up the guillotine scene for the climax of *Orphans of the Storm*. This is the same set as the revolution scene with the fountain removed.

Monte Blue as Danton stirs the crowd, *Orphans of the Storm*.

Danton leads the "ride to the rescue," *Orphans of the Storm*.

Lillian Gish comforts her "blind" sister Dorothy, *Orphans of the Storm.*

Joseph Schildkraut and Lillian Gish, *Orphans of the Storm.*

Arthur Dewey as George Washington, *America* (1924).

Arthur Donaldson as King George III, *America*.

Neil Hamilton as Nathan Holden, *America*.

Lionel Barrymore as the villain Captain Butler, *America*.

King George and his court, *America*.

Nathan Holden receives his charge, *America*.

Paul Revere gives warning of the British approach, *America*.

The battle of Concord, *America*.

The British advance, *America*.

George Washington prays at Valley Forge, *America*.

The morning food line faces inflation in post-war Germany, *Isn't Life Wonderful* (1924). Carol Dempster leans out from the end of the line.

W. C. Fields faces the judge in *Sally of the Sawdust* (1925).

Adolphe Menjou and Ricardo Cortez, *The Sorrows of Satan.*

Satan and his evil angels cast out of heaven, in the Norman Bel Geddes setting for *The Sorrows of Satan* (1926).

Lupe Velez in *Lady of the Pavements* (1929).

Walter Huston as the young Lincoln, *Abraham Lincoln* (1930).

Walter Huston as
President Lincoln,
Abraham Lincoln.

Walter Huston and Una Merkel as Lincoln and Ann Rutledge, *Abraham Lincoln*.

Young Lincoln fights for the right, *Abraham Lincoln*.

The Union Army advances, *Abraham Lincoln.*

Hobart Bosworth as General Lee, *Abraham Lincoln.*

The signing of the Emancipation Proclamation, *Abraham Lincoln.*

Lincoln confers with Generals Grant and Sheridan. Fred Warren as Grant and Frank Campeau as Sheridan, *Abraham Lincoln.*

The Lincoln family in the White House. Gordon Thorpe as Tad Lincoln and Kay Hammond as Mary Todd Lincoln, *Abraham Lincoln*.

The assassination at Ford's Theatre. Walter Huston as Lincoln, Kay Hammond as Mary Lincoln, and Ian Keith as John Wilkes Booth, *Abraham Lincoln*.

Zita Johann and Hal Skelly, *The Struggle* (1931).

Hal Skelly, Zita Johann, and Evelyn Baldwin face the first crack in the family prosperity, *The Struggle*.

Hal Skelly as "the life of the party" starts down the road to alcoholism, *The Struggle*.

A drunken Skelly arrives late at a sedate party, *The Struggle*.

Hal Skelly, Zita Johann, and Evelyn Baldwin, *The Struggle*.

Hal Skelly and Zita Johann, *The Struggle*.

Hal Skelly in an alcoholic frenzy breaks in on his mistress, *The Struggle*.

Hal Skelly, *The Struggle*.

The drunkard faces his little daughter, *The Struggle*.

Final redemption, *The Struggle*.

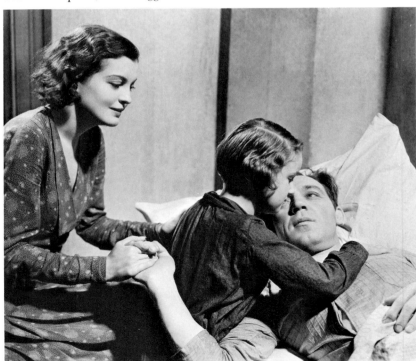

him that one good hit film would wipe out all past financial failures. Like the proverbial horseplayer, Griffith knew that just one big "score" would be enough to put him on "easy street." Subsequent history has now shown that movie companies, like horseplayers, die broke. Griffith was to have one more big "score," the film he began in the summer of 1920, *Way Down East*. It would finish its primary showings with profits second only to those of *The Birth of a Nation*.

Lottie Blair Parker's melodrama *Way Down East* was noted in 1911 by critic Montrose J. Moses as a "standardized" play that had become one of the staples of stock companies throughout the country and was "familiar to everyone." Lottie Parker had written the play in 1897 following a brief career as an actress opposite Dion Boucicault among others. All the rights to her play had been purchased by William A. Brady, a specialist in the production of melodramas. The original suggestion that Griffith might acquire the rights and film this old war horse came from Albert Grey, Griffith's brother. Like many of Albert's suggestions, this made little theatrical sense. The era of such plays had passed. But a play from 1897, in fact, a great popular hit, was still fresh to Griffith, who remembered his own stock company barnstorming with affection. William Brady managed to take shrewd advantage of Griffith's sentimental judgment and sell the rights dearly. Griffith paid Brady $175,000 for the film rights to the play, and then another $10,000 to Anthony Paul Kelly to write a scenario. Albert's idea had already cost Griffith $68,000 more than the production costs of *The Birth of a Nation*. Lillian Gish has reported that the members of the Griffith company thought their director had gone quite mad in buying this tired old play. But Griffith's instinct told him that there was still a quality in this story that could reach the public. This time he was right. The public still responded to melodrama, particularly a familiar one.

The cast for *Way Down East*, with Lillian Gish as Anna Moore, the heroine, and Richard Barthelmess as the farm boy, David Bartlett as the man who falls in love with the "fallen angel," and such other Griffith stalwarts as Creighton Hale, Porter Strong, Kate Bruce, and Lowell Sherman, went into rehearsal for ten weeks at the Hotel Claridge in New York in January 1920. Griffith had

taken a suite at the Claridge, across the street from his favorite
hotel, the Astor, in order to be close to rehearsals. It was not quite
so convenient for Lillian Gish because she, her mother, and her sister Dorothy had rented an old house in Mamaroneck in order to
be close to the new studio.

Tragedy plagued the path of the *Way Down East* production. As
previously mentioned, Clarine Seymour, the most promising of the
Griffith newcomers, died shortly after Griffith went into rehearsal.
Clarine was missed. Allison Smith in *Theatre Magazine* had written of her performance in *The Idol Dancer:*

> Claurine [sic] Seymour is featured as the volcanic little hula
> dancer; she is a colorful little creature with provocative eyes and
> movements, and her dance in the third reel shocked all the mis-
> sionaries in the cast and those (if any) in the audience.[163]

Bobby Harron, the one-time Biograph office boy who had become
Griffith's leading juvenile actor, was left out of the cast of *Way
Down East*. Griffith intended to use him in a comedy series much
like that featuring Dorothy Gish. The first of these, *Coincidence,*
directed by Chester Withey, was almost completed by the end of
the summer of 1920. Just before *Way Down East* was to be premiered, Bobby Harron shot himself fatally in his hotel room. The
verdict was that the shooting happened accidentally when Harron
dropped a coat containing a loaded revolver in one pocket. When
the coat hit the floor, the revolver fired, wounding him critically.
He died a few days later. The circumstances surrounding his death
have remained a subject of some controversy, but the principals in
the case have stoutly maintained, despite the oddities of the evidence, that the shooting was accidental. Not the least of their arguments was that Harron, a Roman Catholic, would not have taken
his own life against the teachings of his faith. There was no hint, of
course, of any of the tragedies to come as *Way Down East* was
being filmed. It was enough for Griffith and his acting company to
cope with the rigors of a late winter in New York and Connecticut
while shooting the winter and blizzard scenes on location.

Griffith had no choice except to shoot the blizzard scenes and
the other winter scenes in the midst of the real thing. The studios
of 1920 were not prepared to execute realistically snowstorms, wa-

terfalls, and rapids choked with ice floes inside their walls. If they were called for, it was necessary to don overshoes and heavy coats, light the spirit-warmer to keep the camera working, and film in whatever gale blew their way. This was exactly what Griffith and company had to do. The working conditions were dreadful. A storm descended on Mamaroneck just in time, so that Griffith could film those scenes just outside his studio on Orienta Point. The same location was used later in the spring after the trees had acquired leaves. Additional winter scenes were made in White River Junction, Vermont, and in Farmington, Connecticut.

According to Lillian Gish, only one small part of Anthony Paul Kelly's scenario was actually used in the film. This was a scene in which Lillian is helped out of her coat by a rigidly proper butler while her rich cousin tries to remove Lillian's gloves. The gloves are attached to the coat by elastic and promptly snap back. Miss Gish remembered that Griffith thought the sequence was very funny and well worth the fee to Kelly. Epping, for one, didn't agree that one joke made a $10,000 fee worthwhile.

Among added expenses were a number of insurance policies that Griffith took out. One of the policies was designed to compensate the company if a genuine blizzard didn't materialize in time for filming. Other policies were taken out on the principal players. Each had to be examined by the insurance company doctors. Only Lillian Gish managed to come through with flying colors. Ironically, Clarine Seymour was also examined and only a minor ailment was found, no evidence of the condition that was to demand surgery. Barthelmess had sinus trouble. The insurance brokers were only willing to insure Lillian Gish, the frailest appearing member of the group.

While the company waited for a blizzard, scenes were filmed inside the studio. The snowstorm finally arrived in March. There was no time to lose. The scene in which Lillian Gish staggers through the storm down to the river bank became the subject of furious all-day and all-night filming. The crew, and Griffith, were swathed in overcoats, mufflers, boots, and gloves. A fire had to be kept burning on the ground underneath the camera to keep the camera motor oil from freezing. The faces of the crew were encrusted with frost and ice. The only relief was hot tea, and one stand-up meal around a bonfire. The fire under the camera went out and had to be rekindled with frozen fingers. Lillian Gish fainted and was carried back to the studio on a sled. It seemed for a moment that filming would be finished with the star gone, but after a brief thawing out with more tea, the indomitable Lillian Gish continued. Everyone else had remained outside because they felt that any retreat to the warmth of the studio would cause them to lose the tempo of the scene being filmed.

In his drive to complete a sequence in almost impossible conditions, it must have seemed as though Griffith had turned into a Simon Legree with Lillian Gish as "Little Eva" being pursued across the ice, but actually Griffith was always a kind and polite commander. A young man, Frank Walsh, had come to Mamaroneck while Griffith was in Florida and, on his reputation as a child actor and general assistant for a number of film companies in the New York area, secured a job doing extra work and helping out wherever needed. Griffith used him in several small extra roles in *Way Down East,* including a stint in the barn dance scene, and had him help with make-up and wardrobe. Griffith took a fancy to him and promoted Walsh to his personal "gopher," to *go for* tea, cigarettes, or anything else that was needed. Walsh recalls:

> I did everything I was asked. Then Griffith wanted me for rehearsing. He never worked with a script. He would act himself, going through the general movement of the scene, demonstrating for his actors. Then he would shoot until he got what he wanted. Thirty or forty takes was nothing.[164]

The company took the train to White River Junction for the filming of the actual river scenes. Three weeks were spent in temperatures hovering around zero taking the shots in which the principals would be recognizable, the medium and close shots. After the main company had returned to Mamaroneck, other shots were made with Allan Law doubling as Lillian Gish on the floating ice floes under the direction of Elmer Clifton. Griffith had returned with the actors to recover from a slight injury. He had been hit by flying ice when dynamite was used to break up the solidly frozen river into floes. Leigh Smith, an assistant, sent Griffith a wire to inform him that Elmer Clifton had been forced to substitute himself for Allan Law at the last moment when "Allan Law went yellow."

Clifton had arranged to have some fake ice floes constructed of wood and painted to pass for the real article when the genuine ice became too treacherous as the spring thaw got under way.

Griffith's ego, slightly damaged by the reviews for *The Idol Dancer,* was pleased at Allison Smith's comments in the May 1920 *Theatre Magazine:*

> A new Griffith production always marks a red-letter month on the screen. In "The Idol Dancer" this Dean of all screen directors has produced a vivid picture of the South Sea Islands, which is half-like a painting of Winslow Homer and half-like an evening in the Cocoanut Grove roof garden.

On the same evening that *The Idol Dancer* opened, March 28, the Society of Arts and Sciences paid tribute to *The Birth of a Nation* as a major achievement at a meeting in the Biltmore Hotel in New York.

When Griffith gave his speech to the American Newspaper Publisher's Association on April 21, he continued his attacks on the censorship of motion pictures. In general he found a sympathetic audience. He told the publishers before showing a preview of *The Love Flower* that he was still thinking of calling the film *Black Beach.* He noted that it had been titled *The Gamest Girl* at one point. The publishers liked the final title, *The Love Flower,* the best.

As the preparation of *Way Down East* continued, Griffith's money problems increased. His brother had a suggestion for a way to reduce expenses. He told Griffith that Daniel Frohman, brother of the distinguished stage producer Charles Frohman, lost on the *Lusitania* during the war, and head of the Frohman Amusement Corporation, was interested in obtaining the services of Lillian Gish. Albert argued that if Griffith would persuade Lillian to sign a contract with Frohman, her increasingly higher salary would be saved. Initially Griffith rejected Albert's suggestion. Albert continued and proved very persuasive. Griffith agreed to send for Lillian, but at the last moment he changed his mind about telling her. He said that after all these years, and because Lillian had always meant something very special to him, he just couldn't do it. Albert said that he would talk to Lillian.

Albert Grey felt little sentiment toward Lillian, and certainly

her long association with his brother meant little to him. When
Lillian arrived in response to David's summons, Albert explained,
rather bluntly, that Daniel Frohman wanted her services, and with
the completion of *Way Down East,* Griffith would have no use for
her services for some time. Lillian was shocked, and not a little
hurt, particularly since Griffith was not there to tell her himself.
She had somehow always regarded their association as almost insep-
arable, and now that she had made herself useful to him as a director and in other capacities than merely as an actress, she was at a
loss to understand why her services would not be needed. She assuaged her feelings by choosing to interpret Griffith's motives in
the best possible light, and she finally agreed to accept the Frohman offer. The three-year contract she signed with the Frohman
Amusement Company had a short run. The first film, *World Shadows,* was abandoned in the middle of shooting when the Frohman
Company went bankrupt and collapsed. When Griffith heard this,
his troubled conscience forced him to send for Lillian and to ask
her to come back. He painted a word picture of a production of
Faust, drawn from his stock company experience, that would place
most of the emphasis on Marguerite, played, of course, by Lillian.
Miss Gish was happy to return, but she saw through the sham of the
Faust story, and with the help of Harry Carr, argued against it,
seemingly talking Griffith out of the project. Griffith protested that
it would be the perfect film for her. What he managed to leave un-
said was that there wasn't enough money available to finance such
a film on either the scale he described, or, for that matter, on that
subject. It hadn't hurt Griffith, or cost him a penny, to conjure up
a dream film, and he did feel that it had helped bring Lillian Gish
back, and somehow assuaged his guilt at letting her go. After this
succession of events, the relationship between Lillian and Griffith
had changed. Perhaps neither quite realized that the role of master
and pupil was changed forever. Lillian knew that she had a career
of her own to follow, whether with Griffith or without him, and
she was prepared to follow her own star. As amply evidenced in
her own writings and statements over the years, she has remained
Griffith's most ardent supporter and defender, but the girlish ro-
manticism that had caused her to sit near him when he was working, that gave her pleasure to be in his company whenever he

would permit it, that made her half dream that something more might develop between them, was gone. The final factor producing a change in their relationship was Griffith's evident interest in Carol Dempster.

Griffith's contract with First National expired on June 21. He had completed the contract with two of his own films and one film directed for his company by Chester Withey, *Romance,* starring Doris Keane, made while Griffith worked on *Way Down East.* Griffith was now free to form a new company, and on June 30, D. W. Griffith, Inc. was granted a charter by the state of Maryland. The new corporation was designed to go public with a sale of stock. It was capitalized at $50,000,000 with 500,000 shares of common stock, designated Class A, and 375,000 shares of non-voting Class B stock to be held by Griffith. In effect, however, Griffith would not control the corporation, but would be an employee, and, perhaps, its principal asset. The stock offering was made through Counselman and Company of Chicago and Bertron, Griscom, and Company of New York. The incorporation papers named Griffith as president, Albert Grey as general manager, J. C. Epping as business manager, and Albert H. T. Banzhaf as general counsel. Charles Counselman and Lee Benoit were added to the board of directors as representatives of the underwriters. The initial stock offering of the Class A shares was made on July 13, 1920, at $15 a share.

An advertisement of the offering in *The New York Times* stated that the purpose of the offering was to provide *additional* working capital. In truth, the sale was intended to produce the *only* working capital except for the money that might be raised by mortgaging the negatives of any films that Griffith controlled. The only significant asset, other than the talents of Griffith and the debt-ridden Mamaroneck studio, was the one-fifth interest in United Artists.

That one-fifth interest in United Artists might have been regarded at that moment as a somewhat shaky piece of collateral. Oscar Price had been persuaded by a group that had backing by the Guaranty Trust Company to leave United Artists and form a new company to be known as Associated Producers' -Big 6. Hiram Abrams had then been moved into the United Artists presidency, where he was not only assisted but, to some extent, dominated by dynamic B. P. Shulberg. Abrams resented Shulberg's domination and interference. Shulberg took a short vacation in Europe and on his return discovered that Abrams had decided to go his own way, dismissing Shulberg. Shulberg brought a suit against United Artists in August 1920 for commissions that he alleged were due from the sale of Pickford, Fairbanks, and Chaplin films sold to British exhibitors. One of the results of the trial of this suit was the revelation, when the United Artists books were opened by Judge Lydon, that the formation of United Artists had been formulated by Benjamin Shulberg and not the four artists for whom the company had been named.

The only Griffith film released through United Artists until that August had been *Broken Blossoms*. It was the pressure placed by the other partners in United Artists, unhappy with the limited output of that one member, that forced Griffith to buy back from First National the rights to *The Love Flower* and open it under United Artists' auspices on August 22 at the Strand Theatre. Griffith's third film for United Artists was to be *Way Down East*.

The first preview of *Way Down East* was given in Middletown, New York, on August 23. The trip to Middletown, so close to Cuddebackville, was almost a sentimental journey for Griffith. A second preview was presented in Kingston, New York, on August 23. Griffith was determined to get a grassroots reaction to this film, not that of the increasingly sophisticated film people or New Yorkers. After the usual and almost insatiable Griffith editing touchups, *Way Down East* opened at the 44th Street Theatre in New York on September 3.

Although *The Love Flower* had received only a lukewarm reception, *Film Daily* had noted that it was "a beautiful, poetic story with little action; same class as the last picture [*The Idol Dancer*]." Any concern for Griffith's last pictures was submerged in the success of *Way Down East*. *Film Daily* rhapsodized:

> This is a splendidly treated melodrama rising to the greatest climax ever screened; the comedy strikes a false note. It is the biggest box-office attraction of the times; it is artistic, lasting, powerful. DWG's name and that of Lillian Gish will help to put it over too.[165]

Iris Barry's assessment, made during the Griffith retrospective at the Museum of Modern Art in 1940, differed little from most of the critical judgments made when the film opened.

> The extremely improbable plot creaks loudly . . . yet if most of the characterizations are two-dimensional, they are handled with vigor and skill and the study of Anna is entire and convincing.
> . . . the flight through the storm, the ice scenes, and the split second rescue remain triumphs of direction, camera placement, and editing, in which Griffith again attains, though hardly surpasses, the vitality of *The Birth of a Nation* and *Intolerance*.[166]

Not all of the comments about *Way Down East* at the time of its opening were favorable. *The New York Times* editorialized that Griffith was something of a faker for decrying that the movies were composed of gilded hokum while making a similar bit of hokum himself in *Way Down East*. There was some truth in the *Times* position. As his fame had increased, Griffith's ability to issue pretentious statements to the press kept pace. He told an interviewer for the *Times* in November that his reason for making films in the East was the result of his desire to get *real* settings, and New York was the home of "wealth and brains," whereas Los Angeles had been filmed "to death." Griffith should not be taxed with the sins of his rationalizations and occasional hyperboles. One man's "fakery" in the film business is another's showmanship. The irony of Griffith's personal prestige at that moment was that it was at its peak with the public and the press but counted for less and less with the new business barons of the film industry who were increasingly more concerned with clever mergers, larger distributing combines, and tricky stock maneuvering. To these emerging moguls the film director was just another tradesman to be used, exploited, and if, at any point, he was apparently non-productive, in box office terms, something to be discarded. Griffith, in choosing to assert his independence at Mamaroneck, to go his own way, was like King Canute trying to hold back the ocean. Independence was being merged out, and even a Griffith could not change that. Still, the way that *Way Down East* was beginning to return the largest profits since *The Birth of a Nation* must have seemed to

Griffith an omen of success. He believed he could turn almost any tired, worn-out dramatic vehicle into a success. In this over-confident assessment were the seeds of future disaster.

While basking in the success of *Way Down East,* Griffith was at work on his next film, *Dream Street.* He had returned to some of the same Thomas Burke material from which *Broken Blossoms* had been taken. He combined two of the stories, "The Lamp in the Window" and "Gina of Chinatown," into one scenario, crediting this personal compilation to another fictitious writer, Roy Sinclair. Griffith didn't see *Dream Street* as a sequel to *Broken Blossoms,* but he hoped to capture some of the same poetic magic that had made the earlier film a success. It, too, was to be a filmed poem of the slums, and if symbolic wispiness had worked before, here would be something even wispier, something even more symbolic. The characters were to be maneuvered through their lives by the opposing forces of good and evil, translated into the figures of a street preacher, played by the senior Tyrone Power, and a masked violinist, played by Morgan Wallace.

Other significant events were taking place in the courts. Wark Producing Corporation, the company set up to handle the distribution of *Intolerance,* was declared bankrupt in a petition filed on January 5, 1921, by Griffith, Harry Wolfe, and S. Meyer. Griffith claimed that Wark owed him $10,000. The liabilities of the corporation were set at $300,000, and the assets at $100,000. The court appointed Walter N. Seligsberg as the receiver. Griffith's claim was that he had lent the corporation money in 1919 in return for rights to the *Intolerance* negative and its use, re-cut, for other films. He had, indeed, re-cut the original negative into two separate films, *The Mother and the Law* and *The Fall of Babylon,* and released the separated films as part of a "repertory season" of his own films at the George M. Cohan Theatre in New York. The re-cut films were welcomed in modest terms by the New York press, but the entire re-release had added little cash to the D. W. Griffith, Inc. coffers.

Griffith was now discovering the lessons learned earlier by Harry Aitken, that the process of raising money to keep a film studio afloat was continuous and difficult. Griffith had no real judgment of what made enterprises profitable or not. He allowed himself to become involved with promotional schemes that were flattering to his ego even though on close examination they could have been seen to be unsound.

Griffith was taken in by a group of speculators, organized as the Philadelphia Properties Corporation, who purchased a site in Philadelphia on which they proposed to erect a giant motion picture palace to be called the David Wark Griffith Theatre. Griffith was persuaded to take a lease on the property and to be the principal in the erection of the theatre. This building bubble was announced in January 1921 and vanished suddenly with the coming of spring. Griffith was forced to drop his option in April.

Way Down East's increasing profits, coupled with the unloading of the Wark Producing Corporation, did enable D. W. Griffith, Inc. to pay a dividend of $1 on its Class A stock on March 6. This announcement served to bring in the final money needed to complete *Dream Street,* and to enable Griffith to begin planning for his next films.

Dream Street was substantially finished with the editing process by mid-March. Griffith arranged for a preview in Middletown, New York, on March 16. Griffith still felt some ties with this city on the fringe of the Orange Mountains, close to Cuddebackville, and it seemed to him that he would get an honest opinion of his films there. He saw that the film would need some further work before its scheduled opening in New York in April. For some time Griffith had been toying with the idea of adding synchronized sound to the film. This was hardly a new idea; even Edison had encouraged and permitted the work on motion pictures to take place in his laboratories in the hope of developing them as an accompaniment to the phonograph. Griffith had been shown a device developed by Orlando Kellum that synchronized records with the picture by means of a device attached to the projector. Griffith had several records made for selected sequences in *Dream Street,* and, further, he made a short featurette of himself discussing "The Evolution of the Motion Picture" intended as a prologue.

As the final stages of the preparation of *Dream Street* were carried out, Griffith found time to be the guest of honor at a dinner given by the Friars, a theatrical club, at the Astor Hotel on March 27. The Friars hailed him as the motion picture director who had contributed more than any other individual to the development of the screen throughout the world. The dinner was attended by both Lillian Gish and Thomas Dixon, author of *The Clansman.* The principal speaker was State Senator James J. Walker, "Gentleman Jimmy," the future mayor of New York. Walker spoke about the great power possessed by Griffith and how Griffith held it as a sacred trust, never abusing it. How the round full phrases of the political flatterer rolled on, and how Griffith loved it.

While Griffith didn't in fact use the power of the film itself for any personal aggrandizement, he didn't hesitate to try out his public stature to further his favorite political objective, the striking down of growing censorship of films. He took time in April to testify in Albany, as a volunteer witness, against the Clayton-Lusk bill that called for rigid film censorship.

Dream Street opened at the Central Theatre in New York on April 12, 1921. The sound experiments proved somewhat erratic, so the film opened as a silent film with the usual musical accompaniment. The trade assessment, as represented by *Film Daily,* was favorable, if a trifle lukewarm: "This is not a super production, but it is artistic and well acted, though a little long, It will draw because of DW's name." [167]

Frank Vreeland, in *Theatre Magazine,* took a different view:

> In "Dream Street," David W. Griffith has become lost a bit in the mist of the falls that end "Way Down East." This semi-allegorical story, picturing a struggle between good and evil, suggested by a couple of Thomas Burke's Limehouse stories, but acknowledging strict allegiance to no time or clime, seems to be more photography than Griffith. A violinist, with a beautiful mask hiding a diabolical face, is supposed to incite the slum dwellers to evil, though it takes the form of a kind of nervous wiggling. The rivalry between two brothers, one a swaggering sport and the other a weakling, for the hand of a music hall dancer, has moments of charm and inspiration, but it ends in the bathos of a noble benefactor making everyone happy and giving the sport and the girl a chance to accumulate a baby and a kitten. If he produces "Faust," Griffith will have to do better than the paper-mache inferno in this picture. But a dash of colored scenes and synchronized phonographs made some incidents vocal, give the picture a show for the money. [168]

Vreeland's references to the use of synchronized sound show that he didn't view the film at its opening, but some four weeks after when Griffith had the film transferred to Town Hall. The sound experiments were never satisfactory to Griffith and they were abandoned after the Town Hall run. Lillian Gish has attributed Griffith's decision to abandon sound as due to his awareness that pictures using one language, English in this case, would lose their power to communicate in the rest of the world. If he told Lillian this, it would seem to be more of his rationalization for public consumption. The truth is that the Kellum process was a bust. Griffith really felt that he couldn't continue with a failure. As to the value of sound itself, when a process that worked was finally developed later in the decade, there was no stopping it, and the silent film was displaced. The problem of language barriers was only considered by those few historians who liked to speak of the universality of the silent film after it had vanished.

Vreeland's comments that *Dream Street* seemed "more photography than Griffith" sounded a note echoed by *Film Daily:* "By and by, what became a Billy Bitzer photography? Henrik Sartov. did Griffith's latest. And the crowd wondered. Because Bitzer has been regarded as part of Griffith." [169]

Griffith had assigned Sartov to *Dream Street* because of his desire to capitalize on Sartov's soft-focus photography throughout the film. Bitzer had been quite willing to step aside and assist in trying to perfect the Kellum sound process. Bitzer privately didn't think that there was anything that Sartov could do that he was unable to do. Karl Brown commented on the relationship between Bitzer and Sartov as cameramen:

> Sartov was a skilled pictorialist. He brought his skill to an unfamiliar field, in which he was not unnaturally slow. He was extremely slow by comparison to cameramen who were working in a familiar field with years of experience back of them—to light a portrait is one thing—to light a moving figure is quite another thing. The time-eating trick of moving picture portraiture is to hold constant quality throughout a shot in which the figure may not only move completely around, but who may traverse a hundred feet or more of a set, through varying lights. Sartov had to learn this. Bitzer already knew it. The upshot was that it was

easier for Bitzer to learn all Sartov knew about portraiture than it was for Sartov to learn all Bitzer knew about cinema lighting. Bitzer therefore beat Sartov to the screen with Sartov's successful soft-focus methods.[170]

To Karl Brown, however, it didn't really seem to matter who might be Griffith's cameraman:

> The brute truth is that Griffith would have succeeded as well with Landers (Sam), or Tony Gaudio, or Art Martinelli, or Lyman Broening as he did with Bitzer. The cameraman was then and is now a very minor factor in the success or failure of all but a microscopic minority of pictures produced.
>
> The cameraman and his camera provide an instrumentality through which the producer expresses himself. The better the instrument, the finer the work—but!—a Kreisler playing a fiddle chosen at random from an orchestra will produce greater music than any fiddler chosen at random from the same orchestra playing Kreisler's pet fiddle.
>
> Griffith was the whole show, and nothing but the show. Others contributed, some greatly—but they were followers, not leaders.[171]

Real rivalry and conflict between Bitzer and Sartov began with Griffith's next film, *Orphans of the Storm,* when Bitzer was to share the filming with Sartov. Lillian Gish has reported that Bitzer refused to assist Sartov and walked off the set. Bitzer certainly never considered himself number two. Griffith let him go, now quite confident, as Brown believed, that he didn't need any single individual.

A minor incident shedding some light on the business affairs of Griffith's film company occurred in April when Robert Edgar Long, Griffith's former press representative, sued Griffith's brother Albert Grey for an accounting of the receipts from the sale of souvenir booklets for *Way Down East.* Long, the author of the first book about Griffith, claimed that he had designed the souvenir booklet under a partnership agreement with Albert covering its sale and distribution. Through his attorney he claimed that Grey owed him $11,625. This minor case was a symptom of the general carelessness with which Albert was managing Griffith's affairs. On the day the suit was filed, *Way Down East* had reached its 450th performance in New York City.

The other person relied upon by Griffith to keep his company afloat amid the rising tide of film company mergers and bankruptcies was his attorney Albert Banzhaf. In 1944 J. C. Epping, the much put-upon accountant for Griffith, evaluated Banzhaf:

> . . . it is true that Mr. Banzhaf was not the kind of lawyer Mr. G. needed. A clever, strong, combative lawyer would have been of much greater benefit to him. That he should fear such a lawyer was an unfortunate personal idiosyncrasy. In my opinion, Mr. Banzhaf gave ineffective and weak counsel on many of the problems presented to him by Mr. G. Personally, Mr. Banzhaf was too cultured, admirable, and conscientious a gentleman to be such a counselor as Mr. G. needed as Mr. Griffith's negotiations were frequently with men who were solely guided by expediency where right and principle were relegated. Mr. Griffith needed a lawyer of very keen mentality and capacity of correct appraisal of the men he was dealing with and their motives. Mr. Banzhaf did not qualify for this.[172]

As to Griffith's reasons for keeping others about him who were really incapable of pulling their own weight in management, Epping also commented:

> If Mr. Griffith kept a few people on his payroll who probably would have been more fit in industry other than motion pictures, it was not so much due to faulty appraisal of fitness for the job, as to his outstanding sense of loyalty and fairness.[173]

Regardless of the increasing financial problems of D. W. Griffith, Inc., with its increasing overhead at the Mamaroneck studio, Griffith could see only one way to keep going, to make the enterprise succeed, and that was to exploit the films in release and to keep making new films in the hope that the next one would turn into another bonanza. It would be some time before a politician would invent the phrase, "prosperity is just around the corner," but for Griffith this was a principal belief.

In May Griffith spent some time making the rounds of the openings of *Dream Street* in Providence and Boston. *Film Daily* reported that the talking sequences of *Dream Street* were tried at the Capitol Theatre in New York on May 2, and that a film clip of Griffith talking to Irvin S. Cobb was also shown. *Dream Street* was not being shown at the Capitol Theatre; instead, Griffith had in-

stalled a revival of *The Birth of a Nation*. This series of showings
was picketed by the NAACP.

On May 31, 1921, Griffith signed a contract with Kate Stevenson
for the exclusive film rights to a successful old stage melodrama,
The Two Orphans. Griffith gave Mrs. Stevenson $5,000 for these
rights, more than he had paid Brady for the rights to *Way Down
East*. Mrs. Stevenson, under her stage name Kate Claxton, had performed in this play throughout the length and breadth of the
country, since its American premiere in 1882. One of the original
stars, who played Jacques Frochard opposite Kate Claxton's
Louise, was Griffith's old director, McKee Rankin. Mrs. Rankin
had played the part of the second of the two heroine sisters, Henriette. Much later Rankin did a version of the play independently
of the touring performances featuring Kate Claxton, and Miss
Claxton instituted suit to stop him on the grounds that she had
purchased the stage performance rights from Palmer. Griffith was
undoubtedly familiar with much of this background, as well as the
play's long-lasting and phenomenal success.

Interestingly enough, and further evidence of Griffith's lack of
proper business advice and research backing that advice, was the
fact that the copyright on the Jackson version of the play had expired in 1917. Kate Claxton did not own the film rights that she
blithely sold to Griffith; the play was now in the public domain.
The indomitable Kate Claxton had, however, successfully sued the
Fox Film Company in 1915 for $100,000, assisted by the Selig Poli-
scope Company, when William Fox had filmed an unauthorized
version of the play. The case was settled for the small sum of
$2,000. Selig had filmed a version in 1911. This case was well
known to Griffith, and this knowledge, coupled with Miss Claxton's
strong proprietary interest in the play, however legally misguided,
convinced him that she owned the play. After all, Kate Claxton
had been the play's best-known star for over twenty-nine years.

One person who knew well the tangled history of the play and
its rights was the dynamic William Fox. When Fox heard of Griffith's purchase and plans to film the play, he managed to secure the
European rights to the play from the estates of the original authors. Eventually Griffith found that he would have to meet Fox's
price in order to release his film in England and France.

Lillian Gish has said that she was responsible for persuading Griffith to purchase *The Two Orphans*. She has described a visit with Griffith to an Italian-language theatre in downtown New York for a performance of the play. This visit had resulted in Griffith's signing one of the Italian actors, Frank Puglia, for a role in his film. There is no doubt, however, that Griffith didn't need such a visit to acquaint himself with this stage warhorse. He did twit Lillian that her interest was primarily in the roles of the two sisters, so suitable for herself and her sister Dorothy. Lillian insisted that this was not the real reason. She said that she had "researched" the audience reaction to the play and knew of its tremendous popularity. Griffith was already aware of this, including a clear memory of the New York all-star revival in 1904 by A. M. Palmer in which Grace George had played Louise, the role that Lillian saw for herself.

There were many who privately felt that Griffith would fail with a film of *The Two Orphans,* insisting that it had long worn out its welcome, but after Griffith's success with an even more shop-worn melodrama, *Way Down East,* they weren't going to make these statements publicly. Griffith himself had no doubt that the play would make a successful film, particularly after he made some alterations, specifically adding the French Revolution to the story. The guillotine would be as effective a climactic device as Niagara Falls had been in *Way Down East.*

Despite the declaration of a dividend of fifty cents on each share of stock on July 1, Griffith's company desperately needed operating capital for continuing work at Mamaroneck. The summer of 1921 was spent trying to raise enough money to continue. Not until October was Griffith able to secure a loan from the Central Union Trust Company of New York for $340,000 against mortgages on the negatives and future box office receipts from *Way Down East, Dream Street,* and even the projected film, *The Two Orphans.* Griffith had now been backed into a financial corner, one in which even a success with *The Two Orphans* would not really bring his company into the black. Griffith and his advisers were unable to see this. Their eyes were still bedazzled by the image of the returns from *The Birth of a Nation.* What they failed to see and sense was the ratio of cost to profits, the ratio that had helped make the returns from *The Birth* so impressive. They did know, of course, that the failure of *The Two Orphans* would inundate D. W. Griffith, Inc. and mean the end of the studio at Mamaroneck. Griffith now had a number of pictures that had failed at the box office, but, with the exception of *Intolerance,* his big pictures had not, and the concept of failure was not part of his thinking. Griffith gave the signal to begin preparations and set construction for making the film.

13

The End of Independence:
Orphans of the Storm

I told Mr. Griffith that I felt he was essentially an artist
and not a promotor and that he could not successfully
maneuver and manage other people. His most important
work of all was producing. He had to be an integral
part of his own productions else he would fail.[174]

Under the direction of Griffith's master builder, Huck Wortman,
almost fourteen acres of sets for *The Two Orphans* began to rise at
Mamaroneck. Hollywood had already become blasé about giant
sets rising above the one- and two-story studio buildings, but this
was a new experience for the residents of New York and Connecticut. Mamaroneck became a sightseer's mecca during the summer
and fall of 1921. For the first time a designer was credited with the
settings for an entire Griffith film, but the designer, Charles Kirk,
was still subject to the imagination and desires of Griffith. Wortman built replicas of the Palais Royale, the cathedral of Notre
Dame, a grand salon at Versailles, and the Bastille. These known
landmarks were coupled with sets of twisted cobblestoned streets,
lavishly rendered in plaster imitating ancient stone, but here and
there a facade finished in New England cedar shingles undercut
some of the authenticity of those old Parisian streets.

Publicity wheels were turning out stories designed to build an-
ticipation of the release of the picture. One article that Griffith enjoyed was the result of a visit to the studio by Richard Savage.
After seeing the grand salon setting, Savage rhapsodized:

Far across the mighty salle—itself a vast checkerboard of ex-
quisite mosaic—wonderful mural paintings of elegant Arcadian
revels in the Watteau manner dominated a regal dais centering
in the chairs of state. The grandeur of entablature, pillar and
plinth; the sumptuous grace and ease of the side wall and can-
opy in fresco and gilt. . . .[175]

Griffith would have liked to have written that florid passage himself, and there is the possibility that he might have suggested some of the language to the writer. Savage also described Griffith's arrival for the interview:

> He was elegantly dressed, this interpreter of dreams; graceful in mien and carriage as any grand seigneur, but brilliant of eye and mobile of face as a Talma or Sully; with a cunning of speech that, but for a smooth Kentucky liquidity, might have doubled the plenipotentiary Talleyrand. I shook hands with the proprietor of the grand salon, the uncrowned king of the French Revolution, none other than David Wark Griffith. He talked. I listened.[176]

Griffith then described to Savage his intentions in making *The Two Orphans:*

> Some of the world's greatest crimes have been committed by well-meaning men. The events leading up to the great Revolution (which I am depicting as the climax to my version of *The Two Orphans*) are very modern in their tale of tyranny, of laws and more laws, even of the income tax, the sensational press and other ills that now irk us.
> . . . With the overthrow of the monarchy men thought they saw the millennium. They awoke to a more bitter reality than any of their previous sufferings. For again—as so often in History—a fanatical minority of "think-as-I-think!" men, the Jacobins, seized the places of power, inaugurated the Reign of Terror and stamped out with the guillotine all who opposed them.
> . . . And the leader of the slaughter was that conscientious public servant, Robespierre—the advocate incorruptible—the patriot who scented the Republic's danger so keenly that in every opponent he discovered a traitor and marched him to the axe forthwith. Russia has been much like that. The people seem to win, but a faction of fanatics defeats their will to govern.[177]

In later years when critics, sympathetic to the Russian Revolution, and particularly to the Bolshevik coup, analyzed the Griffith films, particularly Griffith's version of *The Two Orphans,* they seized on these sentiments as proof that Griffith and the film were anti-revolutionary and reactionary. The truth probably was that Griffith, essentially an a-political man, would say anything that might help sell his film. The mood in the United States in 1921 was anti-Bolshevik, and for Griffith to establish even a modest parallel between his film's using the French Revolution and the Russian experience undoubtedly seemed good salesmanship and nothing more.

It would have taken an egoless man to have withstood the overblown praise from writers like Savage. Griffith managed to maintain an outward appearance of modest self-deprecation, but as he read, he believed.

Savage witnessed and described the filming of the picture's climax. Lillian Gish's head was placed in the yoke waiting for the fall of the blade. Only the sight of the real blade, detached from the machine and resting at one side, out of camera range, reassured the writer.

> An ear-piercing scream . . . congealed my blood with instant alarm lest Lillian's throat be actually cut. I started hurriedly for the guillotine. "Louise!" Henriette was tenderly breathing the name of her beloved blind sister, just before closing her eyes. Gentle Lillian's blonde head was still necked to the lovely Lillian torso. The axe had not fallen, was, indeed, quite out of commission beside the guillotine. The camera stopped clicking. Mr. Griffith raised up the yoke, and the prostrate orphan scrambled to her feet and stepped down a ladder from platform to floor.
> "You often mail advice to aspirants, don't you?" remarked Miss Gish to me. "Please tell them it is no fun dying on the movie guillotine from 10 A.M. to 7 P.M., as I have done this day!" [178]

Lillian didn't mention that film stars were now being well paid to fake their death scenes on the guillotine, but Griffith did give Savage a justification for the steadily increasing salaries paid film actors:

> When a girl's work entertains the patrons of fifteen thousand theatres, it is easy to see how it possesses the cash value of five thousand a week. Whereas, the stage star can entertain but twelve or fifteen hundred individuals nightly, the motion picture star appears before as many individuals in each of a hundred or a hundred and fifty theatres. Her moiety of the small charge of millions is the pay for her services. [179]

Griffith's assessment of a business in which millions of dollars could pour into box offices across the country, and even the world, was based on his own experience as well as observation. But first a producer must have a film to show, and in Griffith's case, the mounting expenses of producing this film were draining away his cash reserves rapidly. The loan from the Central Union Trust Company proved enough to carry *The Two Orphans* to completion. It seems almost an absurdity in light of the huge sums needed to complete a film project that Griffith managed to collect on an insurance policy taken out against the possibility of snow before November 20 when shooting on the outdoor sets would be completed. The snow held off, and Griffith, who had bet that it wouldn't snow, collected $25,000. This may have been the first instance of business interruption insurance in the film industry. That sum once, just a few years earlier, might have represented the entire budget of a feature film; now it was almost meaningless in the total costs.

In addition to the press releases and feature stories built around the film in production, Griffith was aware of the value of anticipating future plans, even when these plans consisted of almost pure conjecture. He issued statements concerning grandiose schemes for future films. The press was duly notified that Griffith had written to the Secretary of the Navy asking for the use in an anti-war film of a flotilla of navy ships that were about to be scrapped. The notion, of course, was for the consumption of the general public, and neither Griffith nor Washington entertained the idea seriously. The next announcement concerned a projected 72-reel film to be released in six related films of 12 reels each. Actually Griffith was lucky to have his cash last to the end of the film then in production. These great schemes did serve their main purpose, however, which was to keep Griffith's name before the public. The public believed that the creator of *The Birth of a Nation* and *Intolerance* would really make these films. In the industry, however, they merely served to make those who were jealous of Griffith's talent and fame derisive. Griffith, the actor always close to the surface, basked and beamed in this artificial limelight.

The Two Orphans was finished and ready for release just before Christmas 1921. The name of the film was changed by Griffith, in recognition of his addition of the French Revolution to the old d'Ennery plot, to *Orphans of the Storm*. The first half of the film, with much expansion and enrichment of locale, stayed fairly close to the play, but Griffith had liberally borrowed from Dickens's *A Tale of Two Cities* for the background and flavor of the French Revolution to bring excitement to the second half, and, of course, to give the circumstances for the obligatory last-minute rescue.

Orphans of the Storm opened in Boston on December 28, 1921, with the New York opening following on January 2. Griffith was easily persuaded to present the film on a road show basis, as had been done with *Way Down East,* only playing a relatively small number of major film theatres across the country. This exhibition technique had worked quite well for the previous film, but it was to prove a severe disappointment this time. It has been suggested that the habits of movie-goers had changed to a pattern of neighborhood theatre attendance, and this may well have had some influence, although more likely the fact that the film was released in the teeth of an economic recession was even more significant. The fate of the film was not helped by the inept management of Albert Grey. Albert convinced his brother to make huge expenditures for promotion at each showing, thus contributing to the road show losses. The settlement with William Fox for $85,000 in order to show the film abroad also hurt badly.

The situation was somewhat further confused by two other versions of the play produced by an Italian and a German film company. Griffith was forced to buy the German film to keep it off the market. Some help in combatting the Italian film came from Griffith's change in title. The Italian film was still called *The Two Orphans.*

Orphans of the Storm was well received critically, and Griffith had to take some pride in and hope from them rather than the box office reports. *Film Daily* reported:

> The power of the film lies in the fact that it is a melodramatic spectacle, huge at times. It is magnificent but not the best of DWG's splendid creations. Some sequences are too long but the close of the first part and the rescue at the end are driven home. Joseph Schildkraut is a definite discovery.[180]

The last-mentioned actor, playing the Chevalier de Vaudry, was the son of a distinguished German Jewish stage star, and had al-

ready gained a considerable measure of recognition in the theatre
for his performance, under Theatre Guild auspices, in the title
role of Ferenc Molnar's *Liliom*. Despite this, Schildkraut, a neo-
phyte in films, was not accepted readily by the actors at Mamaroneck. They thought he was difficult, egotistical, and not the least of
the unkind remarks was Dorothy Gish's remark to the effect that
Schildkraut thought he was prettier than she was. For his own
part, Schildkraut didn't think much of the film people or of the
process of film-making. He was quite willing to go back to the theatre at the end of *Orphans of the Storm* and never return to films.
This initial judgment was eventually reversed and Schildkraut enjoyed a long and distinguished film career.

The power of *Orphans of the Storm* stemmed not only from the
tested ingredients of *The Two Orphans,* the perils of two lovely
girls whirling in and out of the clutches of assorted villains, but
also from Griffith's addition of the French Revolution. The latter
reflected Griffith's borrowing of Dickens's analysis of the Revolution, a British sympathy with the Old Regime. The Revolution
and its handmaiden the guillotine became, for Griffith, the biggest,
blackest villain of them all.

More stories about future productions were being put out by
Griffith's publicity department. The plan of filming *Faust* with
Lillian Gish was revived again. Films for two South American na-
tions were announced. A film about Abraham Lincoln was projected, and Griffith also said that he would make another film in
Florida. The latter film may have been merely Griffith's reaction
to the cold weather in New York. Instead of warm Florida, Griffith
was on his way to the Chicago opening of *Orphans* in February.
The publicists also announced a possible remake of *Sands of Dee*
with Mae Marsh again starring. But the most grandiose project announced was a film based on H. G. Wells's *An Outline of History*.
Of all of these projects, only the film about Abraham Lincoln was
ever to be made, and that would come a decade later as Griffith's
next-to-last motion picture.

Despite these brave announcements, reality for Griffith and his
company was something quite different. In the obviously deepen-
ing financial crisis, Albert Grey persuaded his brother that a significant saving could be made if Lillian Gish were to be persuaded to

take an outside offer and thus relieve the studio of meeting her salary. Griffith was adamant that he couldn't do this. While he had shifted his attention and interest from Lillian to Carol Dempster, he still couldn't bring himself to part with Lillian. Albert was quite persuasive, however, with the assistance of the financial reports, some small help from Banzhaf, and even a promise to take over for Griffith and speak to Lillian himself. Griffith replied that, if anyone was to do it, he himself would have to be the one. Albert smiled at his victory.

It was a painful experience for Griffith to suggest to Lillian that she should go out into the world alone. Never was Griffith's paternalism stronger. In mitigation of the circumstances, he made an elegant little speech about Lillian finally getting, from someone else, what she was worth. Lillian was to say: "Thus, in the most friendly way, an artistic and business association of many years was broken off as casually as it had begun." [181]

Obviously Lillian Gish had then, and has now, something more than the feelings one shares with even the best of business partners. But if she was hurt by this gentle dismissal, she never let it affect her feelings for both Griffith the man and the motion picture artist. There were observers who felt that Lillian was considerably more unhappy about the attention that Griffith was paying to Carol Dempster. Billy Bitzer, in a private letter, years later, wrote:

> He was crazy about Carol Dempster and he just about put himself out of the movie business in trying to make her a star. They didn't like her—I mean the public and film people—but he did. Spent a lot of money on her—took her to Europe—England—Germany . . . made a picture called *Isn't Life Wonderful*. It wasn't very good, but he kept plugging her. He dropped Lillian Gish who he went out with all the time before. Then it seems when Carol realized she couldn't make a go of it and had got all she could in money out of Griffith, she beat it one day and married a younger man her own age.[182]

To make his next film, Griffith was forced to return to the Central Union Trust Company to negotiate another loan. Eli Bernheim of the bank loaned Griffith an additional $267,500 against the negative of a picture tentatively titled *Haunted Grande* on June 15, 1922. Griffith assured Bernheim that this would be a commercial film. D. W. Griffith, Inc. now owed this single bank over a half-million dollars, and the bank was to take its repayment off the top. D. W. Griffith, Inc. would have to wait for any of its returns.

The new film underwent a quick title change to *One Exciting Night*. It was conceived by Griffith as a minor film designed to recoup company losses by taking advantage of the popularity of Mary Roberts Rinehart's stage success *The Bat* and of another "haunted house" stage success *The Cat and the Canary*. At first Griffith thought that he would buy the rights to *The Bat,* but there wasn't enough cash in the bank to negotiate for such a successful property. Griffith then went back to the old technique of writing his own plot, carefully skirting any possible plagiarism. He copyrighted a synopsis for legal purposes, but in the actual shooting of the film promptly departed from that outline. To avoid, as he had done before, any personal identification, he credited the screenplay to a non-existent Irene Sinclair, undoubtedly the sister of his previous nom de plume Roy Sinclair. With the memory of his expensive settlement with William Fox still fresh in his mind, he had Banzhaf search and examine his story to make certain that he hadn't opened himself up to a suit by Miss Rhinehart. From *The Cat and the Canary* there was one thing that could be taken with impunity: the play's star, Henry Hull. Griffith had last worked with Hull when he was a ten-year-old child actor.

The most distinguishing feature of the campaign to turn *One Exciting Night* into a commercial hit was the use of a promotional slogan that proved extremely durable for mystery and suspense films. The audience was asked "not to reveal the ending." Griffith was determined to make a film that was more mystifying than its stage parents. His efforts were so successful that the audiences were never certain that they even understood what was happening in the film. This effect was heightened by Griffith, for once again he was unable to resist to continue cutting in the projection room in an effort to pick up the slow tempo.

Again Griffith took advantage of natural phenomena, in using a real hurricane that struck Long Island Sound on June 11. Griffith hustled Sartov out into the storm to make hurricane shots for the film's climax. This time, unlike the storm in *Way Down East,* the real article seemed out of place amid the sliding panels and clutching hand artificiality of a haunted house mystery. Later film-makers found that there was more point to *opening* a film of this genre with a storm.

One Exciting Night was previewed in Montclair, New Jersey, on September 22. Griffith continued editing the film. A second preview was held at the Colonial Theatre in Newport, Rhode Island. Another week of editing, and the film was opened at the Tremont Theatre in Boston. The film still didn't meet Griffith's standards, so the opening in New York was delayed until October 23. The trade review in *Film Daily* was lukewarm: "The film is good enough but Griffith wastes his tremendous talents. This has box-office, but one expects more from Griffith—this could have been made in his Biograph days." [183]

The review in *The New York Times* generally praised the film and the performances of the cast. It concluded with the comments:

> The film is somewhat too long. It hasn't the photographic finish in all of its scenes one has come to expect from a Griffith production and, of course, there are those subtitles, subtitles that try to make a rampant melodrama into an allegory, or something— think of it. But for all that, and despite everything, *One Exciting Night* is a hilarious thriller. And don't forget the storm. You won't if you see it. [184]

To watch the film today is to find the comedy aspects of the film —surrounding, as they do, the performance of Porter Strong in blackface as a stereotyped, eyeball-rolling, black servant—unsatisfactory, and not very funny. The *Times* account noted at the time, however: "There's Porter Strong, too, as Romeo Washington. . . . His comedy is of the broad and busy kind, but he's funny. . . ." [185] The *Times* also liked Carol Dempster: "[She] gives vitality to the picture."

The failure of *One Exciting Night* lay in Griffith's misinterpretation of the nature of the mystery-melodrama. He thought that the secret lay in the hokum of sliding panels, clutching hands, shrieks in the night, and mysterious characters. He overlooked the need for a tightly constructed plot, the presentation of a logical progression of clues, both visual and verbal, and the rational explanation that must underly the characters' natures, regardless of how suspicious each is made to look. In the filming, and in the final editing, Griffith threw out the logic and the structure, leaving only a catalogue of haunted house set dressings. No wonder that the audience was confused.

The road showing of *One Exciting Night* fell to the increasingly dubious managerial skills of Griffith's brother Albert. Albert was already demonstrating with *Orphans of the Storm* that he could soundly destroy any potential profits with excessive expenses. Under Albert's management, *One Exciting Night* earned the left-handed distinction of losing less money than any other Griffith film of that period.

Despite his shaky financial condition, Griffith had managed to float and finish another film. He still had no money with which to continue, so back to Bernheim and the Central Union Trust Company he went. Griffith was so certain of Bernheim's approval of another loan that he actually began work on *The White Rose* at the beginning of December 1922, before the loan was approved. The bank did come through again, lending Griffith $650,000 against the negative and profits of *The White Rose.*

Masquerading as Irene Sinclair again, Griffith concocted his own story for *The White Rose* around a fallen minister who sins with a young member of his flock. Looking for more strength at the top of the cast, Griffith persuaded Mae Marsh to return and work for him again, and he imported Ivor Novello, a young British matinee idol, to play the minister. As he had done so many times before, he found a small part in the cast for one other old Biographer, Kate Bruce. He had also continued to use Adolph Lestina, although not in *The White Rose.*

Griffith had first met Ivor Novello while making an exploitation trip to London for *Orphans of the Storm.* The meeting was arranged through the acerbic English critic Hannen Swaffer, who thought little of Novello as an actor and said to him: "D. W. Griffith wants to meet you. I told him you were Ivor Novello, but he said that makes no difference to him! Why not give him a ring." [186]

At their meeting in the Savoy Hotel, Griffith kept pacing around Novello, staring intently at him, and remarking how he had been struck by Novello's resemblance to Richard Barthelmess. He also kept repeating that if Novello ever came to America to work for him, he would work harder than he had ever worked before. Novello made the usual actor promises that he would be willing to work twenty-four hours a day with Griffith. Griffith concluded the interview by saying that if he had a role for Novello he would cable him.

Quite unexpectedly the Griffith cable arrived just after Novello had signed a contract to appear in a film for Adrian Brunel to be shot in Italy. Griffith wanted him for the part in *The White Rose*. This was an opportunity that, in Novello's eyes, was not to be missed. The Brunel film could be quickly finished, so he promptly accepted Griffith's offer.

In New York City, Griffith's publicity department arranged to have Novello interviewed, photographed, and lionized almost from the moment he stepped off the ship. The thrust of the campaign was the assertion that Novello was the handsomest man in England.

Novello's reactions to his experience in working for Griffith were stated in an interview given to the London *Daily Herald:*

> I thought when I went out that I would have to do all sorts of stunts in the movie like jumping off the Woolworth Building to save Mae Marsh from being ground in the propellers of the Mauretania! Nothing of the sort. The climax of the picture, for example, is purely emotional.

In answer to the question about how he found Griffith as a director, Novello replied:

> He's wonderful. He never raises his voice in the studio, but he gets everything he wants. His methods are peculiarly his own. The artists do not read the script, but on the first day he tells you the whole story. Then for three weeks, before we ever see a camera, we rehearse the whole picture right through.
>
> It is a great help later when the continuity has to be broken because of scenery necessities. It is also wonderful experience, because, if an actor happens to be absent from rehearsals, his place must be filled by anyone else who is on the spot. So in those weeks I played my own part and several other people's, which helped a great deal in the understanding of the character's motivations.
>
> . . . After the first three weeks' work he was not satisfied with the photography, so it was all taken again. Each scene is taken six or seven times with three cameras, so that he has a choice of

shots. He shows them the 'rushes' of the picture and listens to
their suggestions as to which are the best scenes to keep.

. . . He is frank, too, and always ready to tell you when you
are good—or bad. Some directors let one work on blindly in the
dark.[187]

To get away from the New York winter, as he always liked to do,
Griffith had written the story of *The White Rose* in a manner,
while reminiscent of his own Kentucky milieu, so that it could be
filmed in the bayou country of Louisiana. The company spent two
months in Franklin and St. Martinsville, Louisiana, in the Bayou
Teche country. Ivor Novello, with his inexperience of America
outside New York City, always thought he was in Florida. The
company did go to Florida after the Louisiana stint to shoot the interiors in rented space at the Hialeah Studios outside Miami, so
Novello's confusion was understandable.

During the Louisiana trip, Griffith stayed in a mansion owned
by Weeks Hall, near New Iberia. Weeks Hall became a close
friend, providing Griffith with some relief from bouts of loneliness.
This side of Griffith's nature was hidden from his company. He
needed the kind of personal family contact that had been provided
for some time by the Gish family, and of which, after letting
Lillian go, he now was deprived. Weeks Hall managed to supply
some of the warmth and friendship that he needed. After leaving
Louisiana, Griffith, an irregular correspondent at best, continued
to write to Hall.

Since the plot elements of *The White Rose* were built around
the fallen clergyman, an illegitimate child, and the suffering of the
transgressing couple, Griffith was very concerned about the possible reaction of the clerical community. Various clergymen were
consulted during the filming, and other clerical reactions were
sought during previews. Despite this effort there were still some
church associations that strongly objected to the film, and it was
banned in some areas.

Billy Bitzer was re-hired for *The White Rose,* sharing the photography chores with Sartov and Hal Sintzenich. The most impressive camerawork was done in those scenes using Louisiana exteriors.

The White Rose opened at the Lyric Theatre in New York on

May 21, 1923. Under the headline "The Minister and the Cash Girl," *The New York Times* reported:

> The White Rose . . . in spots is a remarkable but weird offering.
>
> The pains that have been taken with this photoplay are striking throughout most of the scenes, and sometimes the acting is far above the average good picture, and unusually restrained. The artist in Griffith as the master of photoplay photography smites the eye constantly, and occasionally there was applause for the beauty of the scenes. Many women wept and a little commotion in the audience was caused by a girl fainting. Although there is suspense galore and sob scenes aplenty, it is not a picture of great strength, the story being rather worn and thin and much drawn-out.
>
> Mae Marsh . . . did some excellent work, and even in those scenes which called for a bit of overacting she did her utmost to keep her antics from being absurd. In some parts she was as good as one would want any actress to be in a picture, especially when she is supposed to be dying with her child in her arms.
>
> . . . Now we come to Ivor Novello, a handsome young man who played the part of the clergyman, an individual with what might be called a perpetual expression of gloom. Only the flicker of a smile once passes over his face. He is filled with grief for the world just before he becomes a minister, and his expression of melancholia increases when he is ordained.

In summation the *Times* said:

> There are several scenes in which the censor has been a trifle lenient with Mr. Griffith, and titles which are obviously superfluous. Mr. Griffith has attempted deep characterization with a simple story by extending the action. It does not make a great picture as there is little novelty in the situations, except in the splendid comedy obtained through the negroes being attacked by alligators.[188]

About a month after the opening of the film, Quinn Martin, in *Theatre Magazine,* commented:

> Considering the miserable batch of picture plays that have been trotted out for Broadway consumption recently, it would not be doing Mae Marsh justice merely to say that her performance in D. W. Griffith's *The White Rose* is the best performance of the month. I feel called upon to go much farther than that and say that it is one of the very finest pieces of screen act-

> ing I have ever seen. It might very easily be *the* best. Certainly I
> have never seen anything more moving and more artistic (yes,
> here is art) than her Teazie.[189]

When Quinn Martin's notice appeared, *The White Rose* had already closed its engagement. Martin reacted:

> I do not presume to know why *The White Rose* ran only a
> few weeks on Broadway. I do know that the reflection is only
> upon the New York picture-going public. Here was, perhaps, the
> finest picture Mr. Griffith ever did, from the standpoint of
> drama. It ought to have been seen by everyone in town.[190]

The White Rose went into general release by United Artists on
August 19, already, visibly, a financial failure. Ivor Novello returned to England, ostensibly for a short vacation, fully expecting
to be re-called under the terms of his contract for another Griffith
film. The call never came.

The grimness of his company's financial situation was readily apparent to Griffith. Despite his press announcements that he was no
longer interested in spectacle and only concerned with stories that
dealt with one or two human beings who were "far more interesting than a thousand remote persons carrying unfamiliar spears," he
decided that he would have to return to the "big" pictures to recoup the fading fortunes of D. W. Griffith, Inc. Griffith reached
back into his trunk and resurrected his old unproduced play,
War. Now was the time, he felt, for a major film about the American Revolution, and he believed that one sure-fire formula for success was an appeal to patriotism.

Re-reading his play proved an unsatisfactory experience, except
as it suggested the general outlines for a film. He commissioned a
novelist, Robert Chambers, a specialist in historical romances, to
write a story for the film. To indicate the scope of the film, Griffith
called it simply *America*.

Griffith began his approach to *America* gingerly. He lacked the
strong personal point of view that he held about the Civil War,
and he was now overly conscious of the necessity for historical
truth. He sought out the advice and advance approval of the
Daughters of the American Revolution and other patriotic socie-
ties, and he obtained the cooperation of the War Department in
Washington for the necessary troops, particularly the cavalry. All

of these commitments to specific groups, both private and govern-
mental, tended to keep the treatment something less than vigorous
and controversial. Griffith's anglophilia and the kinship with Britain arising from the late partnership in World War I caused him
to place the responsibility for any British villainy during the Revolution on the shoulders of one character, the evil Captain Butler,
played consummately by Lionel Barrymore, a loyalist rather than a
born Englishman. There could be, of course, no suggestion of villainy on the side of the revolutionists.

In October 1923 Griffith shot the battle of Bunker Hill in West-
chester County, New York, and a week later took some members of
the company to Lexington, Massachusetts, for some scenes with the
authentic backgrounds. Later sequences were filmed in Virginia at
Fort Myers, Westover, and Yorktown. By the end of October the
film was about half-finished, but the cash in the company coffers
was used up. At that moment enough money seemed to be coming
in from the previously released films to retire the bank loans, with
even the possibility, despite the brief New York run, that *The
White Rose* might be free and clear of any mortgages, and even
earn a profit. The prospects were good enough for Griffith to pay
another visit to the Central Union Trust Company. Again the
bank was willing to extend a loan for $500,000 at 6 per cent against
the negative of *America*. Filming was able to continue.

As a publicity move, and as an assist in continuing to receive
free help from the War Department, Griffith persuaded Congress-
man Treadway to present him to President Coolidge, and to ar-
range for showing the President some of the finished scenes from
the film. Frank Walsh, now increasingly relied on as an assistant
director, went along on the trip.

> He was the most commanding personality around. I remem-
> ber we were down in Washington . . . Griffith bought a square-
> topped derby to meet the President. The group consisted of Neil
> Hamilton, Charlie Mack, Griffith, and myself. No kidding, you
> would have thought that Griffith was the President. People
> stepped aside for him.[191]

Cooperation from the War Department continued, so that much of
the trip was a success. There was no recorded reaction from the
President, a not unusual situation for Coolidge.

Returning to Mamaroneck, Griffith finished the film in December and January. He edited and changed titles to produce two versions, one for the United States and one for Britain. The British version was eventually titled *Love and Sacrifice.*

The total cast for *America,* including the army troops, was almost of the same size as that for *Intolerance,* but the final version of the film ended with a rather small-scale personal story revolving around Carol Dempster as Nancy Montague and Neil Hamilton as Nathan Holden in opposition to the evil Captain Butler. Louis Wolheim, later to achieve fame in *All Quiet on the Western Front,* played Captain Hare. Four cameramen were used during the filming. Marcel Le Picard was added to the trio of Bitzer, Sartov, and Sintzenich. Charles Kirk again was the art director.

America opened at the 44th Street Theatre in New York on February 21, 1924, and later in Boston on March 6, and Philadelphia on March 31. Griffith faithfully made his usual rounds of the openings. Howard Irving Young, for *Theatre Magazine,* greeted the film:

> I approached Mr. Griffith's latest picture in a diffident mood, expecting the shrewd and ofttimes effective melodramatic dodges that the director has mastered by a somewhat wearisome public practice, but never dreaming that my eyes would be blessed by the loveliest visions the cinema has yet brought to them. In sheer pictorial beauty *America* has no equal among the moving pictures of the past.
>
> . . . The Griffith pictures are ever ripe in vigorous action and *America* is no exception. Cloyed as the movement is with the ponderously patriotic subtitles of the ingenuous historian, the story manages, under the aegis of Robert W. Chambers as fictionist, to break loose from time to time and spread itself over the landscape, both the real and the imaginary.
>
> A pretty romance between two gifted players, Neil Hamilton and Carol Dempster, is embroidered with the human touches that D. W. Griffith manages to impart to his characters. The rift in the lute is caused by those admirable rascals, Lionel Barrymore and Louis Wolheim, but they, with George the Third, are confounded before the final closeup.[192]

The man writing in *The New York Times* was enthusiastic about the first part of the film, but complained about the length of the second part and the amount, as he considered it, of superfluous detail. He admitted that some were exceedingly moved even by the latter half of the film:

> Tears were drawn last night, and sighs and sobs came from trembling women. And if we criticize the length of the latter portion of this artist's work, we must admit that the woman sitting next to us was clutching her hands with frenzied fear that the two Americans who had entered a house would be discovered by Captain Butler and his murderous crew. We thought for an instant that when they were caught she would scream. And, after all, if it affects one woman that way, it may have impressed scores of others, in spite of the drawn-out portions of the latter half.
>   . . . The Battle of Bunker Hill and Paul Revere's ride make up for all the superfluous detail in the latter half of this picture, which is certainly one that will stir the patriotic hearts of the nation as probably no other picture ever has done.[193]

For the trade press, *Film Daily* opined: "Once again DWG triumphs, tho a great epic has been allowed to dwindle at times to sheer melodrama, but the public will probably eat it up." [194]

In *America,* Griffith tried to use the same ingredients that had proven so powerful in *The Birth of a Nation,* concern for individuals in the midst of great panoramic action, historical vignettes, and lusty outdoor photography. But this time the audience's emotions were not stirred by real concern for the characters. The hero and heroine were bloodless and bland. The villain, although played with skill and talent by Lionel Barrymore, could easily be thought of by the audience as one isolated man, and not, as in *The Birth,* as the representative of a race. Griffith's own anglophilia militated against using the British in the same manner as the blacks. The end result was the same tedium that sets in while watching a travelogue that shows the beauty of the mountains for too long.

It took a long time for the public to "eat up" *America.* As Eileen Bowser, in the Museum of Modern Art monograph on Griffith, has pointed out, *America* finally earned back its cost, but only after years of distribution, re-issue, and the sale of stock footage for other films. Any profits would come much too late for D. W. Griffith, Inc.

In the midst of Griffith's promotional rounds, the United Artists board met on March 28th. Griffith was asked if he would be able to fulfill his contract with United Artists. He solemnly promised that he would meet all of his contractual obligations. But the other members of the board were also seeing the published returns from Griffith's films and were keenly aware of his financial plight. Abrams, Pickford, Fairbanks, Chaplin, and their advisers were not impressed with press agentry. They knew that Griffith had taken a financial beating through the premature construction of sets at Mamaroneck for a film to star Al Jolson, only to have Jolson walk out before shooting began, take a boat for Europe, and leave D. W. Griffith, Inc. holding the losses. The board members were particularly unhappy with Griffith's concept of a handshake with Jolson as a contract. Griffith told the board that his attorney, Banzhaf, was bringing suit against Jolson, but this answer was unsatisfactory since they had found little reason to be impressed with Griffith's attorney. Mary Pickford remembered: "As I recall it, his attorney, Banzaf (I am not sure of the spelling) who is now dead, represented him on the board. Personally, I think he could have had better business advisors." [195] Griffith also told the board that a group of Italian bankers had made overtures to finance a film to be made in Rome, and that he would be leaving for Italy shortly to confirm the deal.

Griffith did indeed leave for Italy, accompanied by Banzhaf, a week after opening *America* in Pittsburgh. They sailed on the *S.S. Olympic* and, coincidentally, Mary Pickford and Douglas Fairbanks sailed on the same ship. The boat trip was most pleasant, with Griffith anticipating that the Italian bankers' group, headed by G. Andrea Serrao, would open up a new channel of financing. In explaining his motives for making the trip to Italy to the press, Griffith issued the usual dockside statement about how foreign films were languishing in comparison to American films and implied that they needed his talents to give them a stimulant. He also mentioned that he had been asked to make a film about the life of the Italian playwright Gabriel D'Annunzio by the playwright's brother, and that Joseph Malkin, representing the Soviet film industry, had asked him to direct some films in the Soviet Union. With great satisfaction, Griffith connected the latter invitation with the great success of *Intolerance* in Russia.

While Griffith and Banzhaf were in Italy, the press in the United States carried the announcement of the filing of a suit against Al Jolson by D. W. Griffith, Inc. for $571,969.72 for breach of contract. The suit claimed that the special sets built for the aborted Jolson picture had cost the company $571,969.72. It noted that the *gentleman's agreement* had been made the previous June 15, and was terminated unilaterally by Jolson's sudden departure for Europe.

Griffith's deal in Italy fell through. The Italian bankers were not really ready for the sort of financial arrangements necessary to sustain a Griffith film. Upon Griffith's return from Europe, he would only comment that conditions in Italy were not right for making "big pictures." He did announce that he had agreed in secret to accept $250,000 from Adolph Zukor for D. W. Griffith, Inc. against his own commitment to direct three pictures for Zukor.

Following the March 28 board meeting of United Artists, an optimistic statement had been issued that all of the producing partners would be renewing their agreements, but Griffith knew as he left the room that he, for one, could not continue. The deal with Zukor was his last hope to prevent extinction. He had been informed that no further bank credit would be extended. In making the deal with Zukor, Griffith was forced to agree that even his personal compensation would be pledged to pay back the Zukor loan. To try to improve the picture, Griffith agreed to the release of financial statements by D. W. Griffith, Inc. that would show only earnings above the actual production costs of his films, thus showing a seeming profit, but carefully omitting the high costs of promotion and road show expenses. The true situation was that every picture from *The Love Flower* to date, excepting only *Way Down East,* showed a loss. The distributor, United Artists, however, had earned more from the Griffith films than they had from the output of the other partners. It was a case of everyone doing better from his films than Griffith himself.

On June 10 his press representative put out a statement that the Italian venture was now to be backed by the Banco Commerciale Italiana. If not an outright fabrication, the statement certainly represented wishful thinking.

Actually on June 10 Griffith signed the agreement with Zukor.

With Zukor's backing, the Empire Trust Company advanced $250,000 at 6 per cent to D. W. Griffith, Inc. for a film tentatively titled *Wronged Receipt,* but subsequently called *Isn't Life Wonderful,* to be filmed in Germany. When the official announcement of his deal with Zukor was made on July 16, Griffith was happy to avoid the storm from his United Artists partners by escaping to Germany.

Griffith packed up Dempster, Hamilton, Sartov, and Sintzenich for the trip and departed on the *S.S. Washington* on July 4, twelve days before Zukor released the announcement. Zukor had kept his promise to hold up the announcement until Griffith was out of the country.

Eileen Bowser has speculated that the idea for *Isn't Life Wonderful?,* the story of post-war depression in Germany, was suggested by J. C. Epping. Her reasoning is that Epping had maintained his German citizenship, despite the war, and had paid a visit to Germany after the war, reporting to Griffith an eyewitness account of the terrible conditions in that country. The actual short story on which Griffith based the film had been written by Major Geoffrey Moss, himself an eyewitness to the conditions in Germany. There is no doubt that Griffith would have found almost any excuse to make a film abroad at that tense moment in his financial affairs.

Of somewhat smaller influence was Lillian Gish's report of her successful filming in Italy of *The White Sister* for Inspiration Pictures, and Griffith's desire to follow. There were signs at this moment that Griffith was changing from the innovator who went his own way without paying attention to what other film-makers might do to the less sure posture of a follower. The old Griffith had looked at the films of others, paid a compliment in his spare, lean way, and then gone back to doing something entirely his own. Failure was bringing back some of that uncertainty that had not been present since the first days at Biograph. Now he looked to see what ideas were working for others. He was pleased, sometimes surprised, and now, at times, a little envious when his former players and assistant directors struck out on their own, making money and even achieving artistic success. His former bit player, and quondam assistant director, Erich Von Stroheim, had scored as a major director, and even seemed to be developing into a rival to Griffith as an artistic leader. Richard Barthelmess had become a star, not only in a Griffith film, but with the director Henry King in *Tol'able David*. King had also achieved a solid success with Lillian Gish.

For a time it had seemed that Griffith stood head and shoulders above the competition. Now it seemed that, while he had not hit bottom, he had still slipped back into the pack. If Griffith had any self-doubt, it was not about his skills, but only about why he hadn't found again the magic touch that had catapulted him to the top. He only asked himself just what it was that the public wanted now. If he could find that out, he'd give it to them. He didn't realize, however, that his gift was innovation. To stop stretching his own creativity, to rest on his laurels, to try merely for "money" pictures was courting personal disaster. He was not a hack, but like many men of genuine genius, he felt that he could, when pressed, turn out hack work. He could not.

14

Lockstep to Oblivion: Griffith, the Employee

He did not keep up with the times. You know he was never much of a mixer—didn't go around much—stayed in his rooms at the hotel too much—perhaps he got lazy so he just let things slip.[196]

Less than two weeks after Zukor's announcement of his contract with Griffith, United Artists released a statement that Griffith had previously renewed his contract for a three-year period with them. When *The New York Times* called Albert Banzhaf and questioned these conflicting announcements, Banzhaf replied that the signing with United Artists was a publicity stunt and was invalid. Hiram Abrams at United Artists disputed this judgment and said that Griffith would be held to his United Artists contract. Abrams was the winner over Banzhaf, really no contest, and both *Isn't Life Wonderful* and Griffith's next film, the first under his contract with Paramount, Zukor's company, were distributed by United Artists.

During July and August of 1924 Griffith worked on the exterior filming for *Isn't Life Wonderful*. Scenes were shot in the streets of Berlin, the shipyard at Capenick, the forests in Crampnitz and Sacrow, and the potato fields in Grunaw. Although the story concerned the trials of a German family fighting against the famine-producing effects of inflation and depression following the end of the war, Griffith made a concession to American tastes by turning the family into Polish refugees. Despite this change, Erich Pommer, head of the German film company UFA, advised Griffith that there would be no market for the film in Germany. There have been many comparisons between this film and those films made in Italy at the end of World War II because of their similarities in approach to the grim subject of war's aftermath and their documentary qualities. One other parallel lies in the fact that the Italian films of the late 1940s and early 1950s also failed to attract any business in their home countries despite their success in the United States.

On the way back to the United States from Germany, Griffith paused in England. He attempted to get a ban lifted that prevented *America* from being shown. The title change for the British showings to *Love and Sacrifice* had not been enough. Griffith staged a private screening at Prince's Restaurant in the hope that an engagement at the Scala Theatre would be possible. The film was finally approved after changes in subtitles had been made and was able to open on September 19, two weeks after Griffith's private screening. In the meantime Griffith had made his return voyage on the *S.S. Scythia* with the other members of the cast and crew for *Isn't Life Wonderful.*

The interiors were shot in the Astoria, Long Island, studios of Paramount. A second interim title had been applied to the film, *Dawn,* but this was dropped in favor of the more upbeat title just before the opening at the Rivoli Theatre in New York on December 5, 1924. The preceding evening a premiere showing was staged at Town Hall in New York.

Film Daily, with its eye on the box office, thought that the film was "too sordid," but that it would achieve success "because it is a Griffith." It went on to state that "one admires the subject matter and the handling, but it is not box-office." [197]

Theatre Magazine's reviewer thought:

> D. W. Griffith's latest offering, made in Germany, is a very slight and inconsequential affair. It makes no pretense at drama. It is just a glimpse into the lives of some Polish refugees in Germany, victims of the war, struggling in the face of dire poverty to find a little happiness in their existence of hardship and self-denial.
>
> . . . Griffith is, of course, a sentimentalist. His philosophy which he assays to put into his pictures has no connection with real life; in fact, it is no philosophy at all. But in spite of his fondness for coating his situations with sugar, he manages always to evoke the sympathy of the audience. Can you imagine a gathering bursting into spontaneous applause simply because a bowl

of steaming hot potatoes is set before a family of anemic emigrants? Or can you anticipate anything particularly exciting in two young people running through the night pursued by hungry Bolshevists with covetous eyes on the precious cart-load of this self-same harvest of potatoes? Yet Griffith presents these trivialities as so important in the lives of two young people that tears are being furtively shed because Grannie refuses to give her sanction to a pauper's wedding.

Little Carol Dempster gives a performance that is at once startling because of its beauty and its histrionic power heretofore unknown. She is quite a revelation.[198]

Good reviews do not make a film a success. They didn't help *Isn't Life Wonderful.* Failure was readily apparent. In December Griffith was forced to give the negative and rights to the Central Union Trust Company as further collateral for his outstanding loans. Griffith began work on the first of his films under Zukor's Paramount banner. Both Zukor and his executives were willing to defer to Griffith on the choice of subjects for this film despite what must have seemed an increasingly poor record. Griffith selected Dorothy Donnelly's *Poppy,* a successful play about early show business that had enjoyed a successful run in New York with the comedian W. C. Fields playing the lead. Griffith wanted Fields to repeat his stage role in the film. Zukor agreed with Griffith's choice, and work on the film began as soon as rights to the play were acquired and Fields signed to a contract.

To clear Griffith of the last of his United Artists obligations, Zukor arranged for the distribution of *Poppy,* now re-titled *Sally of the Sawdust,* by United Artists. In the complicated maneuvering to settle Griffith's affairs between Zukor and Abrams, Griffith lost all hope of personal gain from the film.

When Griffith transferred to Paramount and the Astoria studios, he could take few of his old crew with him. Carol Dempster was kept to play the lead in the film, and Hal Sintzenich was retained as a cameraman, although Paramount cameraman Harry Fischbeck was first cameraman. The only other person to go with Griffith was Frank Walsh, who was asked to accompany Griffith as assistant director, a title he had not held at Mamaroneck. Paramount refused to put Walsh on the payroll, so Griffith added him to his personal payroll, paid from his own salary.

Griffith was kind and patient with young Walsh, coaching and teaching as he had done with his young Biograph players a decade before. Walsh remembers:

> He was a gentlemanly guy, always. Even though I was a kid when I was assisting him, it was always "Mr. Walsh," unless he wanted to apologize for something. If he had bawled me out, then he would say, "Frank . . . it was a tough day . . ." Even with the extra people, it was always "please do this" or "please do that." He could get mobs of people to do things for him that they wouldn't do for other people.[199]

At first Walsh functioned as second assistant director behind Erville Alderson, who had been assigned by Paramount. In one of his rare displays of temperament Griffith expressed his dissatisfaction with Alderson and forced him to resign. Walsh moved up to first assistant and held that post through Griffith's next two films.

Walsh had an unobstructed view of Griffith at work. His job began at nine in the morning, setting up for rehearsals, and then taking notes and acting as guardian of the script. For the first time Griffith was given a script, a shooting script, for a film. Walsh testifies that Griffith generally ignored it. "He told one person, 'I wouldn't read the script. It might get you all balled up.' "[200] Walsh's guardianship of the script largely consisted of keeping it out of Griffith's way.

Griffith would arrive for rehearsals between 9:30 and 10 a.m. Rehearsals were not held at the Astoria studios. Instead the banquet room above the 44th Street Keen's Chop House, next door to the Belasco Theatre, was rented. Walsh would have the outline of the set laid out on the floor before Griffith's arrival. Griffith's methods of rehearsal were still much the same as those he had learned in the theatre. From these rehearsals Walsh would gain a solid idea of Griffith's wishes and intentions, and when it was time for that scene to be shot, he could spend most of the night before working with the cameramen to light the set and make certain that everything, including the smallest prop, was in place and ready. Once the shooting began and a new camera set-up was required, Griffith had Walsh take charge. Griffith would ask Walsh for an estimate of the time it would take and then retire to a dressing room for a nap, even for as short a time as three-quarters of an hour. "He could sleep at any time. He would lay down and be fast asleep and wake up in that three quarters of an hour and be back on the set." [201]

Although the working day ran from nine to six, six days a week, Griffith kept Walsh on call twenty-four hours a day. He would sometimes call Walsh at three in the morning with changes for the next day's shooting. Walsh would be summoned to Griffith's suite at the Astor for a conference. If Walsh took advantage of the free tickets for Broadway shows accorded to him as Griffith's de facto casting director, it was necessary for him to leave his name at the box office with his seat number, just like a physician, so that Griffith could summon him from the theatre without delay. Walsh did not realize that he was one way in which Griffith managed to relieve the loneliness of a hotel room.

Griffith's manner of working had become somewhat more erratic, and new ideas came with great suddenness. When Griffith broached a new idea, Walsh found that it was best not to tell Griffith that he had not heard it before but to reply, "It's on the way, Mr. Griffith." The hustle would then begin to fill Griffith's order. Since the Paramount studio was on Long Island, across the East River from the theatrical suppliers in Manhattan, an alternate stall was to answer, "It's stuck on the Queensboro Bridge from Manhattan." If Griffith was satisfied that the costume or prop was on its way, he would continue shooting. If he didn't believe Walsh, or the same excuse had been used once too often, he would stop shooting and wait for the item to arrive.

Griffith's second picture for Paramount was also announced early in January 1925, *The Sorrows of Satan,* based on a popular novel by Marie Corelli. The property had been purchased originally for Cecil B. De Mille. Zukor was aware that De Mille might be planning to defect from Paramount, and there is some evidence that the announcement that Griffith would direct *The Sorrows of Satan* was a weapon in Zukor's dispute with De Mille. Hiring Griffith was thus a form of insurance against a pullout by De Mille, then Paramount's star director. Despite these maneuverings by Zukor, De Mille left within the year to form his own company, and *The Sorrows of Satan* was Griffith's to direct. Griffith later claimed, with some justification, that the picture was forced on him.

Before starting *The Sorrows of Satan,* Griffith was pressured to make a second picture with W. C. Fields to be called *That Royle Girl.* Griffith fought against doing this second film, objecting vigorously to Jesse Lasky that the script was a bad one, rejected by every other director at Paramount. Lasky turned on his charm, barely covering his executive power, and convinced Griffith that only he could turn this drab material into a hit. Lasky's appeal to Griffith's vanity worked. Griffith was now sufficiently unsure of himself and his own judgment to be easily persuaded. There was no one left to whom he could turn for advice.

The filming of *Sally of the Sawdust* had its problems, most of them revolving around the differences between Fields and Griffith. Fields considered the whole process an opportunity for defying the system. He would perform in one part of a scene wearing one costume, and then appear for a second shot in the same scene in a different one. The two shots would not, of course, match. A careful watch had to be kept on Fields to prevent these deliberate attempts to sabotage the scenes. Fields also used a fake clip-on moustache that had been part of his make-up in the stage role. He could not be persuaded that the artificiality showed on film. Fields also brought his own one-man claque with him, a stooge known simply as "Shorty," who could be depended upon to carry out Fields's gags off camera.

Sally of the Sawdust was released by United Artists on August 2, 1925, opening at the Strand Theatre in New York. *Film Daily* reported:

> DWG has forgotten about art and played to the box-office, but the film is still too long. Carol Dempster waves her arms about too much in an attempt to give an impression that she is a kid. W. C. Fields is best; it is his first appearance. This film is box-office chiefly because of DWG's name.[202]

It is obvious, even today, that Fields is the only thing that holds the film together. Carol Dempster's mannerisms become embarrassing, and she was obviously miscast. Still, Griffith had acceded to her suggestions that her role be strengthened. Griffith's brother Albert later claimed that an additional $25,000 was spent shooting extra scenes to build up the Dempster role.

Dempster and Fields were back together in the next film, *That Royle Girl,* but this time Fields's role was cut to a pale shadow. The story of the film was a silly one, and Carol Dempster's performance matched the story. *That Royle Girl* opened at the Strand on January 10, 1926. Mordaunt Hall in *The New York Times* was more concerned with the appearance of Carol Dempster and James Kirkwood in the flesh following the film, and with a projector breakdown during the screening, than with the film itself. Griffith gave Dempster a free rein, trying unsuccessfully to turn her into a Pearl White style comedienne involved in a melodramatic murder plot.

> She first appears as a young hoyden, the daughter of a bibulous reprobate, impersonated by Mr. Fields. Later she figures in a dressmaking establishment where her appearance wins her the position of a manikin, and subsequently she becomes a dancer, disguised so that she can obtain information regarding a murder of which her friend Fred Ketlar has been convicted. Miss Dempster is exceptionally attractive in these chapters, but one gathers that the various villains must be shortsighted not to recognize her as Daisy Royle before they do.
>
> Occasionally Daisy is called upon to emulate Tom Mix, Douglas Fairbanks, and Richard Dix in acrobatic stunts, especially when she escapes through the flustered coterie of scoundrels.
>
> Mr. Fields' more modulated efforts appeal warmly to the gathering such as when . . . he inadvertently picks up a lighted candle and sticks it in his mouth instead of the cigar.
>
> While it would be more encouraging to see Mr. Griffith's genius devoted to a more plausible vehicle, his work on this subject—aside from the wild stretches—proved for the most part a decidedly satisfactory entertainment to the audience.[203]

It might seem that Griffith had found the perfect material for a Mabel Normand at last, but instead he was stuck with Carol Dempster.

There was little doubt on the part of the studio crew and the others working with Griffith that his infatuation with Carol Dempster was clouding his judgment. Carol proved difficult for almost everyone to handle except young Frank Walsh. Dempster did not use the fiery approach, but instead turned a frigid eye on those who displeased her. Griffith had always been attracted to a certain type of young nubile girl. As each of his actresses had matured, he had let them slip away. He was always gallant in telling them, as he had reluctantly told Lillian Gish, to go and seek a greater fortune elsewhere, but it also seems apparent that he tired of them as elements in his own creative fantasies when they no longer fitted his pattern. Anita Loos has unkindly said that the Griffith girls were moronic. She remembered Clarine Seymour bringing a ball to the set to play with. Actually Griffith had been lucky, as well as a judge of talent, in having a string of young girls with rare ability, Florence Lawrence, Blanche Sweet, Mary Pickford, the Gish sisters, and Mae Marsh. None was moronic. With Carol Dempster, however, only the physical appearance really fit the pattern. She, too, was intelligent. In fact, while the other girls had grown to artistic maturity while working for Griffith, Dempster was already a mature woman under the facade of girlish innocence when she first appeared on the Griffith horizon as an extra in *Intolerance*. She knew what she wanted, and her campaign was successful. Griffith at fifty-one was not the first director, nor the last, to try to make a star out of a girl who excited him for other reasons than talent. Griffith refused to see Dempster's failings as an actress.

It was recognized by Paramount that *That Royle Girl* was a dull film before shooting was over, and an additional $100,000 was authorized for the staging of a hurricane as a finish for the film. *Film Daily* found the film long at its premiere on January 17, 1926, but felt that: "Griffith plays it straight to the box-office and hits the mark. The picture runs long but the whirlwind climax is sure to send them out forgetting all about it." [204] Most of the audience forgot about showing up for the picture in the first place.

Despite his falling prestige within the film industry, Griffith was still being lionized by the outside world. The magazine *World's Work* polled motion picture advertisers and found that of the twelve men who had made the "most contribution to the advancement of the art of the film, Mr. Griffith was the only director honored with membership in this Hall of Fame."

As Griffith became less and less sure of himself in making films, his public posture grew increasingly pompous. He looked for alibis to explain both the change in the types of films he was making and their general lack of acceptance by the public. *Collier's Magazine* published an interview in which Griffith stated: "Personally, I believe it is far easier to make an artistic picture, such as would please those whom the majority consider 'highbrow,' than to make one that will be popular." [205]

A year later Griffith wrote an article for *Theatre Magazine* in which he said:

> There were better stories in the early days, like *Pippa Passes* and the works of Shakespeare, but exhibitors would not buy them today. It is above the taste of the masses.
> . . . Pictures are the only medium that can carry big stories, epochal poetry and events—that is what I would like to see, but who knows! If I had my way, I would do Homer's *Iliad, Antony and Cleopatra, The Life of Napoleon, Medea*—things that can never be done as effectively on the speaking stage, stories in which all the illusion of a spectacle and authenticity might be introduced.[206]

All of these grandiose concepts from the man who, when he was independent and able to choose his own properties, filmed two threadbare popular melodramas, *The Two Orphans* and *Way Down East*.

Griffith's suit against Al Jolson, via D. W. Griffith, Inc., came to an end in mid-September 1926, with the award to the Griffith company of only $2,627.28, hardly enough to cover the legal expenses. Griffith's trial lawyer, Arthur Driscoll, announced he would consult with Griffith about appealing the judgment. No further action was taken.

The production of *The Sorrows of Satan* was a descent into disaster. Carol Dempster quickly put her co-stars Adolphe Menjou and Ricardo Cortez into the deep freeze. Frank Walsh found himself carrying the necessary messages back and forth between them. At first Griffith was given a free hand by Paramount's New York studio chief, William LeBaron. Walsh found himself the keeper of the budget among his other duties. "Griffith would have a conference with Bill LeBaron, then head of the studio, and afterwards they would call me in to interpret what was said." [207] LeBaron would ask Walsh, now on the Paramount payroll, about the requirements of the script that Griffith seemed to be ignoring. Walsh would tell LeBaron what Griffith was actually going to do. "They didn't hold him down on anything. Anything he wanted, he got. That was a bone of contention with other directors on the lot, like Herbert Brenon, who did not receive the same treatment." [208]

There were as many as four or five films shooting at the Astoria studio at the same time. Walsh had to manage Griffith's schedule to stay out of the way of the other companies. This schedule was complicated because Griffith liked to shoot in the script sequence: scene 1, 2, 3, etc. The flexibility of a shooting schedule was thus destroyed.

Everything that Griffith shot was printed, even the botched takes. At the end of the day, Griffith would go to dinner and later meet with Walsh, his long-time cutter Jimmy Smith, and frequently Carol Dempster, at Nile's Projection Room on 46th Street between Broadway and Sixth Avenue. They would watch the dailies, the shots made that day, until ten or eleven o'clock at night. As the film rolled on, Griffith seldom commented, communicating in an almost incomprehensible code with Jimmy Smith. Nothing was cut during the filming, and Griffith never had the shots run in sequence. When the shooting was finished, he disappeared with Jimmy Smith for a week to edit the film. Then a rough cut would be screened.

The Sorrows of Satan had been budgeted as a major picture, and the initial planning had called for considerable spectacle. It has been said that Zukor insisted on Griffith's concentrating on the love story and spending more screen time in dull, vapid close-ups of Carol Dempster and Ricardo Cortez. Frank Walsh remembers it as two films: "Griffith cut the picture and it was a good picture. I can remember Richard Dix coming out of the projection room saying, 'Oh, boy! I'm sorry I wasn't in this.' " [209] When Walsh saw the final version of the film at the premiere, he felt that it had been butchered. After that first cut, Griffith was taken off the picture by Lasky and, with Zukor's approval, Julian Johnson re-edited the film.

Actually the disastrous re-editing was not the first example of front office tampering with the film. Griffith's art director and designer, Charles Kirk, had completed all the sets for the film, but the front office decided to hire the Broadway visionary set designer Norman Bel Geddes to design the heavenly stairs setting. The setting was a spectacular one, with angels flown on wires manipulated by the specialists from the old Hippodrome Theatre in New York. Bel Geddes was secretly hired to do more. He was asked to film, without Griffith's knowledge, this final sequence.

> Walter Wanger supplied me with a copy of the Corelli novel and told me to do a treatment of the final sequence as soon as I could. I was ready in thirty-six hours, with a ten page scenario and twelve large charcoal drawings. Lasky and Wanger went over them immediately and pronounced themselves delighted. The next step was to set up a staff to operate under my direction, and get the thing filmed. William LeBaron, Long Island managing director, took charge of this phase of the operation. He endeared himself to me forever by assigning Fred Waller as my cameraman. This was the same Fred Waller who later invented Cinerama, one of the great cameramen of his time.
>
> Waller ran off the latest Griffith rushes for me. They were as close to the drawings of Gustave Dore for *Paradise Lost* as scenery and camera could get, and, as far as I was concerned, totally unrelated to the earlier, or earthly, part of the film.
>
> Almost any change would have been an improvement.[210]

The Bel Geddes set was constructed without Griffith's knowledge, and the resulting footage shot by Bel Geddes and Waller was edited to the same length as the Griffith footage for the sequence. Lasky, Wanger, and LeBaron, the conspirators, told Bel Geddes that they liked it. Without Bel Geddes present, the sequence was shown to Griffith. Griffith watched the sequence run several times, maintained his composure, and even commented favorably on its originality. Griffith then decided to re-shoot the sequence his own way. Bel Geddes felt flattered that his pioneer attempt was even considered by Griffith and was neither surprised nor chagrined when Griffith decided not to use it. Bel Geddes stated that in the final film about half of the footage that he and Waller had shot was used and, perhaps, 90 per cent of his scenario. There was some mention of a directorial position for Bel Geddes, but it turned out to be only talk. He was of no further use to the executives of Paramount.

Bel Geddes described the Griffith of 1926:

> I never saw him dressed in anything but a high, stiff collar, a gray felt hat, high shoes with brass hooks and pulling loops at

the back, and one of a succession of suits none of which could be less than fifteen years old, and all of which were woefully out of style. He looked like a hard-up, itinerant school teacher. His face was grave. When he smiled it was with the benign rigidity of a stone buddha. His nose, like his face, was long and thin, and he had a pronounced under-lip, upon which rested an endless succession of cigarettes.

DW directed thoughtfully, precisely, without demonstrations. I refrained from stepping near when he was doing an intimate close-up. He would pull his chair almost into the laps of the actors involved and speak softly so that only they could hear what he had to say. His face would be nearly hidden under that wide-brimmed gray hat, but the actors would watch it intently and draw from it inspiration for performances far surpassing anything they had been capable of before. Throughout the directing day, DW kept up a calm, quiet, chattering undercurrent of prompting and advice which contributed greatly to the exactness of the timing and mood. Even when he spoke loudly his words were assured and measured. He did scenes over and over again, sometimes as many as thirty times. "Once again, please. We'll try it once again." It was a virtual refrain to his work. He gave little attention to time. Rehearsals continued all day, often until eight in the evening. And after he had let the actors go, he would retire to the projection room and watch the day's rushes until two or three in the morning.

DW stood more than he sat, and when he sat it was in any chair available. There was no chair with his name on it. When he stood, he folded and unfolded his arms constantly and moved slowly about, drawing deeply on cigarettes. . . .[211]

When Zukor saw the re-edited film, he disliked it, and mistakenly blamed Griffith for the disaster. Griffith, who had been so gracious about the Bel Geddes incident, had actually accumulated his own bitterness, charging that the film had not been his alone from the beginning, and that conflicting instructions from Lasky and Zukor had made a shambles of the budget and the picture. When the film opened on October 12, 1926, and proved almost from the outset to be a financial disaster, Zukor was more than willing to break Griffith's contract by foregoing the final film due Paramount. Griffith was just as eager to go his own way.

The film was not unanimously badly received. Mordaunt Hall in *The New York Times* praised the film:

> In swinging from squalor to pomp, depicting wretchedness on one side and passionate orgies on the other, Mr. Griffith reveals himself as a master, and in this present offering he has made a photodrama that excels anything he has done in recent years. . . . It is a marvelously beautiful film. . . .

As to the cast, Hall said of Carol Dempster:

> Carol Dempster's acting is something exceptional. She imbues the part with pathos and eagerness. She presents the portrait of undying hope, and not even in *Isn't Life Wonderful* did she give an idea of the talent she displays in this new film.[212]

What sort of a film was it? We probably will never know now, even if a print is found someday.

A month after the opening of *The Sorrows of Satan*, Griffith went to California for discussions with Joseph Schenck, who had succeeded Harry Abrams as head of United Artists. Schenck, who had his own production company, Art Cinema Corporation, had become production head for United Artists in 1924, and then succeeded to the presidency of UA when Abrams died in 1926. Schenck had managed to keep UA supplied with enough films by developing his own stable of stars, a list headed by his wife, Norma Talmadge, and his brother-in-law, Buster Keaton.

Schenck felt that he could use Griffith as a director, but more importantly, he hoped that he could control Griffith's stock in United Artists. He offered Griffith a contract to direct films for United Artists release through his own Art Cinema Corporation, only stipulating that he retain script approval and the voting rights to Griffith's stock. Griffith was in no position to object. The only other offer that had been made to Griffith had come from Cecil B. De Mille. De Mille had asked him to join De Mille's independent company, backed by Pathé and the Keith-Albee theatre chain. Griffith had sought advice about this offer, and for once, the advice was sound: Griffith should ignore the De Mille offer. De Mille's company foundered. On April 19, 1927, Griffith signed a contract with Schenck, on Schenck's terms.

Griffith had reached the bottom of the ladder, both personally and artistically. Carol Dempster had departed, without warning to Griffith, and married a shipping heir. Billy Bitzer wrote:

> This broke Griffith all up—he took to drinking quite heavily. He goes on an occasional periodical now and then (this is between ourselves Griffith is a fine fellow, always was). During one of his drinking spells he got into a sort of a jam with a girl who claimed he had promised to make a star out of her. She was some outsider who had got into his room at the Astor Hotel etc. She sued him for $100,000. It was in the papers at the time . . . so Griffith's brother got Griffith to put his money in an annuity fund from which only so much could be drawn. If he hadn't done this he would probably be without any money now. . . .[213]

There were some other details from the past that had to be taken care of before Griffith could begin working for Schenck. A young man, Edward K. Bender, had lost a hand during the filming of *America* when a ramrod, left inadvertently in a cannon, had been discharged when the gun was fired. The cannon had been fired by Griffith's former Biograph colleague Eddie Dillon. Bender had sued D. W. Griffith, Inc. for $50,000. Griffith appeared in court on February 9 in Philadelphia as a witness. Bender won his case and received an award of $20,000, although an appeal was filed by D. W. Griffith, Inc. seeking to prove contributory negligence on Bender's part. Presumably this contribution was made by Bender when he put his hand in the path of the flying ramrod.

There was also the matter of Linda Arvidson Griffith. She had stayed out of Griffith's way as long as regular payments were made under their agreement. Griffith had agreed in addition that the sum of $100,000 would cover all of his obligations. In the twenties, of course, he just didn't have the money to make the payments. Linda was now threatening legal action. The action would be brought in New York, another factor contributing to the attractiveness of Schenck's offer of work in California. Griffith was assured that Linda couldn't touch him there. It was never Griffith's desire to run out on any of his financial obligations. J. C. Epping commented:

> . . . if Mr. Griffith paid $100,000 to Linda Griffith, it no doubt fulfilled a contractual obligation. All I know is that all of these obligations were met by Mr. G. at a very great financial sacrifice and often financial embarrassment. . . . Whether this contract was fair or generous, I can neither confirm nor deny. . . . In the

light of subsequent events, the contract seems to have over-antic-
ipated too optimistically into the future.[214]

Linda Griffith kept up the drumfire of demands, however, refusing
to believe that Griffith didn't have the money to pay her.

Griffith didn't help his domestic situation with the continued release of publicity about grandiose film schemes, impossible of ful-
fillment, but designed to restore what remained of his prestige.
Late in October 1926 he announced that George Bernard Shaw
had offered to write a scenario for him to film back in 1917. Griffith said that he had turned the offer down. When Shaw was que-
ried by a reporter from *The New York Times* the day after Griffith's story, Shaw replied that he couldn't remember the *rejection*.
Then, in April 1927 it was announced that Griffith would direct a
film with H. G. Wells as the scenarist. The film, to be called *The
Peace of the World,* was to be made in London and Hollywood.

Reality was far removed from the proposed H. G. Wells film.
Griffith went to California and was given a first assignment by
Schenck. He was to edit and tinker with a bad production of *Uncle
Tom's Cabin,* starring the Duncan sisters, called *Topsy and Eva,*
which Del Lord had directed. Schenck said that he was more than
satisfied with Griffith's improvements.

The next film assignment under Schenck was a film based on
Francesca da Rimini, an Italian melodrama that Griffith knew well
from the play by George Henry Boker that had been a staple of the
late nineteenth-century theatre. It had been a star vehicle for Otis
Skinner. The story was reset from fourteenth-century Italy into
nineteenth-century Latin America, and the title changed to *Drums
of Love.*

The one auspicious sign for *Drums of Love* was the signing of
Lionel Barrymore to play the cuckolded husband, hunchbacked
Duke Cathos De Alvia. To counter that splendid actor, Griffith
had the misfortune to be given Mary Philbin, who was a sufficiently wooden actress to make Carol Dempster seem hyperactive.

Since the story revolved around the act of adultery, there was
only one way to have it end, tragically. When this downbeat ending proved unpopular, Griffith shot another happy ending which
only proved, within the context of the story, ludicrous. The film

was further burdened by pretentiously asinine titles composed by Griffith's former publicity man Gerrit Lloyd. A superb performance by Lionel Barrymore could not save the picture.

At least *Film Daily* got the point of the picture: "It is a tragic love story, beautifully done. It has loads of sex appeal." [215]

Drums of Love opened at the Liberty Theatre in New York on January 24, 1928. It should be noted that Griffith had re-hired Billy Bitzer as one of the three cameramen on the picture. The others were Karl Struss and Harry Jackson. Two other old members of the Biograph acting company were also in the cast, Tully Marshall and Charles Hill Mailes. Griffith continued to be loyal to his old associates when he could.

Mordaunt Hall commented in his review:

> It is a picture with unrestrained love scenes and prolonged kissing episodes. One might imagine that it would be immensely pleasing to a Parisian audience, for the element of sex dominates the whole affair. . . . It has been produced with a certain artistry, except for a closing incident which adds nothing to the picture and might better have been omitted. Mr. Griffith has succeeded in setting forth his narrative with a good deal of suspense, and Lionel Barrymore gives a forceful portrayal of Giovanni, the Cripple, or, as he is known in this photoplay, the Duke Cathos De Alvia.
>
> Following the screening of *Drums of Love*, Mr. Griffith appeared upon the stage and made a short talk, in which he thanked those who had helped him. Among others, he mentioned the players and Mr. Gest.[216]

Laurence Reid in *Motion Picture News* boosted the film:

> Who said Griffith was through? The master of shadings and shadows, the builder of climaxes, demonstrates again that he has a firm hold on the treatment of a film story.
>
> . . . This is all told with the utmost simplicity—and if it builds slowly, the treatment is perfectly excusable to emphasize the tragedy of the climax. The original story cannot be read inside of three days. Why should one scoff over the film which has to be told within two hours? [217]

Reid's review sounds almost like those letters to the editor protesting that the latest Broadway turkey is really a tremendous success, understood, of course, only by the limited few that can appreciate the subtlety of the material. There were "scoffers" at the film. They outnumbered the Reids. Reid did admit that the drawing power of the film lay solely in the Griffith "appeal," and the "beauty of Miss Philbin." The first was almost non-existent, and the second absurd. If these were the cards for *Drums of Love,* Griffith was trumped again.

For his second picture under Schenck's auspices, Griffith decided to re-make his old film *The Battle of the Sexes,* with some changes to modernize the story. The decision to have Griffith make sex farces was a disastrous one. He had a sense of humor, but it was one that grew out of naturalistic effects. His attempts at farce of any sort were always cloying, lacking timing and grace. *The Battle of the Sexes* had only its title going for it. The same Laurence Reid who had been so strong a supporter of *Drums of Love* now said of the new film:

> They've given D. W. Griffith an opportunity to make over one of his early triumphs, and all things considered it doesn't shape up as anything out of the ordinary. The idea has been used many, many times—indeed, ever since it was first exploited by Griffith.
> . . . The picture is obvious all the way, and lacks the Griffith touches of humanity. But he hasn't forgotten his contrasts nor his sentiment, although the latter element looks out of place . . . as if it were added to balance the high jinks and make its bid for sympathy.[218]

Griffith's uncertainty in selecting film subjects and in finding the right dimension for his films, compounded by his heavy drinking away from the set, forced others, all too willing, to make vital decisions about his films. A synchronized score and one song, sung by Phyllis Haver, were added to *The Battle of the Sexes* without Griffith's knowledge. When he heard them, he didn't like them, but was powerless to have them removed.

Schenck now had lost his trust in Griffith, and for Griffith's third film Schenck gave Griffith a complete shooting script written by Sam Taylor. Taylor had based his script on a story by Karl Volmoeller, and intended to film it himself. Schenck took the pseudo-Balkan romance away from Taylor and gave it to Griffith to shoot verbatim, an act that should have earned Taylor's undying gratitude to Schenck. Once again Griffith was called upon to make a film that required a light, deft touch if its marzipan story was to survive. Griffith stamped on it with his high shoes and left it with little life. Griffith took the heroine, Lupe Velez, whose only strong asset was her Latin tempestuousness, and changed her into a vapid imitation of his past heroines. The film, titled with a matching heavy hand *Lady of the Pavements,* opened first in Los Angeles on January 22, 1929. Mordaunt Hall thought the film was "a handsome production, with spacious and lavishly furnished settings, brilliant photography, faultlessly fitting uniforms and voluminous crinoline skirts." He reserved his hardest comments for the hero, William Boyd, who later found more congenial material as Hopalong Cassidy:

> A rather unfortunate choice for the principal male role was William Boyd, who is quite pathetic when it comes to expressing his silent love . . . with his well shaved face and American haircut, he hardly impresses one as being either an attaché or a person of bygone days.[219]

John S. Cohen, Jr. in the New York *Sun* noted:

> Mr. Griffith has turned her [Lupe Velez's] animalism into cuteness. He has done her hair up into little pompadours, made her pigeon-toed and rather coy, and when she begins to upset court functions, one is reminded of the gosling days of the Gishes and the Dempsters.[220]

Griffith had come to New York for the opening on February 16, and started back for the West Coast immediately following. His first press statement wasn't made until he paused in Chicago, in which he stated that the sound film would force the drama from the stage and spell the end of the silent film. He was, of course, right only in the second part of his statement, and by that time his remark was not terribly prescient. The evidence was all at hand. He told the interviewer that he planned to revive *The Birth of a Nation, Intolerance,* and *Hearts of the World* with sound.

The only review of *Lady of the Pavements* with which he could console himself was that from *Film Daily:*

> This is a fine woman's picture, nice love interest played against colorful backgrounds. A beautifully mounted produc-

tion. The first half merely average because of the over-empha-
sized sequences and comedy that doesn't click. The second half
builds up and puts the picture over with considerable to
spare.[221]

Not really much consolation in even that. Griffith was out of New
York only a step ahead of Linda Griffith's process servers.

When Griffith arrived in California, he found that Schenck
avoided him. After weeks of this treatment, Griffith began to tell
his colleagues that he intended to quit. His associates in D. W.
Griffith, Inc. became afraid that any severance of Griffith from
United Artists at that point would sink their foundering company.
They asked Griffith to keep trying to see Schenck.

As the disappointing box office returns mounted, Griffith knew
that the only chance with Schenck, and for himself, was to find
some property that would appeal to the studio head. One idea appealed to him, the old one of making a film about Abraham Lincoln. Griffith had toyed with the idea since his days at Biograph
and the first of his films about the Civil War. This was fortified by
the research that he'd done for *The Birth of a Nation*. Despite his
romantic sympathies with the Confederacy, Griffith, like many
Southerners, admired Lincoln. He was convinced that, had Lincoln
lived, the terrors of the Reconstruction period would not have
been visited on the South.

Out of this old idea, Griffith developed an ambitious plan for a
Lincoln film. When Schenck, at last, was willing to see him, Griffith placed his plan on the table quickly, before Schenck had an
opportunity to fire him. Griffith had anticipated that this was the
real meaning for his appointment with Schenck. Griffith was surprised when Schenck, who had lost confidence in Griffith and listened to the industry gossip that Griffith was through, agreed to let
Griffith make his film about Lincoln. Apparently the boldness of
Griffith's proposal, and the appeal of the subject material as something that had worked so well for the old Griffith, turned the trick
with Schenck.

The situation for Griffith's company, D. W. Griffith, Inc., was
eased somewhat in May with the refund of some $38,000 in tax
over-payments from 1920. Without Griffith's knowledge these
funds were invested in the stock market. In retrospect such an in-

vestment in the market at the time that the country was plunging into its worst economic disaster, the great depression, would seem to have been potentially the crowning debacle of Griffith's business career, but through an ironic twist these investments proved sound and managed to survive the market crash, returning a substantial profit.

Caught up in the Lincoln project, Schenck was willing to allow Griffith the material and support for a top-budgeted film. Griffith cast Walter Huston, a fine actor, as Lincoln, and Una Merkel, once Lillian Gish's understudy in *Orphans of the Storm,* as Lincoln's first love, Ann Rutledge. Griffith brought back his old star Henry Walthall as Colonel Marshall, and Ian Keith as John Wilkes Booth. Jason Robards, Sr. and Cameron Prudhomme were also in the cast. The one expenditure that Schenck would not permit was the hiring of Carl Sandburg to do the script. Instead, Griffith was able to secure the services of the poet Stephen Vincent Benét. The art direction was assigned to the talented William Cameron Menzies. It looked like Griffith's best opportunity in many years. Three factors worked against the possibilities of success: Griffith's drinking, described, even by himself, as an illness; his sense of insecurity; and his inability to keep from "improving" the work of others with sycophantic, but inept, assistance. Griffith and Lloyd tinkered with the Benét script. In the end little of the Benét material was actually used. Later Griffith regretted these changes and felt that a finer film would have resulted if they had stayed with the Benét scenario.

These regrets were, in large part, the rationalizations of a man outside the film industry, made after his career was over, but when Griffith separated himself from his pompous publicity statements he had a strong gift for self-analysis. He was always flexible in viewing his own work. A major part of his failure ultimately was his inability to understand the nature of the intuitive ingredients that made one of his films successful and another a failure. Griffith himself had said that it was necessary for a film-maker to understand his audience. Griffith was remote from his audience, retaining only the vision he had acquired in the 1890s. Times and people had changed, but Griffith didn't realize this.

Lillian Gish has reported that Benét's script was torn apart, in the author's presence, by the front office philistines at United Artists, and that as a result of this humiliating session, Benét caught the next train out of Hollywood, never to return. Griffith might have liked to defend Benét's script, but he was in no position to do so.[222]

As soon as the shooting was finished on *Abraham Lincoln,* Griffith left for an isolated retreat in Mineral Wells, Texas. The final filming of special effects was completed without Griffith present, and the editing of the film was carried out under the supervision of John Considine, Jr. The film was previewed in San Diego without Griffith. Griffith saw the completed film for the first time in New York just prior to the opening on August 25, 1930. He requested editorial changes, but Considine, with Schenck's backing, refused. Griffith was prohibited from entering the projection room or touching the positive print, and, of course, the negative was where he couldn't reach it. Griffith now told Schenck that this was the last straw, and he wanted out. Schenck, who thought that *Abraham Lincoln* had much of the old Griffith strength, but found Griffith undependable, readily agreed to the separation. Griffith's contract called for a fifth picture to be made with Schenck's company for release by United Artists. Schenck was willing to forget it. Griffith, given more time and agility of mind, might have made a more memorable exit from United Artists and Schenck, but he concluded with only a cliché, "Too many cooks spoil the broth."

In a normal situation *Abraham Lincoln* might have meant a resurgence for Griffith. The film was well received. On its strength both *Film Daily* and the *New Movie Magazine* selected Griffith as the best director of 1930. *The New York Times* selected it among the ten best films of the year.

Film Daily called it "A Griffith achievement; this is entertainment plus history." [223]

In many ways *Abraham Lincoln* repeated the mistakes that Griffith had made with *America.* The lack of interest in the principal character, despite Walter Huston's attractiveness in the role, was inherent in the audience's familiarity with the basic story. Only through new insights into Lincoln's character and his relationships with his family and loves, might the audience's interest have been stimulated. No new insights were presented, and the results were like a waxworks. The excitement has been drained away. Animated history is not drama no matter how worthy the subject.

But in the midst of the sort of success that might have launched a young man on a career, Griffith was despondent. He allowed the usual statements to go forth about a giant new undertaking: a film about the history of England, to be called *The Birth of the Empire,* and financed by the British government. Griffith felt that he was still one film short of finding his way back. That film had to be one over which he had total control. No more Schencks, no more Considines. California had been closed out by Schenck. The discovery of the small funds remaining in D. W. Griffith, Inc., the results of the stock investment, plus the bolstering of his prestige by *Abraham Lincoln* enabled Griffith to float another small bank loan to make another film.

With the new-found resurgence due to *Abraham Lincoln, The Birth of a Nation* was revived in December at the George M. Cohan Theatre in New York, with added sound effects and a synchronous score. *The New York Times* noted:

> It is not necessary to accept this interpretation of the South in reconstruction as the product of meticulous research. Construed as sentimental melodrama or as inflammatory document born of race prejudice—it has been called both—it remains poignant and stirring.[224]

Griffith rested for a year, planning what would prove to be his last film, *The Struggle.* Renewing his old contacts with Zukor, he exacted a promise that the film could be made in the Paramount studios in Astoria. With a script based on an Emile Zola novel, *The Drunkard,* written by his former colleagues Anita Loos and her husband, John Emerson, Griffith thought that he could say something pertinent about prohibition. At the moment of beginning work it seemed a timely subject. Anita Loos was to tell Lillian Gish much later that she had meant the film to be humorous, but that Griffith had insisted on doing it as drama. There is no evidence that the film ever had the sort of slant Miss Loos thought it should have, except in retrospect. Such a treatment would have been more in keeping with Anita Loos's undoubted talents.

Griffith's heavy drinking had continued, and though he had

managed to keep it under control while working on a film, his year away from work had the aspects of a long binge. Just before beginning *The Struggle,* he required the services of a nurse to pull him through one bad bout. Knowledge of his condition, combined with the gossip of his detractors, who now referred to him as "hooked-nose Dave," caused Paramount to pull out of their promise to make studio space available. Griffith searched frantically for a studio that could be rented. A small cramped studio, Audio-Cinema, Inc., at 2826 Decatur Avenue in the Bronx, was finally found. The film was cast with New York actors who were willing to work for low salaries. The group assembled, however, was a talented one. Hal Skelly, who had achieved success on the stage in *Burlesque* during the 1927–28 season, was signed for the lead. The female lead was played by Zita Johann, who was viewed as a very promising Broadway actress. Another small ingenue role was filled by Evelyn Baldwin. Griffith had met Miss Baldwin a number of years before at her mother's home. Now he found that he was interested in her as a person, rather than as an actress, in a way that hadn't happened since Carol Dempster left him. When *The Struggle* was finished, he signed Evelyn to a personal contract at $50 a week with a clause permitting him to share in any of her earnings made from other companies. The contract was to run for two years from October 2, 1930.

The Struggle was made between July 6 and August 9, 1931. Griffith took the company out of the stifling confines of the tiny Bronx studio as much as possible and shot in the streets and real surroundings, a return to the location-hunting of his Biograph days. For a time he felt renewed. Ray Klune was hired as the unit manager. In turn he hired two assistant directors, Richard Bladen as first assistant and young Jack Aichele as second assistant. Aichele had never worked on a Griffith picture, and he regarded this as a rare opportunity, and still does today in retrospect.

Aichele remembers a confident Griffith, completely in control of the shooting, supporting the cast and crew, and continuing to encourage innovation just as he had done at the beginning of his career with Billy Bitzer. Joe Kaufman, an electrical engineer, painstakingly constructed a special parabolic reflector from many layers of black paper to surround the microphone. This enabled the sound man to pick up the dialogue from a considerable distance, keeping any extraneous sound at a minimum, and freeing the camera for more flexible use. Griffith was also able to move his actors with something of the flexibility of the silent films.

Aichele found himself in charge of a special panel board.

> Mr. Griffith would say he was ready. I would press a button and the bells would come on. Press another button and the lights would come on. Press another and the studio doors would automatically close. My job was to see that everything was signed, sealed, and delivered, ready for Mr. Griffith to begin work with the actors.[225]

Aichele testifies to Griffith's sobriety during the filming of *The Struggle,* and to his careful, decorous behavior toward Evelyn Baldwin. Aichele was surprised when the announcement was made of Griffith's marriage to Miss Baldwin in 1936. There had been no indication of a romance during the making of the film.

Much of *The Struggle* took on the documentary quality that Griffith had achieved in his early films. Splendid scenes were shot in Springdale, Connecticut, at the Stamford steel-rolling mills.

The only sign of uncertainty about *The Struggle* came during the editing process. This time the film was not shown to the company, even in rough cut. They were to see it completed for the first time at the premiere. Barney Rogan, the film editor, told Aichele that Griffith was cutting, re-cutting, and sometimes putting the out-takes (discarded footage) back in again, almost in a frenzy. Aichele remembers at the premiere noticing whole sequences, excellent ones in his opinion, that were missing.

Never one to miss an opportunity for keeping his name in the papers, Griffith was releasing his usual spate of rumored future productions during the editing period on *The Struggle*. One story was reported that Griffith would direct a "George Washington" pageant in Washington, D.C. A second story carried Griffith's denial. Another reported Griffith would direct a film version of Galsworthy's *Loyalties.*

The Struggle opened at the Rivoli Theatre in New York on December 10, 1931, and lasted for one disastrous week. Mordaunt Hall of *The New York Times* was among the kinder critics.

> With her husband, John Emerson, at her elbow, Anita Loos who made the English-speaking world laugh by her wit in "Gentlemen Prefer Blondes," turned out a story for a picture called

"The Struggle," which was offered with due pomp and ceremony at the Rivoli last night. This effusion, which is damp with tears and whiskey, has the distinction of having been directed by David Wark Griffith, whose last production was that splendid film, "Abraham Lincoln."

Neither Miss Loos, Mr. Emerson, nor Mr. Griffith can be said to have accomplished anything particularly novel by this screen work, for, with strong drink as its menace, it seldom arises above that old time contribution, "The Face on the Bar Room Floor."

And after it was all over . . . a very busy Hal Skelly appeared in dress clothes and, with the aid of men with a spotlight, pointed out former Governor Alfred E. Smith, Nancy Carroll, Clyde Pangborn, the distinguished aviatrix, Ruth Elder, and others.[226]

On the same day Mordaunt Hall gave a better review to a film called *Elisabeth Von Oesterreich,* in German, and directed by someone named Adolf Trotz.

The rest of the reviews were worse than Hall's, and mocked the film. Griffith was accused of having made a cheap melodrama drawn from a despised past. The audience at the premiere had laughed in the wrong places. Griffith was crushed. He had expected to come out after the film with his tested shy speech, but instead he fled to his hotel room, leaving Skelly to face the music. He proceeded to get drunk, and refused to see anyone for days. The unkindest cut came when *Film Daily,* which had managed to see something good in almost everything Griffith had done, dismissed the film: "This is poor entertainment; it is old-fashioned domestic drama with little box-office appeal." [227]

The Struggle was given its national release by United Artists, which had put up a small amount of the production money for the distribution rights, on January 9, 1932. *The Struggle* disappeared quickly from the screens. Few theatres wanted to book the film even with Griffith's name attached. For Griffith now, the money was gone, and, more important, the ability to raise money was gone. Only a hope, sustained by the last remnants of bravado, remained. Griffith still felt that somehow the tide would turn again, but it didn't. Griffith, the film director, was a part of the past. *The Struggle* was his last film. Griffith was fifty-seven years old on January 23, 1932.

15

Postscript:
Accolades and Unemployment

About two years ago Griffith made his last picture here in New York, *The Struggle* it was called—had Hal Skelly in it—that died. I was with him on that one (it turned out terrible) old fashioned. We had some country scenes in this picture and Griffith asked me where might be a good place. I suggested Cuddyback. Oh, boy, what a thrill that would have been . . . but somehow they couldn't figure the sound trucks, lights, and big company for that distance.

To close about Griffith thought you would be interested. He has enough money to keep in comfort for the rest of his life. I don't think he will ever make any more pictures.[228]

If Griffith had been directing his own retreat from the Rivoli Theatre to the safety of his hotel room, he would have probably followed with a slow fade-out. That ending might have made a fair tragedy, or if the fallen king of the film had leaped from the Empire State Building, perhaps, even high tragedy. There was no leap, no slow walk into the ocean (as the aging actor did in *A Star Is Born*). Life seldom follows a script, and Griffith lived for sixteen more years buoyed by impractical dreams and old memories. His few friends sustained him in the feeling that he was on the edge of the motion picture industry and at any moment he would make his triumphal return. A small band of self-styled film historians and critics hailed him as the "father of the film," and their articles pleased his vanity even when they had no effect whatever on his industry.

His retreat from the humiliation of *The Struggle,* a humiliation that latter-day viewers of the film feel was undeserved, lasted for almost six months. Griffith was not the man either to drink or brood himself to death. He was not broke, although his funds were severely restricted, and he was unable to pay Linda. He did manage to keep sending money to his kin in Kentucky, support that he had been extending for years in his role as head of the clan. His public corporation was finished now. Fortunately Griffith was only an employee, and the failure of the corporation cost him nothing. Griffith's greatest strength had always been his imagination, and, whether he was at the top or the bottom, that didn't desert him. In 1933 there was still no indication that his career had been ended by one failure, and the bankruptcy of D. W. Griffith, Inc. was not his first.

By November, although saying that he had no plans for the future, he was turning his attention to some of the plays he had optioned. One of these was *Damn Deborah* by Walter Charles Roberts. In the theatre world, where costs were infinitely lower than those of film production, Griffith felt that he might renew his creative touch. Unfortunately, the theatre world of 1933 was no more receptive to Griffith than it had been in 1907. Griffith submitted *Damn Deborah* to both Katharine Hepburn and Katharine Cornell. Both ladies politely turned it down.

Griffith's last financial ties with D. W. Griffith, Inc. had been cut in December 1931, when Banzhaf notified the corporation treasurer that no more advances were to be made to Griffith from the corporation funds, nor to Albert Grey, nor to Griffith's nephew Willard Griffith, who had been barnacled onto the payroll. Griffith resigned the presidency of the corporation in April 1932 and was succeeded by Robert E. Lent, whose task it was to preside over the dissolution.

Despite Griffith's fall from power and employment, his relatives didn't lose their appetite for living off his largess. Now, when Griffith could have used all the warmth and support that a family might have given him, he received only a stream of letters asking for more money, asking for expensive gifts, demanding continued support. Linda Griffith's demands became more shrill. She revealed that a corollary of her agreement with Griffith stated that in no case were her payments to fall below $400 a week. Niece Ruth Griffith in Kentucky wanted a car. She thoughtfully included an advertising pamphlet showing the Chevrolet Master Six that she wanted in her letter to Uncle David. While Ruth was demanding a new car, Griffith was now only able to purchase a second-hand 1928 Mercedes-Benz for himself, an expensive car originally, but now three years old.

At Christmastime 1932, Griffith came out of his isolation long enough to make a radio broadcast on behalf of the Salvation Army's Christmas fund drive. This radio appearance seemed like the opening of a possible new career for him. Griffith was hired to appear on a series of radio broadcasts dealing with the history of the movies and including dramatized fictional vignettes from his own career. The broadcasts were sponsored by Hinds, the hand lotion manufacturers. Griffith's introductory reminiscences occupied most of the thirty-nine programs in the series. Griffith's tales were romantic distillations of his press agents' stories and his own falsified personal history. Griffith had become quite used to the practice of fictionalizing his career, and he readily extended this technique into his radio broadcasts. The stories he told were anecdotal, and before long the sponsor began to feel that they were irrelevant to the times. The decision was made to drop the series. With this new forum, Griffith was up to his old publicity tricks, announcing that he was looking for a Mary Pickford of the radio. If at that point he was looking for another Mary Pickford, no one else was, not even the original.

In April 1933 Griffith found that he had to sell his United Artists shares. He had long since, of course, lost his voting control in the shares as a result of his agreement with Schenck. He was further rewarded with a small bonanza, $20,000 in cash, that he had left and forgotten in his old California headquarters, the Alexandria Hotel. The old hotel was also bankrupt, and the receivers had discovered Griffith's money while making an inventory of the contents of the hotel safe. Griffith's imagination was fired by this almost cinematic incident, and he embroidered it for an acquaintance by saying that a similar find had turned up in a forgotten safe deposit box in New Orleans when a bank was being rebuilt. There is no evidence that this latter story was anything more than Griffith's imagination at work.

With his new-found nest egg, Griffith went home to Kentucky in his aging purple Mercedes. To the Louisville press he sent word that he was merely trying to stay away for a time from the "studio merry-go-round." He invested in a new wardrobe, and established himself in the Bluegrass Room of the Brown Hotel in Louisville. He had long since found that he couldn't stay with his relatives, so he made only an occasional visit to them.

Just before he left New York, he had accorded an interview to Mildred Mastin. Miss Mastin observed:

> At the windows of a tall Manhattan hotel, a man stood look-ing down at Broadway. From the window, twenty-two stories above the street, he watched hundreds of dancing, burning elec-tric signs, screaming the names of movies and their stars.
> For twenty years the man had been the outstanding creative genius in motion pictures. He was idle now. Out of the game.

Griffith told Miss Mastin:

> "Movies are written in sand. Applauded today, forgotten to-morrow. Last week the names on the signs were different. Next week they will be changed again.
> "I am tired of the movies! To suggest my making another film is like asking a pensioned bricklayer to build another wall." [229]

Before the interview was over, however, Griffith had belied his own words and outlined his desires to make a film about Sam Houston and the development of the Southwest. He showed Miss Mastin his furniture, books, and possessions, making certain that she knew he was financially well. Griffith had learned an old show business axiom well, that one must never seem hungry, one's shoes should be shined, and one's smile bright. Always look like a win-ner. Griffith had seen what little attention was paid to those who had become obvious losers. He had himself been begged for a job by his old assistant director, Frank Powell, whose career had had one high point, the direction of *A Fool There Was* with Theda Bara, and then had gone steadily downhill to oblivion. Harry O'Neill, the actor who had played Paul Revere in *America,* had begged Griffith for a job—any job. Griffith knew that he had to keep up the front.

Mildred Mastin finished her version of the interview with an as-sessment that was accurate, even if it was only reflecting the indus-try's opinion at the time: ". . . his old masterpieces, when run off

on the new and faster modern projectors, jump and flicker fool-
ishly. His glory is in the past."

While Griffith was savoring the delights of the bar in the Bluegrass Room at the Brown Hotel, an unexpected hope suddenly appeared that there was a road back. An offer arrived asking him to
preside over a re-make of *Broken Blossoms* in England. Griffith
had sold the film rights to Julius Hagen of the Twickenham Film
Company. Griffith cabled that he would be delighted to consider
the offer and would come to England at once. He arrived in South-
hampton on the *S.S. Acquitania* in late May 1935, full of anticipa-
tion and bourbon. Griffith loved England, but he was unhappy
this time that his reception was not in the same spirit as his previous trips. The new version of *Broken Blossoms* was to be made
with Emlyn Williams playing the Barthelmess role. Somehow the
casting of British players grated on Griffith's nerves. He grew increasingly irritable. Suddenly he called Lillian Gish at three in the
morning, New York time, and asked her, somewhat incoherently,
to come to London to play again the role of Lucy. Lillian, failing
to understand the true nature of Griffith's position, suggested that
he make some other film and not repeat himself. Griffith asked,
pleaded, and begged that she come to play the part, and then,
without warning, hung up. Lillian was so shaken by the phone call
that she cabled the British film producer Herbert Wilcox to find
out whether Griffith was drunk. She was told that the film deal had
fallen through and Griffith was on his way home.

Griffith's entire stay in England had lasted only three weeks. On
his arrival in New York, he did not stop but went straight through
to Louisville. One reason for this was the fear that Linda Griffith's
process servers would find him.

Despite Griffith's appeal to Lillian Gish, the dispute that had
scuttled the re-make of *Broken Blossoms* had come about when
Griffith had been suddenly taken with a young French girl, Ariane
Borg, as the perfect Lucy. Unfortunately the producer had already
contracted for the role to be played by Dolly Haas. In a dramatic
effort to convince Hagen that his new find should have the part,
Griffith had rehearsed the beautiful but inexperienced Miss Borg
in a scene from the film, and then staged a reading for Hagen in
which he played Battling Burrows himself. The scene was the vio-

lent one in which Burrows discovers his daughter in the young
Chinese boy's room and beats her unmercifully. Griffith put everything he could into the scene, and the reaction of Hagen was one
of shock. He was convinced that Griffith had lost control completely. The scene had an additional and unexpected climax with
the appearance of Miss Haas. The producers then terminated their
agreement with Griffith as quickly as they could.

In October 1935 Judge Murray Hulbert appointed a receiver in
equity, Joseph Gans, for D. W. Griffith, Inc. Gans was immediately
embroiled in stockholders' suits. Griffith, fortunately, escaped any
involvement.

The brief stop-over in New York in transferring from the boat
to the train gave Griffith time to see Evelyn Baldwin. This young
girl of twenty-four and her widowed mother seemed to hold some
of the family warmth that Griffith had once found in the Gish family. At this point in his life, at sixty, the lovely Evelyn must have
seemed like a return to his youth. Griffith was convinced that he
was in love with her, and, fully cognizant of his age and marital status, he proposed to her. Griffith's courtliness and his still imposing
manner undoubtedly had made a great impression on the young
actress. She had watched his battle on his last film, *The Struggle,*
and her heart went out to him. She indicated that, if Griffith were
free to marry, she would accept him. As Griffith rode the train
back to Louisville, his mind dwelt heavily on how he might free
himself from Linda.

The day after Christmas, 1935, Griffith filed suit for a divorce
from Linda Arvidson Griffith in Louisville under a Kentucky law
that provided grounds when a man and woman had not lived together for five or more years. Griffith's suit stated that he and his
wife had lived apart since 1911. The Kentucky court did not require that both partners be present for the divorce proceedings.
The legal process of attempting to notify Linda of the action was
followed. She did not appear, and on February 28, 1936, the divorce was granted. Two days later Griffith married Evelyn Baldwin
in a hotel in Louisville. The ceremony was performed by the Reverend W. R. Johnson, a Methodist minister from La Grange. Many
of Griffith's relatives, including his brother, William, attended.
The bride's sister, Mrs. W. F. Walls of New York, was also present.

When Linda Griffith heard of the divorce and re-marriage, she attempted to institute an action to have the divorce rendered invalid. She claimed that she had not been notified, and even threatened to produce the statement Griffith was said to have made confessing misconduct to her in 1911, the alleged basis for their separation. Linda's suit failed. The supposed confession was never produced.

The highlight of the Griffiths' honeymoon trip was the annual Academy Award ceremonies in Hollywood. During this eighth annual award ceremony, Griffith was presented a special citation for his contribution to the motion picture. He was praised for his "innovations, upon which the industry has built much of its success." The Griffiths remained in California, hopeful that the attention accorded him by the Motion Picture Academy of Arts and Sciences would somehow produce a summons from a studio. It did not. Griffith had that one evening in the spotlight, nothing more.

In May Griffith visited the set of a film being directed by his former assistant director of *Intolerance* days, W. S. Van Dyke. The film was *San Francisco,* and Van Dyke was filming the crowd scenes in which refugees from the earthquake and fire flee the devastation. Van Dyke welcomed Griffith, listened to Griffith's reminiscences of the actual event and how close he had come to being in the city when it happened, and then asked Griffith if he would like to direct the crowd scene then being staged. Griffith smilingly welcomed the momentary assignment, for old times' sake, and enjoyed himself while ordering the actors into a satisfactory composition. To Evelyn he later speculated on how much better he might have handled the assignment for the entire picture if it had been his.

In August he was given a testimonial dinner at the Hollywood Athletic Club by some of his old colleagues, including Mack Sennett. A print of *The Battle of Elderbush Gulch,* belonging to Andre Beranger, was the highlight of the evening.

All of this activity still produced no signs of a job offer. Griffith and Evelyn decided to return to La Grange. Evelyn wished to visit her mother in New York first. Griffith would go with her only as far as Newark, still wary of Linda Griffith's process servers. Linda was attempting to raise the bigamy issue in New York, and was claiming that Griffith was still $50,000 in arrears on his payments to her.

Lillian Gish came over to Newark to see Griffith and his bride.

She remembered that he seemed little changed except for thinning hair—still vigorous and hopeful for the future. Lillian approved of Evelyn Baldwin, as had Griffith's old cameraman, Billy Bitzer.

Griffith remained in La Grange, Kentucky, for the next several years. He wrote some scenarios, started work on an autobiography to be called *D. W. and the Wolf,* and wrote some poetry. He was sufficiently active to make it necessary for him to hire a secretary. He became an honored guest in Louisville amateur theatre circles, and found a champion in Boyd Martin, amateur theatre director and sometime critic. Martin asked him several times to take an active part in community theatre, but Griffith shied away, explaining that he was too busy adding a wing to the house in La Grange and writing. None of these efforts at seeming busy made any impression on Hollywood. Griffith was forgotten.

One significant interest in the Griffith of the past came from John Abbott, director of the new film library at the Museum of Modern Art in New York, and from Mrs. Abbott, who used her maiden name, Iris Barry, professionally. They had approached Lillian Gish in 1937 and asked her to intercede with Griffith in an attempt to secure prints of Griffith's films for the library; otherwise, these films might vanish. They explained that these prints should be properly preserved, and copies made on acetate film stock that would not be subject to the disintegration inevitable with the originals on nitrate stock.

Lillian Gish was excited by the idea and transmitted the Abbotts's request to Griffith. He was not only flattered by this attention, but in a very practical sense he was glad to be relieved of the charges for keeping prints and negatives in storage in New York and Louisville. In March 1938 he presented a considerable quantity of his material—films, business records, correspondence, and press books—to the museum. The materials covered the period from 1913, when he left Biograph, through 1924.

The concept of preservation inspired Griffith to ask Abbott to mount a campaign to save the old sets on the United Artists lot in California that were about to be torn down, particularly the remnants of the *Intolerance* set. The economics of the film industry, as well as the regulations of the fire department, prevented them from being saved.

Finally an offer from Hollywood arrived. Hal Roach, a producer of short comedies, first in competition with Sennett and then as Sennett's successor, had decided to do a re-make of Griffith's old film *Man's Genesis*. Roach had in mind a much more ambitious film filled with prehistoric monsters. He asked Griffith to "supervise" the production. Griffith interpreted this to mean that he would direct. Roach's idea was that Griffith would act in an advisory capacity. Evelyn and Griffith moved back to California in the spring of 1939, and Griffith reported for work at the Roach studio.

In the publicity cranked out by the Roach studio during the spring and summer of 1939, the point was made that the agreement between Roach and Griffith was a purely verbal one. It was announced in August that Griffith would direct *1,000,000 B.C.* with Carole Landis and Victor Mature. No mention was made of the origin of the story. In September the release said that *1,000,000 B.C.* would be produced by David Wark Griffith. A further release to *The New York Times* in October re-stated that Griffith would direct the film for Roach.

Whether Griffith actually directed any of *1,000,000 B.C.* has never been satisfactorily resolved. Hal Roach has stated that none of the footage in the finished film was directed by Griffith. Further, Roach has said that Griffith knew all along that he was to be only an adviser on the film. This is somewhat at variance with the releases from Roach's own publicity department.

Another story had Griffith committing the cardinal sin of ordering Hal Roach off the set. In any event, Griffith was not credited with directing the film, although he drew his salary during the entire production period. When filming was finished, Griffith announced that he was withdrawing his name from any connection with the film. He complained to friends that he had been used by Roach solely for the publicity value of his name. Certainly, there seems to be much truth in this view.

Griffith and his second wife continued to live in Hollywood at the Roosevelt Hotel during the early forties, with Griffith tinkering alternately on various half-completed plays, an attempt at an autobiography, and plans for future film productions. In 1940, the Museum of Modern Art in New York staged a retrospective exhibition of the Griffith films that could be obtained. Iris Barry prepared a monograph on Griffith's career that hailed Griffith as "one of the greatest and most original artists of our time." Griffith came to New York to assist in the preparation of the exhibition, and was barely restrained from taking scissors in hand to re-edit his old films. One vital service he was able to perform was to re-assemble *Intolerance,* although the version shown, and still shown by the Museum, is far shorter and, perhaps, in part edited in different sequences from the original version. Griffith's old cameraman, Billy Bitzer, had been hired by the museum to collate and annotate old Biograph materials donated to the museum's film library. For the last time the two old collaborators could work together, although the reliability of both was doubtful since they both had serious drinking problems. Billy Bitzer was especially grateful for the Beaumont Newhall interview and appraisal of his work that was included with the Iris Barry monograph. The few fierce Griffith partisans had tended, for the most part, to downgrade Bitzer's contribution. On the other hand Bitzer was not reluctant to maximize his own contributions, though he still did not want to detract from Griffith's commanding contribution.

The retrospective gained glowing coverage in *The New York Times,* other newspapers, and magazines, but beyond that its effect was nil. Griffith partisans tried to persuade the film industry to hire Griffith. One of these partisans, Barnet Bravermann, wrote to Darryl Zanuck and upbraided Zanuck and Twentieth Century Fox for not hiring Griffith. Zanuck's reply, while fair and accurate as a personal statement, rather summed up the industry's attitude toward the old director. Zanuck wrote:

> I have your letter of May 29th [1944] regarding D. W. Griffith and confess I am quite puzzled by it.
>
> It is an honor, of course, to be listed as one of D. W.'s contemporaries. He brought much to this industry. He pioneered in many important directions. Very few of us here fail to recognize his solid contributions and great influence in the development of motion pictures.
>
> Yet, there are many important men in this industry who were much more closely associated with him than was I. They were his intimates and co-workers. Consequently, I am at a loss to understand why I was singled out for implied criticism in not providing him with a post worthy of his attainments.

. . . I am perfectly willing—indeed happy—to give D. W. his full due. As I said before, he is one of the great pioneers of this industry. I respect and admire him for what he has done.

As to finding a place for him to suit his talents, that is another matter. D. W. is too big a man to be offered any job. He's a legend in this business. It would be mutually embarrassing, I believe, to offer him something which a lesser person could do as well. To engage him in an important capacity, with a commensurate salary, would require a vote of the board of directors. To be frank with you, I do not know whether we could here gain their consent since the important posts are all filled at present.[230]

A different approach was separately taken by Lillian Gish and Sidney Skolsky, both of whom spent a considerable amount of time attempting to sell a studio on making a film about Griffith's life. Griffith was particularly enthusiastic about Lillian's efforts and was convinced that Lillian's name was big enough, if his own was not, to convince A. P. Giannini of the Bank of America to advance the necessary financing.[231] No one was interested in Gish's proposal, and later even less interested in Skolsky's scenario. Hollywood gossip columnist Hedda Hopper summed up the industry's reaction: ". . . if our producers are going to glorify anybody then it's going to be themselves. They've practically forgotten the man who started their fortunes—D. W. Griffith." [232]

Lillian Gish has written about the studios' attitudes: "It was almost a conspiracy of indifference. Perhaps D. W. had achieved too much fame, and the reigning powers were afraid that he would run away with the picture industry again." [233]

The Griffiths were forced to move from the Roosevelt Hotel when suites were broken up for more profitable use as single rooms. D. W. and Evelyn purchased a small cramped stucco house in Beverly Hills in the less fashionable section of the city. The house was right next to the street so that its walls were easily penetrated by the noise of passing cars. Griffith hated it from the beginning. His only escape was a trip to the ranch property at San Fernando where time might be spent in the cottage-like house occupied by the property's caretaker. Some of his old friends— W. S. Van Dyke, Del Henderson, Marshall Neilan, Herb Sterne, and Lillian Gish—would gather there to reminisce about the old times. The gaiety and good fellowship of those few occasions could not dispel Griffith's feeling that he was being walled in, separated from the only activity that really mattered to him. The frustrations of retired life piled up. He drank too much and began to quarrel with Evelyn. He became increasingly irritable.

In the fall of 1947 matters finally came to a head between Evelyn and Griffith. Griffith moved to the Hollywood Knickerbocker Hotel, and on October 2, 1947, Evelyn filed for divorce. Evelyn's charges of incompatibility were supported by Griffith's statement that he was "a bachelor at heart." There was no need at the divorce proceedings for bitter exchanges concerning the Griffiths's domestic difficulties in a ménage of wife, mother-in-law, and three cats. Griffith was glad to go.

The only recorded version of Griffith's last year of life at the Hollywood Knickerbocker was an interview with Ezra Goodman, a reporter for *PM,* a short-lived liberal newspaper in New York. Goodman's interview allowed Griffith the opportunity of commenting gently upon the current motion picture scene, but Goodman, with an eye obviously on a thesis about Hollywood later realized in his book, also chose to emphasize Griffith's drinking and still predatory, if, at seventy-three, elderly, inclinations towards the nearest blond. Like most elderly men separated from their work, Griffith liked to dwell in the past, but even at this point he clung to the hope that one of his projects might open up a new opportunity for him.[234]

On July 22, 1948, Griffith was struck by a massive cerebral hemorrhage in his room. He managed to leave his room and reach the hotel lobby looking for help. Dr. Edward A. Skaletar was summoned, and Griffith was rushed to Temple Hospital. Little could be done for him. He remained in a coma throughout the night and died the next morning, July 23. His niece and nephew, Ruth and Willard Griffith, were able to reach his side before death, although Griffith never knew they were there. If he had known of their presence, he probably would have thought they were after money.

Funeral services were held at the Masonic Temple in Hollywood on July 28. Griffith had joined the Masonic Lodge in Northern New Jersey many years before during the Biograph days. Eulogies at the services were delivered by Donald Crisp, then acting president of the Motion Picture Academy of Arts and Sciences, and Charles Brackett, the M.P.A.A. vice-president. Crisp said:

I cannot help feeling that there should always have been a place for him and his talent in the motion picture field. It is hard to believe that the industry could not have found a use for his great gift.[235]

The Bob Mitchell Boy Choir sang, and the Reverend Emil Brininstool presided.

Griffith's body was flown to Kentucky and buried in the family plot at the Mount Tabor cemetery. Two years later his body was moved to a new grave marked with a new stone provided in a last act of contrition by the Screen Directors' Guild.

Griffith had written his own best epitaph in 1907 in *The Wild Duck:*

Look! He is falling, falling out to the sea.
Ah, there is mist on the sea!
There is always mist on the sea in the evening.
Perhaps, his nest is beyond, I know not;
Perhaps it is built of the mist, I know not.
Only with tired wings wearily beating
And eyes turned back to the mainland
To the red and white and red,
Waving and blowing together
He is falling out, out to sea.
Poor little wild duck! Poor little wild duck!

The recognition of Griffith's work that had begun in a small way with the Museum of Modern Art's retrospective in 1940 has continued since Griffith's death with retrospectives and memorials both in Kentucky in 1962 and again in New York in 1965. In 1969, the Film Society of Lincoln Center devised a program for the schools of New York State that detailed some of Griffith's contributions to film history. Lillian Gish dedicated a scholarship at Columbia University in Griffith's name. The brightest tribute of all, however, are the intense faces of the young people of a new generation, not even born when Griffith died, leaving a showing of *Intolerance,* announcing that they have just seen "the most exciting film" of their lives.

The Films of D. W. Griffith

The following list of films is divided into two parts: films made during Griffith's employment by Biograph, and subsequent films made for other companies. The Biograph films are listed in the order in which they were made with their release date. More complete information can be found in *D. W. Griffith, The Years at Biograph*, by Robert M. Henderson. The non-Biograph films have been listed with their principal credits in the order in which they were made with their release date.

The Biograph Films

1908

The Adventures of Dollie (7.14;08)
The Redman and the Child (7.28;08)
The Tavern Keeper's Daughter (7.24;08)
The Bandit's Waterloo (8.4;08)
A Calamitous Elopement (8.7;08)
The Greaser's Gauntlet (8.11;08)
The Man and the Woman (8.14;08)
For Love of Gold (8.21;08)
The Fatal Hour (8.18;08)
For a Wife's Honor (8.28;08)
Balked at the Altar (8.25;08)
The Girl and the Outlaw (9.8;08)
The Red Girl (9.15;08)
Betrayed by a Hand Print (9.1;08)
Monday Morning in a Coney Island Police Court (9.4;08)
Behind the Scenes (9.11;08)
The Heart of Oyama (9.18;08)
Where the Breakers Roar (9.22;08)
The Stolen Jewels (9.28;08)
A Smoked Husband (9.25;08)
The Zulu's Heart (10.6;08)
The Vaquaro's Vow (10.16;08)

Father Gets in the Game (10.10;08)
The Barbarian, Ingomar (10.13;08)
The Planter's Wife (10.20;08)
The Devil (10.2;08)
Romance of a Jewess (10.23;08)
The Call of the Wild (10.27;08)
After Many Years (11.3;08)
Mr. Jones at the Ball (12.25;08)
Concealing a Burglar (10.30;08)
Taming of the Shrew (11.10;08)
The Ingrate (11.20;08)
A Woman's Way (11.24;08)
The Pirate's Gold (11.6;08)
The Guerrilla (11.13;08)
The Curtain Pole (2.15;09)
The Song of the Shirt (11.17;08)
The Clubman and the Tramp (11.27;08)
Money Mad (12.4;08)
Mrs. Jones Entertains (12.8;08)
The Feud and the Turkey (12.8;08)
The Test of Friendship (12.15;08)
The Reckoning (12.11;08)
One Touch of Nature (1.1;09)
An Awful Moment (12.18;08)
The Helping Hand (12.29;08)

The Maniac Cook (1.4;09)
The Christmas Burglars (12.22;08)
A Wreath in Time (2.8;09)
The Honor of Thieves (1.11;09)
The Criminal Hypnotist (1.18;09)
The Sacrifice (1.14;09)
The Welcome Burglar (1.25;09)
A Rural Elopement (1.14;09)
Mr. Jones Has a Card Party (1.21;09)
The Hindoo Dagger (3.11;09)
The Salvation Army Lass (3.11;09)
Love Finds a Way (1.11;09)
Tragic Love (2.11;09)
The Girls and Daddy (2.1;09)

1909
Those Boys (1.18;09)
The Cord of Life (1.28;09)
Trying To Get Arrested (4.5;09)
The Fascinating Mrs. Frances (1.21;09)
Those Awful Hats (1.25;09)
Jones and the Lady Book Agent (5.20;09)
The Drive for Life (4.22;09)
The Brahma Diamond (2.4;09)
Politician's Love Story (2.22;09)
The Jones Have Amateur Theatricals (2.18;09)
Edgar Allen Poe (2.8;09)
The Roue's Heart (3.8;09)
His Wife's Mother (3.1;09)
The Golden Louis (2.22;09)
His Ward's Love (2.15;09)
At the Altar (2.25;09)
The Prussian Spy (3.1;09)
The Medicine Bottle (3.29;09)
The Deception (3.22;09)
The Lure of the Gown (3.15;09)
Lady Helen's Escapade (4.19;09)
A Fool's Revenge (3.4;09)
The Wooden Leg (3.8;09)
I Did It, Mama (3.15;09)
A Burglar's Mistake (3.25;09)
The Voice of the Violin (3.18;09)
And a Little Child Shall Lead Them (3.22;09)
The French Duel (5.10;09)
Jones and His New Neighbors (3.29;09)

A Drunkard's Reformation (4.1;09)
The Winning Coat (4.12;09)
A Rude Hostess (4.8;09)
The Road to the Heart (4.5;09)
The Eavesdropper (5.3;09)
Schneider's Anti-noise Crusade (4.8;09)
Twin Brothers (4.26;09)
Confidence (4.15;09)
The Note in the Shoe (5.6;09)
Lucky Jim (4.26;09)
A Sound Sleeper (4.12;09)
A Troublesome Satchel (4.19;09)
Tis an Ill Wind That Blows No Good (4.29;09)
The Suicide Club (5.3;09)
Resurrection (5.20;09)
One Busy Hour (5.6;09)
A Baby's Shoe (5.13;09)
Eloping with Auntie (5.24;09)
The Cricket on the Hearth (5.27;09)
The Jilt (5.17;09)
Eradicating Auntie (5.31;09)
What Drink Did (6.3;09)
Her First Biscuits (6.17;09)
The Violin Maker of Cremona (6.7;09)
Two Memories (5.24;09)
The Lonely Villa (6.10;09)
The Peach Basket Hat (6.24;09)
The Son's Return (6.14;09)
His Duty (5.31;09)
A New Trick (6.10;09)
The Necklace (7.1;09)
The Way of Man (6.28;09)
The Faded Lilies (6.17;09)
The Message (7.5;09)
The Friend of the Family (7.15;09)
Was Justice Served? (6.21;09)
Mrs. Jones' Lover, or *"I Want My Hat!"* (8.19;09)
The Mexican Sweethearts (6.24;09)
The Country Doctor (7.8;09)
Jealousy and the Man (7.22;09)
The Renunciation (7.19;09)
The Cardinal's Conspiracy (7.12;09)
The Seventh Day (8.26;09)
Tender Hearts (7.15;09)
A Convict's Sacrifice (7.26;09)
A Strange Meeting (8.2;09)

Sweet and Twenty (7.22;09)
The Slave (7.29;09)
They Would Elope (8.9;09)
Mr. Jones' Burglar (8.9;09)
The Mended Lute (8.5;09)
The Indian Runner's Romance (8.23;09)
With Her Card (8.16;09)
The Better Way (8.12;09)
His Wife's Visitor (8.19;09)
The Mills of the Gods (8.30;09)
Franks (8.30;09)
Oh, Uncle (8.26;09)
The Sealed Room (9.2;09)
1776, or The Hessian Renegades (9.6;09)
The Little Darling (9.2;09)
In Old Kentucky (9.20;09)
The Children's Friend (9.13;09)
Comata, the Sioux (9.9;09)
Getting Even (9.13;09)
The Broken Locket (9.16;09)
A Fair Exchange (9.23;09)
The Awakening (9.30;09)
Pippa Passes (10.4;09)
Leather Stockings (9.2;09)
Fools of Fate (10.7;09)
Wanted, a Child (9.30;09)
The Little Teacher (10.11;09)
A Change of Heart (10.14;09)
His Lost Love (10.18;09)
Lines of White on the Sullen Sea (10.28;09)
The Gibson Goddess (11.1;09)
In the Watches of the Night (11.25;09)
The Expiation (10.21;09)
What's Your Hurry (11.1;09)
The Restoration (11.8;09)
Nursing a Viper (11.4;09)
Two Women and a Man (11.15;09)
The Light That Came (11.11;09)
A Midnight Adventure (11.15;09)
The Open Gate (11.22;09)
Sweet Revenge (11.18;09)
The Mountaineer's Honor (11.25;09)
In the Window Recess (11.29;09)
The Trick That Failed (11.29;09)
The Death Disc (12.2;09)
Through the Breakers (12.6;09)

In a Hempen Bag (12.16;09)
A Corner in Wheat (12.13;09)
The Redman's View (12.9;09)
The Test (12.16;09)
A Trap for Santa Claus (12.20;09)
In Little Italy (12.23;09)
To Save Her Soul (12.27;09)
Choosing a Husband (12.30;09)
The Rocky Road (1.3;10)
The Dancing Girl of Butte (1.10;10)
Her Terrible Ordeal (1.10;10)
The Call (1.20;10)
The Honor of His Family (1.24;10)
On the Reef (1.17;10)
The Last Deal (1.27;10)
One Night, and Then— (2.14;10)
The Cloister's Touch (1.31;10)
The Woman from Mellon's (2.3;10)
The Duke's Plan (2.10;10)
The Englishman and the Girl (2.17;10)

1910
The Final Settlement (2.28;10)
His Last Burglary (2.21;10)
Taming a Husband (2.24;10)
The Newlyweds (3.3;10)
The Thread of Destiny (3.7;10)
In Old California (3.10;10)
The Man (3.12;10)
The Converts (3.14;10)
Faithful (3.21;10)
The Twisted Trail (3.24;10)
Gold Is Not All (3.28;10)
As It Is in Life (4.4;10)
A Rich Revenge (4.7;10)
A Romance of the Western Hills (4.11;10)
Thou Shalt Not (4.18;10)
The Way of the World (4.25;10)
The Unchanging Sea (5.5;10)
The Gold Seekers (5.2;10)
Love Among the Roses (5.9;10)
The Two Brothers (5.9;10)
Unexpected Help (7.28;10)
An Affair of Hearts (5.19;10)
Romona (5.23;10)
Over Silent Paths (5.16;10)
The Implement (5.30;10)
In the Season of Buds (6.2;10)

A Child of the Ghetto (6.6;10)
In the Border States (6.13;10)
A Victim of Jealousy (6.9;10)
The Face at the Window (6.16;10)
The Marked Time-table (6.23;10)
A Child's Impulse (6.27;10)
Muggsy's First Sweetheart (6.30;10)
The Purgation (7.1;10)
A Midnight Cupid (7.7;10)
What the Daisy Said (7.11;10)
A Child's Faith (7.14;10)
The Call to Arms (7.25;10)
Serious Sixteen (7.21;10)
A Flash of Light (7.18;10)
As the Bells Rang Out (7.21;10)
An Arcadian Maid (8.1;10)
The House with the Closed Shutters
    (8.8;10)
Her Father's Pride (8.4;10)
A Salutary Lesson (8.11;10)
The Usurer (8.15;10)
The Sorrows of the Unfaithful
    (8.22;10)
In Life's Cycle (9.15;10)
Wilful Peggy (8.29;10)
A Summer Idyll (9.5;10)
The Modern Prodigal (8.29;10)
Rose O'Salem Town (9.26;10)
Little Angels of Luck (9.8;10)
A Mohawk's Way (9.12;10)
The Oath and the Man (9.22;10)
The Iconoclast (10.3;10)
Examination Day at School (9.29;10)
That Chink at Golden Gulch
    (10.10;10)
The Broken Doll (10.17;10)
The Banker's Daughters (10.20;10)
The Message of the Violin (10.24;10)
Two Little Waifs (10.31;10)
Waiter No. 5 (11.3;10)
The Fugitive (11.7;10)
Simple Charity (11.10;10)
The Song of the Wildwood Flute
    (11.21;10)
A Child's Stratagem (12.5;10)
Sunshine Sue (11.14;10)
A Plain Song (11.28;10)
His Sister-in-law (12.15;10)
The Golden Supper (12.12;10)

The Lesson (12.19;10)
When a Man Loves (1.5;11)
Winning Back His Love (12.26;10)
His Trust (1.16;11)
His Trust Fulfilled (1.19;11)
A Wreath of Orange Blossoms
    (1.30;11)
The Italian Barber (1.9;11)
The Two Paths (1.2;11)
Conscience (3.9;11)
Three Sisters (2.2;11)
A Decree of Destiny (3.6;11)
Fate's Turning (1.23;11)
What Shall We Do with Our Old?
    (2.13;11)
The Diamond Star (2.20;11)
The Lily of the Tenements (2.27;11)
Heart Beats of Long Ago (2.6;11)

1911
Fisher Folks (2.16;11)
His Daughter (2.23;11)
The Lonedale Operator (3.23;11)
Was He a Coward? (3.16;11)
Teaching Dad To Like Her (3.20;11)
The Spanish Gypsy (3.30;11)
The Broken Cross (4.6;11)
The Chief's Daughter (4.10;11)
A Knight of the Road (4.20;11)
Madame Rex (4.24;11)
His Mother's Scarf (4.24;11)
How She Triumphed (4.27;11)
In the Days of '49 (5.8;11)
The Two Sides (5.1;11)
The New Dress (5.15;11)
Enoch Arden, Part I (6.12;11)
Enoch Arden, Part II (6.14;11)
The White Rose of the Wilds
    (5.25;11)
The Crooked Road (5.22;11)
A Romany Tragedy (5.29;11)
A Smile of a Child (6.5;11)
The Primal Call (6.22;11)
The Jealous Husband (7.10;11)
The Indian Brothers (7.17;11)
The Thief and the Girl (7.6;11)
Her Sacrifice (6.26;11)
The Blind Princess and the Poet
    (8.17;11)

Fighting Blood (6.29;11)
The Last Drop of Water (7.27;11)
Robby the Coward (7.13;11)
A Country Cupid (7.24;11)
The Ruling Passion (8.7;11)
The Rose of Kentucky (8.24;11)
The Sorrowful Example (8.14;11)
Swords and Hearts (8.28;11)
The Stuff Heroes Are Made of
    (9.4;11)
The Old Confectioner's Mistake
    (9.7;11)
The Unveiling (10.16;11)
The Eternal Mother (1.11;12)
Dan the Dandy (9.18;11)
The Revenue Man and the Girl
    (9.25;11)
The Squaw's Love (9.14;11)
Italian Blood (10.9;11)
The Making of a Man (10.5;11)
Her Awakening (9.28;11)
The Adventures of Billy (10.19;11)
The Long Road (10.26;11)
The Battle (11.6;11)
Love in the Hills (10.30;11)
The Trail of the Books (11.9;11)
Through Darkened Vales (11.16;11)
Saved from Himself (12.11;11)
A Woman Scorned (11.30;11)
The Miser's Heart (11.20;11)
The Failure (12.7;11)
Sunshine Through the Dark
    (11.27;11)
As in a Looking Glass (12.18;11)
A Terrible Discovery (12.21;11)
A Tale of the Wilderness (1.8;12)
The Voice of the Child (12.28;11)
The Baby and the Stork (1.1;12)
The Old Bookkeeper (1.18;12)
A Sister's Love (2.8;12)
For His Son (1.22;12)
The Transformation of Mike
    (2.1;12)
A Blot on the 'Scutcheon (1.29;12)
Billy's Strategem (2.12;12)
The Sunbeam (2.26;12)
A String of Pearls (3.7;12)
The Root of Evil (3.18;12)

1912
The Mender of the Nets (2.15;12)
Under Burning Skies (2.22;12)
A Siren of Impulse (3.4;12)
Iola's Promise (3.14;12)
The Goddess of Sagebrush Gulch
    (3.25;12)
The Girl and Her Trust (3.28;12)
The Punishment (4.4;12)
Fate's Interception (4.8;12)
The Female of the Species (4.15;12)
Just Like a Woman (4.18;12)
One is Business, the Other Crime
    (4.25;12)
The Lesser Evil (4.29;12)
The Old Actor (5.6;12)
A Lodging for the Night (5.9;12)
His Lesson (5.16;12)
When Kings Were the Law (5.20;12)
A Beast at Bay (5.27;12)
An Outcast Among Outcasts (5.30;12)
Home Folks (6.6;12)
A Temporary Truce (6.10;12)
The Spirit Awakened (6.20;12)
Lena and the Geese (6.16;12)
An Indian Summer (7.8;12)
The Schoolteacher and the Waif
    (6.27;12)
Man's Lust for Gold (7.1;12)
Man's Genesis (7.11;12)
Heaven Avenges (7.18;12)
A Pueblo Legend (8.29;12)
The Sands of Dee (7.22;12)
Black Sheep (7.29;12)
The Narrow Road (8.1;12)
A Child's Remorse (8.8;12)
The Inner Circle (8.12;12)
A Change of Spirit (8.22;12)
An Unseen Enemy (9.9;12)
Two Daughters of Eve (9.19;12)
Friends (9.23;12)
So Near, Yet So Far (9.30;12)
A Feud in the Kentucky Hills
    (10.3;12)
In the Aisles of the Wild (10.14;12)
The One She Loved (10.21;12)
The Painted Lady (10.24;12)
The Musketeers of Pig Alley
    (10.31;12)

Heredity (11.4;12)
Gold and Glitter (11.11;12)
My Baby (11.14;12)
The Informer (11.21;12)
The Unwelcome Guest (3.15;13)
Pirate Gold (1.13;13)
Brutality (12.2;12)
The New York Hat (12.5;12)
The Massacre (2.26;13)
My Hero (12.12;12)
Oil and Water (2.16;13)
The Burglar's Dilemma (12.16;12)
A Cry for Help (12.23;12)
The God Within (12.26;12)
Three Friends (1.2;13)
The Telephone Girl and the Lady
 (1.6;13)
Fate (3.22;13)
An Adventure in the Autumn
 Woods (1.16;13)
A Chance Deception (2.24;13)
The Tender Hearted Boy (1.23;13)
A Misappropriated Turkey (1.27;13)
Brothers (2.3;13)
Drink's Lure (2.17;13)
Love in an Apartment Hotel
 (2.27;13)

1913
Broken Ways (3.8;13)
A Girl's Strategem (3.10;13)
Near to Earth (3.20;13)

A Welcome Intruder (3.24;13)
The Sheriff's Baby (3.29;13)
The Hero of Little Italy (4.3;13)
The Perfidy of Mary (4.5;13)
A Misunderstood Boy (4.19;13)
The Little Tease (4.12;13)
The Lady and the Mouse (4.26;13)
The Wanderer (5.3;13)
The House of Darkness (5.10;13)
Olaf—An Atom (5.19;13)
Just Gold (5.24;13)
His Mother's Son (5.31;13)
The Yaqui Cur (5.17;13)
The Ranchero's Revenge (6.2;13)
A Timely Interception (6.7;13)
Death's Marathon (6.14;13)
The Sorrowful Shore (7.5;13)
The Mistake (7.12;13)
The Mothering Heart (6.21;13)
Her Mother's Oath (6.28;13)
During the Round-up (7.19;13)
The Coming of Angelo (7.26;13)
An Indian's Loyalty (8.16;13)
Two Men of the Desert (8.23;13)
The Reformers, or *The Lost Art of*
 Minding One's Business (8.9;13)
The Battle at Elderbush Gulch
 (3.28;14)
In Prehistoric Days (Original Title:
 Ware of the Primal Tribes; Re-
 leased as *Brute Force*) (13)
Judith of Bethulia (3.7;14)

The Non-Biograph Films

The Battle of the Sexes
Opened at Weber's Theatre, New York, April 12, 1914. Based on *The Single Standard* by Daniel Carson Goodman. 5 reels.

CAST

Jane Andrews *Lillian Gish*
Frank Andrews *Owen Moore*
Mrs. Frank Andrews *Mary Alden*

The Siren *Fay Tincher*
and *Donald Crisp, Robert Harron*

The Escape
Opened at the Cort Theatre, New York, June 1, 1914. Based on the play by Paul Armstrong. 7 reels.

May Joyce   *Blanche Sweet*
Jennie Joyce   *Mae Marsh*
Larry Joyce   *Robert Harron*
McGee   *Donald Crisp*

Dr. Von Eiden   *Owen Moore*
The Father   *F. A. Turner*
The Senator   *Ralph Lewis*

Home, Sweet Home
Opened at the Strand, New York, May 17, 1914. 6 reels.

I Prologue and Epilogue
John Howard Payne   *Henry B. Walthall*
His Mother   *Josephine Crowell*
His Sweetheart   *Lillian Gish*
Her Sister   *Dorothy Gish*
The Worldly Woman   *Fay Tincher*
II
Apple Pie Mary   *Mae Marsh*
Her Father   *Spottiswoode Aiken*
The Easterner   *Robert Harron*
His Fiancé   *Miriam Cooper*

III
The Mother   *Mary Alden*
Her Sons   *Donald Crisp, James Kirk-
wood, Jack Pickford*
The Sheriff   *Fred Burns*

IV
The Husband   *Courtenay Foote*
The Wife   *Blanche Sweet*
The Tempter   *Owen Moore*
The Musician   *Edward Dillon*

The Avenging Conscience
Previewed in Pasadena, California, July 16, 1914; opened at the Strand, New York, August 2, 1914. Suggested by Edgar Allan Poe's "The Tell-tale Heart" and "Annabel Lee." 6 reels.

The Nephew   *Henry B. Walthall*
His Sweetheart   *Blanche Sweet*
The Uncle   *Spottiswoode Aiken*

The Italian   *George Seigmann*
The Detective   *Ralph Lewis*
The Maid   *Mae Marsh*

The Birth of a Nation
Previewed at Riverside, California, January 1915; opened as *The Clansman* in Los Angeles, February 8, 1915, and as *The Birth of a Nation* at the Liberty Theatre, New York, March 3, 1915. 12 reels.
Directed by D. W. Griffith; screenplay by Griffith, assisted by Frank Woods, based on the novel and the play, *The Clansman,* with additional material from *The Leopard's Spots,* all by Thomas Dixon; photographed by G. W. Bitzer, assisted by Karl Brown; music arranged by Joseph Carl Breil and Griffith.

Elsie, Stoneman's daughter   *Lillian Gish*
Flora Cameron, the pet sister   *Mae Marsh*
Col. Ben Cameron   *Henry Walthall*
Margaret Cameron, elder sister   *Miriam Cooper*

Lydia, Stoneman's mulatto house-keeper   *Mary Alden*
Hon. Austin Stoneman, Leader of the House   *Ralph Lewis*
Silas Lynch, mulatto Lieut. Governor   *George Seigmann*
Gus, a renegade Negro   *Walter Long*

Tod, Stoneman's younger son   *Robert Harron*
Jeff, the blacksmith   *Wallace Reid*
Abraham Lincoln   *Joseph Henabery*
Phil, Stoneman's elder son   *Elmer Clifton*
Mrs. Cameron   *Josephine Crowell*
Dr. Cameron   *Spottiswoode Aiken*
Wade Cameron, second son   *André Beringer*

Duke Cameron, youngest son   *Maxfield Stanley*
Mammy, the faithful servant   *Jennie Lee*
Gen. U. S. Grant   *Donald Crisp*
Gen. Robert E. Lee   *Howard Gaye*
Sen. Charles Sumner   *Sam de Grasse*
John Wilkes Booth   *Raoul Walsh*
and *Elmo Lincoln, Olga Grey, Eugene Pallette, Bessie Love, Jennie Lee, William de Vaull, Tom Wilson*

On the original screen credits for the film only the names of D. W. Griffith and Thomas Dixon appeared, but subsequently the other names listed above were given in the credits and in the programs.

Intolerance
Previewed at Riverside, California, August 6, 1916; opened at the Liberty Theatre, New York, September 5, 1916. 14 reels.
Directed by D. W. Griffith; photographed by G. W. Bitzer, assisted by Karl Brown; music arranged by Joseph Carl Breil and Griffith.

CAST
The Woman Who Rocks the Cradle   *Lillian Gish*

THE MODERN STORY
The Girl   *Mae Marsh*
Her Father   *Fred Turner*
The Boy   *Robert Harron*
Jenkins   *Sam de Grasse*
Mary T. Jenkins   *Vera Lewis*
Uplifters   *Mary Alden, Pearl Elmore, Lucille Brown, Luray Huntley, Mrs. Arthur Mackley*
The Friendless One   *Miriam Cooper*
Musketeer of the Slums   *Walter Long*
The Policeman   *Tom Wilson*

The Governor   *Ralph Lewis*
The Judge   *Lloyd Ingraham*
Father Farley   *Rev. A. W. McClure*
Friendly Neighbor   *Max Davidson*
Striker   *Monte Blue*
Debutante   *Marguerite Marsh*
Owner of Car   *Tod Browning*
Chief Detective   *Edward Dillon*
Jenkins' secretary   *Clyde Hopkins*
The Warden   *William Brown*
Wife of the Neighbor   *Alberta Lee*

THE JUDEAN STORY
The Nazarene   *Howard Gaye*
Mary the Mother   *Lillian Langdon*
Mary Magdalene   *Olga Grey*
Pharisees   *Gunther von Ritzau, Erich Von Stroheim*

Bride of Cana   *Bessie Love*
Bridegroom   *George Walsh*

MEDIEVAL FRENCH STORY
Brown Eyes   *Margery Wilson*
Prosper Latour   *Eugene Pallette*
Her Father   *Spottiswoode Aiken*
Her Mother   *Ruth Handforth*
The Mercenary   *A. D. Sears*
Charles IX   *Frank Bennett*
Duc d'Anjou   *Maxfield Stanley*

Catherine de Medici   *Josephine Crowell*
Marguerite de Valois   *Constance Talmadge*
Henry of Navarre   *W. E. Lawrence*
Admiral Coligny   *Joseph Henabery*

BABYLONIAN STORY
The Mountain Girl   *Constance Tal-
madge*
The Rhapsode   *Elmer Clifton*
Belshazzar   *Alfred Paget*
Princess Beloved   *Seena Owen*
King Nabonidas   *Carl Stockdale*
High Priest of Bel   *Tully Marshall*
Cyrus, the Persian   *George Seigmann*
The Mighty Man of Valor   *Elmo
Lincoln*
Judge   *George Fawcett*

Old Woman   *Kate Bruce*
Solo Dancer   *Ruth St. Denis*
Slave   *Loyola O'Connor*
Charioteer   *James Curley*
Babylonian Dandy   *Howard Scott*
Girls of the Marriage Market   *Alma
Rubens, Ruth Darling, Margaret
Mooney*
Favorites of the Harem   *Mildred Har-
ris, Pauline Starke, Winifred West-
over*

Hearts of the World

Opened at the 44th Street Theatre, New York, April 4, 1918. 12 reels.
Directed by D. W. Griffith; scenario by M. Gaston de Tolignac, trans-
lated into English by Capt. Victor Marier (both pseudonyms for D. W.
Griffith); photographed by G. W. Bitzer; technical supervision by Erich
Von Stroheim; music arranged by Carli Elinor and Griffith.

CAST
The Grandfather   *Adolphe Lestina*
The Mother   *Josephine Crowell*
The Girl, Marie Stephenson   *Lillian
Gish*
The Boy, Douglas Gordon Hamil-
ton   *Robert Harron*
The Father of the Boy   *Jack Cosgrave*
The Mother of the Boy   *Kate Bruce*
The Littlest Brother   *Ben Alexander*
The Boys' Other Brothers   *M. Emmons,
F. Marion*
The Little Disturber   *Dorothy Gish*
Monsieur Cuckoo   *Robert Anderson*
The Village Carpenter   *George Fawcett*
Von Strohm   *George Siegmann*
The Innkeeper   *Fay Holderness*
A Deaf and Blind Musician   *L. Lowy*
A Poilu   *Eugene Pouyet*

A French Peasant Girl   *Anna Mae Wal-
thall*
A Refugee   *Mlle. Yvette Duvoisin of
the Comédie Française, Paris*
A French Major   *Herbert Sutch*
A Poilu   *Alphonse Dufort*
A Poilu   *Jean Dumercier*
Stretcher Bearers   *Gaston Riviere, Jules
Lemontier*
A Poilu   *Georges Loyer*
A German Sergeant   *George Nicholls*
A Refugee Mother   *Mrs. Mary Gish*
Woman with Daughter   *Mrs. Harron*
Wounded Girl   *Mary Harron*
Refugee   *Jessie Harron*
Boy with Barrel   *Johnny Harron*
Dancer   *Mary Hay*

Not credited on the original programs: Erich Von Stroheim as a Hun in
several scenes, and Noel Coward as the Man with the Wheelbarrow and
as a Villager in the Streets.

The Great Love

Opened at the Strand, New York, August 11, 1918. 7 reels.
Scenario by Capt. Victor Marier (D. W. Griffith and S. E. V. Taylor).

CAST
Jim Young, of Youngstown, Pa.   *Robert
Harron*

Sir Roger Brighton   *Henry B. Walthall*
Jessie Lovewell   *Gloria Hope*

Susie Broadplains   *Lillian Gish*
John Broadplains   *Maxfield Stanley*
Rev. Josephus Broadplains   *George Fawcett*
MademoiselleCorintee   *Rosemary Theby*
Mr. Seymour of Brazil, formerly of Berlin   *George Seigmann*

and *Queen Alexandra, Lady Diana Manners, Miss Elizabeth Asquith, and the Princess of Monaco as themselves.*

A Romance of Happy Valley
Opened at the Strand, New York, January 26, 1919. 6 reels.
Scenario by Capt. Victor Marier (D. W. Griffith).

CAST

Old Lady Smiles   *Lydia Yeamans Titus*
John L. Logan, Jr.   *Robert Harron*
Mrs. Logan   *Kate Bruce*
John L. Logan, Sr.   *George Fawcett*
Jennie Timberlake   *Lillian Gish*

Her Father   *George Nicholls*
Vinegar Watkins   *Adolphe Lestina*
Judas   *Bertram Grassby*
The Negro Farmhand   *Porter Strong*

The Greatest Thing in Life
Opened in Los Angeles, December 16, 1918, and at the Strand, New York, December 22, 1918. 7 reels.
Scenario by Capt. Victor Marier (D. W. Griffith and S. E. V. Taylor).

CAST

Jeanette Peret   *Lillian Gish*
Edward Livingston   *Robert Harron*
Leo Peret, Jeanette's father   *Adolphe Lestina*
M. Le Bébé   *David Butler*

The American Soldier   *Elmo Lincoln*
The German Officer   *Edward Piel*
Jeanette's Aunt   *Kate Bruce*
Mlle. Peaches   *Peaches Jackson*

The Girl Who Stayed at Home
Opened at the Strand, New York, March 23, 1919. 7 reels.
Scenario by S. E. V. Taylor.

CAST

Monsieur France   *Adolphe Lestina*
Mlle. Acoline   *France Carol Dempster*
Ralph Gray   *Richard Barthelmess*
James Gray   *Robert Harron*
Count de Brissac   *Syndeconde*
Mr. Edward Gray   *George Fawcett*

Mrs. Edward Gray   *Kate Bruce*
Herr Turnverein   *Edward Reel*
Cutie Beautiful   *Clarine Seymour*
A Man About Town   *Tully Marshall*
Johann August Kant   *David Butler*

True Heart Susie
Opened at the Strand, New York, June 1, 1919. 6 reels.
Scenario by Marion Fremont.

CAST

True Heart Susie *Lillian Gish*	Bettina *Clarine Seymour*
William *Robert Harron*	Bettina's Aunt *Kate Bruce*
William's Father *Wilbur Higby*	Bettina's Chum *Carol Dempster*
Susie's Aunt *Loyola O'Connor*	Sporty Malone *Raymond Cannon*
The Stranger *George Fawcett*	

Scarlet Days

Opened at the Rivoli, New York, November 10, 1919. 7 reels.
Scenario by S. E. V. Taylor.

CAST

Alvarez, a bandit *Richard Barthelmess*

Lady Fair, an Eastern girl *Carol Dempster*

Chiquita, a Mexican dance hall girl *Clarine Seymour*

Randolph, a Virginia gentleman *Ralph Graves*

Rosie Nell *Eugenie Besserer*

The Sheriff *George Fawcett*

Bagley, the dance hall proprietor *Walter Long*

Broken Blossoms

Opened at the George M. Cohan Theatre, New York, May 13, 1919.
6 reels.

Directed and written by D. W. Griffith, based on "The Chink and the Child," in Thomas Burke's *Limehouse Nights;* photographed by G. W. Bitzer; special effects by Hendrick Sartov; technical advisor, Moon Kwan; music arranged by Louis F. Gottschalk and Griffith.

CAST

Lucy, the Girl *Lillian Gish*

The Yellow Man *Richard Barthelmess*

Battling Burrows *Donald Crisp*

His Manager *Arthur Howard*

Evil Eye *Edward Peil*

The Spying One *George Beranger*

A Prize Fighter *Norman Selby* ("Kid McCoy")

The Greatest Question

Opened at the Strand, New York, December 28, 1919. 6 reels.
Directed by D. W. Griffith; story by William Hale, scenario by S. E. V. Taylor; photography by G. W. Bitzer.

CAST

Nellie Jarvis, "Little Miss Yes'm" *Lillian Gish*

Jimmy Hilton *Robert Harron*

John Hilton *Ralph Graves*

Mrs. Hilton, the mother *Eugenie Besserer*

Mr. Hilton, the father *George Fawcett*

Zeke *Tom Wilson*

Mrs. Cain *Josephine Crowell*

Martin Cain *George Nicholls*

The Idol Dancer
Opened at the Strand, New York, March 21, 1920. 7 reels.
Directed by D. W. Griffith; scenario by Gordon Ray Young; photographed by G. W. Bitzer.

CAST

The Beachcomber   *Richard Barthelmess*
White Almond Flower   *Clarine Seymour*
Walter Kincaid   *Creighton Hale*
Rev. Franklin Blythe   *George MacQuarrie*
Mrs. Blythe   *Kate Bruce*
Peter, a native minister   *Porter Strong*
Pansy   *Florence Short*
The Blackbirder   *Anders Randolf*
Chief Wando   *Walter James*

The Love Flower
Opened at the Strand, New York, August 22, 1920. 7 reels.
Directed by D. W. Griffith; based on the story "The Black Beach" by Ralph Stock; photographed by G. W. Bitzer.

CAST

Stella Bevan   *Carol Dempster*
Bruce Sanders   *Richard Barthelmess*
Stella's Father   *George MacQuarrie*
Matthew Crane   *Anders Randolf*
Mrs. Bevan   *Florence Short*
The Visitor   *Crauford Kent*
Bevan's Old Servant   *Adolph Lestina*
Crane's Assistants   *William James, Jack Manning*

Way Down East
Previewed in Middletown and Kingston, New York, during August 1920; opened at the 44th Street Theatre, New York, September 3, 1920. 13 reels.
Directed by D. W. Griffith; scenario by Anthony Paul Kelly from the stage play by Lottie Blair Parker; photographed by G. W. Bitzer and Hendrick Sartov; technical direction by Frank Wortman; art direction by Charles O. Seessel and Clifford Pember; music arranged by Louis Silvers and William F. Peters.

CAST

Anna Moore   *Lillian Gish*
Her Mother   *Mrs. David Landau*
Mrs. Tremont   *Josephine Bernard*
Diana Tremont   *Mrs. Morgan Belmont*
Her Sister   *Patricia Fruen*
The Eccentric Aunt   *Florence Short*
Lennox Sanderson   *Lowell Sherman*
Squire Bartlett   *Burr McIntosh*
Mrs. Bartlett   *Kate Bruce*
David Bartlett   *Richard Barthelmess*
Martha Perkins   *Vivia Ogden*
Seth Holcomb   *Porter Strong*
Reuben Whipple   *George Neville*
Hi Holler   *Edgar Nelson*
Kate Brewster   *Mary Hay*
Professor Sterling   *Creighton Hale*
Maria Poole   *Emily Fitzroy*

The fiddler and many of the dancers in the country dance scenes were native Vermonters.

Dream Street

Opened at the Central Theatre, New York, April 12, 1921. 10 reels.
Directed by D. W. Griffith; scenario by Roy Sinclair (D. W. Griffith),
based on two stories by Thomas Burke, "Gina of Chinatown" and "The
Lamp in the Window"; music arranged by Louis Silvers.

CAST

Gypsy Fair *Carol Dempster*
Spike McFadden *Ralph Graves*
Billy McFadden *Charles Emmett Mack*
Sway Wan *Edward Peil*
Gypsy's Father *W. J. Ferguson*
Samuel Jones *Porter Strong*

Tom Chudder *George Neville*
Police Inspector *Charles Slattery*
A Preacher of the Streets *Tyrone Power*
The Masked Violinist *Morgan Wallace*

Orphans of the Storm

Opened in Boston, December 28, 1921; opened at the Apollo Theatre,
New York, January 2, 1922. 12 reels.
Directed by D. W. Griffith; based on the play *The Two Orphans* by
Adolph D. Ennery; photographed by Hendrick Sartov; technical direc-
tion by Frank Wortman; set design by Edward Scholl; music arranged
by Louis F. Gottschalk and William F. Peters.

CAST

Henriette Girard *Lillian Gish*
Louise *Dorothy Gish*
The Chevalier de Vaudry *Joseph Schildkraut*
The Count de Linieres *Frank Losee*
The Marquise de Praille *Catherine Emmett*
Mother Frochard *Lucille La Verne*
Jacques Frochard *Morgan Wallace*

Pierre Frochard *Sheldon Lewis*
Picard *Frank Puglia*
Jacques Forget-Not *Creighton Hale*
Danton *Monte Blue*
Robespierre *Sidney Herbert*
King Louis XVI *Leo Kolmer*
The Doctor *Adolph Lestina*
Sister Genevieve *Kate Bruce*

One Exciting Night

Previewed in Connecticut, September 12, 1922; opened in Newport on
October 2, 1922; at the Apollo Theatre, New York, October 23, 1922.
11 reels.
Directed by D. W. Griffith; scenario by Irene Sinclair (D. W. Griffith);
photographed by Hendrick Sartov; set design by Charles M. Kirk; special effects by Edward Scholl; music arranged by Albert Pesce.

CAST

Agnes Harrington *Carol Dempster*
John Fairfax *Henry Hull*
Romeo Washington *Porter Strong*
J. Wilson Rockmaine *Morgan Wallace*
The Neighbor *C. H. Croker-King*
Mrs. Harrington *Margaret Dale*
The Detective *Frank Sheridan*

Samuel Jones *Frank Wunderlee*
Colored Maid *Irma Harrison*
The Butler *Percy Carr*
A Guest *Charles Emmett Mack*
Auntie Fairfax *Grace Griswold*
Clary Johnson *Herbert Sutch*

The White Rose

Opened at the Lyric Theatre, New York, May 21, 1923. 10 reels. Directed by D. W. Griffith; scenario by Irene Sinclair (D. W. Griffith); photographed by G. W. Bitzer, Hendrick Sartov, Hal Sintzenich; set design by Charles M. Kirk; special effects by Edward Scholl; music by Joseph Carl Breil.

CAST

Bessie Williams, "Teazie"   *Mae Marsh*
Marie Carrington   *Carol Dempster*
Joseph Beaugarde   *Ivor Novello*
John White   *Neil Hamilton*
"Auntie" Easter   *Lucille La Verne*
"Apollo"   *Porter Strong*
Cigar Stand Girl   *Jane Thomas*

An Aunt   *Kate Bruce*
A Man of the World   *Erville Alderson*
The Bishop   *Herbert Sutch*
The Landlord   *Joseph Burke*
The Landlady   *Mary Foy*
Guest at Inn   *Charles Emmett Mack*

America

Opened at the 44th Street Theatre, New York, February 21, 1924. 12 reels.

Directed by D. W. Griffith; scenario by John Pell from a story by Robert Chambers; photographed by G. W. Bitzer, Hendrick Sartov, Marcel Le Picard, Hal Sintzenich; art direction by Charles M. Kirk; music arranged by Joseph Carl Breil.

CAST

Nathan Holden   *Neil Hamilton*
Justice Montague   *Erville Alderson*
Miss Nancy Montague   *Carol Dempster*
Charles   Philip   Edward   Montague   *Charles Emmett Mack*
Samuel Adams   *Lee Beggs*
John Hancock   *John Dunton*
King George III   *Arthur Donaldson*
William Pitt   *Charles Bennett*
Lord Chamberlain   *Dowling Clark*
Thomas Jefferson   *Frank Walsh*
Patrick Henry   *Frank McGlynn, Jr.*
George Washington   *Arthur Dewey*
Richard Henry Lee   *P. R. Scammon*
Captain Walter Butler   *Lionel Barrymore*
Sir Ashley Montague   *Sidney Deane*
General Gage   *W. W. Jones*
Captain Montour   *E. Roseman*
Chief of Senecas, Hikatoo   *Harry Semels*

Paul Revere   *Harry O'Neill*
John Parker, Captain of Minute Men   *H. Van Bousen*
Major Pitcairn   *Hugh Baird*
Jonas Parker   *James Milaidy*
Colonel Prescott   *H. Koser*
Major General Warren   *Michael Donovan*
Captain Hare   *Louis Wolheim*
Chief of Mohawks, Joseph Brant   *Riley Hatch*
Marquis de Lafayette   *H. Paul Doucet*
Edmund Burke   *W. Rising*
Personal Servant of Miss Montague   *Daniel Carney*
Household Servant at Ashley Court   *E. Scanlon*
Lord North   *Emil Hoch*
A Refugee Mother   *Lucille La Verne*
Major Strong   *Edwin Holland*
An Old Patriot   *Milton Noble*

Isn't Life Wonderful
Premier at Town Hall, New York, December 4, 1924; opened at the Rivoli Theatre, New York, December 5, 1924. 9 reels.
Directed by D. W. Griffith; scenario by D. W. Griffith, based on a short story by Major Geoffrey Moss; photographed by Hendrick Sartov and Hal Sintzenich; music arranged by Cesare Sodero and Louis Silvers.

CAST

Inga   *Carol Dempster*
Hans, son of the professor   *Neil Hamilton*
Grandmother   *Helen Lowell*
The Professor   *Erville-Alderson*
The Brother   *Frank Puglia*

The Aunt   *Marcia Harris*
Rudolph   *Lupino Lane*
Hungry Workers   *Hans von Schlettow, Paul Rehkopf, Robert Scholz*
The American   *Walter Plimmer, Jr.*

Sally of the Sawdust
Opened at the Strand, New York, August 2, 1925. 10 reels.
Directed by D. W. Griffith; scenario by Forrest Halsey, based on the play *Poppy* by Dorothy Donnelly; photographed by Harry Fischbeck and Hal Sintzenich.

CAST

Sally   *Carol Dempster*
Professor Eustace McGargle   *W. C. Fields*
Payton Lennox   *Alfred Lunt*
Mrs. Foster   *Effie Shannon*
Judge Foster   *Erville Alderson*

Leon, the acrobat   *Glenn Anders*
Mr. Lennox, Sr.   *Charles Hammond*
The Detective   *Roy Applegate*
Miss Vinton   *Florence Fair*
The Society Leader   *Marie Shotwell*

That Royle Girl
Opened at the Strand, New York, January 10, 1926. 11 reels.
Directed by D. W. Griffith; scenario by Paul Schofield, from the serial and novel by Edwin Balmer; photographed by Harry Fischbeck and Hal Sintzenich.

CAST

The Royle Girl   *Carol Dempster*
Calvin Clarke, Deputy District Attorney   *James Kirkwood*
George Baretta   *Paul Everton*
The Royle Girl's Father   *W. C. Fields*

King of Jazz   *Harrison Ford*
and *Florence Auer, Marie Chambers, George Rigas, Ida Waterman, Alice Laidley, Frank Allworth*

The Sorrows of Satan
Opened at the George M. Cohan Theatre, New York, October 12, 1926.
9 reels.
Directed by D. W. Griffith; scenario by Forrest Halsey, adaptation by
John Russell and George Hull of the novel by Marie Corelli; photographed by Harry Fischbeck; edited and titled by Julian Johnson; art
direction by Charles Kirk; miniatures by Fred Waller.

CAST

Prince Lucio de Rimanez *Adolphe Menjou*
Geoffrey Tempest *Ricardo Cortez*
Princess Olga *Lya de Putti*
Mavis Claire *Carol Dempster*

Amiel *Ivan Lebedeff*
The Landlady *Marcia Harris*
Lord Elton *Lawrence D'Orsay*
Dancing Girl *Nellie Savage*
Mavis' Chum *Dorothy Hughes*

Drums of Love
Opened at the Liberty Theatre, New York, January 24, 1928. 9 reels.
Directed by D. W. Griffith; scenario and titles by Gerrit J. Lloyd; pho-
tographed by G. W. Bitzer, Karl Struss, Harry Jackson.

CAST

Princess Emanuella *Mary Philbin*
Duke Cathos De Alvia *Lionel Barry-more*
Count Leonardo De Alvia *Don Alvar-ado*

The Court Jester, Bopi *Tully Marshall*
Duchess De Alvia *Eugenie Besserer*
Duke of Granada *Charles Hill Mailes*
Maid *Rosemary Cooper*
The Little Sister *Joyce Coad*

The Battle of the Sexes
Opened at United Artists Theatre, Los Angeles, in September 1928;
opened at the Rialto, New York, October 12, 1928. 10 reels.
Directed by D. W. Griffith; scenario by Gerrit Lloyd, based on the
novel by Daniel Carson Goodman, *The Single Standard;* photographed
by G. W. Bitzer and Karl Struss; synchronized music by R. Schildkret.

CAST

Judson *Jean Hersholt*
Marie Skinner *Phyllis Haver*
Mrs. Judson *Belle Bennett*
"Babe" Winsor *Don Alvarado*

Ruth Judson *Sally O'Neil*
Billy Judson *William Bakewell*
Friend of Judsons' *John Batten*

Lady of the Pavements
Opened at the United Artists Theatre, Los Angeles, January 22, 1929. 9
reels.

Directed by D. W. Griffith; scenario by Sam Taylor, based on a story by Karl Volmoeller; photographed by Karl Struss, assisted by G. W. Bitzer; set design by William Cameron Menzies; synchronized music arranged by Hugo Reisenfeld; theme song by Irving Berlin.

CAST

Nanon del Rayon *Lupe Velez*	Baron Hausemann *George Fawcett*
Count Arnim *William Boyd*	Papa Pierre *Henry Armetta*
Countess des Granges *Jetta Goudal*	Dancing Master *Franklin Pangborn*
Baron Finot *Albert Conti*	A Pianist *William Bakewell*

Abraham Lincoln
Opened at the Central Theatre, New York, October 25, 1930. 10 reels. Directed by D. W. Griffith; scenario by Stephen Vincent Benét; photographed by Karl Struss; set design by William Cameron Menzies; production supervision by John W. Considine, Jr.; music arranged by Hugo Reisenfeld.

CAST

Abraham Lincoln *Walter Huston*	Offut *Otto Hoffman*
Ann Rutledge *Una Merkel*	Armstrong *Edgar Deering*
Mary Todd Lincoln *Kay Hammond*	Lincoln's Employer *Russell Simpson*
Stephen Douglas *E. Alyn Warren*	Sheriff *Charles Crockett*
General Lee *Hobart Bosworth*	Mrs. Edwards *Helen Ware*
General Grant *Fred Warren*	Herndon *Jason Robards*
Colonel Marshall *Henry B. Walthall*	Tad Lincoln *Gordon Thorpe*
General Sheridan *Frank Campeau*	John Hay *Cameron Prudhomme*
Sheridan's Aide *Francis Ford*	General Scott *James Bradbury, Sr.*
Midwife *Lucille La Verne*	Young soldier *Jimmy Eagles*
Tom Lincoln *W. L. Thorne*	and *Hank Bell, Carl Stockdale, Ralph*
Nancy Hanks Lincoln *Helen Freeman*	*Lewis, George McQuarrie, Robert*
John Wilkes Booth *Ian Keith*	*Brower*
Stanton *Oscar Apfel*	

The Struggle
Opened at the Rivoli, New York, December 10, 1931. 9 reels. Produced by D. W. Griffith, Inc.; distributed by United Artists; directed by D. W. Griffith; screenplay by Anita Loos and John Emerson; photographed by Joseph Ruttenberg; edited by Barney Rogan; music arranged by Philip Scheib and D. W. Griffith.

CAST

Jimmie Wilson *Hal Skelly*	Sam *Claude Cooper*
Florrie *Zita Johann*	Cohen *Arthur Lipson*
Nina *Charlotte Wynters*	Mr. Craig *Charles Richman*
Nan Wilson *Jackson Halliday*	A Catty Girl *Helen Mack*
Johnnie Marshall *Evelyn Baldwin*	A Gigolo *Scott Moore*
Mary *Edna Hagan*	A Mill Worker *Dave Manley*

Notes

1. David Wark Griffith, "The Motion Picture and Witch Burners," in Jean Bernique, ed., *Motion Picture Acting*, Chicago: Producer's Service Co., 1916, p. 199.
2. E. Phillips Oppenheim, "The Missioner," *Pearson's Magazine*, October 1907, p. 48.
3. Hector Fuller, "A Review of *The Fool and The Girl*," *Washington Herald*, October 1, 1907.
4. From an unpublished letter in possession of the Museum of Modern Art Film Library (hereafter referred to as MOMA).
5. D. W. Griffith, *The Fool and the Girl*, manuscript, October 5, 1906, rare book collection, the Library of Congress.
6. *Ibid.*
7. *Ibid.*
8. "Plays of the Month," unsigned review, *Theatre Magazine*, May 1908, p. viii.
9. David Belasco, "Picture Craft, David Belasco Discusses the Picture Theatre," *The Film Index*, Vol. III, No. 34, September 5, 1908, p. 20.
10. Unsigned editorial, Vol. III, No. 37, September 26, 1908, p. 6.
11. D. W. Griffith, *War*, an unpublished and uncopyrighted play, MOMA.
12. D. W. Griffith, notes for a projected autobiography, MOMA (hereafter referred to as "unpublished autobiography").
13. *Ibid.*, p. 1.
14. *Ibid.*, p. 2.
15. *Ibid.*, p. 2.
16. *Ibid.*, p. 2.
17. Letter from D. W. Griffith to Barnet Bravermann, May 22, 1943, MOMA.
18. Confederate Records, National Archives, Washington, D.C. Colonel Griffith surrendered with Jefferson Davis at Washington, Georgia, May 11, 1865.
19. Letter from D. W. Griffith to Barnet Bravermann, May 2, 1943, MOMA.
20. *Ibid.*
21. Inventory Book, Somerset County, Maryland, January 20, 1796.
22. War Department, Adjutant General's Office, National Archives, Washington, D.C.
23. Dr. John Groves Speer, *Reminiscences of the Speer Family*, published by the author: Oldham County, Kentucky, 1883, p. 102.

24. Tax Commissioner's Book, Oldham County, Kentucky, 1846, p. 47.
25. Records of the War Department for the Mexican War, 1846, National Archives, Washington, D.C., p. 2453.
26. *Ibid.*
27. Interviews with members of the Oglesby family, Tom Oglesby, Dr. J. V. P. Oglesby, and Gerrit J. Lloyd, by Barnet Bravermann, 1943, unpublished, MOMA.
28. Tax Commissioner's Book, Oldham County, Kentucky, 1852, p. 76.
29. The Frankfort *Daily Commonwealth,* Frankfort, Kentucky, January 11, 1854, p. 6.
30. War of the Rebellion, Official Records, Series 7, Part II, Vol. 31, Chap. 43, National Archives, Washington, D.C.
31. Letter from D. W. Griffith to Barnet Bravermann, 1943, MOMA.
32. Judge Charles Kerr in W. E. Connolly and E. M. Coulter, eds., *History of Kentucky,* Chicago: American Historical Society, 1922, p. 638.
33. Interview with William W. Griffith, La Grange, Kentucky, 1943, by Barnet Bravermann, MOMA.
34. Interview with Woodson A. Oglesby, La Grange, Kentucky, 1943, by Barnet Bravermann, MOMA.
35. D. W. Griffith, unpublished autobiography, p. 10.
36. *Ibid.,* p. 5.
37. *Ibid.,* p. 6.
38. *Ibid.,* p. 8.
39. D. W. Griffith, "Possibilities and Probabilities," *Motion Picture Magazine,* August 1926, pp. 47–48.
40. The Film Index, January 2, 1909, p. 4.
41. Biograph bulletin, No. 3454, July 14, 1908.
42. G. W. Bitzer, unpublished notes about Biograph, MOMA.
43. Linda Arvidson Griffith, *When the Movies Were Young,* New York: E. P. Dutton Company, 1925, p. 51.
44. *Ibid.,* pp. 51–52.
45. *Ibid.,* p. 55.
46. Florence Lawrence, in collaboration with Monte M. Katterjohn, "Growing up with the Movies," *Photoplay Magazine,* January 1914, p. 100.
47. *Ibid.,* p. 102.
48. *Ibid.*
49. *Ibid.,* pp. 103–4.
50. *Ibid.*
51. Biograph bulletin, No. 162, August 18, 1908, italics my own.
52. D. W. Griffith, unpublished autobiography, p. 19.
53. *Ibid.,* p. 9.
54. *Ibid.,* p. 11.
55. *Ibid.,* p. 12.
56. *Ibid.,* p. 13.
57. *Ibid.,* p. 14.

58. *Ibid.*, p. 14.
59. *Ibid.*, p. 15.
60. *Ibid.*, p. 15.
61. *Ibid.*, p. 16.
62. *Ibid.*, p. 16.
63. *Ibid.*, pp. 17–18.
64. *Ibid.*, p. 18.
65. *Ibid.*, p. 18.
66. *Ibid.*, p. 19.
67. *Ibid.*, p. 19.
68. *Ibid.*, p. 19.
69. *Ibid.*, p. 20.
70. *Ibid.*, p. 21.
71. Letter in possession of MOMA.
72. Letter from D. W. Griffith to Barnet Bravermann, May 28, 1942, MOMA.
73. D. W. Griffith, "The Miracle of Modern Photography," *The Mentor,* Vol. 9, No. 6, July 1921, p. 67.
74. Terry Ramsaye, *A Million and One Nights,* New York: Simon and Schuster, 1926, p. 503.
75. Lillian Gish, "D. W. Griffith, The Great American," *Harper's Bazaar,* October 1940.
76. Linda Griffith, *op. cit.,* p. 116.
77. *Ibid.*, p. 119.
78. *Ibid.*, p. 128.
79. *Ibid.*, p. 128.
80. *Ibid.*, p. 129.
81. For a detailed description of Griffith's directing career at Biograph, see Robert M. Henderson, *D. W. Griffith, The Years at Biograph,* New York: Farrar, Straus and Giroux, 1970.
82. D. W. Griffith, "Possibilities and Probabilities," *Motion Picture Magazine,* August 1926, p. 61.
83. Linda Griffith, *op. cit.,* p. 146.
84. Biograph bulletin, May 23, 1910.
85. Mack Sennett, in collaboration with Cameron Shipp, *King of Comedy,* New York: Doubleday & Co., 1954, p. 64.
86. Mary Pickford, in collaboration with Cameron Shipp, *Sunshine and Shadow,* New York: Doubleday & Co., 1955, p. 110.
87. Biograph bulletin, No. 3778, January 11, 1910.
88. Biograph bulletin, No. 3779, January 19, 1910.
89. Lionel Barrymore, in collaboration with Cameron Shipp, *We Barrymores,* New York: Appleton-Century-Crofts, 1951, p. 140.
90. Linda Griffith, *op. cit.,* p. 197.
91. Postcard from Billy Bitzer to Charles Predmore, August 23, 1911, in the possession of Lester Predmore.
92. Biograph bulletin, No. 3792, November 6, 1911.

93. "D. W. Griffith—Film Wizard," *Theatre Magazine,* May 1920, p. 490.
94. Mary Pickford, *op. cit.,* p. 139.
95. Linda Griffith, *op. cit.,* p. 217.
96. Mary Pickford, *op. cit.,* p. 144.
97. *Ibid.,* p. 144.
98. *Ibid.,* p. 146.
99. *Ibid.,* p. 148.
100. Lillian Gish, *op. cit.*
101. Lillian Gish, in collaboration with Ann Pinchot, *The Movies, Mr. Griffith and Me,* Englewood Cliffs, N.J.: Prentice-Hall, 1969, p. 36.
102. Terry Ramsaye, *op. cit.,* p. 605.
103. Linda Griffith, *op. cit.,* pp. 213–14.
104. D. W. Griffith, unpublished autobiography, p. 42.
105. Lillian Gish, "D. W. Griffith, the Great American," p. 37.
106. Blanche Sweet, a taped interview with the author, June 17, 1965.
107. Mary Pickford, *op. cit.,* p. 153.
108. Terry Ramsaye, *op. cit.,* p. 609.
109. Linda Griffith, *op. cit.,* p. 225.
110. Letter from Karl Brown to Barnet Bravermann, May 18, 1943, MOMA.
111. Linda Griffith, *op. cit.,* p. 203.
112. Terry Ramsaye, *op. cit.,* p. 609.
113. D. W. Griffith, "Possibilities and Probabilities," *op. cit.,* p. 47.
114. Roy Wilkins, "Distorted Image," *New York Post,* February 14, 1965, p. 34.
115. An interview with Karl Brown, by Barnet Bravermann, May 18, 1943, p. 11, MOMA.
116. *Ibid.,* p. 9.
117. *Ibid.,* p. 11.
118. *Ibid.,* p. 8.
119. *Ibid.,* p. 119.
120. Austin C. Lescarboura, "Generals of Shadowland Warfare," *Scientific American,* May 6, 1917, p. 459.
121. Letter from William de Mille to Samuel Goldwyn, February 9, 1915, quoted by Lillian Gish, in Lillian Gish, *The Movies, Mr. Griffith and Me,* p. 153.
122. *The New York Times,* March 4, 1915, p. 4.
123. *Ibid.*
124. D. W. Griffith, *The Rise and Fall of Free Speech in America,* Los Angeles, 1916.
125. Karl Brown interview, *op. cit.,* p. 12.
126. D. W. Griffith, an interview with Mildred Mastin, *Photoplay,* May 1934, p. 97.
127. Karl Brown interview, *op. cit.,* pp. 13–14.
128. Karl Brown interview, *op. cit.,* p. 13.
129. "Artisans of the Motion Picture Films," *Scientific American,* September 2, 1916, p. 225.

130. "D. W. Griffith—Film Wizard," *Motion Picture Magazine,* 1920, p. 490.
131. *The New York Times,* September 6, 1916, p. 6.
132. *Ibid.*
133. *Film Daily,* September 7, 1916, p. 7.
134. *Ibid.*
135. Letter from Harry Aitken to Barnet Bravermann, August 12, 1914, MOMA.
136. Karl Brown interview, *op. cit.*
137. Lillian Gish, *The Movies, Mr. Griffith and Me, op. cit.,* p. 193.
138. Karl Brown interview, *op. cit.,* p. 13.
139. Review in *The New York Times,* April 5, 1918, p. 13.
140. Karl Brown interview, *op. cit.,* p. 8.
141. Karl Brown interview, *op. cit.,* p. 9.
142. *The New York Times,* August 5, 1918, p. 7.
143. *Film Daily,* January 5, 1919, p. 5.
144. *The New York Times,* January 27, 1919, p. 13.
145. Charles Chaplin, *My Autobiography,* New York: Simon and Schuster, 1964, p. 233.
146. *The New York Times,* March 24, 1919, p. 11.
147. *Ibid.*
148. *The New York Times,* June 2, 1919, p. 19.
149. Karl Brown to interview, *op. cit.*
150. Letter from Richard Barthelmess to Barnet Bravermann, March 30, 1945, MOMA.
151. *Ibid.*
152. Lillian Gish, *The Movies, Mr. Griffith and Me,* p. 221.
153. *Film Daily,* May 18, 1919, p. 6.
154. New York *Call,* May 14, 1919, p. 8.
155. D. W. Griffith, *Theatre Magazine,* January 1918, p. 65.
156. *Theatre Magazine,* June 1919, p. 400.
157. Iris Barry and Eileen Bowser, *D. W. Griffith, American Film Master,* New York: Museum of Modern Art, 1965, p. 59.
158. Barthelmess, *op. cit.*
159. *Ibid.*
160. *The New York Times,* December 29, 1919, p. 4.
161. *The New York Times,* March 22, 1920, p. 12.
162. *The New York Times,* August 23, 1920, p. 8.
163. *Theatre Magazine,* May 1920, p. 410.
164. Interview with Frank Walsh, by the author, November 30, 1970.
165. *Film Daily,* September 12, 1920, p. 6.
166. Iris Barry and Eileen Bowser, *op. cit.,* p. 30.
167. *Film Daily,* April 17, 1921, p. 4.
168. *Theatre Magazine,* May 1921, p. 38.
169. *Film Daily,* April 18, 1921.
170. Karl Brown interview, *op. cit.,* p. 5.

171. Karl Brown interview, *op. cit.*, p. 2.

172. Letter from J. C. Epping to Barnet Bravermann, June 10, 1944, MOMA.

173. *Ibid.*

174. Letter from Mary Pickford to Barnet Bravermann, June 18, 1943, MOMA.

175. Richard Savage, "Making a Million Dollar Picture," *Theatre Magazine,* June 1919, p. 108.

176. *Ibid.*

177. *Ibid.*

178. *Ibid.*

179. *Ibid.*

180. *Film Daily,* January 8, 1922, p. 8.

181. Lillian Gish, *The Movie, Mr. Griffith and Me,* p. 248.

182. Letter from Billy Bitzer to C. V. Predmore, July 23, 1936, in possession of Lester Predmore, Middletown, N.Y.

183. *Film Daily,* October 29, 1922, p. 4.

184. *The New York Times,* October 24, 1922, p. 17.

185. *Ibid.*

186. Peter Noble, *Ivor Novello, Man of the Theatre,* London: Falcon Press, 1951, p. 92.

187. *Ibid.*, pp. 99–100.

188. *The New York Times,* May 23, 1923, p. 18.

189. *Theatre Magazine,* July 1923, p. 34.

190. "Cinema," *Theatre Magazine,* August 1923, p. 34.

191. Frank Walsh, *op. cit.*

192. "Cinema," *Theatre Magazine,* May 1924, p. 30.

193. *The New York Times,* a review of *America,* February 22, 1924, p. 20.

194. *Film Daily,* March 2, 1924, p. 5.

195. Letter from Mary Pickford to Barnet Bravermann, June 18, 1943, MOMA.

196. Letter from Billy Bitzer to C. V. Predmore, MOMA.

197. *Film Daily,* December 1, 1924, p. 9.

198. *Theatre Magazine,* February 1925, p. 32.

199. Frank Walsh, *op. cit.*

200. *Ibid.*

201. *Ibid.*

202. *Film Daily,* August 9, 1925, p. 10.

203. Mordaunt Hall, "The Screen," *The New York Times,* January 11, 1926, p. 33.

204. *Film Daily,* January 17, 1926, p. 6.

205. An interview with D. W. Griffith by M. A. Stearns, *Collier's Magazine,* April 24, 1926, p. 77.

206. D. W. Griffith, "The Motion Picture To-day and To-morrow," *Theatre Magazine,* October 1929, pp. 21, 58.

207. Frank Walsh, *op. cit.*

208. *Ibid.*
209. *Ibid.*
210. Norman Bel Geddes in William Kelley, ed., Garden City, N.Y.: *Miracle in the Evening,* Doubleday & Company, 1960, pp. 319–20.
211. *Ibid.,* p. 321.
212. *The New York Times,* October 13, 1926, p. 21.
213. Bitzer, *loc. cit.*
214. J. C. Epping, *loc. cit.*
215. *Film Daily,* February 5, 1928, p. 7.
216. *The New York Times,* January 25, 1928, p. 20.
217. *Motion Picture News,* January 26, 1928, p. 282.
218. "Opinions on Pictures," *Motion Picture News,* October 20, 1928, p. 1223.
219. *The New York Times,* March 10, 1929, p. 24.
220. The New York *Sun,* March 10, 1929, p. 18.
221. *Film Daily,* March 17, 1929, p. 9.
222. Lillian Gish, *The Movies, Mr. Griffith and Me,* p. 305.
223. *Film Daily,* August 31, 1930, p. 6.
224. Mordaunt Hall, "The Screen," *The New York Times,* December 22, 1930, p. 16.
225. An interview with John Aichele, Jr., by the author, November 4, 1970.
226. *The New York Times,* December 11, 1931, p. 36.
227. *Film Daily,* December 13, 1931, p. 10.
228. Billy Bitzer, *op. cit.*
229. Mildred Mastin, "The Star Maker Whose Dreams Turned to Dust," *Photoplay,* May 1939, p. 50.
230. Letter from Darryl Zanuck to Barnet Bravermann, June 2, 1944, MOMA.
231. *The New York Times,* September 24, 1935, p. 45.
232. Lillian Gish, *The Movies, Mr. Griffith and Me,* p. 347.
233. *Ibid.*
234. Ezra Goodman, *The Fifty-year Decline and Fall of Hollywood,* New York: Simon and Schuster, 1961.
235. Lillian Gish, *The Movies, Mr. Griffith and Me,* p. 357.

Index